D1542285

CULTURAL AWARENESS
IN THE HUMAN SERVICES

THIRD EDITION

CULTURAL AWARENESS IN THE HUMAN SERVICES

A Multi-Ethnic Approach

James W. Green
University of Washington

Allyn and Bacon
Boston • London • Toronto • Sydney • Tokyo • Singapore

Series Editor, Social Work and Family Therapy: Judy Fifer
Editor-in-Chief, Social Sciences: Karen Hanson
Series Editorial Assistant: Jennifer Muroff
Marketing Manager: Susan E. Brown
Composition Buyer: Linda Cox
Cover Administrator: Brian Gogolin
Production Administrator: Robert Tonner
Editorial-Production Service: Ruttle, Shaw & Wetherill, Inc.
Electronic Composition: Omegatype Typography, Inc.

Copyright © 1999, 1995, 1982 by Allyn & Bacon
A Viacom Company
160 Gould Street
Needham Heights, MA 02194

Internet: www.abacon.com
America Online: keyword: College Online

All rights reserved. No part of the material protected by this copyright notice may be reproduced or utilized in any form or by any means, electronic or mechanical, including photocopying, recording, or by any information storage and retrieval system, without written permission from the copyright owner.

Library of Congress Cataloging-in-Publication Data

Green, James W.
    Cultural awareness in the human services: a multi-ethnic
approach / James W. Green.—3rd ed.
        p.   cm.
    Includes bibliographical references and index.
    ISBN 0-205-28632-1
    1. Social work with minorities—United States—Cross-cultural
studies.   2. Multiculturalism—United States.   3. Ethnicity—United
States.   I. Title.
    HV3176.G73   1998
    362.84—dc21   97-44064
                                                              CIP

Printed in the United States of America

10   9   8   7   6   5   4   3   2   RRD-VA   05   04   03   02   01   00   99

Be not forgetful to entertain strangers;
For thereby some have entertained angels unawares.

—Hebrews 13:2

CONTENTS

FOREWORD

This third edition of *Cultural Awareness in the Human Services* attests to the interest of the helping professions in gaining knowledge of ethnicity, race, and culture, matters that continue to impact various groups and are a significant part of the American mosaic. James Green joins the many social science scholars who see the idea of culture as a vital concept in our understanding of ideas, attitudes, and often the fixed patterns of uncritical thinking in American society. Knowledge among human service professionals of the cultural determinants of behavior is a first step toward enabling those who, for historical reasons, have not been full participants in mainstream culture. This knowledge will prepare the professional to deliver social and health services in a manner that advances the cause of social justice for the individual, the family, and the community. This new edition presents the essence of how cultures historically excluded from the mainstream have devised their own adroit responses to the political realities of power through their distinctive values, religions, childrearing practices, family roles, and sense of what is problematic in their lives.

Cultural imperatives are receiving more attention in the professional literature and gaining ascendancy in the professional education curriculum. We are increasingly asking: What purpose does this knowledge serve in the delivery of social and health services? What purpose does the idea of culture serve in assessment and treatment? What is the impact of an acceptance of cultural diversity on the education of human service professionals and the agencies that employ them? Because knowledge of any group can be used to stereotype, how can human services professionals individualize others and still acknowledge their cultural integrity? Should techniques of enabling be geared to the cultural framework of the individual and his or her community, or should they be made to fit smoothly with the demands of the mainstream culture?

Questions are addressed in this book where the concept of culture is shown to be vital to identity and to the integrity of others. This edition contains case studies and chapter-by-chapter guides to emerging cultural issues in the social service literature. It emphasizes in-class activities, topics for research and discussion, and self-evaluation and skills development. New topics relevant to social services, ranging from current discussions of postmodernism, narrative as an intervention tool, and the significance of the latest edition of the *DSM* series, are discussed in ways that challenge students to develop their own capabilities as cross-cultural service providers. We owe our students, and their clients, nothing less.

James W. Leigh
School of Social Work
University of Washington

PREFACE

This new edition of *Cultural Awareness in the Human Services* brings together current information and recent theoretical advances in cross-cultural practice. It is designed to guide students through service issues similar to those they will face as professionals and provide conceptual explanations for the unique challenges of multicultural service delivery. Activities at the end of each chapter are keyed to chapter topics and can be used by individuals and small groups, in classes and workshops, to promote specific skills.

A number of new topics are introduced, reflecting current research and discussion in the human service journals. They include evaluations of the new *DSM-IV,* the growth of biracial and bicultural consciousness, postmodernist critiques in social services, and issues of organizational cultural competence and individual evaluation. Each chapter ends with a new section that features case studies for discussion, ways to experiment with ideas discussed in the chapter, and a short, annotated bibliography designed to help students follow up each chapter's topic in the professional literature. Indeed, leading students to greater use of the journals in social and health services is one of the goals of this new edition.

The idea behind this book, like that of the previous editions, is my conviction that human service professionals can be more effective in cross-cultural settings when they (1) know something about the historical background of the communities they serve; (2) are able to develop interviewing skills that make them sensitive listeners and practitioners; (3) have a clear idea of how "race" and ethnicity are meaningful in both public life and personal experience; and (4) have tools for learning and self-evaluation that apply to any multicultural situation.

On this latter point, I recognize that many of the users of this book are white and some of their clients are from ethnic and minority communities. But in cross-cultural work we need a model that is good in any setting. It should work for an African American professional interviewing a Latina child and for a Japanese American gerontologist seeking to understand the concerns of a Puerto Rican grandmother. Nor are the barriers to cross-cultural understanding those of ethnicity and race alone. Age differences, cohort experiences, religious affiliations, gender identity, and sexual preference present special challenges to clear, contextualized understanding and service as well. My hope is that the model presented in this book will be useful in all those settings and more.

The approach to culturally competent practice outlined here is adapted from my own training as an anthropologist, training that has been shaped by my experience with child protective services, my teaching interests in cross-cultural aging and how people deal with death in different societies, years of leading training workshops for public and private social service organizations, and my ongoing interests in medical anthropology and its critique of health and human services.

Whether you are a student, instructor, or practitioner, I am very interested in how the ideas in this book work for you. I would like to know how you modified them to suit your own circumstances because I am always looking for variations to try in my own teaching. I am attentive (some say addicted) to my e-mail, so if you write me (address below), I will be sure to get back to you.

ACKNOWLEDGMENTS

No one ever writes a book alone, and I want to thank a number of people who helped along the way. James Leigh, social work educator extraordinaire at the University of Washington, has been a companion in training workshops for many years, and no one could be as good at it as he. Michael Austin of the University of California at Berkeley had the original idea for training materials and then a book, and he patiently nurtured both. Many individuals offered helpful advice on this edition, and various authors gave permission to use some of their materials. I want to thank especially Anna R. McPhatter, Morgan State University; Lynn Pearlmutter, Tulane University; Irene Glasser, University of Connecticut; Ronald H. Rooney, University of Minnesota; Anthony A. Bibus III, Augsburg College; Jean M. Granger, California State University at Long Beach; Carmen Aponte, State University of New York at Brockport; and Juan Guerra, Martha Richards, Sharyne Thornton, and Maureen Schwarz, all of the University of Washington. David Davies prepared the charts with his usual attention to detail. Carol Green helped me stay on track until the book was done. I thank them all for their assistance and generosity.

Finally, the obligatory disclaimer: what you read in these pages is there because I put it there. No one made me do it. If something doesn't seem right to you, e-mail me, not the people I've quoted. I look forward to hearing from you.

James W. Green
University of Washington
jwgreen@u.washington.edu

CULTURAL AWARENESS IN THE HUMAN SERVICES

CULTURAL DIVERSITY AND SOCIAL SERVICES

Part I is concerned with four major issues: race and ethnicity; culture and help-seeking behavior; cross-cultural or ethnographic interviewing; and the goal of cultural competence in professional practice. Familiar social service topics—individualizing the client, rapport and empathy, the cultural context of problem resolution, and communication skills—are examined. Newer issues are also addressed: biracialism and biculturalism, narrative approaches to intervention, postmodernism, self-evaluation, the significance of the new *DSM-IV,* and effective use of the professional literature. This section introduces you to the basic themes of cross-cultural human services.

1

RACE, ETHNICITY, AND SOCIAL SERVICES

The Reverend Martin Luther King, Jr. gave his famous "I Have a Dream" speech from the steps of the Lincoln Memorial on August 28, 1963. A quarter million people were there on a pleasant summer afternoon for what was then the largest demonstration in American history. They knew what they wanted to hear, but they did not know how famous the words they heard would become.

The press coverage was good. The March on Washington dominated network television. Every large newspaper sent reporters, and the national news magazines featured the event. The morning of the March the *New York Times* ran a front-page photo with the caption "Nuns and other volunteers worked in hall of Riverside Church," where they made 80,000 lunches to be sold to the marchers for fifty cents each. The next day the *Times* ran seven pages on the event. In one photo President Kennedy smiled with leaders of the Southern Christian Leadership Conference, the United Automobile Workers, the American Jewish Congress, the United Presbyterian Church, the NAACP, and other civil rights groups. Other photos showed the massive crowd, completely surrounding the Reflecting Pool in front of the Lincoln Memorial, black and white faces together. The pictorials were surrounded by comforting headlines: "Gentle Army Occupies Capital," "Three Faiths Join in Rights Demand," "Marchers Sing and Voice Hope." Seventy-five Senators and Representatives sat on the Memorial steps with civil rights and labor dignitaries. Later, a delegation of March organizers met with President Kennedy for more than an hour, after which the President praised the "deep fervor and the quiet dignity" of the demonstrators, adding that the nation could be "proud" of what had occurred.

That day King's themes, and the expectations of his audience, were optimistic, hopeful, and Biblical. His thoughts were on history (the Constitution was a "promissory note to which every American was to fall heir") and geography ("from the red hills of Georgia to the snow-capped Rockies of Colorado"). He was philosophical and lyrical but he also demanded action, including "freedom now." The audience responded with appreciation and frequent amens. It is easy (and not at all unrealistic) to imagine King there as a latter-day Jeremiah, standing in the public square, scolding and coaxing any who would listen:

> *Now is the time to make real the promises of democracy; now is the time to rise from the dark and desolate valley of segregation to the sunlit path of racial justice; now is the time to lift our nation from the quicksands of racial injustice to the solid rock of brotherhood; now is the time to make justice a reality for all God's children.... No, we are not satisfied, and we will not be satisfied until justice rolls down like waters and righteousness like a mighty stream. (Washington 1986:218, 219)*

That was 1963. Had King lived, would he want to give that speech today? Would we still be moved by his repeated calls to "let freedom ring" or by his vision of the children of former slaves and former slave owners sitting together at "the table of brotherhood"? What might people do now in response to what he said then: "Go back to Mississippi; go back to Alabama; go back to South Carolina; go back to Georgia; go back to Louisiana; go back to the slums and ghettos of the northern cities, knowing that somehow this situation can, and will be changed." Would we understand his words the same way? In some different way? Would he still have a quarter million listeners?

More than three decades later, the landscape is different. Segregated drinking fountains are not the issue; affirmative action is. Crude racial stereotypes in advertising and the media are out, yet hate groups vigorously promote their lies on the Internet. Minorities are prominent as celebrities in sports, less likely to be decision makers in corporations. The workplace is more integrated than it has ever been. Yet many people think a cross-cultural experience is a visit to an ethnic restaurant.

Some insist we are now officially "color blind," armed with a new ethic of personal responsibility that puts the individual, not "quotas," at the center of things. Work hard, play by the rules, and the old impediments of race, gender, or class will not get in your way. But others argue that only the rules have changed, not the game. Michael Eric Dyson puts it neatly when he says that "in our more racially murky era—an era in which the ecology of race is much more complex and choked with half-discarded symbols and muddied signs—our skills of interpretation have to be more keen, our readings more nuanced" (Dyson 1996:215).

More nuanced indeed. Nuances are the new rules of a very long running game.

DIVERSITY AND HUMAN SERVICES

How should those who define their profession as service to others in a multicultural society respond to the changes since King's day? We do have choices. As policy and service professionals, we could assume that racial and ethnic divisions are so deep running in our history that practical limitations of time and money make it impossible to address them all. We can try to muddle through, as has been done in the past, hoping that everything will turn out for the best. Or we might trust that sufficient good will and energy will overcome old divisions, if we just try hard enough. After all, we all want to get on with just being Americans, and hard work and dedication are basic to the American ethos. Finally, we could acknowledge that there are many agendas operating in Dyson's new racial ecology, some presented more articulately than others, but all available as resources for promoting a legitimate and egalitarian pluralism. My view, and that of this text, is that the first choice is that of the pessimist, the second that of the romantic, and the third that of the serious change agent who sees human difference as an opportunity to help and to learn, not as a problem to be overcome.

It is useful to remember that cultural and racial variation are among the most enduring characteristics of our species. Diversity is certainly a fact of our past, about three to four million years of it, and we can be reasonably assured of it in the future. The recent interest in finding one's ethnic "roots" in faraway places suggests that even in a society in which the imagery of the "melting pot" is widely held as a proper model of ethnic interaction, people still feel a need to define their distinctiveness. Cultural differences reflect not only a history but also fundamental variations in what people hold to be worthwhile. As long as variations persist, they will invite comparison and questioning of the practices and preferences of others. It may be disconcerting to have to acknowledge that members of historically stigmatized racial and ethnic groups often do things their way, not just because they have been excluded from mainstream institutions by prejudice and discrimination, but because they find the values and institutions of the larger society inferior to their own.

The preference for cultural homogeneity, whether expressed as ethnocentrism, racism, or some other principle of exclusion, runs deep in any society. In a multi-ethnic society such as our own, it is a source of conflict between groups and individuals. That is particularly troublesome in social services, where social workers often deal with individual problems of the most intimate kind, brought to them by people they do not always understand. As professionals with authority and power, they can have enormous influence on people's choices and values. But that creates a dilemma. In providing services to ethnically distinctive clients, should a worker's suggestions for problem resolution be based on a belief in the essential similarity of all people's needs and desires? Or should social workers attempt to solve problems in terms of the distinctive values and community practices of their clients, however "unusual" they may seem?

The argument made here, and made very explicitly, is that social services can and should be provided to people in ways that are culturally acceptable to them and that enhance their sense of ethnic group participation and power. When Barbara Solomon referred to this as "empowerment" in 1976, the term caught on as a general point of view within human services. Although for some empowerment has become more a buzzword than a practice, her idea was that workers, service agencies, policies, and educational and training programs must work to meet client needs in ways that are congruent with each individual's cultural background and community setting. More than that, empowerment to her meant that people and communities should be encouraged to define their own best interests, promote their self-sufficiency, and be free to live out their historical values. But how can that be done when the institutions that are to provide empowering services are essentially monocultural, and their dominant perspective is that of one group—college educated, English-speaking whites mostly of middle-class origins and with professional class aspirations?

The problem is *not* that it is inherently bad, or good either, that most social workers (and nurses and teachers) are white, or that most speak only English, or that most are middle class. That is simply what they are. The problem lies in the inevitable limitations of those who are monocultural and monolingual in a society that clearly is not. Despite much discussion about "pluralism," most Americans do not think about what that term implies and, comfortably monocultural, they do not believe it has much to do with them. Social service and health professionals, however, cannot afford that level of comfort, and there are important reasons for them to consider the implications of pluralism for their work. The challenge of cultural diversity is the future of us all. Responding to it is a professional obligation since ethnic and minority group clients are as entitled to sensitive and competent services as anyone else.

Like minority clients, minority professionals look forward to an end of tokenism, both in services and in professional employment and advancement. They expect and sometimes insist that programs and policies change to accommodate their concerns and those of the people they represent. Majority group workers, especially those who cannot perceive the coming changes and who may not be prepared for them when they arrive, may find themselves more a part of the problem than contributors to solutions. That would be an awkward position for individuals and for a profession explicitly committed to the welfare of others.

There is an additional reason why social workers should give careful attention to the quality of their cross-cultural work—their own unfortunate history of insensitivity to ethnic and minority groups. That is an odd thing to say about people whose profession is caring about others. As a teacher and trainer who has worked with a variety of service professionals, I have known white counselors, nurses, social workers, teachers, occupational therapists, agency administrators, and others who are exquisitely sensitive to the formalities and nuances of face-to-face encounters with minority persons. But I have also come to see that their dexterity in "handling" racial otherness is not always a sign of cultural sensitivity; sometimes it is a response to a professional imperative to appear competent, officially color blind, and never, ever, confused with Archie Bunker. The language and style of how one "cares" can mask great ignorance or even hostility, which, even when Archie doesn't see it, Edith Bunker in her unadorned innocence usually does.

A case illustrates this nicely. Applied anthropologist Barbara Joans (1992) reports on a group of Bannock-Shoshoni Native American women residing at the Fort Hall reservation in southeastern Idaho. Their supplementary security income (SSI) was cut off by a local service agency on the grounds that they had not reported all their income. In this economically poor region of their state, some of the women who owned small plots of land had rented them out to local farmers, making a profit of about a thousand dollars. The agency wanted the money back, money the women no longer had and could not return. To help resolve the dispute, Joans was asked by a legal aid service to determine how well the women understood English and if they had understood what was expected of them by the agency. Her evidence would be used in court proceedings.

Through carefully planned interviews, Joans discovered that all the women were familiar with everyday English as they used and heard it on the reservation, in local shops and businesses, and in conversations with whites. But only one woman understood simple jokes, puns, double-entendres, and other subtle nuances of usage, all evidence of her ability to understand fine gradations of meaning. Further, most of the women were not able to use or understand English in other than casual conversations; they had difficulty with the English of whites who represented social service, law enforcement, and other mainstream institutions. Their misunderstandings were compounded by their lack of familiarity with the rules and procedures of off-reservation bureaucracies.

Through participant observation, Joans found some of the reasons for the women's difficulties in understanding whites who spoke with them in an official capacity. For example, SSI people who came to the reservation often met with groups to discuss the aid program in general terms. They did not usually meet with individuals who had specific concerns about the use of funds. In describing SSI, they used the language of their own culture, the professional and bureaucratic culture in which they were immersed all day, and spoke of "regs" and other features of agency policy and practice. Much of this information was poorly understood by the Native American women, partly because it relied on vocabulary they did not know but, more importantly, because the vocabulary assumed knowledge of a system entirely outside their experience. In the critical area of SSI compliance, the differing usages and understanding of English were sufficient that the judge ruled in favor of the Native American women. Joans's research demonstrated the importance of "linguistic patterns as criteria for cultural understanding" (Joans 1992:148) even when the nominal language of communication, English, was the same for everyone.

An additional reason for examining cross-cultural encounters in social work has to do with how the profession has conceptualized its involvement with ethnic communities generally. Despite years of work with minority clients, practitioners have only recently considered their relations with minority communities systematically (Rodwell and Blankebaker 1992; Christodoulou 1991). Descriptions of social work among minority clients, which are now more common in social work journals, emphasize a client's individual characteristics, or problems in communicating with service workers. Much less attention has been given to understanding the cultural background from which these clients speak, or of finding ways to translate cultural understanding into improved social, health, and counseling practices. Even those who prefer "ecological" approaches have generally limited themselves to immediate family relations or personal networks, with little reference to the larger cultural settings in which family life and social networks are embedded. And only recently have texts in the field made other than passing reference to ethnicity as a factor in human services, community organization, or policy and planning. The National Association of Social Workers has on occasion addressed the issue (White 1984; Jacobs and Bowles 1988). But with the exception of a few texts and readers such as Lum (1996), Sue and Sue (1990), Devore and Schlesinger (1995), Ho (1987, 1992), Dana (1981, 1993), and McGoldrick (1982, 1996), ethnicity in the social work literature and teaching is hardly prominent. It is more often treated as an adjunct to other substantive concerns such as mental health or child welfare.

There are many reasons for this, but several are worth mentioning because they remain problems in developing an informed and truly holistic approach to multicultural social services (Pedersen 1985). First, there are disciplinary barriers. Sociologists, psychologists, anthropologists, and social workers rarely show much interest in one another's research. They are even more reluctant to teach in one another's programs. Turf issues are as common in academe as elsewhere. That may never change, but a few brave individuals will always be needed to work at overcoming this insularity.

Second, demonstration projects and intervention research are usually limited to abnormal behavior, viewed in clinical settings. This kind of research looks at individual pathology, not the communities where pathology is generated. There is rarely any attempt to discover a "cultural baseline" against which behavior, intervention, and outcomes can be compared or evaluated. In addition, many social service researchers have an overriding concern with variables that can be isolated and described quantitatively. Their faith in the predictive control they expect their research to produce divorces them from the human context and the lived realities of personal problems. Meaning-centered or ethnographic research is often thought of as yielding data that is "soft" (unquantifiable) and therefore less desirable. Consequently, the issues that might be most interesting to a teacher, a social worker, or a nurse are avoided.

Finally, the current popularity of the family systems approach tends to exclude cultural features that may be important in understanding the sources of some problems. Menicucci and Wermuth (1989), for example, contrast individual, family, and cultural approaches to drug treatment. They note that in cases of clients with long histories of abuse, individual and family systems treatment modes are less useful than treatment that takes account of cultural variables such as life cycle, gender, and social variations within target communities. In their view, overlooking cultural data makes impossible a truly holistic framework for problem assessment and treatment. Where clients come from ethnic and minority communities unfamiliar to the worker, the risks of misunderstanding and treatment failure are simply compounded.

Regular contact between social workers and ethnically distinctive clients, ignorance of cultural differences that may be present, and the absence of a cross-cultural theoretical framework within social work—all seem to suggest a need to look more carefully at client diversity in human services. What, really, are "problems" for some people? What different patterns of problem resolution are common in various ethnic and racial settings? Other than social workers and those in institutional positions of authority, who do troubled individuals turn to in their own communities? And with what impact? What exactly is an intervention "outcome" and who decides if it is a useful one? These are just a few of the issues that a comprehensive program in multicultural services must resolve. They call for a research and practice agenda that would help improve both our understanding of ethnic communities and the quality of services that are provided.

At a minimum, a model for culturally responsive social and health services would require us to do the following:

1. Define a model of cross-cultural social work and caring services. The model must be systematic, and it must take account of cultural complexity in a genuinely pluralistic society. But it must also point to ethnographic features of clients that are explicitly salient to presenting problems and to the services offered. Generalized models of ethnic difference, with generalized principles of cultural awareness, may have been acceptable in the 1970s and the 1980s, but they will not do now. Something more analytical and more client-specific is needed.

2. Describe how the model is applicable to any cross-racial or cross-ethnic relationship. The model must be useful regardless of the participant's cultural identity. It cannot assume that the service professional is always a member of the dominant group or that the recipient of services is always a minority person. Nor can the model assume extensive background knowledge among workers about the communities they seek to serve.

3. Specify how the model would be useful in a wide range of service activities. The service provider's professional specialty, or the provider's ethnicity, should be irrelevant to the model's utility. We simply require that it be applicable whenever contrastive cultural experiences and perspectives are part of a service relationship. The model should be useful in a variety of service relationships, whether they involve social workers, nurses, teachers, career counselors, ministers, doctors, administrators, volunteers, or others.

4. Generate explicit training procedures for improving skills. Training must have a knowledge as well as a skills component. It must result in improved services as measured by professional and also community criteria. The model should suggest ways of adapting agency procedures, policies, and evaluation criteria to the ethnographic issues that workers meet in their clients and their clients' communities. Without administrative follow-up and support, cultural sensitivity skills training will have minimum impact and might well be construed as little more than a faddish interest or, worse, the current face of tokenism.

My belief is that a cultural or ethnographic dimension will be helpful to professionals serving many people, especially those who identify with ethnic traditions, but also those in other kinds of communities as well. It remains true that the most obvious cross-cultural boundaries in American society are those that differentiate ethnic, racial, and minority groups. But we often differentiate people on the basis of power, age, gender, sexual preference, accent, religion, and education as well. The ethnographic approach directs our attention to the significant *cultural* features of any defined and distinctive community. In that sense, the skills of ethnic competence are widely applicable in human services generally. They should not be artificially confined to professional work with ethnic or minority peoples alone.

RACE AND CULTURE

We can begin with the idea of "race" by stating unambiguously that it has no standing of any kind as a scientific concept. A "race" is neither a culture nor a brute fact of nature, two erroneous beliefs that Margaret Mead and other anthropologists of her generation fully discredited more than half a century ago. Yet the shadow of these ideas still flits through everyday speech. Many of our current folk beliefs about race come from eighteenth- and nineteenth-century ideologies, some of which had their origins in religious thinking. Others derive from political ideas once associated with empire and conquest and used to justify European expansion and the doctrine of Manifest Destiny in the settling of North America. People of various "races" were described then as "primitives," "heathens," or subhuman creatures, all of whom would benefit from exposure to a conquering, missionizing civilization. Their cultural and racial diversity was expected to melt and finally disappear, although what they were to "melt to" was always rather vague. Modern racial supremacists and hate groups, with their calls for separate homelands, still rely on religiously and politically motivated racial stereotypes that originated in that divisive history.

In the natural world there are no clear, discrete things called "races." That term has no scientific validity and there is no way that a "race" can be objectively defined or consistently measured. Physical anthropologists and biologists rarely use the term except to warn the rest of us away from it. They speak instead of populations (more correctly, "gene pools") that slowly change due to the long-term effects of natural selection, genetic drift, mutation, and reproductive behavior. Whatever the seeming diversity of races in the modern world, *all* contemporary human beings trace their origin to ancestral populations that lived in east Africa about 200,000 years ago (Klein 1989). The slow movement of those early people out of their African homeland and into the rest of the world, during a period of tens of thousands of years, is an incredibly complex story. But its essence is that they migrated, diversified, evolved, and became us. The current distribution of "racial" groups, such as the peoples of southern Africa, southeast Asia, or northern Europe, is far more recent than 200,000 years. All populations, be they plants or animals, change over time, and it is a certainty that our species' physical variation was different 10,000 years ago and will be different 10,000 years from now. Race simply is not the immutable, heaven-ordained order of things the hate groups would have the rest of us believe.

It is important to mention this mutable dimension of our biological heritage because Americans tend to think of race or "a race" as something inevitable, as an unchanging part of the "natural" world, even as something ordained by God.

Objections to interracial marriage, dating, eating together, and riding in the same part of the bus have always been based on the seeming "naturalness" of racial divisions. Yet no one is a member of a "race" simply because he or she has a given amount of skin pigmentation or a particular type of nose, eyes, or hair. These physiological features, when we make an issue of them, are really representations of something else, namely our creativity and perverseness in devising social categories, sticking individuals into them, and making moral evaluations.

As an interesting illustration of this, Lieberson (1985:128) has shown the tenaciousness and seeming "naturalness" of racial categorization in everyday habits of speech and thought. Consider the following two sentences:

1. Americans are still prejudiced against blacks.
2. Americans still earn less money than do whites.

Williams (1989:430), who quotes this example, comments that the first sentence is perfectly clear in a quick, casual reading. But the second is not. That is because the conventional use of the word "Americans" assumes a white point of view. "Americans" is a linguistic "cover term" or gloss for whites, and that makes the first sentence "correct" both grammatically and socially. The second sentence initially confounds, however, because "Americans" now stands as a linguistic gloss for blacks. To grasp its meaning, we must consciously extricate the statement from conventional usage and make its unfamiliar categorical logic explicit. It defies both a quick gloss and the routines of thought implicit in our taken-for-granted world of everyday discourse. In this example, Lieberson exploits our linguistic habits to expose the social (and arbitrary) way language implicitly defines experience for us. It is a useful illustration of how the partitioning of the world into races is a social convention that we reproduce every time we speak, thus convincing ourselves that our favorite dissections of reality are indeed "true" in some fundamental, normative, and moral way.

But is the persistence of racial beliefs simply a matter of inappropriate language? Probably not. Many social scientists argue that racial logic expresses a concern, both linguistic and psychological, with orderliness (Douglas 1966) and a need to preserve and enforce order. In the instance of race, orderliness is constructed around notions of descent, exclusiveness, privilege, and most especially notions of moral purity. "Blood" is one of the most common and potent metaphors for that purity. As a consequence of historical assimilation and federal regulation, Native Americans commonly speak of themselves as having varying percentages of "blood," and sometimes that percentage is the basis for who can and cannot claim tribal membership and benefits. African Americans have sometimes referred to one another as "bloods," and the chapter on African American culture discusses the ethnomedical significance of "blood" in some black communities. In the nineteenth and early twentieth centuries, whites often described and evaluated one another in terms of their "breeding," an idea not unconnected with notions of bloodlines. References to one's "breeding" would be quaint and a little humorous now because it is language we usually use to describe the pedigrees of dogs, cats, and horses. Whites therefore usually describe their ethnicity as proportions of nationality, such as one-quarter Irish and one-eighth German, but the implication of "blood" purity and descent is still there.

Speculation about descent, one's blood, and degrees of mixed nationality from European ancestors is more than a parlor game. Serious attention to the purity of metaphoric bloodlines always comes to the fore in discussions of "mixed" marriages. The specter of racially or ethnically "mixed" marriages is, for some people, only slightly more troublesome than "mixes" that cross disapproved religious, language, educational, or class lines. Nor is this concern with preserving purity a problem only for whites. Virtually all ethnic groups in America have strong feelings, if not explicit objections, to "marrying out" for fear that the group's integrity will be compromised or contaminated. Some of my Asian American students have described the less than charitable feelings their parents would have were they to marry someone white. Some Jewish students have expressed a strong preference for marrying within their faith, not only to keep their parents and grandparents happy, but also to minimize conflicts over the religious training and identity of their children. And authorities (of sorts) no less than television talk show hosts regularly capitalize on our fascination with unlikely mixtures of intimate preferences. All cross-racial contacts, whether they involve marriage, sex, or advice on how to manage a personal problem, invoke deeply held beliefs about the purity and separateness of social types. We can appreciate, then, that race is far more than a matter of biology. To reduce it to that is a sentimental and dangerous delusion. Race is always a point of view, not a natural fact. Racial thinking is the modern mythology of purity.

Oddly, Americans remain fascinated with what they believe are the genetic, biological foundations of their racial beliefs, continuing to extend a crude biological reductionism to the realm of the mind. A recent and infamous instance of this is *The Bell Curve: Intelligence and Class Structure in American Life,* authored by Herrnstein and Murray (1994). Now in a paperback as well as a hardbound edition, the book has been a publishing phenomenon, appealing to a wide audience not normally taken with works on demography and cognitive psychology. Herrnstein and Murray mix up a stew of racial ideology, statistics, and bogus science to "prove" once again all the tattered old stereotypes about the alleged differences in intelligence between blacks and whites as revealed in their IQ scores. Their entire premise founders, however, on its assumption that there is some essential, biologically based ability (1) that can be accurately measured (unlikely) and (2) that is free of intervening cultural variables (most unlikely), and (3) that such differences are features of whole groups as well as of individuals (very doubtful). Tests always measure performance; test writers like to believe they are measuring ability. But the link between performance and ability is in large part cultural, not biological, as many critics of *The Bell Curve* have said (Fraser 1995; Jacoby and Glauberman 1995). More to the point, however, there may not be any single, essential, biological "thing" that is responsible for your or my "innate" ability. (The same argument, incidentally, goes on in studies seeking to find a cellular or genetic basis for homosexuality. Biological reductionism is always handy for changing the cultural into something "natural.") We all have many abilities; some of our "intelligence" may be with words and numbers but some may be manifest as kindness and patience. The persistent efforts of some to find a biological condition that "explains" differential performance (thereby justifying differential treatment) are an aspect of the American obsession with purity, especially racial purity.

There is an implication in this idea about purity and race that is worth a pause. In the American world view, if we allow that there might be such a singular thing, two explanations of our difficulties with race are common. First, it is sometimes held that racism continues because of our failure to communicate with one another. If we would just listen more carefully, just try to connect, we would see that our problems are not really so large. In communicating and sharing our needs and feelings with one another, we would find the common ground of our experiences and our humanity. Second, and related to this, is the view that racial misunderstanding comes from our ignorance about each other. Learning more, through open and caring communication, would eliminate much of what separates us. (The logic of these points, and compelling critiques of them, will be found in Wellman 1993; Varenne 1977; and Bellah et al. 1985.) In my classrooms, I hear these explanations for racism regularly. Yet it must be apparent that if racial thinking and behavior are a consequence of our need for social orderliness, and the protection of our place and privileges within a system so ordered, then any frank exchange of views is as likely to polarize differences as to resolve them. Readers who think I exaggerate should review their initial reaction to Lieberson's two sentences quoted above and then think again about the power of racial metaphors to shape the way we mentally construct the world.

The idea of "race" is not helpful in advancing our understanding of difference, but it remains a prevalent notion, which is why we need to deal with it. By contrast, a "culture" is something else. Cultural differences are both real and meaningful, especially when people struggle to protect their group identity and personal dignity. Unfortunately, however, the term "culture" lacks a clear, specific meaning; there are literally hundreds of definitions of culture in the professional literature of sociology and especially anthropology (Kroeber and Kluckhohn 1952). Some of these definitions are cognitive: they stress what people know and how they interpret the world. Culture is thought of as a shared "cognitive map" and the study of culture in this sense is the study of a people's categories of meaning (Spradley 1972, 1979). Other definitions emphasize behavior and customs and their transmission from generation to generation. Here, culture is more like a list of traits handed down over time.

Many social work texts and authors, however, continue to rely on a very general (and older) model of culture taken from Kluckhohn and Strodtbeck (1961), one that stresses values and especially value differences. In this approach, people are said to be culturally similar if they share similar beliefs and preferences. While there is some commonsense truth to this view, there is also a problem. A values theory of culture suggests that the differences between group A and group B can be described simply as an inventory of values propositions and, further, that any individual's identity is essentially the match between that person and a given list of values. Obviously, not only is this a rather wooden view of what a culture is but it comes dangerously close to the kinds of stereotyping that we would prefer to avoid. In addition, the values approach leaves out important dimensions of culture, especially those associated with power and powerlessness, situational expression of ethnic loyalties, and how these play out in interaction between persons of differing and perhaps hostile communities.

Like the terms "life" in biology or "gravity" in physics, the word "culture" has to be given some fairly precise meaning before it can be useful as an analytical tool. An obvious place to start is with differences or contrasts; someone else's culture is most evident when I contrast what I see in that person with what I know about myself. The presence of an "other" makes me self-conscious (perhaps even reflective) of my own cultural distinctiveness. The experience of contrast, the presence of an apparent cultural boundary, is certainly stimulating, perhaps even discomforting. When I confront someone I perceive as different from myself, that person's "culture" might be any number of things—what I believe his or her values or family life to be, what I think about the religious beliefs I presume that person holds, my previous experiences of people "like that" when they are in contact with people "like me." The historical or objective truth of what the other is, and of what I am, is less important than perceptions. In an encounter on a bus, in a classroom, or at the beginning of a counseling session, there is a moment in which we each decide what is important to us about the other and how much of ourselves should or should not be revealed. (The word "decide" barely describes the subtlety of what goes on in cross-cultural awareness, for it suggests conscious decision making. Verbs like "scan" or "react" might be more appropriate.) Not all of my background and experiences, or those of the other, are initially important. What counts is how we narrow and focus the relationship, through verbal and bodily clues both subtle and explicit. In our mutual presentations of self, what passes as "culture" and as ethnic identity is usually brief and very specific, little more than a glimpse of all that we are as individuals.

Culture, in this sense, is not something the other "has," such as a specific value or a physical appearance; it is rather the "perspective" that guides our behavior, however brief the encounter. Culture and ethnicity are not essential or innate properties of persons; they are the meanings that two people act on in a specific relationship. This emphasis on relational rather than essentialist aspects of culture may, in fact, be the only useful way to think about cultural differences in a complex, heterogeneous society such as our own (Hannerz 1986).

Before more fully exploring this notion of culture and its implications for professional practice, I want to briefly say something about minority status and social class. I prefer to think of the term "minority" as referring to something different from ethnicity or culture. Minority standing refers to power, not numbers; it concerns the degree to which individuals identified with a specific group are denied access to privileges and opportunities available to others. One could speak of minorities as "communities of interest" (Weaver 1977), those who share a similar set of values, lifestyles, and expectations but whose most common and definitive trait is that they are exposed to a similar set of limiting political and economic circumstances. In this sense, the term "minority" refers to social and economic disability, not to cultural differences as such.

That viewpoint is well established in social services. In a special issue of *Social Work* devoted to oppression of people of color, the editors explicitly link minority status to oppression: "the term *minority* has been expanded to include many other offended groups: immigrants, all those with Spanish surnames, women, the physically handicapped.... The list continues to grow as new groups are identified or claim minority status" (Hopps 1982:3). The phrase "people of color," as used in the special issue, suggests a dimension of power and relative disadvantage. The usage, however, also reveals one of its conceptual limitations. "People of color" do not constitute a culture; the term is just too broad for that. Since I am concerned in this book with the meaning of cultural differences for individuals, families, and service providers, a phrase like "people of color" has only limited utility. A "new" group, suddenly aware of a collective self-interest, may not be an ethnic or culturally distinctive community at all and it is useful to keep that difference in mind.

Finally, what of "social class"? That term introduces what we normally think of as the objective measures of education, income, religious affiliation, housing standards, and the like. However useful social class may be for categorizing large groups of people, especially for policy purposes, it really has little to do with the central elements of culture as I am presenting it here. Even if the social class affiliation of a client (and a worker) are accurately fixed early in a professional consultation, that information would provide only minimal grounds for exploring the relationship. Most human service workers would want to know much more.

ETHNICITY

The essence of ethnicity is contrast, the recognition of difference. That seems obvious. But when we try to determine what differences mean, the idea of ethnicity becomes complex and frequently troublesome. Ethnicity in a multiracial and multicultural society is often problematic, both in practice and in moral terms. In a piercing critique of contemporary race relations in America, essayist Shelby Steele (1988) put the issue bluntly: "I'm Black, you're white, who's innocent?" Moving beyond innocence, he suggested, means understanding what ethnicity is and isn't, recognizing how it works both for people and against them, and appreciating why ethnicity remains important even when racial barriers to minority disadvantage are overcome through education or earning power.

A number of theories of ethnicity have been proposed, and while I do not intend to review them all here, it is worthwhile to note the major ones because ethnicity is neither a simple idea nor an obvious social fact. Alba (1990) has categorized theories of ethnic identity into four types: ethnicity as class; as a political movement; as revival; and as a token identity (Figure 1.1, page 16). I want to review what these different ideas are about, partly because it is useful to look at the range of meanings commonly associated with ethnicity but also because I think some approaches are more useful for social service professionals than others.

Type	Feature	Example
Ethnicity as class	Distinctive lifestyle	Urban and rural ghettos
Ethnicity as politics	Group mobilization	Ethnic power movements
Ethnicity as revival	Return to traditions	Public and family celebrations
Ethnicity as symbolic token	Minimal commitment	Remembered family traditions

FIGURE 1.1   Four Perspectives on Ethnicity

Based on Alba (1990).

Alba notes that ethnicity is sometimes associated with social class, particularly when it is used to suggest working-class or lower-class lifestyles. This is an often romanticized view of ethnic distinctiveness, one associated with urban groups socially isolated in ghettos and in "little Italies" or "Chinatowns" where there is presumed to be a strong congruence between family life, social networks, world view, and language. There is also a sense that economic disadvantages are buffered by family loyalties that are warm and protecting. This conception of ethnicity is commonly linked with a political and policy agenda of assimilation. It assumes that ethnic identity will be strongest among those least assimilated to the national mainstream and that assimilation is both a possible and desirable strategy for help-ing those who are economically disadvantaged. In this perspective, ethnicity is essentially a relic and a social problem, one to be overcome and left behind.

A second view is of ethnicity as a political process. Individuals whose origins (and perhaps their symbolic loyalties) are in other countries, cultures, or continents have suffered and endured the disadvantages and stigmata typically applied to those who are "different" in the American context. Recognizing this commonality in their suffering, ethnicity becomes for them the basis of a call to corrective polit-ical and economic action. Redressing historical wrongs becomes the agenda of eth-nic group politics. Examples of this might be the various "power" movements of the 1960s and 1970s as well as the efforts of people like Cesar Chávez to organize agricultural workers or the Reverend Jesse L. Jackson to build a "rainbow coali-tion." In this view, ethnic groups are really political interest groups, struggling for their share of entitlements in a ruthlessly competitive political market. To hostile outsiders, the claims of ethnicity made by community advocates are seen as little more than a cloak for political opportunism. To sympathetic insiders, the cultural symbols of ethnicity are the flags of a moral crusade against an oppressive social and economic system.

A third perspective is that of ethnicity as revival, as something "celebrated" in self-conscious returns to ethnic foods and clothing, traditional religious practices, ethnic festivals, adoption of ethnic personal names, and renewed interest in non-Western (or at least non-American) languages and folklore. Alba suggests that these deliberate efforts to return to one's roots occur when a people feel they have achieved some of what they want and, having proven their worthiness as Americans, are in a position to comfortably and safely resurrect "lost" or denied traditions. In contradistinction to the class-based theory of ethnicity, here ethnicity and its revival are not the product of those mired in ghettos but of those successfully reaching for the American Dream. The leaders, and followers, are on their way into the middle class, not stuck at the bottom. One thinks, for example, of St. Patrick's Day parades among the Irish in New York, or of summer music and food fairs built around themes of Norwegian, Greek, or Cajun identity. Some would argue that this expressive ethnicity is a healthy social indicator, not a social problem, for it "proves" the essential openness of our tolerant and liberal democracy. Others, a bit more cynical, would point to these displays as contrivances and self-congratulation, not any real commitment to living out the alternative ethnic realities they celebrate.

The fourth view, perhaps only a watered-down version of ethnicity as revival, is ethnicity as a symbolic token. It is something taken on by individuals whose real interest is maintaining a nostalgic connection to an imagined old country. This theory is often applied to whites, or "ethnic whites" (some East Europeans or Scandinavians, for example) for whom ethnicity is an avocation at best. Most of the time, in most of their concerns, these people mix more or less freely with everyone else in their jobs, in recreation, and in political and religious organizations. In fact, they often pride themselves on their loyalty and patriotism. But they choose to "feel ethnic" to distinguish themselves from others on special occasions, in ways that are essentially ornamental rather than political or economic.

For example, most of my white students define themselves ethnically as fractional quantities of European nation states and languages. Being one-quarter this and one-sixth that, their sense of ethnicity extends little further than a grandmother's Swedish Christmas cookies or bratwurst and beer on a Polish uncle's birthday. (I find it interesting that their *functional* ethnicity—white, mainline Protestant, English speaking, middle class, educated, upwardly mobile, suburban—is apparently invisible to them.) Some students get very creative in locating their European fractions, with a kind of pride of place going to obscure groups (Frisian speakers, Basques, French Huguenots). This perspective is far removed from ethnicity as a political process or as a sense of participation in a distinctive community. It certainly has limited use for social service providers.

These four perspectives suggest the diversity of ways Americans deal with what, for them, is a difficult and contentious topic. But ultimately beliefs about ethnicity are about perceiving difference, accounting for it, and knowing how to respond to it. Ethnicity starts with a recognition of "the other" and imposes a set of learned meanings on what "otherness" represents. Wallman (1979:3) remarks that, "Because it takes two, ethnicity can only happen at the boundary of 'us,' in contact or confrontation or by contrast with 'them.' As the sense of 'us' changes, so the boundary between 'us' and 'them' shifts." She adds that "the difference between two aggregates of people will be *objective* to the extent that an outsider can list items that mark it, but it is inevitably *subjective* to the extent that none of these markers has a necessary or precise significance outside the perception of the actors" (1979:5). With ethnicity, we are dealing, first, with meanings that define separateness and, second, with the enforcement of meanings and separateness through power.

This insistence that ethnicity really is about boundaries, control, and meaning construction is not my attempt to spin an interesting but obscure theoretical point. It addresses directly an issue that social service and health workers need to think more about: how their own activities, behavior, and assumptions affect crossethnic encounters. I will say more about this in the chapter on cross-cultural social work. For now, we simply need to be clear that ethnic identity is not the natural order of things it often appears to be. It is shifting, transactional, sometimes uncertain, and almost always implies an agenda of enforcement. And enforcement is a difficult thing for many well-meaning Americans to think about. Ethnicity as a phenomenon is specific to situations, and its particular meaningfulness at any given moment can be elusive and unresolved. Where the bigot sees certainty in the human condition, the rest of us see a conceptual and behavioral minefield.

CONCEPTS OF ETHNICITY: CATEGORICAL AND TRANSACTIONAL

Theories of ethnicity are not academic contrivances. They are systematic efforts to understand people's perceptions of reality and their characterizations of others as human beings. No service profession, especially one that deals with suffering, can afford not to articulate these matters clearly. To further refine these ideas as they apply to social services, I want to consider a distinction made by Bennett (1975) between what he calls categorical and transactional explanations of cultural difference. This distinction is crucial in thinking about cross-cultural social work (Figure 1.2).

Categorical explanations for cultural difference dominate American popular thought. Categorical accounts of ethnicity begin with assemblages of ethnic "traits," lists of things believed to be descriptive of persons in group X or Y. This approach involves a mental operation of sorting and matching specific traits so that one can locate individuals on a predetermined scale of what people X or Y are believed to be like. It presumes that an individual who "fits" one criteria probably fits many of the others that define the group as well. In categorical thought one would presume, for example, that the well-known social worker Jimm Good Tracks, who has written about these issues, must be Native American simply because Native Americans have names like that. (In fact, some do but many others

Categorical	Transactional
◆ Emphasizes cultural "content" within groups	◆ Emphasizes boundaries between groups
◆ Assumes high level of cultural uniformity within groups	◆ Expects differential expression of surface features within groups
◆ Seeks conceptual simplification in response to cultural "otherness"	◆ Seeks conceptual complexity within a comparative perspective
◆ Assimilation or acculturation are policy and intervention goals	◆ Resolution within indigenous frameworks as intervention goal
◆ Associated with melting pot and pluralistic ideologies	◆ Anticipates resistance to political and cultural dominance

FIGURE 1.2   Models of Ethnicity

do not.) Good Tracks is immediately categorized and, depending on how cavalier we want to be about it, we can also assume we know other things about him based on whatever previous experiences (including watching Hollywood westerns) we have had with other Native Americans.

In this approach, individuals are slotted into a predetermined trait list of surface features that do not explain so much as they impose. The categorizer's intellectual task is to assess the degree to which Good Tracks or any other Native American conforms to a standardized, stereotypical expectation. But if, for example, it should turn out that a client is Native American and also has an advanced degree in mathematics, sent her two children to Stanford, and works as a software engineer for NASA, the question the categorical thinker would ask is: with all that education and work experience, how Native American is she? Categorical thought comes with a set of assumptions about assimilation and the degree of match between the individual and the constellation of traits that are believed a priori to typify all Native Americans. The presence of a software-designing Native American client does not challenge the validity of the categorical approach; rather, the categorizer redefines her to fit preconceived ideas about her ethnicity. This kind of pigeonholing seems obviously misguided, especially in this example, but it is surprising how often it occurs, even in social service settings.

Since categorical thinking about race and ethnicity is the norm in American culture, all of us, whatever our background, indulge the habit at one time or another. Even those who try to be sensitive in these matters find it difficult; the sub-tlety and pervasiveness of categorical thinking is profound. Further, where it is rel-atively easy to identify and correct categorization of surface features of ethnicity, it is more difficult when we are working with the core areas of ethnicity that can be less obvious.

Consider an example that involves one of the core areas of kinship, reciprocity (a derivative feature of the more generalized commensality). During a year of par-ticipant observation and interviewing on issues of race in an integrated dormitory at Rutgers University, Moffatt (1986, 1989) documented racial attitudes among white and African American students. He found that whites categorized blacks according to a white model of friendship. White students emphasized their funda-mental individualism, especially what they saw as their "free," voluntary choice of who would be a friend. Whites assumed that friendship pairing was a purely sub-jective matter, one in which no constraints other than personal preference oper-ated. Only in matters of *style,* which to whites meant food and music, did white students concede any significant differences between themselves and blacks. When some African American students seemed to resist white efforts at making friends, whites concluded that there was an "attitude" problem, "attitudes" being something over which individuals ought to have some degree of control. The white model of friendship was voluntaristic, individualist, and ahistorical and was one source of friction between the two groups of students.

African American students, of course, had their own model for friendship pairing, one guided more by ideas about kinship—something hardly voluntary—than white notions of individualism and unfettered free choice. In the black model, friendship was thought of as something that evolves slowly and not entered into easily. It was intended to be genuinely long term and frequently involved a series of small exchanges such as money and personal items that gradually moved the relationship to the point where someone could be described as a "friend." These reciprocities were at least as important to African American students as the psy-chological compatibility that the white students emphasized. Many of the black students resented what they saw as the easy and seemingly shallower attachments the whites favored and that whites insisted ought to be the pattern for blacks as well. For blacks, the easygoing nature of white friendship seemed casual to the point of being superficial and hence not trustworthy.

This example illustrates several features of categorical thinking that usually lead to fundamental misunderstandings about what people are doing and intend-ing. First, the members of the dominant group in the dorm presumed that every-one shared (or ought to share) their beliefs and practices surrounding a very basic and seemingly simple notion: what it means to be a friend. But that kind of homo-geneity did not exist. Second, the white students did not recognize or allow cul-tural (as opposed to psychological) variations on the theme of friendship. As far as the black students were concerned, there was no "attitude" problem at all and cer-tainly no "problem" that needed fixing. Third, the example illustrates how easily "problems" that arise in cross-cultural relationships are located in the ethnographic "other," never in oneself. Categorical thinking is comparative but only in the most simplistic and ethnocentric sense: it presumes a central point of reference that is a standard, myself, and measures all others against that standard.

Categorical approaches to ethnicity have dominated belief and practice in American popular culture for generations, and their omnipresence is hard to avoid. Both the older "melting pot" ideology and more recent notions of cultural pluralism assume that ethnicity is a cultural fossil, a remnant of the historical past and of our unhappy experiences with slavery, immigrant enclaves, and reservations. In the melting pot model, historically received ethnic traits are expected to recede as each ethnic community adopts features of the dominant culture and gradually submerges its own distinctiveness through education, social mobility, and perhaps (although this is rarely mentioned) intermarriage. Eventually, it is assumed, a new and singular national social identity, one without the divisiveness associated with race or class, will emerge. That this has not happened, and probably will not, seems evident, as Glazer and Moynihan (1963) pointed out many years ago.

(It should be noted that the "tossed salad" model of ethnicity, considered progressive by some, is not an improvement. While it postulates a happier future where everyone "celebrates" his or her ethnicity without hindrance, it still pigeonholes—separating the lettuce from the celery from the olives—as though ethnic identities are fixed, permanent assemblages of traits. It does not understand ethnicity as a matter of perspectives, shifting and changing with time. Why this insistence on the immutability of ethnicity is so persistent in American thought is beyond the scope of this book, but those who want to pursue it should start with Mary Douglas's thoughtful essay on the social meanings of pollution in human relations [1968].)

Although the melting pot model no longer has credence in social science, it continues to function as our unofficial, popular ideology on racial and cultural matters (Wellman 1993). Thus, ethnic groups or individuals are described as more or less "assimilated," a reference to the extent to which they are presumed to have given up their ethnic uniqueness in favor of the generalized cultural characteristics thought to be typical and desirable by the larger society. This kind of explanation often includes an implicit scale of degrees of acculturation. Individuals who retain their native language, food preferences, or occupations fall at the "traditional" end of the scale; those who appear to have given up entirely their ethnic lifestyle are "integrated" into the larger community.

The melting pot approach is severely limited, however, for many reasons. For example, there is no historical evidence that the variety of groups that make up American society are merging into a homogeneous whole. Acculturation for Native Americans has really been a euphemism for cultural genocide. (If the word "genocide" seems too strong, review the statistics of Native American mortality over the past two or three centuries and the impact of federal land and education policies on Native American peoples.) Similarly, the effort to preserve linguistic distinctiveness has become a contentious issue for both English and Spanish speakers, especially in the South and Southwest, where the electorate in a number of states has approved ballot initiatives declaring English the official language. That issue is more than the right of Latino children to be taught in Spanish language classrooms. What is involved is preservation of one of the most powerful cultural identifiers any group can have, its language (Gibson and Arvizu 1977). Finally, studies of Southeast Asian students in American schools reveal that those who are most acculturated to the norms of American life have poorer academic scores than those who are less acculturated. Such findings contradict established beliefs about the value of the melting pot model and suggest instead that many people might be better off maintaining their distance from mainstream culture.

Cultural pluralism, a more recent innovation in popular thinking about ethnicity, is also based on the categorical approach and, as such, shares its limitations. Cultural pluralism stresses the distinctiveness of ethnic groups and the need for them to live in a kind of separate-but-equal harmony, the "tossed salad" theory again. Unlike the melting pot view, however, the pluralist approach appreciates cultural differences and their preservation—up to a point. It argues that ethnic groups provide the individual with a primary basis for loyalty and affiliation; that ethnic differences are good in themselves; and that ethnic variation contributes strength, not weakness, to the larger community. While these claims have a powerful appeal, particularly to those of a liberal or humanistic persuasion, they are not without problems. Pluralism can and has been used as a kind of "enlightened" cultural relativism to rationalize the exclusion of some groups from full social and political participation. An example is the once fashionable "culture of poverty" theory, widely used to explain why the problems of poor people are distinctive to them and why they are the victims of their own bad choices. The current expression of this idea is in the benign pluralism that arose in the 1980s. In that period, when greed and self-aggrandizement almost became patriotic acts, troubled communities were left to "do their own thing," "walk their own walk," and otherwise deal with their problems as best they could. A conservative version of pluralism as national policy called for nonintervention in human issues as though that were a benevolent respect for cultural differences. Of course, it was not.

The categorical approach, whether of melting pot or pluralistic forms, always requires that the observer view the ethnicity of others as a combination of traits that they (rather than us) exhibit: their "color," their musical styles, their foods, and sometimes their poverty. If the fashion of the times romanticizes these things as "their" way, this provides justification for doing little or nothing to change debilitating circumstances. Carrying this view to its most extreme, one could argue that slave plantations, Indian reservations, and World War II detention camps were examples of pluralism. Of course, no one thinks of them that way because they were imposed through force by one group on another. But rural slums in the South, reservations for Native Americans in the West, and crowded Chinatowns with sweatshop labor conditions have at times been viewed by the uninformed as quaint, romantic, and authentic. Pluralism, by itself, is not a theory that can help us understand ethnic and minority concerns because it diverts attention from the fact that many people live as they do because the larger society permits them few alternatives.

There is one additional criticism to make of categorical ways of viewing the ethnographic other. Categorization, like prejudice, would probably matter less if everyone were equally powerful. But everyone is not. In categorical thinking, one *imposes* on another, largely because it is possible to do so. Most minority Americans are acutely sensitive to racial slights from whites, far more than whites generally realize. Verbal gaffes are not mere breaches of etiquette or expressions of insensitivity. Rather, they reveal an arrogance of power, a presumptiveness that one has a right to label others and to get away with it.

In sum, the problem with categorical ways of thinking about ethnicity and cultural difference is that it is ultimately political: the dominant group dictates the categories that help it manage and control uncertain and potentially contentious relationships. The implicit assumption is that cross-cultural relationships are essentially competitive and hostile, competitive for the scarce resources of position, power, rank, authority, goods, time, services, and moral worthiness. Cultural difference is a challenge, even a threat, one that invokes self-protection and personal distancing. In service relationships, that is hardly an effective way of learning about others or of responding to their needs.

I want to end this section with an observation about the longer-term implications of ethnicity. I have already mentioned that there is nothing permanent about the racial or ethnic identities we all claim for ourselves. The so-called races that exist today did not exist 10,000 years ago. Some, in fact, did not exist in North and South America even a few hundred years ago, prior to colonization by Europeans, West Africans, and East Asians. Some races that now exist may be less evident in a few thousand years. Certainly current boundaries will be blurred just as new ones will be emerging. Migration, human contact, sex, and evolution guarantee it.

So what does such a large, historical generalization mean for us now? Consider this: America's complexion is literally darkening, and if current demographic trends continue, that darkening will be more evident to everybody by the early years of the next century. Gibbs and Huang (1989) refer to it as the "browning of America." As the baby boomers begin to retire and vacate the workplace over the next 15 to 35 years, the American economy will face severe labor shortages at virtually every skill level. Immigrants from all over the globe will arrive, as they always have, but in much greater numbers than before. Those immigrants will meet and mix with the indigenous African, Latino, Asian, and white population as they always have, but with greater frequency.

At some time near the middle of the next century, people who are now cultural and racial minorities will be close to numerical and political parity with whites. At that time, they may well demand economic and social parity as well and, for the price of civil peace, they will probably get it. Half a lifetime from now, all the meeting and mixing will be evident in the faces of everyone, and the phrase "people of color" may mean something else or it may mean nothing at all. From an anthropological point of view, that process seems perfectly natural, much more natural in fact than our historic insistence on racial separation.

SOCIAL WORK—ETHNIC GROUP RELATIONSHIPS

If ethnicity resides in the boundaries between distinctive cultural communities, then the persons who mediate boundaries are critical actors in the communication of information and regulation of resources affecting minorities. The social science literature has numerous terms for such persons: mediators, facilitators, ombudsmen, cultural brokers, go-betweens, and the like. In their work with minority clients, social workers are often mediators who help clients get things they cannot get alone. But mediation can be expressed in a variety of ways, and each way presupposes an implicit if not explicit value orientation and matching intervention style.

At least four modes of intervention with minority groups can be defined. Following Cowger (1977), I will identify these as (1) group advocate, (2) counselor, (3) regulator, and (4) broker. Of course, these categories can and do overlap, but they suggest ways of understanding the immense variety of social work–ethnic group encounters.- I will use this simple but useful division of professional-client relationships to consider some of the implications of ethnicity for professional services (Figure 1.3).

One approach to intervention is advocacy, sometimes described as a radical response (Statham 1978). The forms of advocacy vary widely, from efforts to fundamentally reorganize community services in New York's Harlem (Day 1987) to making mental health services more available to people in Appalachia (Keefe 1988). Advocacy assumes that conflict is inherent in minority and dominant group relationships and that the dominant social institutions must be challenged and changed. The advocate views the client's needs and problems as a result of unfair and unjust practices and an inequitable distribution of resources. Advocacy has an explicit value orientation. Taylor (1987) notes that the National Association of Social Workers Code of Ethics calls for "marshaling of community resources to promote the well being of all" and "action for improving social conditions" (1987:4). Advocacy is in fact interference and partisanship, which, of necessity, challenges institutional procedures and habits that interfere with the legitimate expectations of those seeking help.

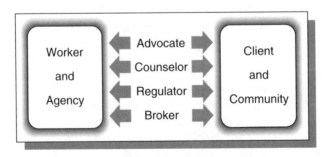

FIGURE 1.3   Worker–Client Relationships

The important issue raised by the advocacy approach is the culpability of dominant institutions, including the institutions that provide social services and social service education, in the problems minority clients experience. Advocates point out that problems are often perpetuated and aggravated by accepted practices: drug misuse by intensive commercial promotion of medications; slums by the investment practice of banks and landlords; job discrimination by the rhetorical insistence on maintenance of hiring and promotion standards. Social work has also been criticized for ignoring the political, social, and economic forces that contribute, in both direct and indirect ways, to the concerns that clients bring to workers.

One of the classic (and controversial) statements of advocacy is that of Cloward and Piven (1975). They charge that schools of social work train students to acquiesce to the organizational demands of social service and government bureaucracies. These demands, they maintain, perpetuate the agency and its agendas at the expense of the legitimate needs of clients. Established service organizations tend to blame the victim for psychological deficiencies, instead of working to change the oppressive social and economic circumstances that are part of the victim's problems. They cite health care: "Social workers are used by hospitals and their medical rulers to appease anxious or dissatisfied patients, to cool out the mark. What we ought to do instead is to challenge the doctors and hospital authorities, and encourage patients to do the same" (1975: xxxiv).

One of the more interesting recent attempts to provide a theoretical basis for advocacy in social services is that of Rose and Black (1985). Explicitly empowerment oriented, they criticize what they call the "decontextualization" of patients and clients—treating individuals as nonhistorical, nonsocial units to be therapeutically acted upon, their background experiences and associations subjectively replaced with a controlling language of procedures and formulas. They find decontextualization evident, for example, in implicit, often unspoken professional criteria of what makes a "good" client:

> *After a time, the externally imposed new social order [of the clinic or hospital] becomes incorporated subjectively—the problem definition coercively held out is tacitly accepted. But in the process, the patient undergoes an experience of anomie—of an abrupt withdrawal of norms and forms.... The experience of such extraction of one's known universe of meaning is profound (1985:30).*

Unlike many of the overtly political models of advocacy of the 1960s and 1970s, Rose and Black's program is intended for work with individuals, not just groups. For them, empowerment is the conversion of dependent help-seekers into self-consciously autonomous persons. Their challenging model calls upon the worker to learn the subjective meanings of the client's everyday world (they use the social science term *Verstehen,* implicit knowledge) and the cultural themes of that world (1985:60–69). The social worker learns of cultural issues prior to making technical assessments and evaluations. This strategy, which makes cultural meaning a central concern, goes well beyond the political mobilization of groups, which is the traditional sense of advocacy. Rose and Black show how their approach applies to case management, legal advocacy, and mental health day-care programs.

While there are many instances of advocacy based on prior cultural knowledge, one older but still excellent example is provided by Jacobs (1974a, 1974b, 1979) in her work with a Midwestern African American community where she helped establish a neighborhood health center. In that community, infant mortality rates among African American children were considerably higher than those for nearby white children, a problem that had become worse rather than better in recent years. The established health organizations attributed this difference to underutilization of existing health services by black families and an apparent unwillingness by expectant mothers to comply with their physician's advice. Jacobs's research and advocacy team discovered different reasons. These included explicit acts of racial stereotyping of black patients by white physicians, collusion among white-dominated health organizations to exclude black physicians, and adoption by health providers of a white model of health services, which at that time was crisis oriented rather than preventive. As she documented these issues, Jacobs also examined the health care preferences and behavior of community residents. Working with black patients, clients, and a variety of black professionals, she helped design health care practices that were more closely aligned with community expectations. The work was time-consuming and difficult, but it resulted in a high level of trust between Jacobs and community members and in a demonstrably more useful health care program. It also showed the utility of an explicitly cultural orientation in taking on a significant community concern. Long-term problems in the transactions between the white health care establishment and black patients had contributed to a serious health problem. Jacobs's work as an advocate unraveled the threads of that problem, thus enabling the community to better plan its own initiatives.

In the second intervention mode, that of counseling, practitioners intervene by focusing on the client's specific problems, particularly on client feelings, ideas, and behavior, and on ways to develop positive responses to specific issues. This is the usual clinical style, with the practitioner functioning as a counselor, and it is the one many social work texts and training manuals address. Professional practice is viewed as neutral in terms of larger social implications. The target of change is the individual, not power structures or class relationships, and change is achieved one-on-one or in small groups. The practitioner's first responsibility is to the client, not to the client's community as such. This approach, as Cowger points out, was codified in an earlier version of the National Association of Social Workers' statement of ethics: "I regard as my primary obligation the welfare of the individual or group served, which includes action for improving social conditions" (1977:27). To change social conditions is usually interpreted as subordinate to changing clients. While the clinical model has the advantage of recognizing that individuals do have concerns that must be addressed through supportive personal services, it often slights the institutionally generated sources of individual difficulty.

A persistent problem in counseling has been the sometimes awkward match between the individual counselor with his or her clinical approach and the cultural diversity of clients. Social work researchers have generally looked no further than the degree of comfort felt by clients and clinicians in same-ethnic and mixed-ethnicity combinations and, in practice, most social workers have relied either on personal experience or empathy to carry them through cross-cultural encounters. This is surprising, because cross-cultural counseling is an area of vigorous interest in such fields as education and psychology and it has a number of applications, particularly in government and business programs involving contact with people in other countries. Anthropologists, although they have not often specifically focused on the interests of social workers, have done extensive work in interethnic communication and in communication issues in medical settings (Kleinman 1980, 1988b), schools (Spindler 1982, 1987; Spindler and Spindler 1994), and specialized areas such as aging (Sokolovsky 1990b), child abuse (Korbin 1981), abortion (Ginsburg 1989), and American marriage and divorce patterns (Johnson 1989). Some have even proposed that ethnographic interviewing has therapeutic functions for minority clients (Davidson 1994; García-Castañon 1994).

But the availability of information, whatever its source, is probably not the real issue. In what has become one of the standard works in cross-cultural counseling, Sue and Sue (1990) list what they see as the impediments to effective communication between mainstream white counselors and minority clients. These impediments include a number of culture-bound values, including extreme individualism in the conceptualization of client concerns; an insistence on verbal and emotional expressiveness as a therapeutic technique; demands for self-disclosure; simplistic, linear cause-and-effect models; reliance on mind/body distinctions in arriving at clinical judgments; and missed body and linguistic cues. Language is of particular concern not only because some clients have difficulties with English but also because social service providers tend to rely on technical vocabulary that mystifies clients. Using euphemisms and jargon, the language of "empathy," "caring," "engagement," "openness," "holism," and even empowerment can inappropriately substitute for learning the meaning of personal issues within the context of another culture.

In a third intervention mode, the practitioner is seen as an extension of the larger society, in effect a kind of regulator who is concerned with helping clients modify their behavior or attitudes. Resocialization of clients, especially involuntary ones, is a standard strategy in this approach. There is an important social control function that clearly reflects society's mandate that some kinds of problems be corrected or controlled. In the area of child abuse, for instance, the idea of serving the "best interests of the child" may be viewed as one of changing family discipline practices. The social worker may indeed act as a counselor to an abusing parent, but the aim of intervention is to modify family patterns. How these patterns are modified, in what direction, and under what authority are critical issues that often reflect the mandate placed on the social worker-as-regulator. Ethnic community leaders often cite this control-oriented function as evidence that the profession is more committed to protecting the status quo than ensuring just and fair treatment for those who need it most. Whatever the merits of these complaints, these critics raise an important issue that goes beyond mere rhetoric. How should deviance, discontent, maladaptation, and nonconformity be defined and judged, and who is to do the judging?

One of the most dramatic illustrations of the regulatory functions of social service providers can be found in the history of control over Native American children, first through government boarding schools (Blanchard 1983), then in attempts to deal with suicide, alcoholism, and delinquency (Wise and Miller 1983; Robbins 1984), and finally in the slow development of Native American–oriented and –operated service programs (Shore and Manson 1983; Grafton 1982). Native American children were often removed from their homes, not because of abuse or neglect, but because of perceived deficits in the home and community environment. Tribal authorities and agencies were not always consulted nor did parents understand the nature of the legal proceedings against them (Blanchard and Unger 1977). In the boarding school system, parents and tribal authorities did not always know where children had been sent. These injustices are far less frequent now, in part because of the militancy of tribal leaders and Native American social workers but also because of the growing sensitivity of social workers generally to the values and strengths of Native American communities (Edwards and Edwards 1984). But this example raises larger issues about the regulatory role. In managing the expression of apparent deviance, who decides what is and is not acceptable, and by what standards? To whom ought social service providers be accountable for their decisions? This is both a cultural and a political issue, and the culturally sensitive worker will need to be able to defend counseling, referral, and placement choices in ways that make sense not only to individual clients but to their families and communities as well.

In the fourth intervention mode, the practitioner functions as an intermediary or broker. This approach stresses the practitioner's dual responsibility to the individual and society. Many social workers probably function as brokers as part of their professional activity, particularly when they work to mediate the needs of clients and the limitations of the service system. It is frustrating and often thankless work and, for some social workers, a primary cause of burnout.

There is more than one way to be a broker or mediator. McLeod (1981) summarizes these ways in an interesting discussion of mediation as a professional skill. She notes that the most superficial kind of mediator is the "trader," whether a trader in goods, ideas, or services. The trader is primarily interested in his or her own enterprise, the personal benefits that might accrue, and the success of the larger agenda of the "home culture," whether that is the "culture" of the trader's company, profession, or local office. A detailed knowledge of client needs and interests is secondary since clients are viewed essentially as consumers (however unwilling, at times) for whatever the trader is offering. In this relationship, one client is much like any other and moving them through the system, "processing" cases, is the trader's goal.

By contrast, the "diplomat" requires a deeper knowledge of the client's culture because he or she will be called upon to deal with unhappy "incidents" in which some member of the client community feels aggrieved. A bit more sophisticated than the trader, the diplomat is still an extension of the home territory's agendas;

the services offered justify the sponsoring organization's staff and budget and the diplomat functions to advance the home culture's goals however they may be defined.

The "missionary" is a third kind of mediator, but one whose first loyalties are not to the home office or the client but to the mission itself. To be successful, the missionary must know more of the client culture than either the trader or the diplomat, but that knowledge is intended to serve first the needs of the mission. Clients, of course, are the presumed beneficiaries, but it is the mission that is at issue. Missionaries are usually individuals with zeal, something that may not typify the trader or the diplomat who has more circumscribed interests. Fueled by enthusiasm for their cause—cracking down on crack, extracting support from errant fathers, gaining convictions against abusive spouses—the missionary is really a crusader, concerned more with a principle than the idiosyncrasies of individual cases.

The fourth kind of broker McLeod calls the "teacher." She states, "I use the word *teacher* to refer to the true mediator, because his success can be measured in terms of what is learned by those with whom he has contact" (1981:40). Teachers undoubtedly have vested interests, just like other kinds of mediators, but they succeed when they can persuade members of differing cultural communities to better understand, respect, and perhaps care about one another. Both sides receive benefits. Not all teachers (in the occupational sense) are mediators, but all good mediators are teachers because their professional work leads to new levels of understanding by everyone.

What special skills do mediators as teachers have? First, not surprisingly, they have knowledge, lots of it, about the communities they serve. Their knowledge is neither superficial nor encyclopedic; it is specific and deep. Second, they have communication skills. That does not mean they know two or three languages but that they understand the importance of vernacular in discussing and clarifying personal and family problems. They know how to use language in specific ways that are helpful in their work, a skill I address in a later chapter. Third, teachers have technical skills, acquired through formal training and refined through apprenticeship. Fourth, they have social skills that enable them to perform effectively in confusing, ambiguous, or even hostile environments. They can articulate some of the "rules of the game" of another community and recognize when rules are being violated, although they may not always know why. For effective mediators, their knowledge of another culture is a kind of master skill that allows them to know that culture much as community members do (Taft 1981). The mediator who recognizes and understands the culture-specific emotional responses of the served community has achieved the highest level of skill. At this point, he or she is truly bicultural.

Is this kind of capability too much to ask, something beyond which social workers need aspire? The answer is an unequivocal no. Many people already have these skills and presently work in human service occupations. They are social work's minority professionals, individuals who occupy a middle ground between their communities of origin and their acquired, professional ones. Whereas most white social workers probably do not experience a significant cognitive and emotional dissonance between what they do on the job and what they believe the larger society supports, minority workers often confront this dilemma. They have grown up in a minority community and perhaps continue to live and participate in it. As most minority communities in America now have a significant and growing middle class, they often share in that. But the universities in which they were trained are still predominantly white and, in at least some of these schools, the debate continues about the place of minority issues in the curriculum, what emphasis they should have, and whether or not courses designed around minority content ought to be required for everyone. Where minorities were once referred to as having a "dual perspective" (Norton et al. 1978), it may now be fairly stated that they have multiple perspectives: a community of origin, their middle class status, and a professional community. On some occasions, professional responsibilities and personal interest may collide.

I would even suggest that in some quarters a degree of ambivalence toward minority professionals remains. Their priorities, if not loyalties, are a question mark to some of their colleagues. I do not think this is due to explicit racism, although that may sometimes be the case, but to the fact that minority professionals do indeed have multiple perspectives. They are in a good position to make comparative, even critical judgments about policy and practice. Being multicultural, the authoritative basis of their insight is hard to ignore. And as professionals, they know the customs, etiquette, and preferences of the professional subculture and how that subculture is generally expressive of the value system of the politically dominant white middle class. Their "quiet presence," as I once heard a sympathetic but troubled trainee describe it, was a daily reminder that his agency's goals and activities were not always accommodating to those who had different ideas about what could or should be done.

SOCIAL WORK AS AN ETHNIC COMMUNITY

Are the differences between minority and dominant group social workers really that great, or are they minor matters of etiquette, communication styles, and personal preferences? One way to think about that is to turn the ethnographic approach onto the service professions directly, treating the subculture of social workers as an ethnic community like any other with its own arcane rituals, in-group jargon, overt and covert values, and boundary-protecting mechanisms. Using our model, we could say that social workers as an "ethnic group" share kinship (common socialization through degree-granting and training programs), commensality (shared physical working spaces, bureaucratic routines, time put in on tasks, and private understandings about work and the agency), and cult (motivations for entering social work as a career, the values that prompt one's labors, and a share in the legacy of the profession and one's agency). We could also say that some members of the social work tribe are, in their own ways, ethnocentric, just like the members of ethnic communities everywhere.

To understand this tribe, we can compare its distinctive features—communication styles, rituals, or implicit working assumptions, for example—with those of other ethnic communities. Native American social worker Jimm Good Tracks has commented that "all the methods usually associated with the term 'social work intervention' diminish in effectiveness" when applied to Native American clients (Good Tracks 1973:30). The more traditional the client's orientation, he says, the less likely the positive effect of normative social work practice. This is because in many Native American communities "no interference or meddling of any kind is allowed or tolerated, even when it is to keep the other person from doing something foolish or dangerous" (Good Tracks 1973:30).

Similarly, Wax and Thomas (1961) contrast the ways in which Native Americans and whites sometimes deal with personal problems. For example, when confronted with a crisis, whites often feel the need to act decisively, to "do something" before the situation gets "out of hand." Activism, courageous decision making, and the appearance of being "in charge" are important values for whites, whether they can do all those things well or not. But many Native Americans respond to problems with quietness, caution, careful observation, and, if necessary, withdrawal. What looks to whites as escapist is, from a Native American perspective, properly careful scrutiny and the avoidance of unnecessary pain. Personal integrity is also protected this way. Rejecting the urge of whites to be heroic and to reach beyond their grasp (failure for whites, if in a noble cause, is still ennobling), many Native Americans prefer to avoid the foolishness of attempting too much. They also value noninvolvement, holding that if something obviously needs to be done, at some point an individual qualified and capable will do it; there is no need for well-meaning bystanders to presume it is their responsibility to act just because they happen to be present. Further, Native Americans avoid direct requests to others. Direct talk, seen by whites as "honest" and "frank," is seen by many Native Americans as rude, behavior more typical of improperly raised children than of adults sensitive to what is going on around them.

Native American communities, especially traditional ones, have low levels of the kind of demonstrative action that whites accept as normal. Voluntary cooperation, at a time convenient for all concerned, is the way things get done. This is reflective of a fundamental and profoundly democratic orientation, one in which "assertiveness," "being number one," and "standing tall"—popular clichés in the white world—are seen as incredible boorishness if not folly. However well intended, intrusive behavior by whites in Native American matters is quietly noted and sometimes resented, a resentment manifest in silence or withdrawal.

From the point of view of the social work tribe, probably no Native American values are more puzzling and confounding than those associated with time and timing. "White time" is clock time, time organized to serve industrial and corporate purposes. The "fifty minute hour" and task-centered services are examples of extreme clock and calendar awareness. By contrast, Native American time is social time, adjusted to meet personal, family, and sometimes ritual needs. Philips (1974) has described how a Native American sense of time is shaped by a distinctive notion of the progression of events, be they public ceremonies, private conversations, or informal gatherings of friends. To whites, most activities have an implicit order: an identifiable beginning, a middle, and an end. At each stage, the participants know where they are in the sequence and modulate their speech and mannerisms accordingly. But for many Native Americans, events are defined more in terms of the availability of people; the presence of certain persons is necessary before anything can begin. Thus many Native American activities are open-ended, seemingly indeterminate, and appear to whites to have confused and ambiguous boundaries. To Native Americans, there is no confusion at all. As Philips notes, an event cannot happen until the right people are available and, given the value of noninterference, it would not be appropriate to coerce anyone to be at a specific place at a given time. This emphasis on people rather than the abstractions represented by a clock face is an organizational strategy that "maximize[s] the possibility that everyone who wants to participate is given the chance when he or she chooses to and in the way he or she chooses to" (Philips 1974:107). Native American time, therefore, is not an inability to get someplace exactly when one must be there; it is not an "inability" at all. It is a distinctive cultural style, subtle and complex, that is preeminently person-centered.

Are these generalizations true of all Native American communities? Certainly not. To believe so would be to stereotype anew. Not all Native Americans fit this very brief summation of generalized Native American values any more than all social workers would fit a comparably brief overview of what they are like. Rather, the value of the information is in alerting the social worker to issues that may affect a relationship with Native American clients. These generalizations about white time and Native American time cannot be taken as Grand Truth but as a hypothesis, one that might have to be explored in working with specific Native American clients.

We could also compare social work as a distinctive culture with other service or bureaucratic entities in the dominant society. For example, there is a small, emerging field that studies the culture of corporations. It goes behind organizational charts, job descriptions, and management policies and looks at the implicit rules and practices of corporate life. Some of this research has been done by anthropologists, although much of it is the work of people in business studies and corporate psychology. The topics range widely: the hidden values in corporate logos; the management of stress by salespeople; company picnics and other organizational festivals; corporate folklore and myth making among top management; the manipulation of customer relations; the funeral director as ritual choreographer; and the "glass ceiling" and its effects on the promotion of women and minorities. (See Jones, Moore, and Snyder [1988] for an interesting introduction to this field.) These matters are not only interesting but useful for understanding the hidden dynamics of behavior in what seem to be highly structured, preeminently rational human associations.

For example, Deal and Kennedy (1982) describe what they call "corporate tribes," each of which has a distinctive way of doing their work. They offer amusing accounts of corporate dress, housing, sports, language, greeting rituals, and officially disapproved relations between coworkers. Deal and Kennedy do not describe social services organizations directly, but close approximations are those they typify as "process cultures," low-risk, slow-feedback organizations (insurance companies, universities, utilities, much of government) in which "no one transaction will make or break the company—or anyone in it" (1982:119). Lacking good feedback on outcomes (sometimes even lacking clear definitions of outcomes), members of these corporate tribes are obsessed with procedures, memos, paper trails, low profiles, "cover your backside" tasks, and hunkering down when evil administrative winds blow. They are marked by an inordinate concern with titles and rank, most dramatically evidenced by office walls papered with framed certificates awarded for attendance at workshops and conferences. Their favorite rituals center on procedures: long meetings on how to organize and reorganize and endless discussions of the micropolitics of departments, personnel, and policies. There is a studied wariness of institutional brush fires and fear of where they may erupt next. The ability to survive procedural challenges and internal power shifts makes one a hero in a process culture tribe. Heroes are also the mythological progenitors of agency policies and practices, all carefully explained to new hires but quickly forgotten when one reigning hero is displaced by another.

The literature on the corporate culture of social work is not great, and what little exists is scattered in many sources, but I want to cite briefly two examples that help us go beyond the generalizing (and sometimes amusing) descriptions of "tribal" corporations. They illustrate how the culture of a service organization can collide with the will and expectations of its clients, creating conflicts for reasons that neither client nor worker quite clearly see.

In describing what she calls "splintered visions," Wharton (1989) analyzes competing views of family violence held by staff and clients in a shelter for battered women. Her case study shows how conflicts can arise when the corporate culture of the staff is not shared by those served. Wharton states that the shelter "was founded by a grass roots feminist group, who adopted the self-help model that battered women realize their own capabilities" (1989:54). But that approach did not lead to actions desired by the residents. The staff encouraged women to separate, permanently if possible, from their offending partners; they referred to the women's abusive husbands as "assailants"; and they defined the dominant emotion of the women in the shelter as "anger," anger that must be turned into "positive energy" to put the residents "in touch" and in charge of their own feelings.

Yet the women who came to the shelter as short-term residents were not interested in permanent separation from an abusive spouse. Their goal was to wait out a husband's anger until it was safe to return home where, they hoped, things might get better. (That may or may not have been a realistic goal, but Wharton's concern was a separate issue, the imposition of staff ideology on residents.) Many of the women resented hearing their husbands or boyfriends referred to as "the assailant" since they knew their situations were more complex than that. The word "assailant" suggested to them a legal category, not a description of a lengthy and complicated relationship. Some of the client-residents became anxious about a "bunker mentality" that permeated the shelter, an us/them dichotomy that dominated staff conversations and counseling. In addition, through interviews and participant observation, Wharton came to understand that anger was not the predominant emotion of these women. They were depressed, tired, frightened, and confused but they did not define those feelings as "anger." Nor did they perceive that dwelling on "anger" and its "venting" would help them deal with hostile and even dangerous men once they returned to their homes. The client's view of the shelter was as a "people-processing" place, one where women in need could come for a short respite. But the staff saw the mission of the shelter as "people changing" according to a predetermined model of residents' "needs." When disputes among the women occasionally broke out— usually over feeding schedules, child discipline, and privacy—staff blamed clients for not really wanting to change their lives. Clients blamed staff for demanding that they accept goals they did not really want.

If ideology, and conflicts about it, is one of the things that defines an organization's culture, so too is behavior, especially behavior that is a response to internal cleavages of power. Wiener and Kayser-Jones (1989) describe what they call "defensive work" in a nursing home: protective strategies intended to shield the institution and staff from outsiders, especially state inspectors and patients' families. For example, the authors found that informally agreed-upon rules had evolved for filling out forms so that the real causes of death or illness were given different names and descriptions. One staff member told the researchers that this was known as "buff[ing] the chart" so that state inspectors would not find fault with the nursing home's procedures. The fact that the nursing home was generally well run did not matter; the nit-picking of state inspectors, with potentially damaging legal results, was perceived to require defensive work simply so the home could carry out its legitimate functions with minimal intrusion. Defensive strategies proliferated, and staff time gradually became more taken up with extensive documentation, even though the documents were unreliable. Defensive work became embedded in all staff activities, creating a massive, complex, and implicit structure of agency-specific understandings that would be as daunting to the state inspectors as it was to newly hired staff. Not only did the preoccupation with defensive work make life in the facility inordinately difficult for everyone, it also drained off the enthusiasm of those who were genuinely concerned for elderly patients. The agency's culture, with its thematic core of defensive work, made realization of that worthy intent unnecessarily difficult.

The nursing home and the women's shelter are examples of just two corporate service cultures. Obviously, corporate cultures can evolve in other ways, some more "user-friendly" for clients and staff than others. But the cultures of many service bureaucracies are similar in one respect: they tend to be grounded in an ideology of "professionalism." Older organizational research describes professionalism as a commitment to rationality, universalism, disinterestedness, and functional specificity (Becker and Carper 1956; Cogan 1953; Goode 1957). That is, professional organizations and activities have a culture that emphasizes reason over tradition as the basis for action, the uniform delivery of quality services regardless of the client's idiosyncrasies, and the provision of services without intrusion into inappropriate aspects of the individual's life. Obviously, any cultural critique of an organization and how it does its business will quickly puncture these bland dicta, revealing a much more complex world than administrative flowcharts and mission statements would suggest.

Any agency, from a state bureaucracy for adult and family services to a neighborhood office of part-time staffers offering walk-in counseling to teenagers, has a complex culture. That culture is based on shared understandings that are contingent on the organization's history, the staff's experiences, and the policies and philosophy of the funding source. Every client confronts this complex mix, usually without any awareness of its controlling effect on the quality of services. The issue for culturally alert human service professionals is to begin thinking beyond the limitations and restrictions of embedded routines, to see their office and their agency as a corporate tribe, with all its attendant strengths and limitations. They also need to consider how clients perceive and respond to agency culture and what that suggests about utilization rates and compliance with professional recommendations. Both at the personal and organizational level, workers need to think about what tribal boundaries mean and how brokering those boundaries, using the skills of "ethnic competence," can lead to greater client as well as worker satisfaction.

A HUMAN SERVICES MODEL OF CULTURAL COMPETENCE

This chapter began by introducing some of the critical concepts for an ethnographically sensitive approach to human services. I discussed a number of issues related to race, culture, and ethnicity because clarity about the meaning of these things is important, both conceptually and in human services practice. Especially practice. My view is that a commonsense approach to race and ethnicity will not carry the worker very far, no matter how well intended and how receptive to others he or she might be. The distinction between categorical and transactional views of ethnicity is vital. It should be obvious that my concern here is not simply intellectual neatness; rather, it is that ideas have consequences for others, and the transactional and categorical ways of looking at human differences express very different ideas about the world and how one operates in it. I have tried to clarify this by discussing some of the possible relationships between social workers and ethnic communities. I then pushed the culture idea a little farther than usual by suggesting that the human services profession is a kind of culture itself, one with its own ways of doing what it does.

These topics, important as they are, are really only matters of clarification. In preparing for practice, we need a model that will help us organize our thinking, perceptions, responses, and professional behavior in cross-cultural encounters of many kinds. Sue and Sue remark that "becoming culturally skilled is an *active process*," one "that it is *ongoing*, and it is a process that *never reaches an end point*" (1990:166). How, then, can we understand what this process involves and what must be done to become proficient in it?

The model proposed here is intended to add an additional and, I believe, essential dimension to service practice: the *comparative* basis for learning and for action in cross-cultural relationships. The comparative emphasis derives from ethnography, the descriptive study of cultures, and cultural anthropology, the comparative study of variation both within and between differing cultures. Figure 1.4 shows the major elements of the ethnic competence model, each of which is developed more fully in subsequent chapters. As an introduction, however, I want to offer a brief overview of the model and its components.

One of the most important elements of the model is the knowledge base for effective cross-cultural social work. But what kinds of knowledge? What is impor-

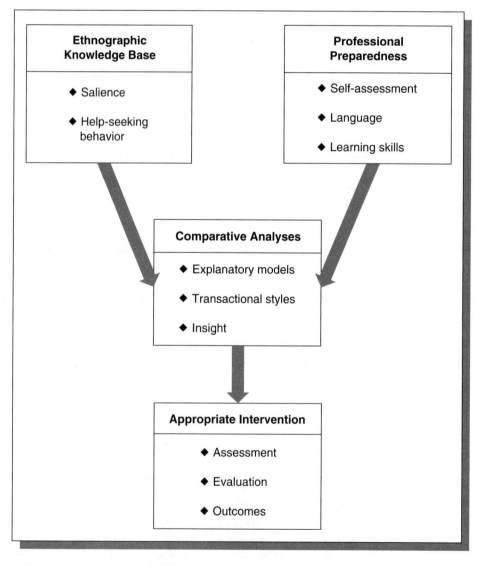

FIGURE 1.4   The Cultural Competence Model

tant, and how can the worker find it? No one can possibly know everything about all the clients he or she sees, especially when in a single day clients may come from many traditions and backgrounds. Overviews of the history of specific groups, or brief summations of their preferences in, say, child rearing might be useful and interesting, but they are at best a beginning point and may not be helpful for working with a particular client trying to manage a difficult child. Some other kinds of learning must prepare the social worker.

In this model, the knowledge base for cross-cultural human services work begins with identifying what is salient in the client's culture for the problems that routinely come before the worker. Once that is clarified—and salience is never as obvious as it seems it ought to be—the model provides a framework for filling in knowledge gaps with culturally appropriate and useful information. This is not particularly difficult, but it does require a systematic approach and a particular kind of perspective about working with and learning from others who may be culturally different from oneself.

A second element of the ethnic competence model is that of honestly addressing the personal meaning of racial and cultural differences for one's professional work. Articles in social service journals, statements of professional ethics, and the goals of workshops and training programs often sound as if all human service workers everywhere are fully aware of their biases and prejudices, have them under full control, and suffer no fear or anxiety of any kind when they are with minority clients. But when I go to training workshops and note what is being said and not said, when I discuss the problems of service delivery for minority clients with supervisors, when I listen to workers in minority directed and staffed agencies, I am forced to reconsider what I thought the professional position papers were telling me. Although I certainly do not believe that gross and blatant racism is a problem in social work, I am troubled by the expressions of insensitivity I sometimes hear. They are usually masked and cautiously phrased: assertions of special insight encoded in buzzwords and jargon; acceptance of superficial knowledge as adequate to one's professional tasks; and presumptions of innocence that distances the worker from culturally threatening others.

These anxieties and reactions are both reasonable and unreasonable. They are reasonable because we do live in a racially divided society, one that has never been color blind and may never be. We have all learned the mannerisms, fears, and etiquette that get us through even the briefest of interracial contacts. But they are unreasonable because they are misperceptions, even dogmas, and offer easy truths as a substitute for the real effort one would have to make to work effectively with others. I would argue that no one can really understand the differences in others without confronting directly one's own limits and capabilities. The chapters on preparing for cross-cultural social work and on language describe ways of beginning that process.

A third element of the model proposes a form of comparative analysis for identifying in detail the salient cultural elements of a client's presenting problems. But the approach does not offer a "trait list" of the characteristics of people in cultures X, Y, or Z. Rather, it emphasizes client concerns within an explicitly comparative framework. This component of the model discusses the importance of understanding culturally different world views, of individualizing clients in reference to those differences, and exploring ways of developing analytical insight and appropriate empathy. A discussion of some of the salient human service issues and needs in a number of ethnic and minority communities follows.

Finally, the model points the social worker toward ways of thinking about appropriate forms of intervention. This is really the "frontline" work for future cross-cultural human services. Early reports from the 1990 census suggest a rate of growth among ethnic and minority groups that will put them on numerical par with whites in a few decades. Some of this growth will occur within indigenous minority groups; some of it will be from foreigners, especially migrants from Asia and Central America, who will come to fill the jobs the baby boomers leave behind. And some parts of the country are already seeing an influx of people from Eastern Europe and the Middle East. Their presence may grow depending on the vagaries of international politics and trade agreements. Methods for learning about all these new people and of meeting their needs appropriately may become a political demand as much as it is an ethical one.

Taken in total, the cultural competence model I will describe in later chapters is really a system of learning. That is what it must be. There are simply no shortcuts. No one-day workshop or list of intervention tips and guidelines will give anyone the skills for working well with others, especially others whom one does not know or understand. The traditional service phraseology of rapport, empathy, empowerment, diversity, and caring is too vague. These terms often hide from the social services provider the true complexity of what he or she is attempting. If we really are committed to doing well by those who seek our help, we have few choices other than to spend the time and energy necessary to understand the context of their lives so we can more effectively respond to the needs and concerns they bring us.

POSTMODERNISM, AN EMERGING APPROACH

Responding to others in culturally appropriate ways is a complex experience. It involves a lot of learning, patient watching and listening, and rethinking some of the familiar assumptions of the discipline and profession. Postmodernism is an emerging model in human services, one that offers its own solutions to the challenges of multicultural work. Recent editorials in the journal *Social Work* by Hartman (1990; 1991) and Pardeck, Murphy, and Choi (1994) have given "official" recognition to postmodernism as a significant paradigm for human services. Because it is an emerging perspective, one that will be discussed and probably debated with intensity in the near future, we need to have an idea of what it is about. On occasion I will be referring to concepts related to postmodernist thinking, so I want to briefly introduce in this first chapter some of the issues that are involved.

Briefly stated, postmodernism is a theoretical critique of how relationships are formed in mass consumer- and information-oriented societies, and especially how people in those relationships use language to make claims about the kind of persons they are and the kind of power they believe they possess. As a contemporary stream of ideas and theorizing, postmodernism comes from several sources. One is literary criticism and its focus on texts and especially narrative. A second is anthropological linguistics with its emphasis on oral traditions and the multiple meanings of discourse. A third is the feminist critique of power in gender-biased societies, a discussion already well advanced in social services. Postmodernist thinking has been stimulated by world events as well. Satellite television, electronic mail, cheap airline flights, and the huge international movement of migrants trying to connect with jobs, rejoin dispersed families, or escape regional wars help generate all the bumping together of ideologies and cultures we now see and even take for granted. Postmodernism is an attempt to understand how people make sense of their disrupted lives under these seemingly chaotic conditions. It assumes that in narratives of experience, individuals assert and reclaim images of who and what they are. The postmodernist task is to interpret those narratives, recognizing that in speech the speaker/interpreter and the hearer/interpreter are both involved in a "constructionist" or reality-creating activity.

Two aspects of narrative are critical: power and voice. In her *Social Work* commentary, Hartman put it very neatly: "The words, interpretations, languages, and social discourses of people in power tend to become privileged and accepted as truth or knowledge, whereas the discourses of disempowered people tend to become marginalized" (1991:275). This happens because words and language are more than basic communicative mechanisms. They are world-creating devices: "In the postmodernist view, speech is an action, not simply a reflection. Words carry intentionality" (Hartman 1991:276). The idea of intentionality suggests that "facts" and information are created in voiced narratives and are the products of interaction and interpretation ("intersubjectivity") between speaker and hearer. Any set of "facts" is, in some significant degree, a product of human perceptions and communication. Talk is not so much about reality but is reality under construction. People generate a world view as they speak, both by reaffirming what they already know and in creatively applying that information to their own situation. "In this regard, normalcy is a linguistic habit" (Pardeck et al. 1994:344), and our sense of normalcy is something we continuously produce as we think, as we feel, and especially as we talk.

To understand what makes this approach distinctive, we can begin with its name. Although not everyone agrees exactly what "post" is, the "modern" part is fairly clear. Modernism refers to science as we conventionally understand it with its empirical or "objectivist" view of the world. Science as a distinctive way of thinking about how things have come to be as they are first emerged in Europe in the early 1600s, although its status as a legitimate way of acquiring information was by no means accepted or ensured. What was then thought of as "science" was seen as a challenge to the religiously inspired models of the period and their emphasis on the primacy of sacred texts and the sufficiency of revealed knowledge. (That argument still goes on, at least in some quarters, in the debates about human evolution.) What the scientific view suggested was that "reality" is both external to human beings (existing in the natural world) and objectively measurable and knowable. Through the correct application of increasingly logical and technological procedures, we can understand the realm of the natural and eventually control and even dominate it. From medicine to space flight to genetic engineering, objective, scientific knowledge can put human beings in charge of their future.

The obvious success of scientific empiricism in the study of natural phenomena inspired some to speculate about the possibility of a science of human relations as well. Like their natural science cousins, Enlightenment philosophers began to think of human social and psychological characteristics as objectifiable phenomena having measurable "properties," after the manner of physicists who studied the "properties" of electricity or light. Some of the early attempts at this now seem ludicrous, but at the time people believed they were extending scientific procedures to the understanding of human activity. One well-known instance was a celebrated eighteenth-century Austrian physician named Franz Anton Mesmer, who believed our bodies are magnetic in the same way as the earth and stars. Logically enough, he treated his patients' neuroses by applying large magnets to their heads to adjust what he called their "animal magnetism." In addition to "mesmerism," the "science" of phrenology was very popular in the nineteenth century. Phrenologists rubbed the bumps on their patients' heads to take "readings" of their personalities and health. But the work of people like Mesmer and the phrenologists were scientific attempts in the hands of popularizers and sometimes cranks. Others, like Karl Marx and Sigmund Freud, sought to put the understanding of human relations on firmer foundations. Marx believed in the possibility of a scientific analysis of power in industrial societies and its manifestation in the class system. He proposed testable ideas about the economic basis of social relations. While Marx's work led to the study of economies as systems, Freud proposed models of the human mind that could be experimentally analyzed and tested. Both Marx and Freud laid the foundations for what have become enduring systems of analysis with the potential for application of scientific procedures to the human realm. Their work was both philosophical and critical in the best sense of scientific study and led, in part, to the founding of the modern social and behavioral sciences.

That empiricist tradition, applied to human beings, has bequeathed an enormous intellectual legacy, ranging from the United States census with its systematic attempts to count us all to the *DSM* series, which replicates what it claims is a scientific viewpoint in its classification and descriptions of mental states. A dedicated empiricism is also on display in many academic journals, especially those that feature tables of data, correlations, probabilities of certainty, and other statistical manipulations as evidence of the soundness of their conclusions. Good, bad, or otherwise, so-called normative science is the way many people in the social and behavior fields now do their business.

The human services have their own tools modeled on modernist, empiricist assumptions. Examples include standard intake interviews, assessment protocols, diagnostic categories, family evaluation schedules, and much of the technical language appearing in the glossaries of textbooks and the pages of social service journals. Others are the banks of computers and the masses of "objective" data gathered from and about clients by service bureaucracies. With our growing data bases we track trends, measure intervention outcomes, and buttress planning and policy. As in medicine, machines and electronics are now a central part of the "helping technology." And like the sixteenth century's first scientific revolutionaries, we too hope that the result of all these objective, fact-finding procedures will be greater understanding of the problems that beset suffering human beings and more certainty about how to resolve them.

This is an ambitious and even glorious project. Its obvious success in the physical and biological sciences, and in applied fields like engineering and biomedicine, has encouraged generations of social science researchers and practitioners to attempt the same. The professional journals are filled with confident papers announcing the latest scientific results from "controlled" studies and "test" cases drawn from scientifically selected samples. This style of research does indeed provide rigorous and hard-won knowledge about very precisely defined slices of human activity.

But there remains the problem of how to interpret and use all that information in specific cases. For example, if careful surveys led us to find a strong correlation between unemployment and the likelihood of family violence in a sample of urban households in a working-class area of a large city, how would that fact help us devise a treatment plan for a specific couple from the sampled neighborhoods as they sit across the desk from us? Even before we begin planning intervention, how do we as helpers know what is going on in the couple's daily life? What credence and weight are we to give to what they say about their life together? How do we integrate what we know about their neighborhood, their style of dress, or their verbal mannerisms into our understanding of their situation? At bottom, how do we activate that social service truism—starting where the client is—when we are backed by the scientific data from our careful surveys? Unfortunately, human beings have never been as predictable as molecules or frogs, and successful intervention with them is not ensured despite the most rigorous scientific analyses of human problems. The postmodern critics have suggested ways we might think differently about our work, ways that do not rely solely on "normal science" and the hidden intellectual baggage it may bring to the helping relationship.

Writing on postmodern issues in her specialty of family-centered practice, Laird (1995) cites several ways this approach offers something new. First, therapeutic dialogue is not translated by the worker/listener into the globalized, totalizing categories that are the hallmark of much academic writing, research, classroom lectures, and the *DSM* series. As sympathetic hearers, we do not mentally bracket our clients' comments with labels such as "complex grief" or "anxiety disorder." Rather, we seek to understand what to our clients is local knowledge (that of home life, neighborhoods, relationships) and—most important—how that knowledge is expressive of certain kinds and qualities of experience. Stories and narratives are the sources of that information. A client is encouraged to pursue a personal narrative that, over time, builds the story of a battered wife's experiences or an alcoholic teenager's struggles. As clinicians we attempt to understand both the explicit and implicit meanings in the story and why they are powerful for the people who tell them. If we explore stories as texts about experience, we eventually come to see how each story generates a world view, one where blame, responsibility, power, and causation are allocated. Feminist critiques have been powerful on exactly this point: why is it that people sometimes collaborate in their own marginalization and disempowerment? What metaphors and story lines do they use to diminish themselves? How does language trap them, and how might narratives be re-edited so that they do not need to feel disadvantaged anymore? What actions are people impelled to take once they rescript personal narratives? Where does narrative analysis fit in the helping process?

Second, Laird's view is that the therapist's job is to open up a conversational space where narrative construction can begin. There must be an atmosphere for the discussion of experience—not just "problem behaviors." As therapists we willingly confess to not knowing a lot about many of the situations our clients describe, and we may even bring our own experiences to the conversation for the purpose of drawing out comparisons. In this "reflexive" or "intersubjective" style, each individual has a story to develop, although that of the client takes priority, and each participant in the conversation is in a position to comment on the other's story and to explore its implications. Rather than seeking to cultivate empathy, as we are normally taught to do, we take the role of the reflective, respectful stranger who is an appreciative learner and astute commentator on the client's experiences. Shared narrative building takes precedence over diagnosing and assessing, which only come later as part of planning and intervention. This narrative-driven approach, says Laird, "invites participation and collaboration. A respectfully curious stance also 'de-privileges' (but does not obviate) the therapist's prior texts or preunderstandings.... Such prior maps tend to lead us to conjure up what we expected to learn and prevent us from hearing the client's narrative" (1995:156).

This style of practice, I want to emphasize, is not just one of becoming a good and agreeable conversationalist, and, in the chapter on language, I will discuss some of the specific interviewing skills needed to make it work. Narrative production and analysis are central to our efforts to understand and change the disabling experiences of those we serve. Pozatek writes that "clinical social workers can be truly helpful to their clients by facilitating their *naming* of an experience: giving *voice* to something previously unacknowledged can be incredibly empowering for clients. Providing an opportunity for this new awareness to happen can be a *transformative* moment for both client and worker" (1994:400; my italics). Nor is the dimension of power, and the need to take action on the revealed discoveries of a fresh insight, left out of this paradigm. Hare-Mustin (1994) discusses not only how discourse in therapy often reflects our culture's dominant, gendered ideologies that put men and women in differing positions of privilege and power, but also how these same discourses may mask through a rhetoric of equality the very disenfranchisement they promote. If that is common in the ways we routinely talk about gender, how much more so is it true in matters of race, ethnicity, and class. Getting outside the rhetorical boundaries of the self with the aid of a skilled helper who is our "reflective other" can indeed be transformative.

I want to end this section by saying that in this book I do not disparage the worth of information gathered according to the canons of rigorous scientific method. Scientific data has an important place in human services. My concern is over the willingness of some to use ideas that appear to have scientific validity as justification for hasty diagnoses and interventions that may be class or culture bound. None of us is in a position to "size up" a client's issues by extracting a label from a *DSM* handbook as an "explanation" for what we see and hear. We can know people only as we understand their experiences and as we develop the skill to be reflective listeners and commentators on what they have to tell us. I am not a partisan of any particular theory of postmodernism. But I see this "critical theory," as some call it, as a powerful adjunct to cross-cultural methods in human services. Postmodernism has the useful effect of exposing the ambiguities of all human relationships, revealing their subterranean dimensions of power and complexity.

FOLLOW-UP

1. Considering Cases

Case 1: What Is the Issue Here?

In a sophisticated and sensitive discussion of cultural sensitivity as a child welfare practice issue, Rooney and Bibus (1996) describe a Native American family whose experience brings some of the competing issues of cross-cultural social work into focus. The facts of the case are simple; their meaning is not.

In Rooney and Bibus's example, firefighters are forced to break into the home of the Smiths, where they find an oven being used to heat the house and a small fire in progress. The two adults in the house are asleep, apparently from excessive drinking, and two of their four children are not at home. When the Smiths are finally aroused, they do not know where the other two children are but state that the children often stay with various relatives who live nearby. Mr. Smith is unemployed (his company recently closed) and he was once an in-patient in an alcoholism treatment facility. He has been drinking more heavily recently. The house lacks food, the mattresses are on the floor, and neighbors have complained about the condition of the property and the comings and goings of strangers to the house.

In their model, Rooney and Bibus speak of five "multiple lenses," their model of five ways to interpret this case. (1) A "color blind" worker might see it as a straightforward instance of children exposed to potential danger by inattentive parents and take whatever legal measures are needed to protect the children. (2) An ethnically sensitive worker might argue that things aren't what they seem. The children are used to staying with other family members and what is needed both for the adults and the children is to connect them with tribal resources for help with employment and drinking issues. (3) Viewed through the lens of empowerment, a worker might argue that the clear needs of this family are education and job skills, development of social networks, and advocacy with those agencies that can assist them. (4) Another perspective involves decisions about professional roles and responsibilities. Does this family need a child protective service person, a family counselor, or some other kind of professional service? (5) Finally, a health worker might focus on the drinking, adopting either an AA model or suggesting tribal religious ceremonies as part of intervention. Any or all of these alternatives may be "right" in some sense, but given the constraints of time, personnel, and budgets, some priorities will have to be set and action begun.

- What implications for treatment do you see through each of these "lenses" or service relationships?
- What are the strengths and disadvantages of each way of viewing this case?
- What would a culturally sensitive treatment plan look like, and how would you know it is culturally sensitive as far as the Smiths are concerned?

Case 2: How Subtle Can Cultural Differences Be?

We have all seen homeless people in large cities and know that some of them go to shelters for the night or to get out of bad weather. But few of us have seen how these facilities operate or have taken the time to get a sense of their social dynamics. Robert Desjarlais did extensive interviewing and participant observation in a shelter in Boston in 1991 and 1992. He wanted to know how the culture of street life and shelter living produces a distinctive kind of psychological experience. In listening to everyday conversations, he was both tracking experience and attempting to give "voice" to those who knew the homelessness experience best.

People staying in the shelter Desjarlais studied suffered from a variety of mental disabilities and all were poor. Their days were spent walking the streets, looking for food and ways to make a few dollars, sitting in public places for long periods of time, and attempting to maintain a low profile as protection against danger and violence. Both inside and outside the shelter, people's days were filled with long stretches of boredom and inactivity punctuated by episodic exchanges of conversation or briefly shared cigarettes and coffee. In this environment there was almost no opportunity for personal privacy, and many individuals were hypersensitive to noise, especially loud radios, television sets, and nearby conversations. Some hoarded small objects in shelter lockers or in the stuffed grocery store carts they pushed around the streets. Life was structured around boredom, vigilance, small annoyances, and attention lavished on small items of personal property. Desjarlais writes that "for the residents of the shelter, a politics of displacement, an episodic sequence of events, and a world of constant public transactions contribute to a certain tack on life" (1994:898).

That "tack on life" is "an acutely tactile engagement with the world, a constant focus on daily concerns, a distanced style of communication, a poetics of pacing and talking centering on unconnected episodes, a makeshift economy of cigarettes and loans and conversations, and a ragtag collection of words, memories, images, and possessions.... The aesthetics of this form of life center on the pragmatics of stasis, expediency, staying calm, and holding oneself together" (Desjarlais 1994:896). Desjarlais suggests that extreme marginalizing produces a distinctive kind of mental state that can be contrasted to what we sometimes think of as "normal" experience. It is a state that is explicitly focused on the physical environment, one that is highly tactile, very immediate in its focus, and seemingly without the interior ruminations many of the readers of this book probably employ when reflecting on who they are and what their lives are all about. The "interior self," taken as normative in the Western view of what a person "truly" is, hardly exists for many of the homeless. Their sense of self is virtually out of time, a self that is as fractured as their short and abrupt conversations and as brief as their episodic encounters. They do not construct narratives linking themselves to a past or a future. Their lives are oriented toward the present, and their vision of their future is almost nonexistent. They repeatedly said to Desjarlais that they "struggle along," and that is the most apt image for their lives on the streets and in the shelter. If we think of the "self" as a social construct, theirs is one finely attuned to the immediate dangers and opportunities of a hostile, existentially fractured environment.

- What physical and social aspects of the environment might you want to change (or could you change) as part of any kind of "intervention" with shelter people?
- What might you do as a "street wise" mental health professional to get to know these people better?
- In considering Desjarlais' perspective on the psychic life of street people, how appropriate might "talk therapy" or other conventional service models be in working with them? What might you do instead?

2. Test Drive an Idea

Everyone has an ethnic identity of some kind, but in American society we often merge talk of race, culture, and ethnicity as though they were about the same thing. Skin color is conventionally taken as the marker of that identity. Even our awareness of our ethnicity is an ethnic issue; some students, usually white, have told me that they are "not ethnic" because they are "just Americans." What they do not appreciate is that their statement is itself an ethnic marker, one that foregrounds their privileged position as someone who can afford to ignore ethnicity as a routine feature of everyday experience.

Three core elements of ethnicity have been described by Nash (1989). They are kinship and affiliation (relatives, friends, and groups both formal and informal where we feel we are comfortable and belong); commensality and intimate sharing (food preferences, where and with whom we like to eat, with whom we share and exchange both favors and goods, and—the ultimate reciprocity—who is and is not an appropriate life partner); and belief (personal preferences, family and group values, and ideologies of all kinds). Nash deliberately means these to be broad categories of identity, and, taken in sum, they describe our ethnicity. Obviously, some people and families may stress one set of features over others.

If you make three circles on a page, one for each of Nash's categories, and start filling in the content for yourself, you will discover two things. First, your own ethnic markers, both those you know and those you think are noticed by others, are probably more varied than you thought. You will also find—and this is really the point—that when you compare your information with that of others in your class or workshop, you have more diversity in the group than you expected. It will become quite clear how limited and limiting are the labels we conventionally use for describing ethnicity in ourselves and in others. We are all more complicated than the stereotyped markers of identity suggest.

3. More on the Issues

- Cultural Competence

Elaine Pinderhughes argues the need for greater attention to cultural competence as a basic empowerment strategy. See her article "Empowering Diverse Populations: Family Practice in the 21st Century," *Families in Society* (76:131–140, 1995).

- Trends

Professional interest in culturally relevant human services is fairly recent, and the history of that awareness points to what future needs and issues are likely to be. An overview will be found in H. Steven Moffie and J. David Kinzie, "The History and Future of Cross-Cultural Psychiatric Services," *Community Mental Health Journal* (32:581–592, 1996).

- Training

How important are cultural issues in human services training now? Consider the discussion of the "communication process model" in Delores Dungee-Anderson and Joyce O. Beckett, "A Process Model for Multicultural Social Work Practice," *Families in Society* (78:459–468, 1995).

- The Bell Curve

Social service professionals have involved themselves in *The Bell Curve* controversy, as have psychologists, sociologists, biologists, and others. For an example, see Asa G. Hilliard, "Either a Paradigm Shift or No Mental Measurement: The Nonscience and the Nonsense of *The Bell Curve*," *Cultural Diversity and Mental Health* (2:1–20, 1996)

- Reshaping the Curve

A special section on children's cognition and mental testing in the journal *Cultural Diversity and Mental Health* (1997) offers alternatives to bell curve simplicities. Three papers cover limited-English children, a "bio-ecological" approach to cognitive assessment, and a case study of a child from Guyana. The bio-ecological article, featuring an excellent interview and testing instrument, is Sharon-Ann Gopaul-McNicol, Stephanie Clark-Castro, and Karen Black, "Cognitive Testing with Culturally Diverse Children," *Cultural Diversity and Mental Health* (3:113–151, 1997).

- Postmodernism

If you are interested in more information on postmodern approaches in human services, a good source with an excellent bibliography is Rachel T. Hare-Mustin, "Discourses in the Mirrored Room: A Postmodern Analysis of Therapy," *Family Process* (33:19–35, 1994).

- Important Journals

Although most social service journals occasionally carry articles on cross-cultural issues and on minority and immigrant groups, several specialize in these areas. Particularly useful are the *Journal of Multicultural Social Work, Cultural Diversity and Mental Health, Journal of Multicultural Counseling and Development, Journal of Cross-Cultural Psychology,* and *International Social Work.* There is a special issue on ethnicity and biculturalism in *Social Work With Groups* (13:4, 1990). See also the special issue on social work with minorities and ethnic groups in the *Journal of Sociology and Social Welfare* (22:1, 1995).

Some publications are devoted to specific groups. Examples include the *Hispanic Journal of Behavioral Sciences, American Indian Culture and Research Journal, American Indian and Alaska Native Mental Health Research,* and the *Journal of Black Psychology.*

2

HELP-SEEKING BEHAVIOR: THE CULTURAL CONSTRUCTION OF CARE

During a training workshop on "reaching minority clients" that I attended several years ago, an African American social worker listened quietly to the advice offered by a panel of speakers during the morning session. They discussed ways adult and family services staff could demonstrate their interest in the well-being of minority individuals and why it was important that both staff and administrators appreciate the cultural diversity of their "catchment area populations." They urged the workshop participants to revise their admissions and "people-processing procedures" (as they described it) to make their agency more "user-friendly" (again, their term). During the question and answer period, the social worker rose to say that she was encouraged by all she had heard but that it probably would not make much difference to her black clients since many of them had alternatives to going to a social service agency. Indeed, she said that on occasion she had referred clients to a local "root worker" where, she felt, they sometimes got better help than her own agency provided. She added that she did not list "root worker" in the client's records nor did she clear the referral with anyone. As the only African American social worker in her agency, she felt the reasons for her clinical decisions with black clients would not be understood and would take more time to explain and justify than she cared to do.

Needless to say, there ensued a lively discussion on who and what a "root worker" is, under what conditions referrals to root workers are appropriate, and what the presence of a large number of "alternative" mental health providers in a "catchment area" means for social service providers. The discussion was animated but inconclusive. Yet the mental health worker had made her point: there are alternatives to official, publicly sponsored versions of care, alternatives that represent choice and even community preferences. Care includes proper staffing, worker empathy, adequate funding, and prompt service delivery, but it also includes a cultural dimension. Care giving as a cultural system is tied to the experiences, perceptions, and needs of specific communities (Albert 1990).

Care giving and care seeking are as influenced by cultural considerations as anything else we do. McMiller and Weisz (1996) studied pre-intake help seeking among a sample of African American, Latino, and white families. They hypothesized that there are culturally specific pathways into child mental health clinics and that families in these three groups would show significant differences in how they approached and utilized care systems. While waiting for their initial appointment at the study clinic, adults accompanying their children were asked a series of questions such as: *"I would like to know all the people and places you went to for advice or help about [child's name].... What did you do first to get advice or help with [child's name]'s problems"* (1996:1088). The outcome of the study confirmed the hypothesis. Just over half the white families consulted with professionals only, whereas just under a third of the African American and Hispanic families limited their help seeking to professionals. Why this difference in help seeking?

A variety of factors may have influenced minority families' decision making. They could include financial limitations, suspiciousness of professionals, and inconvenience in finding and meeting with staff in agencies. But McMiller and Weisz add, "Viewing the findings from another perspective, it is possible the low rate of professional contact by minority parents reflects the availability of alternative social supports" (1996:1091). These alternative supports were significant because for more than two-thirds of the minority families in their sample, "seeking help from professionals and agencies was not their first choice...and a majority of all preclinic contacts in these groups were nonprofessional and non-agency-related" (1996:1092). This pattern contrasts with that of whites, who are both more familiar with how professional services operate and more comfortable with them. It also suggests a need to understand care and service delivery in cultural terms.

CARE AS A CULTURAL SYSTEM

If we think of care as part of a larger system and, more important, as part of a process (much of which may be hidden from our view), we can begin to understand its cultural dimensions. First, care is a part of everyday experience. It is not limited to clinics and consultations. People experience distress and they do something about it, even if that doing is ignoring it, passively accepting what bothers them, or taking an aspirin. In this sense, care systems are about choices and decision making. We all make choices daily, most of them routine, and they all reflect preferences about how we want to manage our lives. Choice making also involves self-diagnosis, self-treatment, and selection of others for advice and confirmation of our decisions. Ultimately, care has a moral dimension. We may or may not articulate that very well, but it is part of our sense of who we are as capable persons and as able bodies. It may not be clearly or explicitly "presented"—you probably don't feel the need to explain your understanding of the supernatural as your dentist prepares the novocain needle—but it is still part of your conventional understanding of how you manage your affairs. (The moral dimensions of visiting the dentist might be your tolerance of pain, whether you thought you did something or omitted something in the care of your teeth, what your good intentions about that are for the future, and how you are going to manage your anxiety as the dentist does with the needle what has to be done.) When we work with people who suffer not with bad teeth but with bad relations, the moral dimension may be even more significant. The puzzle in any counseling relationship, and most especially relationships that cross racial or ethnic boundaries, is that much of the decision making, the help seeking, and the understandings that drive the consultation are implicit and may not be voiced. The more "different" from you your client or patient seems to be, the less likely you are to know about that person's moral universe and the big and little choices he or she makes to build and maintain it.

Second, everyone's distress is both a personal and a communal experience. Obviously it is personal, which is the whole point of psychiatry and psychology, but the issues involved in any form of suffering imply the participation of others. Recall the previous chapter's discussion of "voice" and multivocality. At times of distress we may make our experience known to others because we want their advice about what the problem seems to be, what its name is, how they might have experienced it, how they resolved it, and what we might do to find relief as well. Since all communities are diverse, we may talk with a number of people, some of whom give differing and even contradictory advice. After just a few discussions, however, and long before we have gone to someone for professional guidance, we have formulated a view of what is normative and what has gone wrong. We have compared our distress against the knowledge and practices of others (our "discourse community" as linguistics like to call it) and have come to a "cultural formulation" (a key idea, coming up shortly) of what the problem is and what we can do about it. These inquiries are our personal search for the "sense" of a painful experience, a search that explores what Geertz (1983) calls "local knowledge." If we think of "culture" as all that went into that search—the ideas, beliefs, responses, conversations, shared wisdom, bodily gestures, invoked emotions, attempted solutions, revised hopes and expectations, and, perhaps, even invocations of the supernatural—we come to a view of culture that is much more interesting than the simplistic idea that distinctive values make one group different from another. "Culture" refers to a process whereby people try to solve their problems. Appropriate intervention means knowing something about how that process plays out in a localized community and where we as help providers might fit in.

Third, the body of "local knowledge" into which we dip in the hope of finding solutions is always available to us. It is a historical product, which is why in later chapters a brief overview of the historical experience of ethnic communities in America is presented. It is also a result of contemporary group relations, especially relations of power and relative advantage and disadvantage, including the complex and subtle etiquette of maneuvering that every human encounter involves. It is the collective wisdom of generations of experience and it contributes to our personal slant on the world. It is quite literally the "common sense" of a community, the view of "how we do things here."

This is an important point because the objection of many culturally responsive counselors, nurses, and physicians to highly abstract, "culture-free" diagnoses and disease categories (such as many of those described in the *DSM* series) is that they ignore or push to the sidelines all the cultural "stuff" that is exactly what most engages those seeking help. It is the means by which they make comprehensible, to themselves and to us, what they are going through. If we need to label their pain with professional or medicalized terminology, that comes later, much later, and only with qualifications and inclusions that respect the cultural grounding of their experience.

If care is really all this, in addition to being a helping, empathic, and individualizing service relationship, then how can we get beyond the anecdotes and the testimonials that make up much of what the research literature reports about cultural differences and minority clients? And how can social workers develop a cultural sense of care in their own work, one that will lead them beyond generalizations?

The model followed in this book is one called "help-seeking behavior." It is an adaptation from the work of Arthur Kleinman (1978a, 1978b, 1980, 1988a, 1988b, 1992), his associates, and others of what they have called "health seeking behavior." In the last decade, in fields as diverse as psychiatry, nursing, student counseling, and occupational therapy, Kleinman's model has become recognized as a powerful tool for comprehending the diversity of peoples' responses to crises, whatever their cultural orientation (Shweder 1991). Essentially, the help-seeking behavior model is a discovery procedure, not a formulaic code, and its value to human service providers is as a guide to learning what they can do to work well with culturally distinctive clients.

As a discovery procedure, the model rests on several assumptions. First, language is of special importance since it is the symbolic device by which the flow of experience is categorized, labeled, evaluated, and acted on. Shared cognitive and affective events and the language through which they are communicated are the ultimate bases of a common culture. Any approach to understanding the distinctive cultural characteristics of others must begin with what they say, exactly as they say it. The discourse of personal crisis carries a heavy cultural as well as emotional charge and is the means by which inner states are given shape and conveyed to others.

Second, the model recognizes that any need or problem is both a personal and a social event. It is personal in that it disrupts daily routines by creating discomfort and pain. It is social and cultural in that the labeling of damaging experiences often involves confirmation by others as a preliminary step to corrective action. The model recognizes the role of culturally significant others in diagnosis and evaluation. Indeed, in some situations lay consultation may be more important to a client's response than is information supplied by certified experts and professionals.

Third, the help-seeking behavior model rests on a fundamental dichotomy between illness and disease. Disease is a diagnostic category, a conceptualization originating in a professional subculture and expressive of the procedures and preferences of that subculture. Illness, by contrast, is the experience of suffering. It is how people perceive and live with their symptoms, how they imagine them to be caused, and how they cope with them. Illness includes categorization, explanation, and resort to culturally available hierarchies of care in the expectation of relief. It is personal, localized, shared, and validated by others. All illness experiences are culturally formed, whatever (and sometimes without regard to) the "real" causes of suffering postulated in medicalized or psychologized discourses of disease. Illness complaints are a genre of commentary or narrative, a genre that addresses fundamental questions: What is my problem? What is its cause? What course will it take? How will it disrupt my life? What do I fear about it? Who can help? What might help? What will not? Why me? Why now?

Kleinman (1986:145) suggests three possible ways of thinking about illness. First, there are overt and obvious symptoms of disability: an injury, a deformity, an accident, a personal crisis. One's community of family, friends, and co-workers has a pattern of discourse about symptoms, what they mean, and how well or how poorly individuals cope. Second, there are understandings about the larger meanings of illnesses. These understandings and the discourses that accompany them are not biomedically neutral. (They may not be biomedically well founded either.) Perhaps the most obvious example is the acquired immune deficiency syndrome—AIDS. In families in which it occurs, its meaning is certainly much more than a biological event; it has overtones of choice, lifestyle, and morality. AIDS even becomes a subject of national commentary for some media-oriented religious leaders who find in it evidence of celestial condemnation. Public dialogue on other issues such as abortion, child abuse, doctor-assisted suicides, and gang violence are also rich with rhetoric that mixes beliefs about individual behavior, public morality, and the fate of the nation. None of us ever has a crisis that is fully, ideosyncratically our own.

Third, if we think of illnesses or personal crises as disvalued experiences, the importance of their social and cultural moorings becomes apparent. Kleinman illustrates with several examples:

> Heart disease for the failed businessman in Western society can become embedded in disintegrating marriage, alcohol abuse and related family violence, a demoralizing relationship with a boss, a midlife crisis in which change in body image and coming to terms with one's mortality assault a fragilely constructed ego. Or, for Chinese society, think of a thirty-year-old, disaffiliated worker, a former Red Guard and rusticated youth, whose bitterness, cynicism, and mourning over multiple losses in the Cultural Revolution (of education, career mobility, family harmony, and so forth) are absorbed into the symptoms of a chronic illness so that treatment of the physical complaints needs to include response to the particular psychological and social distress that are likely sources of symptom amplification and worsening disability (1986:145).

In this model, the illness-afflicted individual is a moral agency, the immediate crisis an occasion for dramatizing fractured connections from some normative, perhaps idealized notion of functioning. All cultures provide explanations to which suffering individuals can turn for relief. They range from food as medicine among health food aficionados to personal prayer choreographed by broadcast evangelists. In a culture as diverse as America, with its engulfing media presence, there is a democratizing of information and advice, however useful or useless it might be. That is part of the broader meaning of cultural pluralism. But something different happens when the sufferer, trailing a concentrated mix of belief, imagery, and anxiety, appears before an authorized, professional healer. The disvalued experience is transformed into the clinical "presenting problem." The erupting emotions in one's personal life become "symptoms" to be "managed." Clipboards, file folders, closed doors and modulated voices subdue, at least for the moment, disallowed interpretations of crisis. In the clinics and offices of institutional medicine and counseling, physically and functionally set apart from the client's daily life, the interplay of history, biography, and cultural context is usually subordinant to symptom identification, classification, and assessment.

The help-seeking behavior model is an attempt to reconcile these contrasts and bring together the domains of the personal and the institutional for a more complete, holistic appreciation of the client's experiences and what can be done about them. The model is constructed around a division between what individuals know and do in their privatized responses to problems and what professionals and experts know and recommend. It postulates a client culture and a professional culture (or more accurately, subcultures), each marked by a distinctive set of assumptions, narratives, beliefs about causation, and expectations for resolution (Figure 2.1). Within these contrasting domains, any specific problem initiates differing kinds of questions, discourse, and behavior. Generally, the greater the cultural distance between help seeker and help provider, the greater the discrepancy in their perceptions, labeling, and responses to a given issue. These differences are significant for client compliance and the success of service outcomes. At a minimum, the culturally responsive social worker will assume as a working hypothesis that divergent interpretative and communicative domains accompany all presenting problems and that they will have consequences for the worker–client relationship.

HELP-SEEKING BEHAVIOR: A MODEL FOR CROSS-CULTURAL SERVICE RELATIONSHIPS

The help-seeking behavior model has a number of components, each of which is part of the "cultural baggage" both clients and workers bring to a service encounter. From the client's side they include (1) recognition of an experience as a "problem" of a particular kind, one that is conceptualized out of the individual's stock of knowledge and the prevailing local knowledge of the community; (2) a narrative that establishes the conceptual framework within which the problem will be controlled; (3) knowledge of helping resources in the community and the decision making involved in their utilization; and (4) criteria for determining that a satisfactory resolution has been achieved. For example, in an ethnographic discussion of

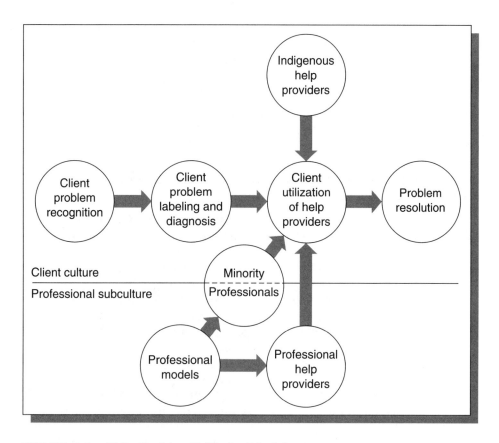

FIGURE 2.1   Help-Seeking Behavior Model

(Based on Kleinman 1977, 1978a.)

chronic pain sufferers, Kleinman lists some of the issues that make their illness more than physiological:

> *What is at stake for the sick person and family? What is learned from the encounter with pain by those who undergo it and those who provide care? How is the meaning of pain created, expressed, and negotiated? How are meanings reflected or constituted in stories people tell? What is the relation between such narratives and lived experience (Kleinman 1992:15)?*

Issues like these are part of the cultural context of problem resolution and understanding them is essential in planning intervention. Kleinman is very specific that patients and clients of all kinds have a "stake" (his word) in their problem, that their concerns are not just "how do I find relief?" but also "what in my life is at risk?" The client's stake, always culturally specific, is part of what the culturally responsive social worker will want to understand before moving on to the technical procedures of diagnosis, treatment, and evaluation.

To make more evident the cultural dimensions of this model, with its dichotomy between disease and illness, pathology and risk experience, I will illustrate each component of the help-seeking behavior model with examples from the ethnographic and human services literature. All of the examples are intended to show that informed ethnographic understanding is critical to planning and delivering culturally responsive social services.

The Individual's Definition and Understanding of an Experience as a Problem

The presenting problems of clients and patients may be general or specific: vague feelings of pain, loss of appetite or a job, a death in the family, violence. But how these objective conditions are interpreted is also a significant part of the experience. This is particularly true when issues of mental health are involved. Any culture provides a repertoire of explanations for problems, explanations related to etiology, symptom recognition, and the course of illness episodes. A culture also provides a sick role for those who suffer, expectations concerning treatment, and a definition of desirable outcomes. These explanations and expectations amount to a "cognitive map" (Wallace 1970) more or less shared by members of the culture. This map or "explanatory model" (Kleinman 1978a) is part of the conception of the problem the client brings to the service provider. Some individuals may be better able to articulate their experiences of suffering than others but all know the local, implicit knowledge of body and self that makes interpretation possible.

But are "folk models" of illness true or false, and how seriously should we take them? Should the trained expert correct an incompletely formulated explanatory model or an illness narrative that may be medically or psychologically "faulty"? Are some clients' beliefs akin to folklore and superstition? Or are clients' perceptions of a different nature altogether, suggestive of ideas and explanations quite different from those of helping professionals but valid within a particular body of local knowledge? This question goes to the core of cultural difference. My view is that if clients routinely draw on localized knowledge to find meaning in illness or trouble, then professionals cannot afford to ignore localized interpretations of misfortune, however odd they may seem.

The examples that follow are really vignettes, chosen only to clarify specific parts of the help-seeking behavior model. They are *not* intended to be representative of whole ethnic groups and should *not* be read as "typical" or "exemplary" of behavior or belief in any particular community. That distinction must be kept very clear so that stereotyping does not occur. Rather, the vignettes show how ethnographic data can help us understand the cultural realities behind specific problems faced by some individuals in particular communities.

The ethnographic description of Native American drinking is one illustration of how the world view of one community can differ significantly from that of another. Years ago Zola (1972) noted that the recognition of symptoms and the concept of "trouble" are not value free. Problem recognition occurs in a values context, and there may be instances where what is perceived by clients as normality, or as the working out of some inevitable sequence of events, is to outsiders an instance of pathology. The question that must be asked at this stage of the help-seeking behavior model is: "What is a problem?" What has been a problem for the white community may be something else for some Native Americans.

Native American Drinking

Alcohol is a significant risk factor in the lives of many Native Americans, more so than for other communities. The Indian Health Service reports that nearly one-fifth of all deaths among Native Americans involve alcohol, compared to less than 5 percent for the U.S. population as a whole. Alcohol risk is especially high for young adults and for urban Native Americans and has recently been documented as a serious health issue for urban Native American women (Walker et al. 1996). No people have been more stereotyped in reference to drinking behavior than Native Americans. The orthodox view on alcohol and Native Americans is that of a whole continent of uncivilized tribes, incapable of resisting the white man's "fire water" and reduced by it, along with warfare and the reservation system, to near total loss of their lands, livelihood, and dignity. This popular image of Native Americans and their drinking has remained, despite changes in thinking about alcoholism as a disease rather than a personal moral failing.

In its most naive form, speculation on Native American drinking has assumed that all Native Americans are possessed of an inordinate desire for alcohol, coupled with an unfortunate genetic incapacity for dealing with it. Neither of these beliefs is true. More sophisticated approaches have associated problem drinking and alcoholism with the social disorganization created through white contact, particularly when access to economic rewards is blocked (Graves 1967) or when individuals feel that they have no sense of belonging to either traditional or white communities (Ferguson 1976). These studies suggest that the incidence of Native American drinking can best be taken as a measure of cross-cultural relations and their difficulties, not as an indicator of biological deficiency. This does not explain, however, what drinking means to Native American individuals, nor does it offer insight into the social context of drinking.

If one looks at the historical and ethnographic record of drinking among Native Americans, a complex picture emerges. There is instead an infinite series of gradations in drinking practices and experiences, ranging from individuals who become boisterous and violent to those who remain sedate or only titillated when inebriated. Among some groups, such as the Menomini of Wisconsin, religious ceremonies focused on the attainment of visions and dreams, and alcohol was used, often generously, within carefully controlled ritual settings to advance that aim (MacAndrew and Edgerton 1969:118). Lemert (1954) notes that there was little aggression associated with heavy drinking among the Northwest Coast groups he observed, and Levy and Kunitz (1974), in a careful and thorough study of drinking in the Southwest, found that the Hopi who abjured public drunkenness were very heavy drinkers in the privacy of their homes. They also found that Hopi drinking contrasted markedly with that of the neighboring Navajo and Apache, both of whom practiced public drinking and the public intoxication that went with it. In Canada, Kupferer (1979) found that among the Cree of Ontario drinking contributed to a sense of community solidarity. Because the Cree valued individual autonomy and normally shunned emotional intensity in their relationships, weekly drinking was an occasion for relaxed animation and the venting of strong feelings. From these few examples, hardly a random sample but at least illustrative, one could not conclude that there is a uniform effect of alcohol on all Native American individuals nor a homogeneous response to alcohol by all Native American groups. Similarly, we could argue that these ethnographic findings are consistent with an approach to providing services that does not generalize from a few cases but rather is specific to the needs and experiences of particular communities.

Drinking among Native Americans, when it becomes a problem for the dominant society, is handled in two ways. One is by police and courts. Arrest and incarceration rates for Native Americans are generally higher than they are for whites, even when whites consume greater quantities of liquor (Price 1975:22). A second approach is Alcoholics Anonymous. But AA is a white model, both in the perception and definition of the problem (it is a "disease") and in the treatment required (abstinence and public confessions). It cannot be assumed that all Native American communities, reservation or urban ones, will find AA perceptions of drinking behavior and drinking treatment compatible. How many Native Americans, for instance, think of heavy or compulsive drinking as a "disease"? Or do they see it as something else? And would they see public confessions as a reasonable method of control? Is there precedent for confessional behavior, of any kind, and would Native Americans see that as an appropriate response to a disease? These are cultural issues that need to be considered as part of implementing a treatment program.

Drinking in many Native American communities is a major problem. That seems clear enough. What too often is not clear is the kind of problem it is. That will vary among Native American communities and perhaps even within them. The point here is, simply, that drinking is culturally conditioned behavior like any other; it can become "excessive," but the meaning of excess is subject to the normative expectations of drunken comportment specific to a group. When and where drinking is determined to be a problem is something dependent on the beholder's point of view. One cannot know a priori that a "drinking problem" exists, or the kind of problem it is, unless one knows how drinking is experienced within a given ethnographic context.

Native American drinking, as briefly as we have considered it here, points to one of the important issues in all cross-cultural problem identification and labeling. Alasuutari (1992), a Finnish sociologist, recently completed a provocative study of worldwide drinking patterns and their management. He notes that the meaning of drinking is highly dependent on cultural variables, especially ideas about individualization, beliefs about the body and its reactions to alcohol ingestion, and expectations of drinking outcomes and their control. He concludes that in an important sense, heavy alcohol consumption is a culture-bound syndrome, a constellation of features that vary from community to community and lack any universal etiology, and therefore any universal treatment. To successfully interdict the outcomes of drinking, if and when that is deemed necessary, requires an exquisite knowledge of the local conditions under which drinking takes place and the cultural evaluations that go with it. Not all drinking is pathological, although it may be, and no control program can succeed unless the local meanings of drinking behavior are fully understood and built into the management regimen.

The Client's Semantic Evaluation of a Problem

In one sense, a culture can be described as what people know—the knowledge, information, and beliefs they share with one another, Geertz's notion of local knowledge. Shared cognitive materials mark off one group as culturally distinctive from all others. Even if one is not willing to accept the argument that culture is equivalent to what people know, it remains true that much that is culturally distinctive within any society is its stock of information, including everything that is linguistically labeled and communicated in speech. Identifying linguistic labels, therefore, and exploring their meaning, is critical to understanding how people construct their world.

The organization of information in any society is partly a matter of categorization. Thus, the semantic label "family" refers to a culturally specific category or domain. Of course there are different kinds of families, and the variations among them are important. These variations are called the "attributes" of the members of the domain. Thus, in American popular culture, we have the domain of "families," and we recognize such attributes as "nuclear," "broken," "extended," "mixed," "single parent," and the like. The attributes themselves can be more minutely divided in order to give finer shades of meaning. Thus, "single parent" families may have a male parent, a female parent, biological parent, or adoptive parent. Similarly, an attribute such as "mixed" can be further subdivided. In its most general usage, the folk attribute "mixed" refers to adults of differing "racial" background (Root 1992) but it might also refer to married adults of "mixed" religious background. In addition, there are gay and lesbian couples who already have or who adopt children, and there are other people who refuse to think of them as having a "family" at all. The complexity of the domain "family" is made more evident when we appreciate that in our culture native speakers not only use the term "family" in a descriptive but also in a metaphorical sense, applying it to entities that clearly are not families. Thus, someone could suggest that the members of a large corporation are "one big happy family," and religious figures sometimes refer to their congregations or denominations as "families."

This latter usage of the native label "family" suggests one of the critical features of folk thinking and the semantic labels attached to folk categories. Semantic labels have both a "referential meaning" and a "social meaning" (Spradley and McCurdy 1975:541). The referential meaning of "family" is its dictionary definition or, when more precision is required, the kinds of definitions found in a sociology text on family life. The social meaning, however, refers to usages that are contextual: appropriate times and places for using the term, its metaphorical associations, or the emotional weight it carries among those who hear it. Appropriateness has to do with subtle variations in meaning that are contextually dependent and that would be recognizable only by those who are members of the speech community. (Humor, for example, is probably the most contextually sensitive form of speech.) This level of understanding is called "communicative competence" (Gumperz and Hymes 1972). Speakers who have communicative competence are intimately and intuitively familiar with both the referential and the social meanings of language in a specific speech or ethnic community.

Language is the storage medium of any individual's stock of cultural knowledge, his or her "cognitive map" or "explanatory model" as Kleinman (1978a) would call it. For example, a parent comes to a worker concerned about a child's health. The parent has an implicit explanatory model of how the child became sick, the probable meaning of the symptoms, what has been observed to be effective with such symptoms before, why certain therapeutic procedures are deemed useful or not, and why some kinds of health advisors are preferable to others. All this conceptualization of the child's illness is something that the client knows, whether or not it is articulated well. It is knowledge that may or may not be held with conviction; the explanatory road map might not be very reliable. But it is the framework within which new information is stockpiled. If the worker is concerned with truly knowing where the individual is "coming from," then the semantic dimensions of the client's explanatory model are the only place to reasonably begin. To start with the client's emotions, as many social workers are prone to do, presumes that the worker *already* understands, exactly like a native, the sensibilities and meanings those emotions express. But if one is not a native in the client's culture, then such a presumption is dubious and exploration of emotions may be superficial at best.

The section below explores exactly this point—the complex features of an explanatory model of illness and health. In this instance, it is one that is at some variance with established, biomedical knowledge. Yet it is a model that is widely known (but not universally practiced, and that should be noted) by Spanish-speaking persons in the United States.

Hispanic Disease Categories

Among Spanish-speaking persons in this country, beliefs and knowledge about disease derive from at least four sources. Medieval Spanish traditions were brought to the New World by colonizers, and these influenced and were influenced by indigenous Native American beliefs. Elements of white popular traditions, particularly as represented in the mass media and advertising, and "scientific" or biomedical knowledge are also part of the body of medical concepts found in many Latino communities. But these diverse disease concepts are not equivalent to those of scientific biomedicine. They have their distinctive etiology, nosology, symptomatology, and treatment methods (Maduro 1983; Gleave and Manes 1990). An examination of several major disease categories, as they are defined by many Americans of Spanish heritage, reveals something of their cultural significance.

Hispanic disease categories do not rest on a dichotomy between the physical and mental sources of *enfermedad,* or illness. Rather, they come from a notion of disturbed balance in one's physical and social well-being. As in the ancient Hippocratic system, the individual in a healthy state is believed to be a harmonic mixture of contrasting elements: hot and cold, wet and dry, and the various "humors" of the body. The ethnosemantic labels for three significant disruptions of this balance are *empacho, mal ojo,* and *susto.* These medical categories have been described in a number of studies carried out in South and Central America and in communities in this country (Martinez and Martin 1966; Madsen 1964; Clark 1959; Saunders 1954; O'Nell 1976). The detailed descriptions provided by Rubel (1960, 1964, 1966, 1984) and Finkler (1985) are particularly useful because of their emphasis on the social functions of these disease concepts.

Empacho is a physiological condition, affecting both children and adults, in which the manifest symptoms of stomach pains are believed to be caused by food that cannot be dislodged from the sides of the stomach. The food is said to be in the form of a ball that can be broken up and eliminated through back rubbing and the use of purgatives. A diagnosis of *empacho* is made only after other problems, such as indigestion, have been considered.

Mal ojo is the result of dangerous imbalances in social relationships and, in its advanced form, can be fatal. Its symptoms include headaches, sleeplessness, drowsiness, restlessness, fever, and, in severe cases, vomiting. The individual's sense of equilibrium is in danger of being disturbed in any encounter with other people. Particularly if one has been the subject of covetous glances, admiring attention, or intense interest by another, *mal ojo* is likely to result. The eyes of another person can be the virulent agent for initiating this condition, although evil intent need not be present. Children are particularly susceptible to the admiring looks of adults, and women may be exposed to danger from the glances of men. This unnatural bond of power that one individual may hold over another can be broken by prayers, by gently rubbing the body with a whole egg, or by having the perpetrator touch the victim's head, thereby draining off the threatening power of the relationship. *Mal ojo,* or the "evil eye," is one of the widely distributed value complexes in the world, found in cultures from India through the Middle East, North Africa, southern Europe, and South and Central America. By no means is it limited to Spanish speakers, although it is associated with Spanish cultures in this hemisphere. As a value complex it was not common in northern Europe nor among the English speakers who came to dominate much of North America.

The *susto* syndrome has a number of characteristics widely dispersed among both Spanish and Native American cultures in South and Central America. *Susto* means fright, and a victim of *susto* is one who has lost some of his or her spiritual essence as a result of an upsetting experience. The source of the fright may be trivial or truly life-threatening, but the symptoms are the same: depression, lack of interest in living, introversion, and disruption of usual eating and hygienic habits. Cure requires coaxing lost spiritual substance back into the individual's body. This is done through prayers, body massage, spitting cold water over the patient, and particularly by sweeping the body with small branches while "talking" the spirit back to where it belongs. Curing is usually undertaken by someone familiar with the condition and known to be successful in treating it. The family and patient are consulted as part of the diagnostic process to determine that *susto* is in fact present. Not all frightening experiences lead to *susto* but many can, and a link between an earlier experience and manifest symptoms must be established before treatment can begin. Clearly, a lot of individual and family counseling and intimate knowledge of the nature of this condition, are a part of the treatment.

One view of these folk illnesses, particularly the methods of diagnosis and treatment, is that they are simply historical survivals from older, now discredited, Iberian and southern European systems of medicine. They persist only in impoverished, backwater areas where people lack access to the benefits of Western medicine or are ignorant of modern medical practice. Another view, however, is that these beliefs and practices are consistent with the culture in which they occur quite apart from their historical origins. They express an underlying logic that is convincing to many people and through which they find relief for some (but perhaps not all) of their problems. Rubel (1960) has argued that the experience of stress is common to all these illnesses. In small communities, where one's position in life is a matter not only of economic success but reputation, respect, and esteem, challenges in the form of unwanted endearments or jealousy and envy are highly stressful. *Mal ojo* is resolved, balance is restored, when the unwitting perpetrator of the disease touches the victim, assuring that there is no intent of inappropriate desire to control the other. Stress is also experienced when individuals are unable to meet their role expectations. Children who feel they have disappointed their parents, particularly in a culture that emphasizes ideals of family honor and the shame that disrespectful behavior entails, may well develop the symptoms diagnosed as *empacho*.

The role stress theory of *susto* has been refined by O'Nell (1976), who suggests that it takes two forms: rationalized and precipitating fright. In the rationalized form, there is a lengthy period between the onset of symptoms and the experience of fright. In addition, fright is usually initiated by nonhuman agents such as an attacking animal or the accidental breaking of household utensils. The patient explains the appearance of symptoms by locating a frightening experience in the past that is deemed to have been causal. This is not, however, an irrational, post hoc procedure. Rather, the patient uses this explanatory principle to define himself or herself as sick, thereby utilizing a defined sick role to withdraw from relationships that generate stress. In this way, a sense of failure in role expectations is institutionalized, and a means of treatment is made available.

Precipitating fright, by contrast, involves human causes, and in this form the appearance of symptoms is rapid. Confrontations with others, exchanges of insults, or threats of violence are all events that challenge the individual's sense of self-control and decorum. Loss of control or a sense of balance in personal relationships precipitates the fright symptoms. This is most likely to happen within the family or among kin, where the frustrations of daily life serve as tests of the individual's ability to preserve a sense of calm and composure. The appearance of symptoms is a signal to all that withdrawal and an easing of tensions are needed to restore the normal order of relationships, the balance and self-control that represent normality and good health.

Far from being an irrational manifestation of folk superstitions that have survived into the modern world, *susto* is a syndrome that is culturally specific, couched in the language of health and illness, one that many (but certainly not all) Spanish-speaking individuals use to adapt to the stresses of everyday life. For *susto* sufferers, both rationalized and precipitating frights "serve to validate the(ir) problems in culturally meaningful terms, (and)…facilitates the rehabilitation of the individual in social context" (O'Nell 1976:61).

How widespread are these beliefs among Spanish-speaking persons in this country? Martinez and Martin (1966) found that in a sample of urban housewives, virtually all the respondents had heard of these illnesses, and 85 percent of them knew therapeutic measures for treating the symptoms. In addition, 95 percent either had experienced a folk illness or knew someone who had. It is significant that Martinez and Martin reported their findings in the *Journal of the American Medical Association*. Physicians are not usually called on to treat *susto* or *mal ojo* because, as the housewives in the survey pointed out, doctors neither understand these diseases nor are they trained to treat them. Most physicians would probably agree! As long as that situation persists, patients will seek help from alternative health care providers who better understand the reasons for their problems.

Should we assume that all Spanish-speaking patients or clients will be familiar with these disease entities and rely on them in personal evaluations of misfortune? Certainly not. Some individuals will be fully committed to these ideas, some will regard them as nonsense, and others will be ambivalent. That is why the explanatory models of illness employed by any given client are always an important topic of inquiry in an assessment. Until we know what shapes an individual's sense of order and disorder, we are not really in a position to make therapeutic recommendations.

Indigenous Strategies of Problem Intervention

There is an enormous range of help-seeking activity in all cultures. These activities are guided for the most part by lay interpretations of personal problems and by informal consultations with persons who are already within the troubled individual's network. Some types of lay intervention and help-seeking are more familiar than others: reliance on family members and friends; solicitation of advice from a minister, pharmacist, or faith healer; use of special diets or drugs; exercise or meditation; resort to religious or secular rituals to manipulate unseen forces; membership in support groups for almost every concern imaginable. There are also help-seeking activities distinctive to specific groups, such as the utilization of *curanderos* among many Spanish-speaking persons and the active use of religion in the treatment of illness in some black communities and among many whites. Even the degree to which contemporary Americans rely on television commercials and the popular media as sources of guidance for problem identification and resolution has been a topic of interest.

The point to be emphasized is that in virtually all communities, including highly urbanized ones that are well supplied with professional healers and therapists, there are many alternative sources of help. Over the last several decades, these alternatives have expanded both in number and in the variety of services they offer. What was once widely considered quackery is now firmly enshrined even in some segments of the middle class (Hess 1993). Indeed, so-called mainstream professionals may be the least and the last consulted for some kinds of personal or family concerns. Especially where minority communities view the social service system as a threat or as a source of social control, social workers may be the last link in the chain of help-seeking contacts.

In pluralistic societies such as our own, one of the critical problems in providing social services is the relationship of the dominant provider system to indigenous alternatives. Where service professionals are selectively recruited, trained in specialized techniques, socialized into the ideology and folklore of their profession, and certified and licensed as a condition of employment, there can be an enormous social gap between them, their clients, and community-based alternatives. The lack of trust many social workers experience in minority communities can have severe consequences for the success of their best efforts. But the social worker who tries to utilize rather than replace indigenous resources may have fewer problems. If there are local individuals or organizations with histories and reputations for providing assistance, the social services worker should seek them out, determine what needs they meet, and strive to deliver services in a complementary way. As an outsider, the worker may never enjoy the prestige of such persons or groups, but he or she can work to supplement the forms of care they provide.

African American Community Resources

For a significant portion of the black community in the United States, and also in some Southern rural areas populated largely by whites, there exists a common set of beliefs about health, illness, and general well-being derived from old European as well as African sources. The African origins of these beliefs are bodies of local knowledge common to the west coast of Africa during the time of slave trading in the seventeenth and eighteenth centuries. The European sources are just as old and were brought to North America by the earliest immigrants. There is no generalized name for this system of knowledge, although terms like "witchcraft" or "spiritualism" have been used. In its contemporary form in some areas of the African American community, it is a consistent, self-contained set of principles for accounting for some of the problems that beset individuals. In addition, it is associated with a set of practitioners who, under certain circumstances, provide effective assistance to those who seek it.

This system of belief has been studied by a number of anthropologically oriented researchers, not only in this country but also in the West Indies and in Africa (Snow 1973, 1974, 1977, 1978, 1993; Whitten 1962; Wintrob 1973). It is very widespread and, in its geographical dispersion, surprisingly homogeneous as well. The system is based on a fundamental division of physical and mental illness into two kinds: that which is natural and that which is unnatural. It is important to understand this distinction in order to appreciate the power of those individuals who are recognized within their own communities as proficient healers.

Natural illness results from the individual's failure to properly care for the body. It may also come about as divine punishment for one's misdeeds. In either event, a lack of wellness is due to an improper relationship with natural forces. Cold air, strong drafts, misuse of alcohol, or poor diet can all be responsible for illness and can signify the individual's inattention to basic health and hygiene requirements. Similarly, illness that is a consequence of God's displeasure results from failure to respect principles of decency and morality as they have been established by Biblical and church authorities.

Unnatural illness, however, is the result of evil influence. It may range from obvious physical ailments to psychosomatic symptoms to problems commonly classified as mental health concerns. But these are all similar in that their origin is in the evil intentions and hostile actions of others. Unlike natural illness, unnatural illnesses are initiated by a human agent against a victim, and they fall outside the orderly domain of the universe established by God and in nature. Various terms for this activity are "hexing," "rootwork," "fix," "mojo," and "witchcraft," but these words change and new ones come into being as needed. It is believed that evil intentions and actions are efficacious because all events in the universe are interconnected. If one knows the interconnections and how to use them, one can have a measure of influence and control over them. It is the wrongful use of this power, not knowledge of occult things per se, that is evil. Thus, individuals who suffer with inexplicable physical or mental problems have reason to suspect that someone else is the cause of their misery. It is important, therefore, to find a specialist who can identify the source of the problem and who can deal with it effectively.

Clearly, neither mental health specialists nor biomedically oriented professionals are in a position to respond to individual complaints based on this model of illness and misfortune. But there are individuals in the African American community who are effective as far as they and many of their clients are concerned. These healers are variously known as psychics, "root workers," counselors, "root doctors," conjurers, and sometimes witches. Snow (1973, 1978) has described in detail the skills and procedures of a woman she calls a "voodoo practitioner," and what is remarkable are the similarities of her techniques to those of mental health professionals. The woman's practice was located in her home in the downtown section of a large southwestern American city. Her clients included African Americans, whites, Native Americans, and Mexican Americans. Snow had difficulty locating the woman because she was known only by word of mouth. Yet her place of business was similar to that of many doctors, counselors, and other professionals. She had an office, she kept nine-to-five hours, and patients met her in a waiting room. The woman had received her training from her grandmother, an individual who also possessed special powers of healing and who was widely known among local blacks for her skills. The training consisted of learning ways to utilize her "gift" in helping others, a gift with which she was born and which could not have been obtained any other way. Portions of her therapy involved touching and massage but much of it involved talking through a problem with the patient. Using an idiom with which most black patients were intimately familiar—the personalities and events of the Bible—she was able to illuminate the source of personal difficulties and suggest practical ways of coping with them.

This practitioner acknowledged the critical distinction between natural and unnatural forms of illness, claiming no medical skills for those problems that were clearly within the domain of medical providers: "Now an unnatural sickness, well, that's a person that's sick in the mind. Mentally sick. Doctors can't find that. They Xray and they can't find it.... And yet they are sick, mentally sick in mind. And then, I'm a counselor, I counsel them.... I give 'em medicine you know, through their mind. I call that spiritual medicine" (Snow 1973:278). Judged by the enthusiasm of her patients and the size of her clientele, this woman was very successful in her community. She did not compete with established medical professionals since both she and her patients recognized that she dealt with problems such practitioners were not trained to handle. Furthermore, she had an intimate knowledge of the pressures of life in her community and of how poor people are vulnerable to forces they cannot control. Many of her patients came to her after having seen professional counselors. They were disappointed with the kind of treatment they received and concluded that professionally trained experts could not treat the kinds of things that afflicted them.

It is important to note, as Snow does, that these beliefs in unnatural illness are not simply the legacy of prescientific superstitions. It would be a serious error to interpret them that way. Rather, unnatural illnesses "are those which have to do with the individual's position as a member of society.... Some arise from the tensions and anxieties of everyday living. Worries about money or family problems, for example, may produce a variety of symptoms that informants call 'mental' illness. Hostility in interpersonal relationships, on the other hand, may cause the individual to become the target of witchcraft" (Snow 1973:272–73). When social relationships are strained because of the problems of poverty, discrimination, and exclusion from full participation in the larger society, beliefs in the efficacy of evil influences are one response to the abrasiveness of everyday living (Rainwater 1970). The problems persist, and so does this culturally defined answer to them, as Snow's (1993) most recent research makes clear.

Foster and Anderson (1978) have identified a number of the characteristics of healers and curers, traits that they believe are the marks of indigenous helpers in many societies. They include selection and training, specialization, certification, projection of a professional image, expectations of payment, and, significantly, an ambivalent public image. Snow's practitioner fits all these criteria. She had a specialized store of local knowledge—the treatment of "unnatural" forms of mental and physical illness—and she was specially selected and trained for her task. That selection came about through the influence of her grandmother, but it was also a divine choice. "I was born just exactly with the gift," she said. The idea of a "gift" to be shared with others was important to her legitimacy in the community. Certification of competence came from patient testimony and did not require framed certificates issued by hallowed institutions attesting to her skills. Further, this healer conducted her practice as a business and, as she herself admitted, her public image was a mixed one. Some in the community accused her of manipulating dark and forbidden forces. Yet she responded that she was simply implementing the power, the "gift," that God had given her.

To the extent that Snow's respondent had success with her patients, it must be attributed not only to her personal skill in counseling others but also to a local awareness of the value of her services to the community. It is this latter quality of legitimacy that professionals who are cultural outsiders, and who are stationed in agencies that are themselves outposts of larger, alien bureaucracies, will always find difficult to obtain. Formal training and the completion of specialized, degree-granting programs are not effective substitutes. But professionals can acknowledge the importance of indigenous help providers and, to the extent feasible, attempt to learn something of their methods and the reasons for their success. Cultural awareness does not require imitation of the skills of knowledgeable insiders, however desirable that may sometimes be. It only requires an honest sensibility as to who and what is really helpful for persons seeking advice on matters that trouble them deeply.

Culturally Based Criteria of Problem Resolution

One of the core tasks of any care system, according to Kleinman (1978a:87), is the "management of a range of therapeutic outcomes." This is a particularly difficult issue in social services, where the specific relationship of treatment to outcomes is not always obvious. That difficulty is compounded when cultural differences contribute to failures in communication and misunderstanding of intent. In transactions with clients, particularly minority clients, social workers have traditionally responded to this problem in two ways, neither of which is useful in enlarging the worker's sense of cross-cultural effectiveness.

One response has been to focus on the idiosyncratic characteristics of each client, taken one at a time. Differences in ethnicity, race, or power between the client and the worker are underplayed or ignored altogether. The rationalization for this strategy is the often expressed desire of workers to "individualize the client" and get straight to diagnosis and treatment. There is a great deal of support for this position in the social work literature, and, indeed, it is one of the implicit if not explicit values and ideological components of social work's professional subculture. But from an ethnographic perspective, this orientation can have the effect of stripping the individual of just those things that may be supportive of a healthy sense of individual identity and capability: familiar communication styles; use of indigenous resources; accustomed family patterns; standards of reputation and respectability with family or peers; and styles of demeanor and conduct that are recognized and meaningful among those who count in one's life. To perceive the client's individuality as something beyond, behind, or irrelevant to these ethnographic features leaves only an insubstantial ephemera of what the individual must really be like. It also leaves open the possibility of easy stereotyping, justified by whatever theory of human behavior the worker brings to the client encounter, whether Freudian, behaviorist, or eclectic. Pursued vigorously, the decision that one need only "individualize the client" in order to come to a full understanding of his or her needs is really a decision to ignore the greater part of the individual's identity.

The other response is the urge to find cultural "reasons" for client "problems" that cannot be accounted for in any other way. In this approach, what clients do or say is viewed as causally related to something in "their culture." A social worker worried about an "inability to self-disclose" among his Asian clients once commented to me that "their quiet culture" was the cause of their reticence to speak about painful family issues. Sometimes workers relying on common, everyday explanations for cultural differences make superficial, even stereotypic judgments about their clients, judgments they believe show them having "insider" information. Typically, the more difficult it is to account for the behavior in question, the more intense the search for some "likely" cultural generalization that explains everything. This reliance on ethnographic trivia, things known anecdotally rather than from systematic observation and analysis, suggests the truth of the cliché that "a little knowledge is a dangerous thing." Lacking an organized, comparative framework for accommodating cultural data, anecdotal information can become the worker's primary, and most misleading, source of knowledge.

One way of resolving this difficulty is to gather information about how people solve problems within their own communities and what, to them, are reasonable outcomes to those efforts. If the social worker is knowledgeable about the recent history and the day-to-day experiences of the client's home community, there is little likelihood that inappropriate intervention techniques or goals will be pursued. Similarly, the worker who is alert to cultural variations within the client's community will have some sense of how different individuals respond to specific therapeutic techniques. Of course, the greater the cultural difference between the social worker and the client, the more the worker will need to learn in order to be effective. Diagnostic and intervention techniques must always be adapted to the needs of specific communities; there is no such thing as a generalized cultural awareness (Chin 1983). The recent immigration of Southeast Asians to this country, particularly the Vietnamese, provides one example of how social workers can respond to clients in ways that build on reliable cultural knowledge.

Asian Immigration

The evacuation of Vietnamese from South Vietnam in 1975 represented a major challenge to social service organizations in many parts of this country. Unfamiliar with American culture and the English language, many Vietnamese discovered too late that what they thought was to be a temporary retreat before returning to their homes was instead permanent exile and relocation in a strange country. Many apparently came to accept the fact that their future would be an American one (Kelly 1977). But this acceptance was not easy, given the suddenness of their emigration and the difficulties of life in the refugee camps (Rahe et al. 1976). The need for social services, both advocacy and long-term counseling, was and still remains great. It is a need that is complicated by the fact that the refugees came from a culture with little tradition of publicly sponsored social service programs and with considerable stigma attached to the kinds of problems that practitioners in this country are trained to help resolve (Rutledge 1992).

As is true of most areas of the world, the population of Southeast Asia is culturally diverse. Excluding tribal peoples, of which there are numerous distinctive ethnic groups, there are two major civilizations in the region (Keyes 1977). Buddhist-oriented traditions evolved as the result of extensive borrowing from India. That borrowing was followed by the cultural infiltration of people and ideas from southern China. Consequently, refugees from Thailand, Cambodia, or Laos are commonly affiliated with a Buddhist world view. The Vietnamese, by contrast, represent a distinctly Chinese tradition, one influenced more by Confucian ideals and Chinese patterns of social organization. The historic Vietnamese "push to the south" along the eastern edge of the mainland led to a lengthy period of instability and conflict, a condition that still persists. Part of that conflict came from colonizing activities by the French, whose influence is seen in the colonial and postcolonial importance of Catholicism in the country and among many Vietnamese in America today.

Aside from these major variations, however, it is important to mention several general themes that are common to the region. One is the exceptionally high value placed on family life. Asians and Pacific Islanders have been called "the most family-dependent" among America's ethnic communities (Sokolovsky 1990b:208), and the Vietnamese are an example of that. Their pattern is based on a Chinese model of the patrilineal extended family, one in which the senior male has high status as head of the family unit. In predominantly Buddhist areas, less emphasis is given to lineality in family and kinship structure, although the predominant importance of senior males is often preserved.

The refugees who came to America were a special, perhaps atypical, segment of Vietnamese culture. Although many came as family groups, rather than as lone individuals, most refugees were young, half of them under the age of eighteen. Almost half were Catholic, over a quarter were Buddhist, and two-thirds were from highly educated, well-to-do, urban and professional households (Montero 1979). Confronted with American cultural traditions and offered jobs that were for the most part menial and low paying, the refugees were certain to face adjustment difficulties. A number of problems have occurred repeatedly.

Many Vietnamese have experienced disturbing readjustments in family roles, a matter of particular concern to social workers. Under crowded, less affluent living conditions, inherent strains in family life have become more apparent. These include potential conflict between the wife and her mother-in-law and the resultant strain for the husband, who must balance important filial obligations with his responsibilities to his spouse. Similarly, the strict obedience expected of children in their relations with parents, relatives, all adults, and older siblings is challenged by American practices that foster a sense of independence, assertiveness, and inquisitiveness. The American preference for autonomous action conflicts with Vietnamese notions of subordination of personal interests to those of the family group. In addition, physical violence, drinking, divorce, open criticism of others, and direct, face-to-face confrontation are all highly offensive.

Yet sometimes these traditions can be turned to advantage and great success. One of the most striking features of the Vietnamese adjustment to American life has been the success of children in the public schools and universities. Many have been drawn into the natural sciences and engineering, areas where the analytical skills of mathematics are more important than full native fluency in English. Others have been attracted to business programs, partly in response to enormous family pressure to achieve in education and in the commercial sector. Recent research by Caplan, Choy, and Whitmore (1992) has suggested that it is the preservation, rather than acculturative abandonment, of traditional family practices that accounts for this remarkable academic success. For instance, they found that among Vietnamese students who were high achievers, there was no perceived discontinuity between family life and what went on in the classroom. At home, older children tutored younger ones, parents insisted on a nightly study table that lasted nearly three hours, and learning was verbal and interactive in a group setting. In fact, group learning, with parents in attendance even when their English was markedly weaker than that of their children, was a normal part of family life. By contrast, the Vietnamese children most acculturated to American youth culture and to American family norms did consistently poorer in school. The researchers concluded that cultural factors, not academic ones, accounted for Vietnamese school success and that the preservation of ethnic distinctiveness and more traditional family values was important to that achievement.

The Vietnamese represent only one kind of Asian adjustment to American life, and it would be a serious error to assume that all Asians have experienced America in the same way. Yet there are some overall uniformities about which a culturally sensitive social worker would be aware. These include a concern with orderliness in relationships, especially hierarchical orderliness with deference to those older than oneself. The preservation of order includes control of emotions and emotional displays. "Talk therapy," as a standardized therapeutic style, does not always fit well with this kind of cultural and personal predisposition. Family responsibilities and family preservation, with a clear sense of internal roles and obligations, are important. Ideas about family protectiveness include concealment of stigmatized conditions from outsiders, especially mental illness, drinking, and related behavioral issues.

Tsui and Schultz (1985, 1988) have described some of the problems that occur when outsiders (usually white) attempt therapeutic work with Asian clients. Group work in particular is a Western invention as far as many Asian clients are concerned, and the insistence that they participate often has predictable results: a surface pleasantness and willingness to be agreeable, indirection in discussion, sometimes withdrawal into silence. Some social workers may become overprotective or oversolicitous with individuals they (correctly or not) identify as spokespersons for the local group. Tsui and Schultz suggest several ways of avoiding these problems in service work with Asian clients.

First, recognize that personal and family problems are often presented as physical symptoms. That is logical in cultures where "mental" problems are heavily stigmatized and certainly not discussed with strangers. Clients often come to social workers, whom they see as authorities (again, the hierarchical idea), seeking very specific suggestions for treating symptoms. Tsui and Schultz describe a client who recounted her physical symptoms to a therapist, to which the latter replied: "Do you feel depressed? That is, feeling sad and possibly hopeless?" The client was confused by the question because to her it wrongly attributed physical illness to "underlying" mental conditions. She reversed the causal sequence when she replied, "Yes, I feel very ill, and my illness is making me sad" (1985:563). At the very beginning of the encounter, the worker and client invoked differing "causal" models, for differing cultural reasons, and the worker missed what it was that the client was trying to say.

Second, Tsui and Schultz urge therapists to consider how the therapeutic alliance is created. Many Asian clients respect the education and academic degrees held by professionals. But responses to a question such as "Tell me more about that," or "When these things happen, how do you feel?" or "Can you tell me something about the things that happened to you when you first came to America?" tend to undermine the perceived authority and expertise of the social worker. The client wonders: Why is he or she asking these questions? Is this inappropriate prying by a stranger? Is it evasion because the counselor really doesn't know what to do? Does the therapist not care about my problem? Is dislike of Asians behind an apparent refusal to take on the issue authoritatively? These are the images some workers create when they impose, at least at the start, a distinctly American, middle-class model of therapeutic questioning. It is a model many Asians do not recognize either as an intervention technique or a useful rhetorical style. Tsui and Schultz state that such interviews may go well on the surface, with a gentle kind of agreeableness all around, but that the Asian client may not come back. To some workers this unaccountable lack of compliance evokes images—more often thought about than spoken in these politically correct times—of "inscrutability" or of "model minority" clients who can be left to fix things up for themselves. Is that response racism? Perhaps, perhaps not. But it *is* ethnocentric and, for the social services professional, it is an opportunity lost.

DSM-IV *AND THE CULTURAL CONSTRUCTION OF CARE*

The help-seeking behavior model has been enormously productive in generating new, culturally sensitive information on illness and distress in a variety of communities. Recent examples, among many that could be cited, include multiethnic child mental health (McMiller and Weisz 1996), black and white elderly (Husaini et al. 1994), depression among Chinese American women (Ying 1990), anxiety disorders (Kirmayer et al. 1995), mental health referral patterns among different ethnic groups (Akutsu et al. 1996), and disability services for West Indians in New York City (Smith and Mason 1995). Despite its success, however, the model is not the best known nor has it received the same level of publicity (including commentary in the *New York Times,* the *Los Angeles Times,* and the *Washington Post*) as a widely used alternative.

In 1994 the fourth edition of the American Psychiatric Association's *Diagnostic and Statistical Manual on Mental Disorders* was published. For the first time it included a small but significant amount of material on the cultural dimensions of disorders. I want to review briefly what the new *DSM-IV* has to say on these things and then consider some of its implications (and limitations) for advancing culturally competent care and service.

The Introduction to *DSM-IV* defines a "mental disorder" as "a clinically significant behavioral or psychological syndrome or pattern that occurs in an individual and that is associated with present distress (e.g., a painful symptom) or disability (i.e., impairment in one or more important areas of functioning) or with a significantly increased risk of suffering death, pain, disability, or an important loss of freedom" (1994:xxi). Disorders in *DSM-IV* are listed as discrete categories, each having its distinctive attributes. Since individual illnesses rarely match these "textbook" descriptions, the *DSM-IV* authors recommend that the categories are best understood as guidelines. They are not to be applied mechanically and should be used only by those trained to do so. These limitations are amplified in a section called "Ethnic and Cultural Considerations":

> *Clinicians are called on to evaluate individuals from numerous different ethnic groups and cultural backgrounds (including many who are recent immigrants). Diagnostic assessment can be especially challenging when a clinician from one ethnic or cultural group uses the DSM-IV Classification to evaluate an individual from a different ethnic or cultural group. A clinician who is unfamiliar with the nuances of an individual's cultural frame of reference may incorrectly judge as psychopathology those normal variations in behavior, belief, or experience that are particular to the individual's culture…. Applying Personality Disorder criteria across cultural settings may be especially difficult because of the wide cultural variation in concepts of self, styles of communication, and coping mechanisms. (1994:xxiv)*

In addition to this advisory, the *DSM-IV* Appendix provides two items of interest. The first is a glossary of twenty-five "culture bound syndromes," which, oddly enough, omits an important home-grown variety, anorexia nervosa (Weiss 1995), apparently not as exotic to the authors as Southeast Asian "latah" or Middle Eastern "zar."

The second is a very brief but more important "Outline for Cultural Formulation" (1994:843–844), buried at the back of the book but nevertheless significant because in making a bow to the cultural dimensions of illness, a topic that did not appear in *DSM-III,* the authors grant the importance of social and cultural factors in understanding mental disorders and in responding to them appropriately and effectively (Mezzich 1995). They acknowledge that there is much more than manifest symptoms when clients and patients "present" in clinical settings.

Manson (1995), a Native American medical anthropologist, has worked long and diligently with others to see that cultural material be included in *DSM-IV.* He argues that a cultural perspective on mood disorders, for example, directs our attention to (1) cultural variations in beliefs about the self and the sources of emotion, (2) variations in the way language is used to report affect, (3) differences in emotional experience in distinctive communities, (4) varying forms of somatic expression in what is called the "ethnophysiology" of experience, and (5) culturally specific styles of narration that may be distinctive not only to particular ethnic communities but to age and gender cohorts within them. These are all areas in which culturally sensitive care providers must have knowledge, practice, and experience as a precondition of clinical effectiveness with *DSM-IV*'s myriad illness categories.

DSM-IV's Cultural Formulation guidelines are a useful beginning point for developing this kind of professional capability. The manual lists five areas that are pertinent to developing a clinical cultural formulation. They are:

1. The individual patient's cultural identity
2. Local explanations for a particular kind of illness
3. The psychosocial environment
4. Client–clinician relationships
5. Cultural features of diagnosis and care

There is, however, no discussion about how to prepare a cultural formulation, the kind of training or experience one would need to do so, or how one would know they "got it right" once a formulation was devised. That task has been taken up in the research literature of medicine, psychiatry, and medical anthropology, usually by people with strong social science backgrounds. Examples include Fleming (1996) on a Native American woman suffering from alcoholism and depression, Cervantes (1994) on Hispanic children and adolescents, Manson (1996) on a Native American man who is socially withdrawn, and Lewis-Fernandez (1996b) on a Puerto Rican woman with *nervios*. Lewis-Fernandez (1996a), who is leading an international effort to collect appropriate cases, is also a contributor to the discussions of *DSM-IV*'s cross-cultural adequacy. In addition to the standard analytic categories, he would add information on language, cultural reference groups, differential involvement with one's community of origin, relations with the dominant culture, social stressors, and help-seeking processes within the client's community.

Rogler (1996), also with long experience in the reformulation of the *DSM* series, is even more expansive about what ought to be included in a cultural formulation. The body of the *DSM-IV* is organized around five major "axes" of illness: clinical disorders, personality disorders and retardation, general medical conditions, psychosocial and environmental problems, and global assessments of functioning. Rogler contends that each of these areas is rich in potential ethnographic or cultural context, not only for minority populations but for various segments of dominant racial and ethnic groups as well.

What can be said of the *DSM-IV* that might be useful here? First, consider symptoms. Following the standard medical model, the *DSM* program has always been to narrow the therapeutic gaze to more accurately recognize symptom manifestation without the intrusion of "extraneous" ideas or subjectivities. The emphasis is on the malady and accuracy in gauging its presence. A cultural approach, while it does not reject this search for clarity of symptom recognition, explicitly calls attention to the social embeddedness of the patient's experiences and suffering and *also* the therapist's position, knowledge, and point of view. Rogler quotes Mezzich et al. (1994:19) on exactly this point: "What the patient reports is itself an interpretation of suffering based upon his or her own cultural categories, words, images and feelings.... The psychiatrist's view is, then, an interpretation, with its own cultural categories, of that interpretation." In effect, two translations of experience, not one, are part of any consultation. In fact, they *are* the consultation. Culture is implicated throughout.

Second, if we think about the so-called culture-bound syndromes and their relationship to the rest of the manual, it is not clear whether they are simply local manifestations of disorders already described in the more "scientific" part of the text or distinctive conditions in their own right and additive to what *DSM-IV* already supplies. In any case, they are idioms of distress probably familiar in the client's community and meaningful both to the people who experience them and who witness them. Think of anorexia nervosa, already mentioned, or such afflictions as "heartbreak," "shot nerves," "middle-age crisis," or "a cold," terms that are complex and meaningful for many people but didn't make it into the *DSM-IV* taxonomy. They are nevertheless useful precisely because they are rhetorical openings to hard experiences and because they function at the level of "folk knowledge" or local reality. The exoticizing of comparable folk concepts from other cultures and relegating them to a list of museum-piece oddities in the back pages of an otherwise "scientific" handbook is a distraction. It slights the importance of local beliefs and practice in our own society, not only among ethnic populations but among the white, educated, middle classes who have preferences and peculiarities of their own.

We need to recognize that the inclusion of a cultural dimension in the new *DSM-IV* is both a good and a potentially risky thing. It acknowledges that a cultural dimension colors every illness experience and shapes the reporting and hearing of it. But the volume's sheer intellectual weight and systematic organization invites mechanical attribution of disease states as a substitute for real cross-cultural insight into what bedevils people, although the authors rightly warn against that. At the level of everyday practice, we need to move beyond the limitations of *DSM-IV*'s systematic elegance. The help-seeking behavior model is one way in which we can reframe our clinical style so we can position ourselves to do that more effectively.

CULTURAL COMPETENCE AS A WAY OF WORKING

If care is in some significant way culturally constructed, what is the "cultural competence" part that is so much discussed in the human services literature? Only a few years ago people talked about "cultural sensitivity" and "cultural awareness," but these are not enough any more. Pinderhughes (1995) has outlined some of the dimensions of "cultural competence" as that idea is now evolving. Her list includes the following: (1) not only respect for others but the much more difficult capacity "to perceive such individuals through their own cultural lens" (1995:133); (2) knowledge of specific beliefs and values in the client's community; (3) personal comfort with those differences; (4) a willingness to change previous ideas; (5) the ability to be flexible and adapt one's thinking and behavior in novel settings; and (6) the skill of sorting through diverse information about a community to understand how it might apply to particular individuals.

What I want to call attention to, in anticipating the next several chapters, is the idea that cultural competence is learnable. There are specific activities that, when pursued energetically, do develop individual capability. McPhatter puts it nicely: "*Skill proficiency* is not a haphazard process; it is focused, systematic, reflective, and evaluative" (1997:272). That is important to state precisely because of the limitations of the workshop format that is common in human services training. I have led many workshops and usually find them a disheartening experience, not because the people who attend aren't interested but because we all know that without follow through and reinforcement back at the office, all that expensive and time-consuming training rarely "takes." And the administrators who could make that happen are rarely in attendance at the workshops along with their staff.

Beyond on-the-job reinforcement, the skills of cultural competence grow when there is some sustained level of immersion in the community of clients. Reading a novel about Chinese immigrants on the West Coast, attending a community festival in a Chinatown, and having a friend who knows the territory take you to a Chinese restaurant is all fine if you are a tourist. It is not fine for developing cultural competence, yet I have heard people use examples like this to explain why they have proficiency with Chinese clients. Immersion is something else. No one is expected to do long-term field research and participant observation as though they were a cultural anthropologist. But everyone can treat his or her job as a site where, with a little extra effort, a lot can be learned, recorded, reflected upon, and tested in new cases and with interested and sympathetic co-workers. It does not call for rewriting job descriptions or agency mission statements; it does require taking a reflective and sometimes critical stance toward what goes on in intake interviews, assessments, consultations, home visits, placements, and terminations. A systematic learning style and a supportive agency environment, aimed at recognizing culturally distinctive modes of behavior and interpreting them in a community context, will go a long way toward developing both personal and organizational cultural competence. The rest of the book outlines how those skills are acquired.

FOLLOW-UP

1. Personal Assessment

Anna R. McPhatter states that "the process of becoming culturally competent begins with an honest assessment of one's level of functioning with culturally different others" (1997:275). She feels that most practitioners (as well as educators) commonly overestimate their cross-cultural capabilities. A realistic assessment, however, can be helpful in identifying personal strengths as well as limitations. At the end of her article in a recent issue of *Child Welfare* she poses nine questions, reproduced here with her permission and that of the journal, which can and should be used as the basis for discussion and personal reflection.

When you read through her list, you will see that McPhatter's questions are simple and direct. They are also tough. They demand an honesty that may be intimidating to some. But cross-cultural work of all kinds—in social services, health care, teaching, or research—demands no less and it should be done by people who have struggled a bit with their capabilities and commitments. Responding to McPhatter's questions is a good place to start.

A Cultural Competence Assessment

1. How much personal/social time do I spend with people who are culturally similar to or different from me?

2. When I am with culturally different people, do I reflect my own cultural preferences or do I spend the time openly learning about the unique aspects of another person's culture?

3. How comfortable am I in immersion experiences, especially where I am in a numerical minority? What feelings and behaviors do I experience or exhibit in this situation?

4. How much time do I spend engaged in cross-cultural professional exchanges? Is this time spent in superficial, cordial activity, or do I undertake the risk of engaging in serious discourse that may divulge my fears and lack of knowledge?

5. How much work have I actually done to increase my knowledge and understanding of culturally and ethnically distinct groups? Does this work include only an occasional workshop in which I am required to participate? What are my deficiencies and gaps in knowledge about important cultural issues?

6. What is my commitment to becoming culturally competent? What personal and professional sacrifices am I willing to make in the short term for the long-term benefit of all children and families?

7. To what extent have I nondefensively extended myself in approaching professional colleagues with the goal of bridging cultural differences?

8. Am I willing to discontinue representing myself as knowledgeable and as having expertise in areas of cultural diversity that I have not actually achieved?

9. If I am unwilling to commit to a path leading to cultural competence, will I take the moral and ethical high ground and discontinue providing services to people I am unwilling to learn about?

Copyright 1997 Child Welfare League of America. Used with permission. This article was originally published in Child Welfare, volume LXXVI, Number 1, January/February 1997.

2. Test Drive an Idea

Help-seeking behavior is ubiquitous, which is why it is sometimes hard to see. But if you think of it as a mental map, as suggested in this chapter, you can literally draw yourself a picture. View yourself as a client or patient and construct a personal help-seeking behavior diagram of how you deal with a specific problem. A small number of possible "problem topics" are listed. Choose one you have experienced or select something else that you prefer. Examples include:

a bad cold	an obsession	contemplating divorce
a hangover	a religious crisis	coming out
quitting smoking	scary dreams	unexpected pregnancy
chronic fatigue	low-grade depression	loss of a job
insomnia	loss of appetite	a death in the family
fear of flying	anorexia	
failure in love	a diagnosis of cancer	

Now consult the help-seeking behavior diagram. For the issue you have chosen, and based on your own experience and understanding, fill in the categories with as much detail as you can. For example, the first category asks for identification of the signs that the problem exists. Think beyond the obvious. Did you anticipate this? Did you have suspicions? What experiences, intuitions, or doubts led you to these possibilities? What feelings were invoked? How did you manage them? What made you decide, finally, that some kind of problem had to be confronted?

Category two asks for diagnoses and labels. Again, think beyond the obvious. Who else do you know who has had this problem or one like it? What did they do? Did it work? Who helped them? Would you do the same? What words did you use to describe the situation? List them. Which ones moved you to thought and finally to action? How did you explain the problem to others? What was the "narrative line" you developed in discussing it? Were there different versions of your narrative for different people? Was moral as well as naturalistic language used? Was your language gendered in any sense that you can recall? Finally, what terms best describe the situation as you look back on it? Which ones would you use with a doctor, a pastor, a significant other, with children, with your parents?

Continue on with the other categories in the help-seeking behavior map. When you are finished, discuss your case with a partner. If that person worked on a similar issue, what were the similarities and what were the differences in your experiences? Are there age, gender, race, ethnic, or social class factors in the similarities or differences in your responses? How do you know that? If your partner worked on a different issue, explain why your responses might have been the same or different and, again, what in your social background would have led you to construct things the way you did?

An exercise like this makes it apparent how complicated these maps and experiences can be. In discussing your own experience or hearing that of someone else, it is important for you to articulate your sources of information, what I have called "local knowledge," in addition to specifying whatever social supports helped you manage the issue. In my experience with this exercise, I occasionally need to push people to develop more detail than they think they either need or know. My insistence on details, lots of them, is part of the learning since that is the ethnographic or cultural element of all cross-cultural work. Exploring and systematically collecting the details of people's responses to a crisis is hard work; it is time consuming and takes lots of patience. But it is the most efficient method for learning about that experience, and, as will be discussed later, it is one of the significant ways we empower others. There are no shortcuts.

3. More on the Issues

- Help-Seeking Behavior

Hard-nosed survey procedures and culturally sensitive intake interviews produced help-seeking maps among African American, Latino, and white children and youth. The differences in their maps were real and important for evaluating services. See William P. McMiller and John R. Weisz, "Help-Seeking Preceding Mental Health Clinic Intake among African-American, Latino, and Caucasian Youths," *Journal of the American Academy of Child and Adolescent Psychiatry* (35:1086–1094, 1996).

- More Help Seeking

How specific and practical can the model be? This article is a culturally sensitive demonstration of the model's utility for understanding substance abuse, with good bibliography and a critique by invited commentators. Maryann Amodeo and L. Kay Jones, "Viewing Alcohol and Other Drug Use Cross-Culturally: A Cultural Framework for Clinical Practice," *Families in Society* (78:241–254, 1997).

- Local Knowledge

A fascinating and lively book, *Controversial Issues in Social Work Practice*, edited by Bruce A. Thyer (1997), features debate style yes/no exchanges on cutting-edge topics. Chapter 18 is "Should Medical Social Workers Take Client's 'Folk Beliefs' into Account in Practice?" Letha A. See says yes; David Klein says no. Since local knowledge is the ethnographic basis of cross-cultural skills, you should analyze their arguments and then formulate your own response.

- Cultural Competence

Family-centered practice, where minority children are at risk due to poverty, is an area where cultural competence is critical. The authors explain why, both in terms of the need for services and as an aspect of legislative mandates. Kathleen A. Rounds, Marie Weil, and Kathleen Kirk Bishop, "Practice with Culturally Diverse Families of Young Children with Disabilities," *Families in Society* (75:3–15, 1994).

- Constructivist Models of Care

The constructivist model, akin to some postmodernist ones and built around a careful consideration of local belief and practice in specific communities, shows how intervention can be culturally responsive. Several case studies, including Americans of South Asian, Chinese, and Hispanic heritages, are included to illustrate the points. Mo-Yee Lee, "A Constructivist Approach to the Help-Seeking Process of Clients: A Response to Cultural Diversity," *Journal of Clinical Social Work* (24:187–202, 1996).

- *DSM-IV*

It is easy to get lost in the *DSM-IV* controversies, but our concern really ought to be with how that model plays out in professional practice. One good article is that by Richard C. Cervantes and William Arroyo, "DSM-IV: Implications for Hispanic Children and Adolescents," *Hispanic Journal of Behavioral Sciences* (16:8–27, 1994). They emphasize contextual variables, especially language, and include an excellent list on pages 18–22 of child and adolescent disorders with problems of cultural bias in the application of *DSM* categories to Hispanic clients.

- More *DSM-IV*

If this subject is of theoretical as well as practical interest to you, there is no shortage of commentary. Lloyd H. Rogler has a critical but sympathetic discussion in his article "Framing Research on Culture in Psychiatric Diagnosis: The Case of *DSM-IV*," *Psychiatry* (59:145–155, 1996). A number of very sophisticated papers appear in a special issue of *The Psychiatric Clinics of North America* (18:3, 1995). Topics include diagnosis, family therapy, anxiety disorders, and cross-cultural psychiatry. There are also web sites on the Internet. My inquiries using "DSM-IV" as the search term brought in more stuff than I really wanted, but it was interesting and occasionally even useful.

- History of Ethnic Sensitive Practice

An excellent overview of theories and methods in cross-cultural social work as they have evolved over the past twenty to thirty years is presented in Elfriede G. Schlesinger and Wynetta Devore, "Ethnic Sensitive Social Work Practice: The State of the Art," *Journal of Sociology and Social Welfare* (22:29–58, 1995).

3

METHOD IN
CROSS-CULTURAL SOCIAL WORK

How far must one go to learn about the experiences of others, the differences that make a difference to them? There is a cliché that we must walk in someone else's shoes if we want to know what their world is like. Several years ago, a 26-year-old product designer in New York City did just that. Not only was Pat Moore dissatisfied with her gerontology courses at Columbia University, she resented commercial products that are difficult for the elderly to use and architectural design that assumes everyone is young, athletic, and fully able to move about. So with the help of an NBC makeup artist, she transformed herself into "Old Pat," an elderly woman of limited means who for three years ambled along the streets of New York and over a hundred other American cities.

As reported by the British newspaper *The Guardian* (August 1, 1989), Moore wore a wig and latex mask, put steelworker's wax in her ears to impair hearing, and used baby oil drops in her eyes to cloud her vision. A heavy wrap forced her to walk stooped. Balsa splints taped to the back of the knees both shortened and slowed her steps, and heavy tape on her hands, hidden under bulky gloves, simulated the restrictions of arthritis. Crayon stains were applied to her teeth, and she gargled a pasty saltwater mix, deliberately irritating her throat in order to create a raspy voice. Columbia students did not recognize her when she attended her own classes as "Old Pat."

Out on the streets, Moore experienced directly the life of an elderly woman. She was shortchanged by merchants and muscled out of her place in lines. People pointedly talked down to her, she was physically assaulted, and at one time she was left for dead by teenagers looking for drug money. At times she was so frustrated "it was all I could do to stop myself from ripping off my wig and giving them a very unladylike piece of my mind" (1989:17). But she didn't, and over time she felt herself becoming increasingly timid and submissive, doing and saying whatever was necessary to get through each demeaning situation with a little dignity. Once during the research she revealed her identity to a small group of elderly women she knew and trusted. Seeing who she really was and wanting to help in the research, they took her shopping, explaining the nuances of getting through the hazards of each day. From them she discovered why the elderly have a reputation among some researchers for concealing, even lying, about how they live. Secretiveness and reduced visibility are important strategies for survival in a world that does not care if you are old. She recalls that one of her best memories as "Old Pat" was a conversation with a six-year-old boy at a beach. He responded to her presence naturally and without affectation because, she said, "he didn't know any better."

Moore's experiment suggests some of the interesting research issues one confronts in learning about any culture one does not know. For example, what is the research technique we call "participant observation"? Why is direct experience useful as a precondition for cross-cultural understanding, especially the kind of understanding that is sometimes described as "empathy"? Is it necessary for those who want to be of service to all the "Old Pats" in the world to have an experience of participatory involvement? Are there other ways of expanding one's personal and professional sensibilities? What is cross-cultural learning anyway, and how can human service workers use it productively?

Cross-cultural social work is both similar to and different from other kinds of human service activity. It is similar in that it can be integrated into the vocabulary and procedures common to any health or social service facility. It is generic, not a distinctive field of practice such as substance abuse or community development. But it is different in that it requires explicit, informed utilization of ethnographic information for planning, service delivery, and evaluation. That information must be specifically and demonstrably salient to client issues within a communal context. Cross-cultural social work is much more than regular contact with clients who are culturally or racially different from oneself. Certainly, it is more than vague and simplistic notions of "acceptance" or "awareness," which sometimes come from casual association with minority staff or clients.

Effective cross-cultural social work combines deliberate preparation with an alertness to the cultural as well as clinical features of the client–worker relationship. It involves specific ways of acquiring the knowledge and skills appropriate for working with ethnically distinctive clients. It supplements traditional social service training methods, and it is eclectic, relying on a number of academic and professional fields in which cross-cultural learning and communication are critical. Finally, it is a discovery procedure, a way of accessing and learning about the world of people different from ourselves.

There are several reasons social workers would want to acquire cross-cultural knowledge and capabilities. First, many workers know little of the *cultural* characteristics of the client communities they serve. This is not surprising as it is only in the last decade or so that multicultural counseling has appeared in the curriculum of many social work training programs (Ponterotto and Sabnani 1989). Unfortunately, many course offerings in this area are little more than supplements to existing curricula, in effect ghettoizing the topic in specialized, "minority issues" courses rather than integrating it into the widest possible range of social work teaching. Much that passes for "cultural sensitivity" training, be it in university classes or on-the-job workshops, is simplistic and anecdotal. Frequently it relies on minority representatives who are asked to give what amount to testimonials. Sometimes it is polite and academic, offering "background" information that is interesting but lacking any clear relationship to specific client issues. It can be simplistic and distorting, emphasizing "norms and values," as Longres (1991:55) put it, avoiding the realities of power and systemic inequality. In addition, a lack of interest among administrators and a lack of willingness to follow through on training initiatives often limit the degree to which cultural awareness penetrates the profession.

Although this situation has begun to change, and some of these changes are an improvement over past practice, still the best current efforts are minimal when compared to the needs involved. It is necessary, therefore, to think about ways of acquiring cultural information more systematically and more efficiently than has been done in the past. Anecdotes, testimonials, role plays, and short-term workshops with no follow-up are no longer adequate. Gallegos put it harshly but succinctly by suggesting that "social work practitioners who lack the skills, attitudes, and knowledge to work effectively in cross-cultural settings are incompetent" (1984:1).

A second reason social workers would want to acquire cross-cultural capabilities is that problem solving with those who are culturally or racially different from oneself can be highly stressful. That will not be news to most minority social workers, who deal with people different from themselves everyday! But to many whites, especially those whose contact with minority persons is infrequent, working with minority clients may be particularly difficult. Ratliff (1988) lists some of the symptoms of "burnout" in the helping professions. Among them are stereotyping clients, judgmental attitudes toward clients who seem particularly difficult, discussion of clients in distancing, jargonistic terms, and a sense that whatever one does with a particular individual, it will never make a difference. These reactions are exacerbated when workers do not comprehend their client's moods and motivations and the cultural sources of them. There is a need for training that goes beyond altruistic desires to help, and well beyond cultural "awareness" workshops that "raise consciousness" but provide little more.

Third, among most Americans the expression of prejudicial attitudes in public and professional settings is much less acceptable than it was even a decade ago. In educated circles, at least, bigotry is boorish. But institutional forms of insensitivity and discrimination persist. As I suggested in Chapter 1 on the relationship of ethnicity to social work, institutional forms of mistreatment are harder to see and more difficult to correct. That is partly due to the fact that sometimes individuals benefit, in direct and indirect ways, from the status quo. Privilege is at stake. A cultural approach to social services, however, makes explicit the dichotomy between the values and procedures of those who provide services and the values and responses of those who receive them. Much of the dynamics of cross-cultural social work involves the juxtaposition of these two, often contrary, traditions, that of the profession and that of the client's community. Recognizing the reality of this contrast can make it easier to identify and change institutional deficiencies.

Finally, it is important to recognize that within social work even our counseling theories presume that some cultural values are "better" than others and hence more deserving of our attention and encouragement with clients. This kind of "theoretical ethnocentrism" can be as detrimental to effective communication as outright bigotry. For example, Ponterotto and Casas (1991) note that psychodynamic approaches to therapy, with their emphasis on intrapsychic conflict rooted in early childhood events, often discount the small, day-to-day stresses of racism and prejudice. They also favor a verbally active expressive style in counseling, something that may not be appropriate or encouraged in some communities. The person-centered approach of existential and humanistic theories, commonly associated with Carl Rogers and Viktor Frankl, emphasizes self-awareness, self-esteem, and self-acceptance. Yet these values are just the opposite of those preferred in communities where the welfare of the group—family, kin, ethnic or linguistic compatriots —is more important than that of the individual. Even behavioral approaches, generally preferred by ethnic and minority therapists and their clients, still assume the central importance of middle-class, white values associated with self-directed independent action, task-centered problem solving, and a linear construction of time (Ponterotto and Casas 1991:61). The task of developing a genuinely cross-cultural, ethnically sensitive social work is just that much more difficult when the discipline's guiding paradigms assume (without making their assumptions explicit) the greater importance of one's own community's values over the standards and preferences of others.

CROSS-CULTURAL LEARNING

It is an axiom of social work that the successful worker must establish rapport and develop empathic relationships in order to further treatment objectives. A number of training approaches have been devised to promote acquisition of these "helping" capabilities. The literature on skills development in social work is very large, covering many kinds of intervention activities, and cannot be completely reviewed here. But it is common in these approaches to stress the student's need for enhanced perception of verbal and nonverbal cues, attentiveness to emotional states during interaction, and sensitivity in questioning and responding. Typically, rather general kinds of desired behavior ("self-involving," "encouraging," "assertive," "engaging," and the like) are described, and then problems for practice and relationship-building are presented. The goals of this kind of training are usually (1) empathic understanding that results from putting oneself in the other's place; (2) nonpossessive respect and warm, unconditional regard for the other; and (3) genuineness in the therapeutic relationship so that what one seems to be is in fact what one is. There is no holding back of one's full attentiveness to the other.

Useful as these may be as goals, they are also limited and limiting concepts. Behind them is an assumption that a specific "helping skill," when sufficiently practiced, ought to be helpful when employed with most clients. There is also an emphasis on personal "style," on practicing the techniques with which one feels "comfortable." Practice should lead to "skills" that help one develop the trusting relationships that are the mark of the competent professional.

Egan (1986), however, has described certain problems that can arise from the simplistic application of these high-sounding communication ideals in social service encounters. He calls them "counterfeits of accurate empathy." Examples include (1) inaccurate responses to the client because the interviewer is excessively focused on technique; (2) inattentiveness because the social worker is mentally anticipating what to say next; (3) assumptions that the client will understand the worker's "validating" gestures and "affirming" subvocalization; and (4) restatement of what the client has said as a device to maintain the worker's end of the conversation. Egan believes that empathy is not really a "skill," certainly not a trained "bedside manner" that can be turned on and off at will. Rather, he sees it as something that is part of how good professionals deal with others all the time. He argues that the way to avoid counterfeit empathy is to look instead for the "core messages" that clients attempt to express, the messages that emerge from their life experiences.

Egan's concern with "core messages" points to one of the essential tasks of effective cross-cultural communication. I want to suggest that interpersonal skills or techniques are not in and of themselves a sufficient basis for working with minority clients. (They may not be adequate for working with many non-minority clients either.) Although personal qualities of warmth and caring may be important as work styles, they are not an adequate basis for comprehending what troubles another person or for knowing how that individual may be helped. Rather, we need some way to identify and learn the significance of our client's "core messages," especially when we are with clients whose cultural background we know little about. Further, we need a way of learning that can be adapted to a variety of cross cultural situations, since it is impossible for any of us to know enough to effectively serve clients from every cultural community in a large, pluralistic society.

How, then, does one learn about another culture? Children learn the patterns and pieces of a culture as they are presented to them, somewhat randomly and over a long period of time. A monocultural adult entering an unfamiliar social world is forced to learn the same way. Anyone who has served in the Peace Corps or who has had overseas experience knows that events, objects, and language may appear strange at first but that strangeness recedes into the background as places, people, and contexts become familiar and taken for granted. The adult's advantage over the child is the capacity for critical assessment of the pieces as they are presented. The disadvantage is that a lifetime of learned preferences can act as blinders to much that is going on, or may lead to erroneous interpretations of the "core messages" that others transmit to us.

The framework developed by Taft (1977) suggests several beginning steps for acquiring knowledge of other cultural systems. The first level of learning is cognitive.

One must simply go to the trouble to learn some of what members of a culture know, including their beliefs about their history, their values, and what they see as their relationship to the rest of the world. At this stage of learning, it is not necessary to rely solely on library-type research and generalized, background reading. What matters is what people believe to be true about themselves and others, since that is what is most real to them. At the cognitive level, then, the task of the skilled learner-practitioner is to try to determine something of the normative beliefs and behavior of a given community as the members of that community perceive and act on them. The social worker must be concerned with a new version of "common sense," the taken-for-granted things that people in a particular community rarely question. For example, there are ways of treating children, of serving food, and of offering greetings that are "right," and ways that are "wrong." The worker will simply have to learn what they are—by combining reading, listening, watching, and consulting with knowledgeable insiders. By paying attention to the regularities of conduct and finding out what they mean in context, the worker begins to discover "core messages" and to acquire empathy as a personal and professional trait.

But knowledge of another culture is more than information. What people do and what they prefer are always associated with an expressive tone. Sometimes that tone is identifiable in such overt activities as singing, dancing, arguing, playing, and working. But affective or expressive tone can also be discovered in offhand comments, facial expressions, joking relationships, exchange of favors, and styles of demeanor. In all cultures, people play largely predetermined roles: spouse, child, friend, or co-worker. But how they play their roles, how they incorporate expressive gestures into what Goffman (1959) called the "presentation of self," is a clue to the affective tone of a community. Affect, feeling tone, and intuitive sensitivities are subtle, complex, and sometimes difficult to detect, but they suggest the gut-level realities of people's experiences and cannot be ignored. It is probably impossible to appreciate them fully in a tradition that is not one's own. To pretend that one has fully crossed into the expressive realm of another culture is not only preposterous but usually embarrassing to onlookers. But to be able to recognize the core messages of expressiveness, and to respond to them even somewhat appropriately, is a sign of growing empathy. Rapport comes from one's willingness to learn about others at that level and intensity. Rapport *cannot* come from a practiced technical style.

One implication of this approach is that the competent learner–practitioner may on some occasions attempt, but with a great deal of caution and humbleness, to simulate culturally appropriate role performances if invited by others to do so. For example, I have seen white social workers who were totally at home in a Northwest Coast Native American potlatch, an all-night ceremony of dancing, eating, speech making, and ceremonial gift giving. Some joined in the dancing because they were qualified and capable of doing so and their presence was acceptable. This is, as Taft notes, the "ultimate test of enculturation" (1977:136), when one can recognize and respond appropriately to the feelings of the members of an ethnic community. When one can act "correctly" and have the act recognized by others as culturally genuine, then one has achieved the broadened understanding that exemplifies the best in cross-cultural social work.

Perhaps that level of capability is beyond what most practitioners really need to do their jobs. Yet it would be difficult to argue that a profession committed to helping others in sensitive personal, family, and community matters could proceed in ignorance of those realities. The typical injunctions to be patient, genuine, and open fall far short of real cross-cultural comprehension.

We need to put a label on this elusive capability, for it represents the essential characteristic of the social worker who knows, appreciates, and can utilize the cultural background of another. The term "cultural competence" has come into general use over the past few years, so I will use it here. *The service provider who is culturally competent can deliver professional services in a way that is congruent with behavior and expectations normative for a given community and that are adapted to suit the specific needs of individuals and families from that community.* Figure 3.1 summarizes the minimal components of the cultural competence model.

It is important to understand what the definition of cultural competence says and what it does not say. It does not say—and I want to be emphatic on this point—that the trained individual will be able to conduct himself or herself "as though" he or she were a participating member of a client community. That is clearly absurd and to make that capability a personal or professional training goal would be misleading and dangerous. In my own workshops, I am always amazed at how regularly someone announces, usually in a holier-than-thou sort of way, that he or she has worked with clients from the "X" culture "for years" and so is authoritative on how the "X" feel about things. No training program can deliver that, and I distrust the claims of those who think simple longevity guarantees that level of understanding. Cultural competence means only that the worker has a systematically learned and tested awareness of the prescribed and proscribed values and behavior of a specific community, and an ability to carry out professional activities consistent with that awareness.

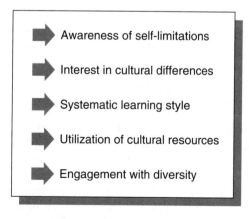

Awareness of self-limitations

Interest in cultural differences

Systematic learning style

Utilization of cultural resources

Engagement with diversity

FIGURE 3.1   Cultural Competence as Practice

CULTURAL COMPETENCE

In some ways, it is easier to define what cross-cultural sensitivity is not than to pinpoint what it is. Pedersen (1997) describes what he calls the "culturally encapsulated counselor," an individual unable or unwilling to engage the client on any but the counselor's own terms. Such a counselor capitalizes on the status differences that separate him or her from the client and uses those differences to manage the relationship. The client's life circumstances or personal problems are evaluated according to criteria more suitable to the personal or professional milieu of the counselor than to the day-to-day realities of client experience. Only minimal reference may be made to the client's larger social setting, with the possible exception of family life. But that too is seen as an isolated site, a locale of pathology, to be diagnosed and treated. From the point of view of the encapsulated counselor, each client is a unique, nonhistorical, culturally unconnected entity.

Given this narrowly conceived orientation, the professional's clinical task is to "strip away" or "get behind" cultural appearances that mask and confound the "true" or "deeper" meaning of the client's problems. The encapsulated counselor has an a priori commitment to a set of beliefs about "processes" and techniques, themselves part of established professional and institutional loyalties. Given that most social service workers have great latitude in the micro-management of their contacts with clients and patients, it seems natural to the encapsulated counselor that dominant agency perspectives would be reproduced in worker–client relationships. In effect, what the encapsulated worker brings to an encounter is ideology as a substitute for the openness and risk taking that real empathy would require.

Perhaps this is an unfair and exaggerated characterization. Much more has been written on cross-cultural counseling and communication for social services specifically, although much of it remains narrowly descriptive (sometimes in ways that are painfully brief) or is limited to anecdotes and short descriptions of single cases. We can begin, however, with some general features of cross-cultural capability that Mayes (1978) suggested some years ago and that are still useful in contrasting cultural competence with other kinds of social service training. I will list these and discuss some of their implications for the model to be developed here.

Cultural Competence as Awareness of One's Limitations

Barbara Solomon's work on "empowerment" is well known in social services. Usually, empowerment is thought of as a quality to be encouraged in the client or as an activity that "aims(s) to reduce the powerlessness that has been created by negative valuations" (Solomon 1976:19). That seems rather obvious and simple, almost a cliché. But I believe it is very difficult for some workers to grasp and accept because it goes to the heart of what Solomon was talking about—power. The worker who has academic degrees, who has attended all the right workshops and has the framed certificates to prove it, who has the job title and career aspirations, may find it quite difficult to grant a teaching role to those he or she is paid to serve. Why should that be so hard?

Think again about the "culturally encapsulated" counselor and that individual's commitment to an a priori set of beliefs. What kinds of beliefs might they be? Some years ago Stewart (1969) listed five values or assumptions he thought characterize mainstream American culture, values often translated into institutionally dominant modes of planning and delivery in mental health services. Those values are (1) active self-expression; (2) equality and informality in social relationships; (3) achievement and accomplishment; (4) control of self and one's destiny while in pursuit of a better future; and (5) individualism and autonomy experienced in democratic, nonauthoritarian relationships with others (Stewart, Danielian and Festes, 1969). A more recent commentator discussing American popular culture developed what he called a "mantra" of white, middle-American virtues: industry; success; civic-mindedness; usefulness; antisensuality; and conscience (Brookhiser 1991). And in a work of great erudition, Bellah and his associates (1985) described individualism and its two subvarieties, utilitarian individualism and expressive individualism, as master metaphors of American life.

These are all admirable values, at least to persons whose socialization has included years of public education followed by advanced training in university programs marked by liberal, humanistic learning. But they may not be the values of those who are immersed in a subculture more oriented toward day-to-day survival, or who participate in a community that has preserved old, even ancient, traditions transplanted from another continent to an American setting. For example, some clients may have a sense of impropriety in discussing intimate matters outside the family, and for them the notion of "active self-expression," especially with a stranger, may be offensive. Nor can it be assumed that the ability to articulate for others one's most private feelings is a sign of a healthy mental state. In some settings, it may not be appropriate for the individual to independently "assert" himself or herself, for doing so could be interpreted as a sign of instability or insensitivity. Similarly, we cannot take it for granted that all cultures have a notion of "personal growth" tied to expectations of individual accomplishment. Indeed, many cultures do not, and "personal growth" that distinguishes one from others might be viewed as arrogant and unseemly.

What all this suggests is the applicability of the old anthropological truism, cultural relativism. Cultures are in fact different, and most of the differences are subtle and not always visible to outsiders. People occasionally get a sense of this when they participate in "values clarification" workshops and similar kinds of exercises. Although we may not all agree that Stewart's five postulates do indeed define the core values of mainstream American culture, we can probably agree that *any* set of values, including professional ones, is culture-bound and that we are all myopic at least to the extent that we operate with one set of beliefs to the exclusion of others. That need not be a cause of despair. It only means we need to see our own actions and values in an explicitly comparative way so that our personal choices do not keep us from perceiving why others may have different ones. Relativism is a beginning, at least, to appreciating that.

Cultural Competence as Openness to Cultural Differences

The belief that "underneath we are all the same" and that we all share a basic understanding of what is good and valuable might well be added to my list of common American values. This idea derives from the melting pot ideology, with its assumption (and hope) that the cultural differences that separate people are less important than the things that unite them, and that manifestations of differences are best underemphasized in order to ensure personal tranquility and civil peace.

Even as the word "pluralism" has become fashionable, both as a description of tolerance and even an appreciation of the idiosyncrasies of others, it remains true that cultural dissimilarity is much less highly valued than cultural homogeneity. In fact, many people are threatened by the promotion of cultural differences, especially if they think that "special privileges" may go with them. This is dramatically clear when themes of ethnicity are explicitly linked with political demands for change in the distribution of status and power (as in the Black Power movement of the 1960s and 1970s) and in the realignment of economic privileges (as in Native American land and fishing claims). Cultural differences are threatening even on the symbolic level, as when seemingly "assimilated" individuals insist that their children receive instruction in languages other than English. Real acceptance of differences has rarely been promoted in the educational, religious, or political institutions of the larger society. It is not surprising, therefore, that the response of social services to ethnic and minority communities would be occasionally awkward and hesitant.

A genuine and open appreciation of ethnic differences, without condescension and without patronizing gestures, is critical for the development of an ethnically competent professional style. At a minimum, that means that the worker ought to have a sense of how the social artifact called the "counseling relationship" fits into a client's normative expectations. Do clients perceive as normal or acceptable a deeply personal conversation with a near stranger, one who has a great deal of authority and who is a representative of another, possibly threatening, ethnic group? Is the social worker expected to give something of value—advice, goods, or an eligibility rating—in return for a proper show of deference or need? What is the agenda, and how is action begun?

One early step is clarifying the expectations in the counseling relationship. This does not mean asking such obvious and abstract questions as "What does your Indianness mean to you?" It means instead some acknowledgment that the client's and the worker's ethnic and cultural identities are different and that the differences may be important to counseling and giving assistance. The skill with which this is done, of course, depends on the social worker's maturity and capability. But it is important in that it makes clear to both worker and client that the latter has more to contribute than the presentation of a problem.

Cultural Competence as a Client-Oriented, Systematic Learning Style

All cross-cultural encounters are potential learning experiences. They may result in the discovery of new information or in a better understanding of something that was not fully appreciated before. But learning depends on the social worker's willingness to adopt something of a student role, something not easy for everyone to do.

This lesson was particularly dramatic for Evans (1988, 1991), a researcher with long social service experience. He describes his activities in a state school for the deaf where he went to study the organization of the institution and its impact on deaf students. Of course, American Sign Language was the lingua franca of the school and, as a hearing-impaired person himself, Evans knew the language needed to communicate with respondents. What surprised him, however, was the degree to which deaf students developed their own, alternative subculture, partly out of opposition to the school's managers but also as a defensive reaction to the larger society. He describes the deep sense of a "wounded self" that typified these students and how that view shaped their responses to the authoritarian culture of their school community. Evans could explore these issues because he knew sign language but also because he allowed himself to be treated in the same way as the students. He experienced directly the slights and not very subtle insults that maintained a "safe" distance between students and staff. By adopting a learner role, he experienced these things directly and came to understand the real culture of the place and why people behaved and felt as they did.

The concept of cultural competence assumes that clients, however plagued by personal problems and uncertainties, know a great deal about what is happening to them. The social worker needs to know the same information—local, contextualized knowledge—so he or she can integrate it into whatever therapeutic model is to be followed (Gubrium 1991).

Cultural Competence as Appropriate Utilization of Cultural Resources

The ability to help others find and make use of resources is one of the critical tasks of the culturally competent worker. It is an important part of what Solomon (1976) meant when she wrote of "empowerment." The culturally competent helper ought to encourage clients to draw on the natural strengths inherent in their own traditions and communities, reducing where possible their dependence on services provided by outsiders or by impersonal bureaucracies. This is not a new idea, although it has become more urgent with the failure of the federal and many local governments to adequately fund critical services. Social services have never been funded at levels that fully meet community needs, but during the past ten to fifteen years federal practice, if not policy, has been to dismantle parts of this "safety net." Out of necessity, self-help has become more acceptable, and perhaps that is a good thing. Minority-sponsored and -operated programs that assist people in the languages and styles of their own communities have become more prominent and will certainly continue to grow.

Despite this change, however, cultural resources are probably those least used by professional social workers in their encounters with clients. One reason for this is the tendency of workers to think of "resources" only as the network of community social service organizations and "referral" agencies that explicitly serve minority groups. But these are only the visible and obvious parts of the human service system, and for many clients they may be the places they go to last. Many people prefer to rely on family, friends, voluntary organizations, ministers, pharmacists, self-help books, and bartenders. Some struggle with their problems more privately, through reading, contemplation, prayer, talking to themselves, compulsive eating, or watching soap operas on television. Choices and decisions are made at many levels, and troubled individuals usually rely on the beliefs and values that are part of their personal and communal networks long before they turn for help to outsiders or professionals.

The capacity for individualizing the client within a specific cultural matrix is the genius and the challenge of effective cross-cultural social work. To reach that goal, the social worker must know all the resources available to the client, especially the less obvious ones, and how they can be used in planning and guiding intervention. The term "resources" means much more than the network of community agencies and referral services. It includes institutions, individuals, and customs for resolving problems that are indigenous to the client's own community. Indeed, these indigenous resources may be the most important, for they are less likely to fade away when public policies or governmental funding levels change. It is critical, then, that the worker know what these resources are and how they can be productively used. That kind of learning requires moving out into the community, not just as a social worker representing an agency and its interests, but as a learner seeking to understand how clients communicate on their home turf and how they participate in the familiar routines of everyday life.

STEPS TOWARD CULTURAL COMPETENCE

The characteristics of cultural competence described above should help orient our professional work toward the needs of minority clients. By themselves, however, they are too general. The route to greater appreciation of the role of culture in human behavior requires direct observation and participation in naturalistic settings, away from the confines of offices and their imposing routines. For instance, the practitioner who has not attended a black church service or talked with a black minister probably does not understand black clients as well as he or she could. The worker serving Native American clients who has not spent enough time in a Native American home seeing how extended families take care of their children and their elderly, or how ritual practices help preserve traditional family ways, really does not know enough about Native American clients. These important events cannot be observed from behind an office desk, nor can they be fully understood through classroom exercises or short-term workshops. Hasty consultations with minority social workers or minority group leaders when a specific problem with a client is overwhelming is not good cross-cultural learning either.

Cultural competence means moving beyond the job description and learning about clients through direct observation and participation in their everyday routines in naturalistic settings. Fortunately, social workers are in a good position to do that, more than most other professionals, because their work takes them into people's homes and into people's personal lives all the time.

In learning about another culture, however, no one can operate alone and without guidance. The overly eager novice often wants to slip unobserved into an unfamiliar community for "study" and "observation." (Unfortunately, this is a too familiar classroom assignment, one that is usually misguided and does little to expand anyone's cultural awareness.) These experiences, usually brief and superficial, create a false sense of knowledge and can be more accurately described as academic voyeurism than as a serious effort at cross-cultural learning. It is better for the social worker to enter a community as a guest, publicly sponsored by someone who understands the learner's goals and who agrees to act as a gatekeeper and guide. Even the task of preparing to meet with a potential guide can be lengthy and tedious, requiring patient negotiating.

I will describe three steps in cross-cultural learning: (1) background preparation, (2) use of cultural guides, and (3) participant observation. The steps are summarized in Figure 3.2. Each is important, and together they amount to a *systematic learning* style that can be easily adapted to the needs of individual learners, small groups, and even entire organizations (Green and Wilson 1983).

Who is a good cultural guide? Guides can be found anywhere, in any community, and they may or may not be community leaders. More often, they are ordinary people who can articulate well what is going on around them. Professionals who are in regular contact with clients ethnically distinct from themselves and who generally work well with them depend heavily on informed and informative insiders. Their use of cultural guides is not occasional, occurring only at times of a case management crisis. Consultation and advice-seeking are ongoing activities.

Workers who are white have a tendency to turn first (and sometimes only) to minority colleagues. That is seen as a "safe" choice. But it also has the potential for exploitation. Many minority social workers rightly view infrequent or uninformed "cultural" questions from white workers as another form of tokenism. However well intended, some whites may be surprised when minority colleagues express irritation at requests for information on why "their people" (an objectionable phrase in itself) think and act as they do. Too often such questions are motivated by the need for a quick fix with a troublesome client, not by a desire to learn something in-depth about the cultural context of a client's needs. Cross-cultural effectiveness is possible only with a committed, long-term effort, not episodic and crisis-inspired ones. The occasional use of a minority colleague's time is not usually very effective.

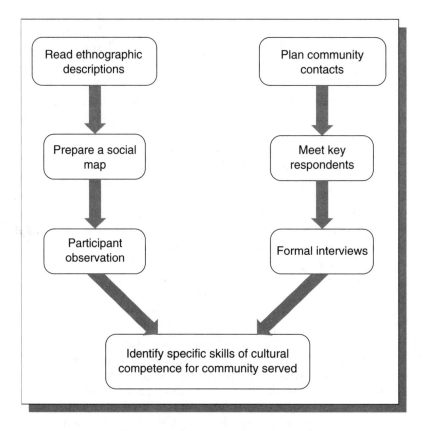

FIGURE 3.2   Basic Steps of Cross-Cultural Learning

Entering an Unfamiliar Community

Learning about unfamiliar places and people often seems to be one of the most difficult and even the most threatening aspects of acquiring cultural competence. It appears difficult, and in some ways it is, because most of the time most of us are not required to accommodate individuals unlike ourselves except on a short-term, instrumental basis. Contact with ethnically distinctive individuals, at least for most whites, is limited to commercial transactions, routine on-the-job activities, and random encounters in public places. For most of these situations, the rules of decorum require studied indifference or cautious politeness; personal opinions about race or ethnicity, however benign or prejudiced, are not allowed to disrupt superficial agreeableness. It requires a real effort, therefore, to show more than a casual interest in others, especially when one is visiting them in their own homes and neighborhoods.

There are two helpful procedures for planning access to an unfamiliar community. The first is preparation through study of available research and documents; the second is a series of visitations for the purpose of "social mapping." These two activities should be carried out at the same time, prior to developing contacts with community members and prior to the extended interviews that will be carried out with key respondents later.

At least three sources of data are available, and all three should be utilized extensively. First, ethnographic accounts in scholarly books and articles have been written on every ethnic group in American society. Indeed, it is difficult to think of any group that has been overlooked by sociologists or anthropologists in their pursuit of a new, "exotic" people to study and write about. As a result of the civil rights movement and affirmative action programs at universities, many ethnic communities now produce their own researchers, and their observations can be particularly compelling. What they write should be examined closely and taken seriously. The perspectives of these writers and scholars must be a major part of any background reading program.

A second source is the literature on ethnicity and race relations that has developed within social work itself. This literature appears in the recognized, established journals and sometimes in obscure, less easily located publications. It focuses on the issues confronting minority persons in social services and on issues in developing sensitive and useful services for minority clients. Unfortunately, much of that literature is highly quantitative, or it relies on brief case reports that do not provide sufficient context. Because of these inadequacies, it must be supplemented with ethnographies or extensive case studies written by minority social workers themselves. The work of Gibbs (1988, 1989) on black youth is a particularly impressive example, and her work should be mandatory reading for anyone wanting to work with this community.

A third source of information is that specific to the community or region. Because of the number of studies conducted by the government at all levels and for all kinds of reasons, it is unlikely that any city or county totally lacks descriptive information on the minority or ethnic groups resident there. The problem with this resource is difficulty of access. It is often buried in the files of government agencies, some of them social service agencies, and one would first have to learn of their existence even to ask about them. These sources, however, can be important for what they reveal about the conditions of life in many communities, and some of them are worth the trouble to find, read, and analyze.

The task of the social worker is to find and assimilate any of this information that is appropriate to his or her work and program needs. There are several reasons for doing this. No one can begin to appreciate what is going on in a community, or why, without digging into background information. A book, a scholarly article, and a government document all have something important to say that cannot be learned any other way. In addition, background research and reading provide an initial familiarity, however limited, that can help reduce the sense of anxiety and uncertainty that may accompany an initial community visit. Avoiding this necessary homework is to slight the seriousness of the job to be done. Computer searching now makes the job easier.

The second procedure is to visit a community for the purpose of social mapping. Social mapping is identifying and recording the cultural resources of a community.

It is making a kind of inventory at the macrosocial level. The minimal data to be included in a social map would be (1) identification and location of an ethnic group in an area; (2) description of the community's social organization; (3) description of the residents' beliefs and ideological characteristics; (4) identification of patterns of wealth, its accumulation, and its distribution; (5) description of the patterns of mobility, both geographical and social; and (6) information on access and utilization of available human services (Cochrane 1979). From a social service perspective, the development of a social map represents an effort to relate the findings of ethnographies, social service research, and other documents to the specific characteristics of the area the worker wants to understand and serve better.

The product of social mapping should be a short document containing one or more physical maps and descriptive information for each of the six items listed above, provided in sufficient detail that a stranger could read it and gain some general sense of who lives in the area, how they live, what they believe and do, and how they use social services. The document should also make clear the outstanding needs of the community, especially as they are perceived by the residents themselves. (Needless to say, that kind of information is invaluable when it comes to writing grants or justifying new services or staff positions.)

There is a good reason for taking the time to do all this background investigation. Most social service workers become aware of the characteristics and the problems of the communities they serve only after a lengthy period. The pressures of the workplace, requiring the worker to begin with clients almost immediately, delay learning about the more general attributes of the community. Information is acquired in a piecemeal way. In contrast, social mapping is highly focused and results in a tangible product; it produces a short and fast learning curve. In addition, a social map can be expanded, revised, and used by other workers in the agency. It can be used in orientations for new workers, training, and performance evaluation. It can guide improvements in the design and delivery of culturally sensitive services. Preparing such a map, especially as a personal or agency project, replicates in a small way the "community study" method that has been so productive in the development of cross-cultural understanding in the social sciences. But its basic purpose should not be forgotten: preparing social workers for a smooth entry into the community they intend to serve.

Entering a Psychiatric Client Community

There have been many studies of psychiatric hospitals and of people who are institutionalized. But with the deinstitutionalization of patients that began some years ago, and the development of halfway houses to assist them, a growing number of the chronically mentally ill have had to take care of themselves as best they could. In a major study of the culture and lifestyles of these people, Estroff (1981) spent two years doing participant observation with both clinical staff and their outpatients in a facility located in a medium-sized midwestern city. She prepared for her work by reviewing the available literature on mental illness and outpatient populations, including literature in social work, psychiatry, sociology, and medical anthropology. But to learn more about how people really lived, how they made daily decisions, and what constraints they faced on an everyday basis, she decided to live among both staff and patients as a participant observer.

Gaining access to the clinic and its staff was not difficult. Her work was in a university town and people understood that graduate students often do community research. Her entry into the client community was more difficult, partly because there were few places where they gathered as a group and partly because they were naturally suspicious of outsiders, especially "researchers" who, for all they knew, might be "spies" from the clinic.

Estroff had to construct her own social map for a diffuse community, which she considered culturally distinctive because of the particular stigmas imposed on the mentally ill. Her first task was to establish her identity and her legitimacy in living among the mentally ill when she was not so incapacitated herself. To do that she spent all the time she could in the clients' natural settings: apartments, coffee shops, parks, storefronts, and alleys. "My general approach was to participate *as if* I were a client in as many treatment and nontreatment aspects of clients' lives as was feasible. The purpose of these activities was twofold: to observe clients across the range of their daily lives and to participate in and experience these circumstances myself" (1981:24). She also attended staffings, participated in group work with clients, got to know community volunteers, and went to social and recreational events planned for clients. Over time, she came to feel that one of the most important elements of her subjects' lives had to be personally experienced: taking "meds." Under careful medical supervision, she took antipsychotic drugs for several months so she could write with more insight about the meaning of "meds" for people who were, in her words, "making it crazy."

Aside from the scholarly contribution of the research and the impact of the experience on her personal life (which was considerable), part of the value of Estroff's work was the policy and intervention recommendations she could make, based on the dual experience of researcher and knowledgeable insider. She had great sympathy for both clients and staff and generally saw staff as both committed and well motivated. But they sometimes worked at cross-purposes to the values and norms of the client subculture and, lacking the kind of understanding she had acquired, they could not always appreciate why their best efforts were never enough. While it is obvious that members of the staff could not spend the time Estroff did to familiarize themselves with their own clients, it is equally obvious that they benefited from the recommendations she could make. Estroff's patience and her bravery made it possible for others to better understand the living conditions and needs of people who are poorly understood even by those who would be their benefactors.

Key Respondents as Cultural Guides

Key respondents are individuals who are knowledgeable about their community and who are able and willing to articulate that knowledge to an outsider. They can be thought of as *cultural guides,* persons who can adopt a teaching role in order to assist the worker in understanding the subtleties and complexities of a particular community. In his book on participant observation, Bogdan (1972) referred to such individuals as "gatekeepers," for they often have the power to grant access to key persons or institutions in the community. Not all key respondents, however, are of equal value either as guides or teachers. All that any individual knows is obviously a function of many things, including the size and composition of one's personal network, degree of participation in community organizations and activities, access to community leaders and decision makers, and ascribed characteristics such as gender and age. All these things facilitate access to some kinds of information and inhibit access to others. In judging the value of a key respondent's knowledge, therefore, the issue is not simply what information seems correct and what incorrect. The issue is assessing the significance and limits of each respondent's knowledge and knowing when it has to be supplemented or modified by information from another guide.

Simply getting information, however, is not enough. The culturally sensitive observer is often interested in things that a key respondent may take for granted, or in details of daily life that some respondents may prefer to conceal. In his well-known dramaturgical model of social behavior, Goffman (1959) argued that we are all actors putting on social performances for each other. But some performances are in the "front region" of the stage, for everyone to see, and others are clearly "backstage" and partially concealed. Front region behavior is relatively open and public, and individuals conduct themselves in ways that support recognized standards of decorum. Front region behavior presumes a critical audience, present or not, to comment on the actor's behavior. In backstage regions, however, the more hidden and sometimes contradictory features of everyday life are evident, and individuals behave in ways that, while predictable or rational by certain standards of their culture, nevertheless do not coincide with publicly espoused definitions of reality.

Family life, for instance, is relatively well concealed in our own as well as many other cultures, and it could be considered a backstage region. It may be, as Leach (1968) once pointed out in an infamous remark, that the "tawdry secrets" of each and every family constitute one of the most remote and difficult-to-access backstage areas of any culture. Obviously, a key respondent, acting as a cultural guide, is not going to eagerly enter into a discussion of sensitive, often concealed matters with someone who represents an ethnic group or profession that lacks high esteem in the respondent's community. The result is that the worker seeking information is most likely to hear what the respondent believes ought to be told and little more. The solution to this difficulty is a carefully cultivated relationship of trust with a small number of individuals, relationships built over a period of time, so that the learner and each respondent come to understand and respect one another's position and purposes.

There is a tempting shortcut to working around this kind of relationship with key respondents. It is to rely on someone who identifies himself or herself as an "old hand" in the community of interest but who is a member of one's own racial or ethnic group. People like this are easy to approach, seem to be well established in their work, and appear to have all the answers and lots of "insider" information.

But there are two distinct disadvantages in relying on the special cultural insights they claim to have.

First, just because someone has long association with a community does not mean they know and understand it well. Individuals can and do spend years working among persons they little comprehend, and their longevity is sometimes used as justification for flawed judgments and even obvious prejudices. From my first foreign research, I well recall white North Americans (locally called "continentals") who had lived in the Caribbean for many years and who claimed to know all about West Indian culture just because of the time they had resided there. When I started collecting my own data, however, cultivating my own guides, and spending time with West Indian families, I began to see how shallow and stereotypical the knowledge of those "old hands" really was. In workshops, I occasionally meet whites who are quite willing to "one up" others in the group with claims about their special knowledge of local Native Americans or Asians. Sometimes I suspect, however, they may never have extended themselves beyond a few clinical sessions with minority clients, or occasional visits to ethnic restaurants, in their pursuit of so-called "insider" information.

Second, sole reliance on a senior worker or others in an agency deprives the social worker of direct encounters outside the safe but enclosed world of bureaucracy, experiences that are essential to anyone who wants to learn about and appreciate cultural distinctiveness. Whatever knowledge the worker gets from kindly co-workers is essentially secondhand, screened through persons whose ignorance or biases may not be obvious. The kind of information they offer too often bears the mark of gossip and office folklore. It is a poor substitute for real learning about real people in situations where they, not the worker, are at home.

An additional point about key respondents is worth noting. People do not usually give their time and energy without some expectation of a return. Any relationship between the learner and a key respondent implies that a "bargain" has been struck, implicitly or explicitly. A respondent may want to aggrandize his or her own position in the community through functioning as "the expert." He or she may have a complaint concerning social services, or social workers generally, so that the appearance of the learner is an opportunity to make those opinions known. Or a respondent may expect special favors at some future time. These motives have to be kept in mind when asking anyone to commit time as a cultural guide and gatekeeper. It would be naive to act otherwise. Consequently, the learner needs to know what he or she can offer in exchange for a respondent's confidence and information.

The Joy of a Good Cultural Guide

One of the most remarkable and enduring ethnographies on the elderly is Barbara Myerhoff's *Number Our Days* (1978), a study of a Jewish senior center in California. It has become a classic in social services, anthropology, gerontology, and sociology. Myerhoff was concerned with how elderly Jews, immigrants and survivors of World War II, established and defended their Jewishness in a country where most expressions of ethnicity are suspect. The people of the center were proud, almost desperately so, of their personal and communal struggles. But as elderly parents of children who had succeeded well by the standards of the American dream, they were pained that their children had less commitment to their ethnic and religious heritage than they did.

In many ways, the senior center was a closed community. It had its formal and informal leaders, its factions, its rules of etiquette and decorum, and its prohibitions, all of which were well known to the regulars who spent their days there. Myerhoff drew the suspicion of some of the older women because she was busy being an anthropologist rather than staying home and tending to her husband and children as some of them expected. In addition, she was unfamiliar with the rural Polish and eastern European background of many of the seniors, and that too put her outside their community of familiar and comfortable things. Nor did she share in many of their Old World beliefs, including the "evil eye" and the magical power of formulaic words and recitations. Being Jewish like them was not enough and did not ensure her easy entry into their small world.

To understand how these elders saw themselves—their sense of being old, Jewish, American, ethnic, and apparently forgotten by their adult children—Myerhoff worked closely with a man named Shmuel. He was well known in the center but not popular with everyone. Like many of them, he had been an internationalist, a socialist, and a Zionist, and he still was. But he also criticized freely and frequently. His targets included the policies of the Israeli government, the folk and magical beliefs of the seniors, and the compromises they made with their Jewishness as they struggled to preserve their ethnicity while affirming their Americanness. Although Shmuel sometimes referred to the others as "peasants," they respected him for his brutal honesty and his ability to articulate the subtle implications of their endless and sometimes philosophical arguments. They kept themselves warm and lively through enthusiastic talk and ingenious insight, and for that Shmuel was one of the best.

In the early weeks of her research, Myerhoff had a vague sense of the center's factional life and its leaders. The contentiousness of some in these factions astounded her. But she lacked specifics about the history and significance of their disputes. Shmuel had the answers. She also wondered why the elders were reticent to accept charitable donations when many seemed so obviously in need. Shmuel and the center manager, also a key respondent, knew why, and they demonstrated for her what correct conduct required. She was puzzled as well that the elders were so concerned that they be visible to themselves and to outsiders. She saw that visibility was a master metaphor in much of their talk. Again, Shmuel knew why that was so and he gave Myerhoff important insights that guided her work.

Could Myerhoff have written about this community with the understanding and sympathy that she did if she had not had a Shmuel to guide her? Perhaps, but he made critical observations that directed her attention to what was important to the people there. He also alerted her to missteps and misstatements and helped her understand why some things she had said meant something very different to those who heard them. Shmuel was not a formally educated man, having been a tailor most of his life, but his knowledge of the local scene was critical to her success and to the vivid picture of aging her ethnography presented. For the social worker desiring to serve Jewish elders, Myerhoff's book is obligatory reading. And Shmuel is what every social worker and social researcher would want in a cultural guide.

Participant Observation

Participant observation is a research style most commonly associated with cultural anthropology. Unfortunately, it has suggested to some investigators, particularly novices, a loose and unstructured way of acquiring information, as though one learned just by "soaking it up" through simple proximity. There is also a view among some that participant observation is a "soft," qualitative technique that results in "soft" and unreliable data.

It would be better to think of participant observation as an orientation toward research rather than a "method" as such. It is distinguished by long-term commitment to learning in detail something of the life of a community, conducted in a way that minimizes overt intrusion into the day-to-day activities of residents. Obviously, that is very different from the kinds of activity that typify most psychological and sociological research. The latter in particular, with its reliance on interview schedules, brief and highly controlled encounters, relative passivity of the interviewee, and generation of computer-friendly data, yields information that is largely divorced from social context and constrained by the preexisting categories of the interview schedule and the research team's interests. Quantitative research places the voice of the researcher in the foreground, not that of the researched. By contrast, one of the strengths of participant observation is the priority it gives to the words and behavior of people on their home territory, making it possible for the outsider to perceive subtlety and appreciate nuance.

Participant observation requires that the observer first determine, with the assistance of a cultural guide, that there are persons in the community who have specialized knowledge that is of interest for some practical reason. Then one of the specialists must be located. That is not always easy because, for a variety of reasons, people may not want contact with investigators from outside their community. That is particularly true where generations of student and academic researchers have entered and sometimes overwhelmed minority communities in their quest for data for term papers and dissertations. Because most of these outsiders have been white, there is now (with good reason) a manifest resentment of further intrusion. Where social workers are concerned, there also may be ambivalence toward the profession or toward particular social service organizations. Even other social service agencies, including those organized and staffed by minority professionals, may be uneasy about the presence of outside "observers." The learner may have to depend on a cultural guide to act as a broker in finding contacts and making the necessary introductions.

It is a truism that anyone who wants to be an observer of almost any kind will have to prove that he or she is worthy of being given information. This is simply a matter of trust, and it may not come easily or painlessly. If the student-to-be can make an effective argument that, as a social service or health worker, he or she can do a better job for the people involved, it may be possible to build a working relationship with a local specialist. But that argument can also backfire, especially if the activities of the worker's own agency have not been acceptable to the host community. I vividly recall a community meeting between minority social workers and the mostly white representatives of a local university and several county and city departments, all of whom wanted to be involved with a research proposal on the minority aged. But none of the social workers wanted to be affiliated with the university or with one of the city agencies that was represented. Throughout the meeting, I had the distinct feeling that long knives had been drawn and placed on the table. A community study of the minority aged, including participant observation, could not even begin until agreements on access and modes of cooperation could be established, and, in this instance, they never were. I remember how, after the meeting, an Asian worker thanked one of the white city agency representatives for her "bravery" in coming to this failed planning session. They both knew what the difficult history of their respective organizations had been.

Once involved in a community, what should one observe? That depends on what needs to be learned. Equally important, it depends on the conceptual framework one will use in guiding observation. An explicit conceptual model is important because it identifies the issues that are important, builds on what other researchers (especially minority researchers) have previously found, and keeps the observation process "on track." In participant observation, as in any learning activity, the investigator must have some idea of what kind of information is important and what is not. It does not work to approach people with a blank or "open" mind, although inexperienced researchers and interviewers often attempt to do just that. One must have a researchable topic, some hypotheses, propositions, or testable statements. The learner needs to examine the research literature so he or she can formulate some ideas about what to look for and why it is important.

Individuals who fail to develop an informed conceptual orientation for their participant observation inevitably make two errors. First, they attempt to register and remember everything they see, thus inviting confusion, information overload, and burnout. Second, they assume a stylized (and occasionally silly) way of looking, listening, and even staring at their "subjects," using mannerisms that broadcast to everyone in the vicinity that they are being "watched" and "studied." Perpetrators of these errors invariably complain later that the situation was too complex for them to learn anything or that everything happened too fast for them to notice it all. My view is that those who indulge the conceit of the hard-boiled clinical private eye are being rude, not observant, and it is unfortunate that teachers and trainers continue to send poorly prepared student observers into minority communities (and sometimes minority agencies) to subject them to this kind of insensitivity. A theoretically explicit research plan combined with informed consent and a good cultural guide can spare both the social worker and community members these embarrassments.

Participant observation is a powerful tool for learning about the cultural features of an unfamiliar cultural scene. It is not the only research approach that can be successfully used, but it is the one most likely to elicit the kind of information that is useful to the social worker who will be confronted with culturally unfamiliar clients. When well done, the procedure alerts the worker to some of the more subtle aspects of behavior and communication and may reveal important data on client expectations that cannot be discovered in any other way. And, as should be evident, it is a technique that requires at least as much discipline as the more structured, highly quantified methods of community study favored by others.

Participant Observation among Intravenous Drug Users

Intravenous drug use is a significant risk factor in the transmission of AIDS. As police work is only partially effective in controlling illegal drugs, the problem for a group of Miami, Florida, public health workers was finding alternative ways to intervene and minimize the spread of the human immunodeficiency virus (HIV). A team headed by Page and others (1990) adopted participant observation as one of several procedures for understanding this issue more fully. Their research model called for a microdescription of the behavior associated with needles and drug paraphernalia.

Through participant observation, the researchers discovered that injection of heroin and cocaine in Miami is commonly associated with a "get-off" or "get-off house," usually a safe house or small apartment where "shooters" can go to take their drugs. "House men," just one of the many petty entrepreneurs the drug culture has created, collect fees from users both for use of the get-off house and for rental of syringes and other gear. House men assist users as needed, usually by tying an arm and locating a vein, and they generally supervise drug taking so that the neighbors or police are not alerted. Drugs are not bought or sold at these houses because penalties for selling drugs directly are more than those for possessing drug equipment (called a "gimmick"). A typical house man keeps a large number of needles in a can and distributes them to those who have paid their fee.

Over a period of time, Page and his observers discovered that in the get-offs there were strict rules for needle use and cleaning and that they were scrupulously followed. The public image of users who share needles is one of crazed and uncontrollable men, passing needles back and forth among themselves. In fact, there was an orderly and complex procedure for cleaning "gimmicks" after each use so that needles were visually clean even though they were not antiseptic. House men supplied cleaning water in small bottles, receptacles for holding "dirty" water, and even tissues for wiping out syringes. Viewed at a microbehavioral level, high AIDS risk was associated with (1) dipping needles for cleaning into the "clean" water used by others; (2) accepting drugs that someone squirted from their syringe into one's own; (3) drawing off melted drugs from a common supply used by others; and (4) contact of a dirty tissue with a needle.

The Miami group's participant observation had clear advantages to them. By observing noninstitutionalized users in a naturalistic setting, they could identify a wider range of user practices and risks than had been found in clinical studies of treatment populations. They also saw that exposure to the AIDS virus was accidental, as needles were not passed directly from one user to another. Perhaps most important, they saw that there was a clear system of rules in the get-offs and they were generally observed: the house men were key figures in ensuring the orderly conduct of their business. Knowing this, health planners and social workers concerned with AIDS were in a better position to intervene by working through rather than against the subculture of the houses and their managers.

The Miami researchers note that the practices and risk behavior they identified probably vary in different parts of the country but that their participant observation would be important in researching and planning AIDS intervention with shooters in other cities: "Intercommunity variations in self-injection practices are potentially infinite, and each variant may be accompanied by different kinds of risk of HIV infection" (Page et al. 1990:69). They add that although their research was time-consuming and sometimes difficult, it was less dangerous than commonly believed and it added significantly to the knowledge base and skills of those who work to control AIDS risk. "In the fight against AIDS, it is worth the extra effort" (Page et al. 1990:69).

EMPATHY AND CULTURAL COMPETENCE

The capacity for empathy is one of the skills most social workers name as central to their profession. But is empathy really a "skill," or is it an attitude toward others that one either does or does not have? If it is a skill, how can it be learned? If it is learned, is its role in social work different when one expresses empathy with a client culturally like oneself? Social workers and social work educators often speak of "use of self" as a professional attribute. But what does that really mean when the professional knows little of the social, cultural, or psychic life of a culturally distinctive client?

These are not easy questions to answer and there is little in the way of a formula for the social worker who wishes to establish solid rapport with clients. Nor are the best of intentions good enough, for they can never substitute for good ethnographic knowledge. (As a trainer, I am always suspicious of those in my workshops who insist that an "open," "caring," or "engaged" approach will carry them through any situation.) Empathy is a complicated emotion, its behavioral expressions subtle and difficult to measure using standardized tests. It is also contextually sensitive, and its meaning for one person may not be the same for someone else. The culturally sensitive worker will want to be alert to how his or her expressions of empathy are read by clients, especially clients unfamiliar with (or even hostile to) the habitual gestures, facial expressions, and language intonations some workers cultivate in their service relationships.

A number of researchers have looked at empathy in an effort to isolate some of its characteristics. For example, Hogan (1969) and Mehrabian and Epstein (1972) developed empathy scales that have been tested for reliability and validity and are now commonly used. Hogan found five traits often associated with empathy: perceptiveness to social cues; awareness of one's impressions on others; imaginativeness, especially as it relates to humor and to verbal play; interest in motivations, both one's own and those of others; and a high interest in verbally exploring motivations (1969:309). Empathic persons have also been shown to be nonconformists in some of their thinking and behavior, to have a strong interest in ethical behavior, and, interestingly, to be facially expressive. Empathy also involves communication. Empathic counselors are clear and unambiguous in their speech, often use words descriptive of emotional states, do not interrupt, and pace their own speech to that of their client.

But shared feelings of warmth and regard, a common view of the meaning of empathy, probably are not sufficient where the goal of the social worker is effective communication and common understanding with persons operating from different cultural starting points. Indeed, one could argue that in *any* profession that is people centered and people intensive, the capacity for "shared feeling" and "vicarious introspection" may be the minimal and weakest form of empathy. A stronger expression of empathy can be envisioned if we move away from the descriptive features of empathic persons and their capacity for introspection and focus instead on empathy as a particular kind of communication event. This is the approach adopted by Squier (1990), whose model of empathy is critical to the cross-cultural approach proposed here.

Squier argues that empathy really has two components, perspective taking and affective responsiveness. Perspective taking refers to the willingness and ability of the practitioner to elicit the client's implicit understanding of his or her needs. It also involves communicating that the client's position has been heard, that he or she may want to say more about it later, that hearing it said is important and appreciated, and that the client's views will be important in planning any services offered. Perspective taking in this sense is primarily informational. But it is also affirming or "validating" in that the social worker clearly signals that what the client has been willing to communicate has been taken seriously and the topic is still "open" so that more can be said about it later.

Affective responsiveness is the feeling tone associated with what is essentially an information exchange. Gestures, mannerisms, body movements, eye contact, and facial expressiveness must all support perspective taking. Affective tone is not in itself empathic. Rather, it is an endorsement or underlining of the importance of the information exchange. The focus of affect, at least initially, is *not* on the internal state of the client since the social worker really cannot know much about that anyway. Pretending to "feel for" or "feel with" a client is usually obvious and therefore minimally helpful. Where the worker can legitimately show great concern and interest, however, is in the client's words, thoughts, and patterns of expressiveness. These things can and should be given great seriousness in any discussion, however brief it may be. Words, not feelings, are the objects of interest. Nor is that interest an academic one. The seriousness one shows about what the client says is the core of empathy. All else is embellishment.

When empathy is understood this way (Figure 3.3 on page 106), what does it look like when it is present in a professional relationship? Squier uses a medical

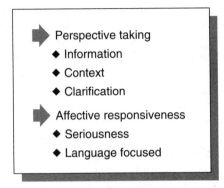

FIGURE 3.3   Empathy and Cultural Competence

(Based on Squier 1990.)

example to help illustrate the difference between an empathic and nonempathic response. In the first, a physician says to her patient: "It must seem almost impossible for an active person like you to come to terms with having the kind of heart condition that might limit your activities." In the second, the physician says "You are to stop all strenuous activities immediately in order to avoid any further heart attacks" (Squier 1990:332).

As examples, these two bits of discourse only begin to suggest the differences between an empathic and a technocratic care provider. Clearly, the first statement was preceded by a discussion of the patient's routine activities and what the patient hopes to return to after recovery. The empathic physician heard what the patient wanted to discuss and has acknowledged that those concerns are important. She has also conveyed that she understands that the patient's crisis is not simply a medical event but is also about a way of living. Her phrase "come to terms" indicates that she understands that "coming to terms" is the work the patient must now do. The second statement, that the patient "stop all strenuous activities immediately," is a command, not an acknowledgment of anything the patient said, and is issued from an authoritarian standpoint. It leaves nothing to discuss; it certainly does not address the readjustments that the patient must make while his health is returning.

Why does the idea of empathy as a specific kind of communication event, rather than an urge to emotional engagement, make sense in a cross-cultural model of cultural competence? Part of the answer has to do with the culture-bound nature of emotions and an appreciation of how middle-class, generally educated Americans (including those who are help providers) usually think of them. In a critique of popular American folk beliefs about what constitutes a "person" or "self," Lutz (1988) argues that Americans tend to think of emotions as "natural," as experiences that are distinct from thought or reasoning. In contrast, ideas, preferences, values, and principles of morality are believed to originate in learned experiences, taught to us by our parents, teachers, and friends as we grow up. Learning is cultural. But emotional states—fear, desire, empathy—are seen as natural, innate processes that some people have more of and some people less. She explains that:

> *emotions [in American culture] are primarily conceived of as precultural facts, as features of our biological heritage that can be identified independently of our cultural heritage. Although there is variation in the* evaluation *of the effect of culture and the natural substrate of our emotions on each other, the element of natural emotion counterposes itself to either the civilization of thought or the disease of alienation and forms the basis for much everyday and academic talk about emotions. (Lutz 1988:70)*

When emotions are thought of as "natural" rather than cultural processes, it is a simple and obvious step to the conclusion that the same emotional experiences are widely and commonly shared by all peoples, regardless of their cultural affiliations. In this view, it is self-evident that what I feel in response to a need must be what everyone would feel. Empathy is my demonstration to you that I literally know how you feel. However, if we put this concept of emotions within its own cultural context, we can see that it is only a variant of another American folk belief discussed above in connection with ethnicity, the belief that "under the skin" and at our inner core we are all "basically the same," desiring the same things and responding to the world in the same ways. Differences of emotional experience, like differences of ethnicity and race, are little more than ornamental covers hiding the presumed sameness of our common human nature.

Clearly, from a cultural competence perspective, assumptions like these (and the practices that derive from them) must be approached with a most determined skepticism, especially in a field where working with the inner states of others is a significant professional activity. People of varying ethnic, racial, linguistic, or religious communities *may* share with many other Americans a bundle of similar psychic experiences and a common language for communicating those experiences. But there is no certainty that they do, and in cross-cultural relationships such similarities cannot be assumed. I would argue that where significant cultural boundaries exist, it is far more reasonable to work with the hypothesis that worker and client do *not* share an emotional universe, and that even where their language of emotional states derives from a common grammar and lexicon, that is not proof that they are expressing identical emotional states. As a rule of thumb, it makes much more sense to assume that the more remote the client's culture and experiences are from those of the social worker, the greater the possibility for distortion and failed understanding of emotional signals, whether those signals are communicated through words, body language, or facial expressions. All the more reason that empathy should be recast as attention to communication and information, not displays of emotional congruence.

As a communication event, how might we demonstrate empathy? Writing on empathy and power in clinical relationships, physician Lucy M. Candib (1994) cites the work of Kristi Malterud, a Norwegian general practitioner, on how empathy emerges as a feature of well-constructed phrasing in questions. Candib discusses the impact of several questions she uses in her own work, especially with women patients (1994:141–143). I paraphrase her as follows:

1. What do you most want me to do for you today?
2. What do you think are the real reasons for X (the issue)?
3. What has been the best way for you to handle this up to now?

Question one, which opens the dialogue, allows the patient to "set the scene" by explaining what she would like to have happen as a result of the consultation. This often generates background information on what the patient has been living with and what changes she hopes to experience as a result of the clinical visit. Expectations of the clinician are made explicit. Question two creates an opportunity to explore details of the presenting problem and is the area where the physician can (and should) probe for local knowledge, the ethnographic setting for the patient's concerns. Question three moves the discussion toward action, what the patient has done so far and why it has or has not helped resolve the difficulty.

There are two reasons this short set of questions is significant for building empathy. They bring forward local knowledge and local experience that the clinician needs to know as a precondition of intervention. Without that information, the clinician can only fumble for what he or she hopes is a useful response. But questions put this way also demonstrate that the clinician takes the client seriously, allowing her choice in the expression of information and a measure of control in the encounter. The construction of a narrative is begun, one that features the pain the patient has already experienced. As communication, empathy is really a verbal "sharing of the stage" without implications of who has authoritative knowledge and who does not. According to Candib, this style of communicating is also empowering because it "includes appreciating the context from which a person comes or in which she lives (especially her oppression as a woman), taking her seriously as a person, valuing her own experience as a source of understanding about the world, hearing her narrative as it fits into her social context and into her life story, recognizing her changing abilities and potential for further change, supporting the mutuality of the relationship, and using self-disclosure on her behalf" (1994:149). "Empathy" is the experience of these things.

The insights of Squier, Lutz, and Candib undercut any claim that empathy is a matter of imaginatively putting oneself in the other's shoes. Rather, empathy is a deliberative effort to learn what one's clients or patients are trying to convey, of adopting a learner stance toward their perspective and their words. It comes not in trying to feel what the client feels but in *discovering* that there is a covert set of meanings, the "core messages," that drive the client's concerns. Language is the most important and most powerful tool the social worker has for acknowledging that. Key words, metaphors, modifiers, and other linguistic elements are direct pathways to the implicit knowledge underlying client behavior, beliefs, and expectations.

ORGANIZATIONAL COMPETENCE

Cross-cultural skills are not just for individual clinicians. Agencies and bureaucracies, the sites where most of us work, can function to promote (or inhibit) the delivery of culturally responsive services as well. Chapter 1 suggested that the human service field can be viewed as a kind of ethnic community: it has its own codes, written and unwritten; it has a history from which it draws lessons and which it uses to formulate a view of the future; and it gives its members a sense of their identity, professional and sometimes personal. But how can we know if a particular organization—be it a clinic, field office, or a distant, central headquarters—is "friendly" as a service provider to people who have urgent needs? And if it is not, what can we do to change things?

In an ethnographic study of labor in a nursing home, Foner (1994) wanted to know if the frustrations of care giving, for both givers and receivers, are an inevitable feature of institutions. She found that what she called the "hidden injuries of bureaucracy" came from a number of sources including legal mandates, regulatory demands and procedures, limitations of funding, inadequate training, internal hierarchies, office politics, policies, and reward structures. Race and gender occasionally figured into these dimensions. When conflicts occurred, among staff or between staff and patients, services to the residents deteriorated and relations between employees soured. The "work culture" of the institution was the arena where conflicts often played out, sometimes in subtle ways. By looking at that culture, Foner determined, among other things, that one of the constant sources of conflict was the need of the institution to be efficient and accountable (expressed through managers and supervisors) and the desire of many of the direct service staff to give quality care with only secondary interest in time or financial constraints. Different agendas, formal and informal, were operating in different parts of the organization, and all were influenced by the personalities of the participants and the history of their relationships in the home. How could the managers, supervisors, and staff proceed to clarify some of their difficulties and redirect their energy in more productive ways?

Evaluation is a word that makes some people nervous. It suggests scrutiny by outside experts who think they know what they are doing by reducing the complexity of human behavior to statistics and variables so administrators can read the results and think something has been achieved. But qualitative evaluation is an established idea as well, and so far people have not been quite as intimidated by the idea of keeping the focus on the humane features of their work. Empowerment evaluation (Fetterman et al. 1996) is an even newer idea that has yet to show that it has staying power among all the "technologies" for measuring organizational fitness. Yet it has much to recommend it. Dugan (1996) argues that empowerment evaluation is basically participatory: it "is something ordinary people can do" (1996:284). Its focus is usually on process, not outcomes, so that as the result of a useful experience in self-critique, people can generate insight into other areas of their work as well. Success is measured by how well people can identify their problems and work toward a consensus for resolving them.

Evaluation from a "constructivist" perspective is one of the empowerment strategies and, as a procedure for increasing organizational responsiveness to human need, Rodwell (1995) suggests some ways it might be done. Not surprisingly, her proposals sound like good ethnography. Thinking in terms of evaluation of family-based services, she argues that a qualitative analysis starts with the following assumptions (1995:192–193):

1. All services and sites have multiple realities. They are different events and places for different people (the "stakeholders"), and each of their perspectives has to be made explicit in the evaluation.

2. There is no "objectified" relationship between observer and observed (expressed, normally, in numbers) but rather mutual participation (expressed in discourse, case studies, descriptions of conflicts and cooperation).

3. The aim of evaluation is "thick description" of cases, not quantifiable comparison with other studies or attempts to find single "causes" for one outcome or another.

4. Evaluation is itself an organization-changing activity, not a snapshot taken from on high, and reflects an explicit value by all concerned to rethink what their work means to them.

To illustrate how these principles might be applied, I will use a hypothetical example based, in part, on my experiences some years ago with a family services agency that wanted to extend its placement services to minority families. Most of the staff were white and some were more enthusiastic than others about engaging clients about whom they knew little. The director, also white, had extensive international experience, wanted the staff to share his fascination with other cultures, and supported a recommendation from his board of directors that the organization pioneer cross-cultural services in this city. The assessment was to determine how well the staff was prepared to carry out that mandate, what internal changes would have to made to make it professionally rewarding for them, what had to be done to make the program attractive to minority clients, and how a future assessment of outcomes might be made.

Rodwell's procedures for doing this are straightforward but logistically demanding. First, all the stakeholders have to be identified and their interests in the program determined. This means in-depth interviews with staff, supervisors, the director, and trustees about their expectations and what they see to be problems. If well done, the interviews can be expected to give a rich picture of the culture of the organization and how those in it assess its capabilities for taking on the new mandate. The interviews would also identify early problem areas and issues that must be resolved before the organization can move ahead with its plans.

Second, small groups within the organization would have a chance to comment on the preliminary findings of the interviews, summarized and distributed in advance. These groups would be asked to respond with their own written statement of whatever consensus they achieved in their discussions. This information, along with summary data from the interviews, would be compiled and distributed throughout the agency. Points of difference as well as agreement would be honestly presented.

Third, some kind of forum (focus groups, a general meeting, a retreat) must be arranged so that items around which there is little or no consensus can be further discussed. The point is to identify what can be done now, what can be done later, and areas where there is still lack of agreement. According to Rodwell, the goal of the evaluation at this point is to reduce differences. "Those themes or interpretations where consensus exists become a part of the final report. Those remaining unresolved may serve to set the stage for another round of evaluative negotiation or become a part of a minority report" (1995:201).

Finally, a report is prepared that presents the consensus of all the stakeholders, identifies areas of lack of agreement, and suggests topics for another round of evaluation once topics of consensus are made policy, implemented, and given a period of "settling in" as agency practice.

What are the tools of this kind of evaluation? They are in-depth interviews, time spent participating in and observing all phases of the discussions, mediation with individuals and subgroups not yet convinced about the emerging consensus, and keeping everybody in the conversation up to the end of the process. From all this activity, summaries, case examples, and varying points of view are written up, distributed to others, and included in discussions as much as possible. Educating everyone about what all the others do and what their goals and frustrations are is part of the process and should be one of the evaluation's effects. No one should be left untouched or without a point of view at the end of the procedure. Everyone should be more of a stakeholder than they were when it all began.

In the case in point, one of the activities devised for staff were week-long visits to minority child welfare and health service agencies where, as "guest service providers," they were expected to work alongside a minority professional. This had the useful effect of educating the visitors about the realities of social services in organizations less well funded than their own as well as about the considerable professional capabilities of their host. It also established alliances between the participating organizations, and between specific workers within each one, so that outreach could proceed through mutual cooperation and shared resources. In effect, the evaluation exercise became an opportunity to change an agency and to enrich its operations in demonstrably helpful ways.

How adaptable is this experience to other organizations? It is only one example of many ways to do a qualitative evaluation, and, in some settings, agreeing to do that rather than the more conventional kinds of assessment may be the issue that is fought over. Qualitative evaluation takes time, lots of it, and usually by people who already know their situation fairly well and don't come into it cold. It also implies a commitment to do something differently and, perhaps more important, a commitment to let the directions for change come from within the ranks rather than from above. It presumes a high level of trust among the participants and a willingness to let democracy play out in the workplace. Finally, it can lead to unexpected outcomes, and everyone must be ready for that. It is not for the timid.

FOLLOW-UP

1. Test Drive an Idea

Idea 1: Entering an Unfamiliar Community

Recalling Pat Moore's adventures as "Old Pat," described at the beginning of this chapter, it is easy to imagine that we too must create an alternative persona to enter a community normally closed to us. Moore's charade was effective for what she set out to do, but it is better that the rest of us do something different. Learning to work cross-culturally is more a matter of skill and attitude than of costuming. It requires a willingness to take some risks and a certain spirit of adventure, but also some modesty about what we can (or might be allowed) to do. It also means respecting those we visit, recognizing that we meet them on their turf and have no particular right to "observe" whatever it is they are doing.

It is common for students in social and health services to be assigned internships or "placements" as part of their training. A placement can be seen as a boundary-crossing experience if you are unfamiliar with how the work is done, who the clients are, what their needs are, and what is expected as a professional level of service. One way to think of any organization is its having two dimensions: a front stage and a back stage. The stage analogy is deliberate, front stage being understood as public image and public areas (reputation, part of town, type of building, layout of waiting rooms, dress codes, promotional materials, public relations, and the like). Back stage (and, by extension, off stage) refers to offices and meeting rooms, intrastaff hierarchies and relations, governance and factions, standards of conduct, perceptions of clients, coffee room conversations, even permitted styles of joking. Typically, front stage areas are just that: they show what the cast and director want the audience to see, foregrounding official definitions of reality at the site. Back stage and off stage areas are less visible, protected from public gaze, scrutiny, and audience speculation about whether the actors really are what they seem to be. Obviously, back stage areas are more difficult to access, but they are where the real work of the organization is done. Good ethnographic understanding of a site involves detailed knowledge of what goes on in both realms.

At this point in your career, you probably have a good idea of the kind of health or social service work you prefer and the kind of organization you would like to work in. Imagine, then, a specific site (one you know about or one you have already worked in) and develop a strategy for a month of participant observation and ethnographic study leading to a reasonably full report of what really goes on there in both its front and back stage domains. Figure 3.2 outlines a general plan of action, but for your project you want to make it as specific as possible. If you like to work in teams, several individuals can work up an agency study plan. You should address each of the following items:

1. What is the site, who works there, and who do they serve? What do they claim to achieve?

2. What are three or four things you don't know about the site and want to learn about its operations? Be specific because these are guides to making observations and formulating interview questions.

3. Who has written about sites like this one in the research literature, and what have they said?

4. When you arrive, who will serve as a Cultural Guide and what do you expect to learn from that person? Will you have more than one guide?

5. How are you going to explain to staff or clients what you are doing at the agency? Do you anticipate objections, and how would you answer them?

6. If you plan participant observation, what specifically are you looking for?

7. If you plan interviews, who will you interview and what are some of the questions you will ask?

8. How are you going to protect the privacy of the people who work at the site, as well as the privacy of the clients or patients you might happen to see there?

9. What would you do if you discovered something that was personally distasteful or practices you consider professionally unethical at the site?

10. Assuming you are asked to make an oral report of your findings to the Board of Trustees, what would you stress and what might you omit?

If some of these topics seem political as well as service oriented, that is because most organizations have a political dimension. That is neither good nor bad; it is just the way organizations are, and participant observation is a powerful technique for understanding the dynamics of this kind of human activity. Neighborhoods, businesses, schools, and especially families have their front stage as well as their back stage areas. You can adapt the above ten questions to those sites as well. If you are working in a community or agency in which you stand out for some reason (because of your race, age, gender, affiliations, accent, or dress, for example), you can expect back stages to be more difficult to access. All communities are protective of their members when inquiring outsiders appear, and that too is neither good nor bad; it is just the way things happen.

Idea 2: Doing a Qualitative Evaluation

How would you plan a qualitative evaluation for an organization where you have worked? How would you defend it as an appropriate methodology? Eisner (1991:32–41) lists six features that make a study qualitative: (1) the study must be *field focused* (this includes all the settings, formal and informal, that are relevant to the study); (2) *the self is an instrument* (we can clearly specify what information we are looking for and then systematically observe and record it); (3) *interpretation and meaning* are central to data collection (we want to know what sense people make of what they do, their reasoning and rationales); (4) *our voice is present* (in our report as author, we are reflectively presenting what we have learned, without the lordly, impersonal voice common in social science writing); (5) *illustrative details are important* (grand, sweeping generalizations without supportive "thick description" do not count); and, finally, (6) *qualitative work reveals insight* into local knowledge and local processes. Our final document is made believable and persuasive because it is written in honest English, without mystifying jargon, and shows that the researcher was present and seriously engaged in the effort. Those who doubt the validity of the findings must support their own position with equally rich and detailed data.

Select an organization you know, either because you have worked or volunteered there or because you received services from the organization. Imagine the director coming to you and saying, "We want to know if our programs are really doing for people what we say they do. Can you help us find out if we are making an impact in our clients' lives and, if we aren't, why?" Of course, you will be well rewarded for a good effort, with love if not much money.

Using each of Eisner's six points, plan a qualitative evaluation. List what you would do and, specifically, how you would do it. Draw up your plan as though it were a contract with the agency. The outline of a sample plan might look like the following, although you should modify this list if you need to:

1. The nature of the agency, its services, staff, and mission
2. Issues the agency wants you to address in the study
3. Sites where you will carry out the study, who you will talk to, what topics you will discuss with them, and specifically what you want to observe
4. How you will involve staff in the study and how you will protect confidentiality
5. What you hope to learn at each site
6. How you will present your findings: cases, flow charts, interview summaries, etc.

2. More on the Issues

- Self-Assessment

How skilled or experienced are you in cross-cultural relationships? A process-oriented Ethnic Sensitive Inventory (ESI) that is easily administered and scored will give you a good, general measure of your capabilities. The ESI can be found in Man Keung Ho, "Use of Ethnic Sensitive Inventory (ESI) to Enhance Practitioner Skills with Minorities," *Journal of Multicultural Social Work* (1:57–67, 1991).

- Empowerment

Effective cross-cultural service skills have been linked to empowerment for both clients and providers. A useful discussion of this large topic, with specific suggestions for practice, appears in Cynthia M. Gibson, "Empowerment Theory and Practice with Adolescents of Color in the Child Welfare System," *Families in Society* (74:387–396, 1993).

- Competence and Social Service Generalists

A case study, discussion questions, and practice guidelines are presented in the excellent overview article by Karen M. Sowers-Hoag and Patricia Sandau-Beckler,

"Educating for Cultural Competence in the Generalist Curriculum," *Journal of Multicultural Social Work* (4:37–56, 1996).

- Agency Cultural Competence

The characteristics of culturally competent agencies, as reported in the research literature, are described by Richard H. Dana, Joan Dayger Behn, and Terry Gonwa, "A Checklist for the Examination of Cultural Competence in Social Service Agencies," *Research on Social Work Practice* (2:220–233, 1992).

- Supervision

Cross-cultural work has its organizational component, and training follow-up is crucial to successful implementation. Supervision is one area where agency commitment is carried forward. A useful discussion, in the context of Hispanic interests, is Natalie Porter, "Empowering Supervisees to Empower Others: a Culturally Responsive Supervision Model," *Hispanic Journal of Behavioral Sciences* (16:43–56, 1994).

- Administration

Issues in implementing cross-cultural mental health services, including staffing, training, bureaucratic resistance, and community acceptance, are analyzed in Lillian G. W. Fong and Jewelle Taylor Gibbs, "Facilitative Services to Multicultural Communities in a Dominant Cultural Setting: An Organization Perspective," *Administration in Social Work* (19:1–24, 1995).

- Community Work

Involving communities in planning, as well as taking proactive stances on critical public issues, is critical to multicultural social services. The rationale for such an approach and suggestions for action are outlined in Loraine Gutiérrez, Ann Rosegrant Alvarez, Howard Nemon, and Edith A. Lewis, "Multicultural Community Organizing: A Strategy for Change," *Social Work* (41:501–508, 1996). A similar discussion, but one oriented toward protecting children, is in Margaret Boushel, "The Protective Environment of Children: Towards a Framework for Anti-Oppressive, Cross-Culture and Cross-National Understanding," *British Journal of Social Work* (24:173–190, 1994).

- Qualitative Methodology

Qualitative assessments are likely to become more important in all human services in the future. A sophisticated overview, with examples and bibliography relevant to social services, is in Cynthia Franklin and Catheleen Jordan, "Qualitative Assessment: A Methodological Overview," *Families in Society* (76:281–295), 1995.

4

LANGUAGE AND CROSS-CULTURAL SOCIAL WORK

The African American actor Ossie Davis once complained that the English language was his enemy (1969). Bigots and discriminatory hiring practices offended him, but so did the language itself. English, he argued, perpetuated in its vocabulary all the habits of mind and verbal responses that are associated with racially founded inequities. Davis's point is obvious enough if one thinks of the slang terms used for labeling members of ethnic groups. But words do more than label. They impose an order on perception; they create categories of things and suggest something of what the categories are worth. Perhaps it was a victory of sorts when "colored" became "negro," then "Negro" was capitalized, and finally "black" replaced "Negro." Labels identify, but they may also prescribe and limit the possibilities of the persons to whom they are applied.

Words are weapons, and in Davis's view they have to be handled as such. Misuse of words can be a kind of aggression. Individuals are labeled and boxed into categories that do not apply to them. Or words are used to "mystify" others, to suggest the speaker's expertise and superior insight (Jones 1976). Language commonly becomes a weapon when people rely on clichés and buzzwords, particularly the clichés and jargon of institutions, professions, and higher education. For many in minority and ethnic groups, such use of language is threatening and offensive because it is, among other things, the language of power and coercion. The recent "English-Only Movement" is a political example of the same process, operating as it does through state legislatures and the initiative process, seeking to impose a single language throughout the country despite the significant linguistic diversity that has always characterized the American experience. Blatantly hostile to immigrant communities, such movements create special problems for those who deliver social and mental health services to non-English speakers (Comas-Diaz and Padilla 1992; Padilla et al. 1991).

But words are more than weapons. They reveal a "mental lexicon" (Aitchison 1987), the individual's storehouse of information about how the world is organized and how it operates. Words are the conveyers (and some would say the creators) of a world view for they reveal a particular and distinctive construction of reality. This is obvious enough when we think of individuals who speak languages different from our own. But it can also be true when two people use the same vocabulary and grammar. They may have different mental lexicons and distinctive if somewhat overlapping world views.

This point has been demonstrated dramatically by Gilligan (1982) and her colleagues (Gilligan and Murphy 1979; Gilligan and Belenky 1980), who looked at the speech of English-speaking men and women to see what gender differences, if any, were revealed by common speech conventions. They found that by puberty, American males and females had acquired sharply contrastive attitudes toward the world. Gilligan tested her hypothesis about gender differences by asking her subjects to discuss a number of issues bearing on personal responsibility, including responsibilities toward parents, friends, partners, and society at large. The males she interviewed commonly used a *categorical* frame of reference. That is, they described responsible conduct as a social, moral, and sometimes legal imperative, believing that "proper" behavior was best understood as rule-governed activity. They were especially concerned with restraints on action and with finding the balance between individual freedom and obligation to others. For them, responsibility was a matter of achieving that balance within a defined framework of permissible action. In their conversations with Gilligan, many men felt impelled to invoke large, abstract principles, and their primary way of thinking about personal morality was through general principles. For men, matters of fairness, justice, rights, and privileges were important, and these concepts organized even their informal, casual talk.

Women, by contrast, answered the same questions with language that was *contextual*. They described personal responsibility as the extension of self through action, as in noticing the needs of others and then doing what was necessary to meet them. Care and reciprocity, not rule formation and rule qualification, were the underlying themes in their answers. "The moral imperative that emerges repeatedly in interviews with women is an injunction to care, a responsibility to discern and alleviate the 'real and recognizable trouble' of this world. For men, the moral imperative appears rather as an injunction to respect the rights of others and thus to protect from interference the rights to life and self-fulfillment" (Gilligan 1982:100). Women also showed a tendency to think of personal responsibility in terms of relationships, in how their actions might affect others, and whether those effects were desirable in some concrete sense. In contrast to men, their thinking was "horizontal" rather than "vertical," and they cast their discussion in terms of networks and linkages rather than conceptual hierarchies.

Does this mean that women are by nature more focused on specifics, whereas men are more conceptual and abstract? Certainly not. What it suggests is that men and women in English-speaking American culture have learned to formulate their understanding of personal responsibility in ways that are both distinctive and gender-specific. To some degree, men and women live in differing cultural universes, and that is revealed in the implicit organization of their speech. Gilligan concluded that men and women spoke not only "in a different voice" but that they approached a basic American value—responsibility—in fundamentally different ways.

Gilligan's argument contains several important implications for how social workers can think about and understand cultural diversity. First, she suggests that even where men and women are homogeneous in matters of income, education, class, and race, they may still live in differing conceptual and experiential subcultures. Those differences are more than minor variations in beliefs and attitudes. They have to do with how the individual confronts the world and perceives himself or herself as a participant in it. The appearance of cultural similarity or of shared language is to some degree illusory and should not be accepted at face value.

Second, Gilligan is explicit that language is a very sensitive and revealing device for identifying differences. In seeking to understand another's perspective, she looks carefully at the choices of words, phrasing, implicit and explicit themes, metaphors, and stories—exactly as they are stated by interviewees in open-ended and gently guided conversations. This linguistic data is her prime source of ethnographic information and the basis of her insight into another's world.

More recently, social workers, health workers, and various kinds of therapists have begun to rethink the role of language in their practice. This is an important development because Americans commonly view language as a neutral feature of everyday life. Oral and written language are popularly seen as devices for conveying information, and the information, not the way it is delivered, is all that is of interest. But language is more than referential. Sands (1988), for example, has shown how a sociolinguistic analysis of a mental health interview can lead to important insight into the client's sense of self. She found that for a depressed client, verbal repetition was a means of "cognitive rehearsal," that is, of trying out new ideas and testing old assumptions during therapy. She suggests that language analysis has an important place in the organization and evaluation of intervention. Similarly, Rumelhart (1984) has identified strategies commonly invoked by both social workers and clients in interviews to keep the discussion deliberately off target, to impose new agendas, and to manage asymmetrical power in the relationship. Her language-sensitive approach is an indication that many social workers are moving beyond language as a "tool" and thinking of it reflexively and critically.

The emerging view within social and health services is that language is a cultural product, a behaviorally active agent, as well as a signifier of an individual's ethnic affiliations. Thinking self-consciously about language is one way the culturally sensitive worker can move beyond personal and professional ethnocentrism. The worker who wants to humanize the service relationship will find a focus on language helpful because it makes explicit the ways in which clients also use specialized or esoteric language to depict their particular concerns and loyalties. As does language among social workers, client language defines boundaries, conceals "insider" information from those who would attempt to penetrate group boundaries, and helps preserve a sense of specialness and dignity among those familiar with the jargon. In this sense, "language is more than a means of communicating about reality: it is a tool for constructing reality. Different languages create and express different realities" (Spradley 1979:17) and different uses of a single language create alternative realities as well.

LANGUAGE AND WORLD VIEW

Although the connection between speech and thinking is not entirely clear, one important hypothesis suggests that language influences the way people perceive the world, that it has an important role in molding the individual's perception of reality. The linguist Edward Sapir argued that language "defines experience for us by reason of its formal completeness and because of our unconscious projection of its implicit expectations into experience" (Sapir, as quoted in Mandelbaum 1949:578). He suggested that the natural world bombards our senses with stimuli and that these stimuli are sorted according to learned linguistic categories. These categories are in some sense "real" for us and are the fundamental tools of our thought. Assuming that we require language to think, and knowing that languages vary, Sapir felt that speakers of different languages will perceive and therefore construct reality in ways as distinctive as their languages. "The fact of the matter is that the 'real' world is to a large extent unconsciously built upon the language habits of the group. No two languages are sufficiently similar to be considered as representing the same social reality. The worlds in which different societies live are distinct worlds, not merely the same world with different labels attached" (Sapir, as quoted in Barnow 1963:96).

Benjamin Whorf, also a linguist, took a similar point of view and argued that the ways in which individuals organize their perceptions of the world do not constitute a uniform process that can be assumed to be the same in all groups or cultures. He argued that for any individual, the world is not objectively known, but is filtered through a cultural lens, the most important feature of which is language. He agreed with Sapir's statement that the "real world" is constructed according to the received linguistic traditions of a culture. "We see and hear and otherwise experience very largely as we do because the language habits of our community predispose certain choices of interpretation" (Whorf, as quoted in Carroll 1956:134). The work of these two linguists is well known as the Sapir-Whorf hypothesis, and it has been one of the most interesting and challenging ideas in linguistics for many years.

It is useful to see how and why Whorf came to this point of view. Before he was a linguist, he worked as a safety inspector for an insurance company. He was impressed that the name for something could influence people's behavior, even when that behavior was "objectively" inappropriate or even dangerous. He noted, for instance, that people working around gasoline storage drums and pumps were appropriately cautious in order to prevent fires. But where people worked with "empty gasoline drums," they were careless with the equipment and with their cigarettes and matches. The phrase "empty gasoline drums" suggested an absence of danger, when in fact the empty drums were at least as hazardous if not more so than the full ones, as they contained highly explosive vapors. Dangerous behavior, such as smoking, was a response to a linguistic cue, not an objective condition. In this way, language habits masked the reality of the situation and substituted a conventional and, in this example, dangerous interpretation.

Semantic labels are part of the reality-defining process. They are also indicative of sharp variations in how people classify and interpret behavior. This is well illustrated by research done some years ago on how linguistic labels were used by policymakers and researchers to categorize ghetto residents in Washington, D.C. Liebow (1967), an anthropologist, was concerned with the needs of poor people in general and of urban blacks in particular. He recognized that much of the academic research carried out among economically depressed African Americans had either implied or concluded that they were largely responsible for their own problems. While paying lip service to such factors as societal racism and unemployment among the poor and poorly educated, existing studies normally concluded that there was something pathological about urban black life itself. These studies usually identified the "female-centered family" as the scapegoat, but they often cited other things as well: "faulty childrearing practices," "illegitimacy," "absentee fathers," "inability to use money wisely," "low value placed on formal education," and a "psychological inability to make future plans and to work consistently toward the realization of those plans." This last factor has often been described as an "inability to defer gratification" and a poor sense of time management. Thus, it was assumed, poor people are poor in part because they have never learned the importance of planning and saving for the future. When they get something in the way of a financial surplus, their impulse is to spend wildly and then come up short before the next payday or the next welfare check. Indeed, this is one of the most common stereotypes about the poor and is often used to justify reductions in assistance programs.

The terms I have put in quotation marks here are semantic labels that both classify and "explain" the behavior of the people in question. But the terms are not "objective" in the sense that they represent critically examined, unbiased, and cross-culturally applicable analytical constructs. They are, rather, the linguistic habits of a particularly small segment of the larger society: largely white, highly educated researchers and policymakers, whose own value orientations derive in part from their participation in highly structured, bureaucratically organized research, teaching, and government institutions. Their language reflects some of the concerns of those institutions: pathology, legalism, analytical understanding, "intervention," and abstract generalization. The issue I raise is not whether these concerns are legitimate; for some purposes they may be. The issue is whether the labels are appropriate for understanding the people they claim to describe. How might that appropriateness be tested?

Living in close contact with those he called street corner men and their families, Liebow looked at these "problems" but from the inside, from the perspective of those involved with getting along on very little. He discovered that to phrase the issue as one of middle-class financial prudence ("deferred gratification") as opposed to lower-class psychological hedonism simply obscured the reality of the situation. From the perspective of economically poor black men and women in urban ghettos, planning and saving for the future made very little sense. They could look around at those older than themselves and see what the future would be like, and it was nothing much worth investing in. Most of those who did have jobs were in dead-end positions. No matter how hard one worked at sweeping floors or washing dishes, these things never made anyone anything other than a hardworking floor sweeper or dishwasher. Liebow's respondents perceived the future only as a continuation of the present, and the life experiences of friends and relatives were evidence for that perspective. Although the middle-class virtue of thrift may be appropriate for those who have a future to work toward, for those who do not, investing in the future makes little sense.

To understand in a cultural sense the world of Liebow's street corner men—or the world of any unfamiliar community—requires us to move outside our own linguistic habits. We need to hear and respond appropriately with what is called "communicative competence" to the language habits that are familiar to someone else. If semantic labeling is in fact a reality-defining process, the most efficient way we can access the experience of others is through our grasp of their terminology. The word "emic," which has begun to appear in the social services journals, is linked to this kind of inquiry.

Emic comes from the word "phonemics," the study of the sounds that are distinctive to a given language. As an English speaker, for example, I know that the differences between "t" and "th" are meaningful and would never confuse the words "tin" and "thin" when I hear them. My understanding at that level is emic—it is familiar and "real" for me, although someone using a language where the t/th contrast does not occur might not notice the difference at all. (In fact, "th" is a very unusual phoneme and is rare among languages around the world. It is critical to the spoken English I use, but it is not necessary for all English speakers. In two years of research among West Indians on the small islands of the Eastern Caribbean, I never heard the "th" sound except among those who learned British English in local schools. Everyone else did just fine without it.) Once we move beyond our own language community, emic variations become more obvious. American English speakers have a hard time with French phonemes and an even harder time with those of Arabic or Japanese. The point is that no language can be easily translated into another, and no learner of a second language can succeed just by memorizing vocabulary and rules of grammar.

Subtle and not so subtle differences in speech are important because the sounds and meanings seem reasonable and "natural" to those who share it. Jokes are the most evident example of this. All speech communities have their insider jokes, which rely for their punch on exaggerations of regional or ethnic accents or on the stranger's confusion about things that to native speakers are self-evident. If you think of some of the ethnic jokes you have heard—we all hear them because all groups have jokes, usually disparaging, about other ethnic groups—you will see how humor turns on mispronunciations, exaggerations of accents, the double meanings of common terms, and inappropriate responses to routine situations. Jokes point both to the ethnocentrism of all speech communities and also to how finely speech communities cut up and parcel the world of experience. Language and reality fuse in ways that are obvious to the insiders but arbitrary if not incomprehensible to outsiders. That is why language and care in its usage are such critical factors when we are dealing not with jokes but with the issues and all their fuzzy edges that troubled people bring to help providers.

WORDS, MEANINGS, AND CLIENT PERSPECTIVES

An old idea in psychological anthropology is that the human mind organizes information by filtering it through linguistic "mazeways" and that they constitute a template that is a mental "map" of the culture in which we grow up (Wallace 1956, 1970). Thus we create order, specifically a cultural order, out of the chaos of stimuli to which we are exposed. Of course, "maps" and "mazeways" are metaphors, ways of expressing an idea for something difficult to grasp. But the principle of mapping is useful as a way of thinking about how people know what they know and how their language reveals some of what is important to them.

In this metaphor, specific words can be thought of as points of interest on a map, the cities, roads, and topographical features that are landmarks for the user of a particular language. This point has been made by Aitchison (1987), who proposes a way of thinking about the relationship of people to their culture that, as in Gilligan's research, emphasizes words. Words are useful as indicators of how people construct meaning because we use so many of them and because they are organized in a particular way. Aitchison estimates that the average, reasonably well educated person may know as many as 250,000 words, although most people underestimate their word inventory by half or more. Not only is there an abundance of thought topics contained in so many words, but the fact that we can find and organize the topics we want as quickly as we do suggests very sophisticated patterns or "mazeways" of word organization inside the brain. Aitchison's metaphor for this complex system of word storage and organization is the "mental lexicon."

In a mental lexicon, words have an "identification function." That is, they stand as a proxy for specific things, ideas, relationships, and actions. This identification function is more than a matter of dictionary-type definitions, however. Word meanings in the mind can change, quickly if necessary, and, unlike dictionaries, they are never out of date. In addition, the amount of information each of us has about a single word is far more extensive and complex than the amount of information supplied in typical dictionary entries. But the most important feature of the mental lexicon is that the meaning of words in the mind is not fixed. Their appearance on a printed page suggests that words have clarity, solidity, and permanence. But in the mind they have a different aspect, one that Aitchison calls "prototypical." That is, words only approximate the natural world we see and hear. They represent prototypical characterizations of our experiences rather than dictionary descriptions of an external reality. This makes it possible for us to use language with flexibility, economy, and especially efficiency.

It is important to have a clear sense of this seemingly obvious distinction between dictionary and social usages of language. Lakoff (1972) has said that words in natural languages (in contrast to words for technical or scientific use) have "fuzzy edges." That is, they don't have crisp, highly delimited definitions because that is not the way they are used. Their fuzzy edges are what make them prototypical. Suppose that on a hot summer day a friend says to you, "I could go for some ice cream about now," and you agree. What meaning has been communicated? Does your friend mean "a rich, sweet, creamy, frozen food made from variously flavored cream and milk products churned or stirred to a smooth consistency during the freezing process and often containing gelatin, eggs," etc.? That is what the second college edition of *Webster's New World Dictionary* says. Does that mean your friend won't settle for nonfat ice milk? How about sherbet, or frozen yogurt? Would a root beer float be out of the question? Is the part that melts and runs down the cone onto your thumb no longer "ice cream" since it is not "frozen" as the definition specifies? And what of the drips (again, no longer frozen as required by Mr. Webster) that dried, leaving a chocolate stain on your freshly laundered jeans? Is that still "ice cream"? Unless you want to get caught up in quasi-legalistic formalities with your friend, it is far better to think with words that are "fuzzy." Maybe what was being asked was if you wanted something cold, wet, and sweet, and for that a cola or even a flavored ice cube will do. One has to be a bit dense to miss the point, especially on a hot day, but we are not dense precisely because natural languages are more than compilations of dictionary renderings. They are full of nuances and implied meanings, sensitive to culture context and known, emically, by cultural insiders.

The ability to use words prototypically, as fuzzy entities in a mental lexicon, rather than as eternal verities stored up in dictionaries, is what gives spoken language its richness and flexibility. Each word doesn't have to be a perfect match to each object or action in the natural world. It is sufficient that it contain (1) identification criteria (the ice cream in our example and what a native English speaker knows "ice cream" as a physical substance happens to be) and (2) an area of reference (ice cream as cooling on hot days, something fun to eat, and associated with relaxation or even moods of nostalgia or romance).

If we make the jump from ice cream to something more serious, for example the conditions we label "depression," "abuse," "disability," or the recently fashionable "co-dependent," it becomes obvious that in ordinary talk the fuzzy edges of these words are sometimes very fuzzy indeed. Like "ice cream," they all have dictionary definitions intended to give them legal or clinical precision. But also like ice cream, they carry a richness of prototypical meanings that can make their use ambiguous in legal, clinical, or everyday conversations. Moreover, these words originated in popular speech and were imported into the thought and speech habits of professionals. That alone ought to make us even more concerned about what it is that is being communicated by clients as they describe in their own terms their emotional states, domestic crises, or accounts of recent illnesses.

We all use technical language to describe, mostly among ourselves, the issues clients bring to us. That language is important in making accurate assessments and planning effective intervention. But it is not the same language clients use among themselves, with family members or friends. Where professional language is intended to be diagnostic, everyday speech, including our own, is expressive of experience. It is colloquial, colorful, and laced with metaphor and implication. Richly connotative as well as denotative, it is intended to convey the tone of everyday life, not its analytical dimensions. To really know what and how people experience the things they do, to be truly empathic, we have to focus first on their language because language is our most direct window onto what they know and feel. But what about language are we to look for?

Shweder (1985) discusses the cultural context of the language of crisis, illness, and pain, language that has incredibly fuzzy edges and is rich in nuance and localized meaning. To access the lived experience of others, he suggests we initially drop our analytical categories and look for something else. There are five areas where we must be linguistically alert to what people are saying (see Figure 4.1).

First, Shweder suggests that the culturally sensitive counselor must know something of the types of emotional states commonly reported for a given population. Even if we assume that all people have somewhat similar emotional lives and consequently suffer from a common set of emotional problems, the distribution of mental illnesses such as depression may vary by social class, ethnic group, or other social markers. Having information about that distribution is obviously useful to the counselor or social worker simply as a hedge against making gross errors of diagnosis. Data on that topic is scattered throughout the research literature of social work, psychology, and psychiatry, and the ethnically alert worker would want to make some effort to be informed simply as a matter of professional preparedness in addressing the needs of a specific population.

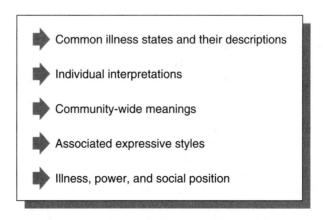

Common illness states and their descriptions

Individual interpretations

Community-wide meanings

Associated expressive styles

Illness, power, and social position

FIGURE 4.1 Cultural Modifiers of an Assessment

(Based on Shweder 1991.)

Second, he suggests that all emotions, illnesses, and problems have a situational or ecological aspect. The problem for the social worker is to identify those components. What specific situations in culture X are likely to invoke depression or anger or generosity? Some workers try to individualize clients by separating them from their social and cultural context. But every client is a representative of his or her own culture, and every biography is part of a group history. Individualizing the client in a culturally sensitive way means locating that individual within a specific context. Client tellings and retellings of personal concerns are usually rich with clues about what is believed about causes, circumstances, and aftereffects of illnesses or crises. These private understandings are also culturally grounded, and knowing the range and types of cultural scripts associated with particular difficulties will greatly aid the worker in deciding what can and cannot be done with a particular client bearing a specific problem.

Third, the social worker needs a sense of the culturally generated meanings attached to specific emotions or conditions. For example, in culture X is depression and discussion of it highly psychologized and individualized, as among many middle-class Americans? Or is it understood in terms that are equally metaphorical but different, perhaps through somatizing or reference to the supernatural? The meanings assigned to emotional states in many ethnic communities can go well beyond standard *DSM-IV* categories and may involve foods conceived as medicine, mental states understood as physical sensations, and maliciousness in others attributable to hostile spirits. (It should be pointed out that highly educated middle-class whites are "ethnic" in this sense as well: hence the presence of chapels and chaplains in most hospitals and even airports.) Client accounts of their private grievances are not devoid of standardized (if fuzzy) meanings shared with ethnic compatriots, and an awareness of those meanings is essential for the ethnically responsive worker.

Fourth is the communicative aspect of emotional functioning. In some cultures, expression of emotions such as depression, anger, hate, or pride is viewed as dangerous, if not to oneself then to others. In other settings, the danger is in not expressing them but burying and avoiding them. Much of the current national interest in what is loosely called the "men's movement" focuses on acceptable ways of being masculine in a post–John Wayne era. This and other issues are the fodder of well-known television and radio talk shows in which celebrity guests help their viewers and listeners articulate their personal and emotional problems. Given this national mood of expressing what was once "hidden," it is no accident that the common metaphors of middle-class speech about communicating emotions are metaphors of physical containment ("bottled up my feelings") and explosive release ("blew my stack," "venting"), a long list of which has been compiled by Lakoff and Johnson (1980). All communities have their styles for the expression of emotion and their implicit rules on managing talk about misfortune. Indeed, in all cultures communicative competence in reference to misfortune is one of the criteria by which onlookers judge the veracity of statements about private emotional and physical states. The ethnically competent worker needs to have a sense of what that style is in his or her client's community.

Fifth, and flowing from the previous points, Shweder suggests that there lurks in all descriptions of emotional and problem states issues of power, its distribution, and its availability. How, then, does "depression" or any other debilitating condition signify relations of power and powerlessness? In what ways are personal complaints also social commentaries about other issues? These questions are not posed out of a narrowly academic research interest. Indeed, the ability of the social worker to perceive those connections and to help the client do so as well may be a significant part of intervention and empowerment. How individuals manage their own depression—through bodily denial in fasting or sleeplessness, for instance, or through indulgence or destructive behavior—is more than idiosyncratic. It is an attempt, however ill-advised, at reconstructing one's world and righting perceived wrongs. Shweder and others who favor a culturally informed approach to understanding emotional and personal problems would argue that the appreciation of power, including power differentials between those who are troubled and those who offer comfort, may be the beginning not only of humbleness about one's knowledge and skills but also of effectiveness in working with the problems of those who need our help.

LANGUAGE AND MEANING

Words are more than a quarter-million points of cognitive light in our mental lexicons. Aitchison's model also suggests that words link up to one another to make the lines, boundaries, and connections that are the second feature of our cognitive maps. Words in the mind, she says, are organized into semantic networks or fields so that they tend to cluster, again a feature very unlike a dictionary, which presents each word standing alone as though it were as important and independent as every other one. These semantic networks form in several ways, but we will look at only one because that is sufficient for getting a sense of the importance of word linkages for the skill of ethnographic interviewing, to be discussed later.

One form of word linkage in the mind is "co-location." The idea is simple enough. Several words cluster around a single conceptual location and, sometimes, in the mind of the speaker, they seem "naturally" and automatically linked. This idea recalls psychological tests and word games where respondents are asked to give their first response to word cues. But for the social work investigator, the first response to a word cue is not what we want. Rather, we seek a full, well-elaborated response. We want to know what words the speaker uses to explicate a prototypical cluster and how other clusters are linked to it. The clustering of linked word ideas is an indicator of how the individual is conceptualizing an issue. Examples of co-location in everyday English are fairly easy to find. We commonly use expressions that reveal the power of word linkages to formulate our ideas. For example, when I "catch a cold" I attribute it to "a bug that is going around." There are two different, even contrary, notions of causation implied here but that does not trouble me. My semantic field links the verbs "catch" and "going around" to a folk medical noun, "cold," which does not rely on biomedical notions of cause and effect anyway. The point is simply that my way of thinking about "colds," and what I intend to do when I have one, is very much influenced (Sapir or Whorf might even say regulated) by the semantic network my culture has taught me and on which I rely for a self-diagnosis and treatment. How much more complicated the issue becomes when someone says, "I think I am losing my mind" or "I think people who get AIDS are being punished by God." The semantic linkage networks, and the moral urgency behind them, are truly potent in organizing perceptions and beliefs.

A second example of co-location in a semantic field is more complex and takes in much more territory than my simple example of how some American-English speakers account for their upper respiratory infections. Diabetes is a major health problem in Native American communities, one that has become more pronounced since Native Americans have begun to substitute commodity foods (especially high-fat and sugary ones) for traditional choices. "Traditional" really has a double meaning for it covers pre-contact food sources, which for many Native American communities are still important symbolically if not economically, and government surplus foods supplied at times by Federal programs. In a study of food resources and the conceptualization of disease among the Devil's Lake Sioux in North Dakota, Lang (1990) recorded word-for-word descriptions of diabetes, a disease that is new to the Devil's Lake community. She found that "when I asked about why people thought they had diabetes, conversation invariably turned to the diabetic diet, then to traditional foods, and to reflection on their history" (1990:284).

What has history to do with diabetes? In the minds of the Dakota Sioux, a lot. They had all heard diabetes and its causes described by the mostly non-Native American staff of the local Indian Health Service clinic, and they accepted the medical explanations as probably true. But that was not their interest. In their minds, diabetes was linked with the eclipse of traditional foods and traditional medicine by commercial food and packaged pharmaceuticals. Further, diabetes was linked in their semantic networks with tuberculosis, measles, smallpox, and alcohol, all problems brought by whites. They spoke regularly (and longingly) of "old time cures" that had been forgotten and of medicine men and women in distant tribes reputed to still have healing powers. Thus diabetes, a clinically describable syndrome with a lengthy dictionary-like entry in physicians' reference books, was for the Dakota Sioux an issue of the symbolic boundaries between the Dakota and white worlds.

But semantic linkage was only one part of the Dakota Sioux's alternative construction for the meaning of diabetes. Lang found that the style of talk they favored for explication of a disease model was the personal narrative. When asked to explain how they came to have diabetes, and what they thought diabetes was, her respondents went into lengthy, sometimes rambling discussions of their personal experience, told in a quiet, gentle way. Lang recognized this form of presentation as a common one for the Dakota Sioux, as well as some other Native American groups. To be able to hear and understand the semantic links that govern their ideas surrounding diabetes, she spent hours in active and patient listening. Their emic model of diabetes, once elicited, gave her insight into many other issues of health in the community; she had a "handle" on how the Dakota Sioux relate illness to their everyday experiences.

Was Lang's work (1990) of eliciting semantic data about diabetes a research extravagance, one done largely for the benefit of other research anthropologists? Hardly, and that is the point. Lang spent the time she did with Native American respondents because the local clinical staff either could not or would not. They often expressed their distress that Native American patients were "noncompliant" with dietary and medical recommendations. Lang's ethnographically sensitive approach, directed toward understanding the conceptual system that makes up the Native American view of things, led her to propose ways that clinical staff could work more effectively with their patients. She was able to do this because of her willingness to hear what the Devil's Lake Sioux had to say and why they said it the way they did.

INTERVIEWING FOR EMIC INSIGHT

The goal of the culturally responsive social service worker is to approximate what has been called "communicative competence," that is, to learn "what a speaker needs to know to communicate effectively in culturally significant settings" (Gumperz and Hymes 1972:vii). To accomplish this, the worker needs to have a strong grasp of the meanings that clients attach to behavior, events, other persons, and especially words, just as they occur in naturalistic or "culturally significant" settings. This is an obvious but often forgotten point. The practitioner whose primary concern is "getting in touch with feelings" is unfortunately limiting his or her ability to acquire and utilize cultural knowledge. "Empathy" and "openness" as primary techniques are inadequate because they presume an ability to enter into the sensibilities of another without first learning the context from which those sensibilities arise. The real skill in cross-cultural social work, as in any kind of cross-cultural learning, is to comprehend what the client knows and how that information is used in the mundane traffic of daily activities. Stylized "caring responses" are not an effective way of doing that. Rather, it is what our clients tell us about themselves, and how they do the telling, that is crucial to genuine understanding and insight.

It is surprising that in a field like social work, where interviewing is a primary work activity and where minority clients are served in numbers often higher than their representation in the total population, social work researchers have given so little attention to the dynamics of cross-cultural interviews. There are, of course, a number of studies on racial and cultural matching and the problems that may occur when the interviewer and interviewee are of a different background (Atkinson 1983; Leong 1986). And there are many guides to interviewing as a general social service skill (Benjamin 1981; Barker 1990; Epstein 1985; Schubert 1982; and Ivey 1983 are examples). But what are the special issues for social service providers who work across cultural boundaries?

The classic statement on the social work interview is that of Alfred Kadushin (1990), whose book every practitioner should have as a desk reference. His advice is eminently sensible, presented in such an orderly way that even the casual reader will pick up useful tips on interviewing style. He describes how interviews serve a variety of purposes—exchanging information; establishing trust; and changing people and situations. They have specific phases and sequences, usually determined by the social service provider and the kind of assistance that is available. Kadushin gives special attention to what might be called the subtle intimacies of an interview—humor, knowing glances, posture, silences, mood, and personal style.

One chapter takes up cross-cultural interviewing. He presents the essential problem of communication at the very beginning:

> *The statistically typical social worker is middle class, college trained, white, young, and female. The statistically typical client is an older, lower-class female member of a minority group with less than high school education. The only significant social characteristic they hold in common is that the typical social work interviewer and the typical social work interviewee are both females. (1990:303)*

So what should the statistically typical social worker make of these differences in planning and conducting an interview? Kadushin notes the error of one common worker response: that "race" or "culture" makes no difference because we are all human and pain is no less painful whether one is black or white. Although there is a fundamental generosity in such a response, there is also a fundamental problem. It discounts the value of an individual's heritage as a reservoir of experiences that help define, shape, and perhaps resolve the crisis of the moment. Official color blindness exalts what Kadushin calls the "myth of sameness" (1990:304), as if all the things a person has been over a lifetime are not relevant to what is happening now. The myth of sameness also implies that the worker has a superior insight into the nature of the presenting problem and how it can be resolved. In the color-blind response, generosity is linked with power and difference with deficits (two interesting semantic nodes!). Although the worker may in fact have considerable insight, and that is certainly what she or he is paid to provide, that insight becomes useful only when the worker can approach a problem in ways both affirming and familiar to the client. "There needs to be receptivity toward such differences and a willingness to be taught about them by the client" (Kadushin 1990:306).

What does "receptivity" in interviewing mean? Two caveats about interviewing styles in social services and related fields need to be mentioned. First, there is sometimes a tendency in interview training to promote a "stance" toward clients rather than knowledge acquisition. This idea is really an extension of the "sameness myth." Honesty, genuineness, and caring are urged as appropriate and necessary traits to help the worker break through mistrust or misunderstanding. Although laudable as personal qualities, they are not in and of themselves adequate for developing an understanding of others. Even as traits, they are highly abstract and difficult to translate into directives that can be passed on to a learner.

Being open, patient, and concerned are useful in many relationships, especially those in which troubled individuals need our help, but they are not "skills" to be handily picked up in workshops or through role play.

The second limitation has to do with the skills that are needed in social work interviewing. Because one really cannot teach people to "care" about others in their professional relations, discussions of interviewing often turn from broad generalizations about rapport to specific techniques. Techniques are often described in terms of anecdotes or with reference to the results of controlled studies of interviewing, such as the effects of white interviewers on black interviewees. Generalizations about appropriate behavior are then drawn from the anecdotes and the research conclusions, as guides for students to follow. Techniques, strategies, and tactics are one response to the need to go beyond global statements about helping and caring for others. They are usually specific, and therefore they are learnable with a little practice. But the cultural appropriateness of techniques and their acceptability to ethnic group clients are highly variable. Interviewing skills that may work well with Puerto Ricans (Ghali 1977) may be quite unacceptable to Japanese Americans (Kaneshige 1973) or Native Americans (Youngman and Sadongei 1974). It is difficult to speak of any specific interview techniques that can be assumed to be successful with any or all classes of minority clients.

Ethnographic interviewing from an emic perspective, however, is one way to move beyond the limits of culturally bound tactics in information gathering. It is really an interview style that doubles as a process of discovery. "Its object is to carry on a guided conversation and to elicit rich, detailed materials that can be used in qualitative analysis" (Lofland 1971:76). In particular, the interviewee's voice is given preference, and that has major implications for the helping relationship. It means that in some respects the interviewer, the worker, is also a student, and the interviewee is an instructor, guiding the student through the labyrinth of the interviewee's semantic network and culture. Attentive listening means more than just hearing the client out as part of the therapeutic process. It means that the client is in some sense an expert in defining the depth and breadth of a problem, and that the opinions of this expert must be clearly understood before analysis of the problem can begin. Simply allowing the client to ramble at length will not produce information in an efficient way, nor will it increase the social worker's understanding of the client's problems. The central idea in the ethnographic interview is that the worker channels the flow of the interview by using linguistic features of the conversation as they are provided by the client.

There is no single, standardized procedure for ethnographic interviewing. What I describe here, however, is an adaptation to social services of selected principles and methods common to cross-cultural research in the social sciences. As the preceding discussion would suggest, the model is cognitive and word oriented. It is not untested in social work, however, having been presented in a number of regional and national social work forums (including the Council on Social Work Education) and taught extensively by myself and others to social workers on the West Coast. Where I have offered the model, both in teaching and in workshop settings, I have been gratified by the positive response of both white and minority social workers. The procedures of ethnographic interviewing in social services are straightforward and, once their rationale is explained, really quite obvious. They are an attempt to move beyond exhortations to empathic understanding and make good interviewing and good listening rigorous, teachable, and learnable activities.

PLANNING THE ETHNOGRAPHIC INTERVIEW

The cross-cultural interview in social services is an adjunct to other interviewing styles. It is not intended to be a substitute for what the worker already does but rather to supplement what goes on in the normal course of interviewing, inquiry, and advising with clients and patients. The ethnographic style rests on several assumptions which I will discuss first. The basic elements of the interview are presented in Figure 4.2.

The first and central issue, of course, is language and how it is to be understood in the interview. Kadushin (1990:3) defines the social work interview as "a conversation with a deliberate purpose, a purpose mutually accepted by the participants." There are two elements here, purpose and conversation. Clearly, purpose may be problematic, and client and social worker may have to negotiate what can be "mutually accepted" as the goals of the interview. But the meaning of a conversation is problematic as well, and it is that part of the interview I want to consider in some detail. Language communicates, but it also defines, categorizes, and establishes the meanings speakers assign to their experiences. As I have argued, language is not simply a tool for transmitting information. In the hands of a skillful interviewer, language is a window to the reality that people create and act on. To a considerable degree, then, the focus of the ethnographic interview must be on language, how the client uses it, and what it suggests about the client's state of being and thinking. Language, and especially its exploratory potential, is central to our interest.

A second concern in ethnographic interviewing is salience. In social services, we do not want or need to know everything about the cultural background of

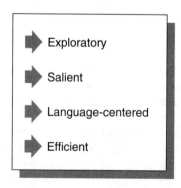

FIGURE 4.2   **Ethnographic Interviewing**

every client. What is needed is cultural data bearing on the presenting issue. If family violence is an issue, then a culture's funeral customs or food preferences are probably not salient to our interests. Family violence is a major topic in its own right, and any social worker will be fully occupied in learning about it without wandering off into other areas that are perhaps interesting but not immediately pertinent. Our concern as culturally sensitive interviewers is, at least initially, the context of the presenting problem.

There is a good reason for keeping the issue of salience prominent in any cross-cultural learning activity. In my own experience as a trainer, I sometimes see a tendency for workshop participants to go off on tangents that are interesting but not obviously relevant. Ethnicity is a field that is ripe for distractions. Some common ones include scheduling workshops around ethnic foods or visits to ethnic restaurants, or bringing in a speaker who may fairly represent the interests of a particular group but who has little knowledge of the audience's specific training needs. Generalized films, artistic performances, and tourist-like forays to minority agencies or community centers are other diversions. Some social workers have immersed themselves in the history of a particular group, a fascinating exercise in its own right but not always useful in face-to-face encounters with someone who needs help with a difficult child. On occasion, I have seen workers overwhelmed by thinking they must learn everything about another culture and, perceiving the clear impossibility of doing that, giving up in frustration. The idea of salience is to keep attention focused on what we really need to know about specific clients, the kinds of problems each one brings to us, the cultural context in which needs are embedded, and the language used to describe personal or family concerns.

A third principle concerns the veracity of what clients say. If someone seems to be stretching a point for the hearer's benefit, in the ethnographic interview that is acceptable because they are still telling us something, however encoded, about themselves, how they perceive us, and how they view the rest of the world. Yet veracity is more than simple truthfulness. We want to recognize that every client or patient has a perspective, however ill formed it might seem to be, and that we need to understand it so we can be more precise with our procedures of assessment, diagnosis, and treatment.

For example, some years ago while doing participant observation among child protective service workers, I was impressed that some workers made a special effort to understand how child abusers conceptualize their violent behavior. They wanted to find out more about what their clients believed about discipline, about child–adult relationships, and about the situations that led to violence in their home life. These workers were most explicit about their desire to get beyond "presenting problems," partly to enhance their professional effectiveness but also because they saw the effort as a means of coming to terms with a stressful and often discouraging job. Their approach was, in some ways, distinctly ethnographic because they were interested in understanding their clients at an emic as well as clinical level. Their reasoning was: Who, after all, is more of an expert on child abuse than someone who beats kids? Assuming that language is a window, and that what people say about their experiences and expectations has some kind of truth in it, working with what people say—exactly as they say it—may be the closest we can ever come to knowing why they respond to crises the way they do.

Fourth, the ethnographic interview, when combined with other kinds of social and health service interviewing, is the most efficient way to learn about cultural differences. No amount of reading in libraries, role playing in classrooms, shared experiences in staffings, or listening to experts in workshops as they go through "how to do it" lists will ever match the learning curve of a dedicated social worker who sees each client not only as an opportunity for service but also as someone who can be a teacher about some aspect of his or her life. That may seem an ambitious statement. But I believe it is true precisely because in too many workshops and years of classroom training I have been one of the so-called experts and I appreciate how my very best efforts are small compared to those of the dedicated worker who wants to add ethnographic procedures to his or her work style. The issues of language and salience combine to create a learning opportunity for the worker that is far more revealing of the realities of ethnic differences than the hours and days so often committed to training sessions on cultural awareness and racial sensitivity. I am optimistic that those practitioners who really want to use the ethnographic approach to inform and guide their efforts will experiment with the method and make it work for them.

Searching for Salience: Global Questions

Finding salience in the ethnographic interview is partly a matter of sorting among possibilities: what do I want to know that might have some significance for my work with a specific client? The technique of the guided ethnographic interview assumes that there is something problematic that is of concern to both the interviewer and the interviewee. Unlike interviews with highly structured, close-ended questions, the ethnographic interview calls for the social worker to identify in advance those aspects of the client's life that may be personally and professionally puzzling. The interviewer can list topics of general interest, write questions, and arrange them in an order that seems to make sense. The choice of opening topic is really one of personal preference. Sometimes, the specific topic is less significant than the fact that the worker is organizing his or her thoughts around some point that will be used to lead off the interview. Lofland (1971) calls this process "global sorting and ordering" and in this practice it is best to define and order problems in a way that is straightforward and obvious. "Deep" sociological or psychological probing about the "true" nature of the client's situation is not appropriate at this early stage.

For example, suppose a mental health worker is assigned to an unfamiliar area of New York City that is Puerto Rican and, further, she does not know Spanish. But as a native of the city, she heard Spanish in stores and on street corners for many years. She takes a drive through the streets with a colleague who is an "old hand" in the area. He reveals that it was predominantly Jewish until the late 1940s when Spanish-speaking people from the Caribbean—Puerto Ricans, Cubans, and others —started moving in. The housing stock is diminishing and disintegrating, the schools are underfunded and not well maintained, and those who have jobs are paid minimal wages. There is increasing crowding and the demands on public health facilities are far greater than the allocations of local government can possibly meet. Nevertheless, street life and neighborhood activities suggest a strong sense of community and a determined effort to preserve West Indian values, especially Hispanic ones, despite the evident poverty.

The new worker notices that in addition to the government-funded health centers and several hospital outpatient clinics, there are a number of private physicians, numerous pharmacies, and a pediatric clinic. There are also *botanicas* or herb shops, and many *centros,* small storefront or basement "churches" in which believers in *espiritismo* gather for services and for indigenous forms of mental health treatment, *consultas,* provided by specially trained folk healers. Although it is true that not all Puerto Ricans in New York City believe in *espiritismo,* many Puerto Ricans, other Spanish-speaking West Indians, and many Roman Catholics of other nationalities know of it, and many of them accept some of its premises and seek out its healers in times of need. Thus, formal adherence to the ideology or even great familiarity with it is not required for the many who, on occasion, make use of these practitioners. Knowledge about and utilization of *espiritismo* is far greater (if sporadic) than a simple count of *espiritismo* adherents would suggest.

This is exactly the situation studied by Harwood (1987) and others interested in indigenous healing systems, how they function as alternatives to scientific biomedicine, and why they not only persist but grow in popularity. Harwood shares a view held by many researchers with interests in Puerto Rican popular culture and its healing traditions "(1) that spiritism resembles mainstream psychotherapies in certain specific ways and therefore undoubtedly works by the same processes and, by implication, at least as well as those therapies; and (2) that spiritist healing rites are consonant with Puerto Rican culture in important ways and for that reason are more likely to be effective than mainstream psychotherapeutic services, which in certain respects are antithetical to Puerto Rican expectations and values" (Harwood 1987:viii). The companion escorting the new worker through the neighborhood explains casually that although there is no "official" use of spiritualist healers by the agency, and certainly no funding for it, nevertheless some in the agency make informal referrals. For many clients a decision is made informally about mixing and matching service modalities. He explains that even though it is not agency practice, encouraging some clients to see spiritualists is at least suggested as a good thing in the research literature (Comas-Diaz 1987). Some workers in the agency are inclined to do that but many others are not. The new worker will need to decide what is best, one case at a time.

So what do these spiritualists do, and what makes them effective? Like all therapists, they treat people's problems, but the symptoms, diagnosis, and intervention may involve supernatural powers. Our hypothetical social worker may need to know more about that and if a visit and a formal interview could be arranged, that would be an opportunity for her to prepare a list of global questions. Starting with what is personally and professionally puzzling, she might come up with these:

1. What are the various activities of the *centros*?
2. How is a healing session conducted?
3. What other persons assist the healer, and what do they do that is important?
4. How are healers trained, and what specific skills do they say they have?
5. What distinguishes problems that are physical, supernatural, or both in their origins?
6. What are some examples of diagnoses the healer makes?
7. What are the causes of the problems healers see in their practice?

In thinking about the coming interview, the mental health worker knows she will probe in order to collect more detailed information than these questions alone would provide. They are simply a starting point. She will continuously refine the global questions, both before and during the interview, relying on the principle of salience to limit the scope of her inquiry. She will continue to ask herself: what remains that is personally and professionally puzzling? (She is, after all, planning to meet with the competition, and she needs to know what they do and why their clients like it.)

One final point needs to be made about the use of global questions in learning from clients, alternative practitioners, and even co-workers. Discourse patterns in American middle-class culture include a marked preference for "filling air time." This is not true in many communities, including many Native American and some ethnic European groups. For them, periods of silence are a normal part of any conversation. But most professionals in most fields are trained to be outgoing and analytical in an explicitly verbal way. As a teacher, I am well aware that I cannot hold the attention of a class if I include long, thoughtful pauses in my lectures. Similarly, interviewers who feel that they are supposed to be "in charge" often express their anxiety by keeping up a heavy flow of words. "Dead air" is seen as a failing, as though there was nothing else worthwhile to communicate. For some, it suggests a loss of control or direction. My recommendation is that when you lead off with a global question, allow the client time to answer, even if there is a period of silence, or a struggle to find the right words. Many trained workers are so anxious to help they want to jump right in and almost literally put words in the client's mouth. Yet it is the client's perspective, and especially the language, that we want to hear. Both what people say and what they don't say are valuable to us. They need to have air time too and permission to participate in the interview as they choose.

The Cultural Guide

In addition to selecting topics for the guided interview, the social worker will need to have an explanation of why the interviewee's cooperation is important. Spradley (1979:58–68) has suggested that an ethnographic interview be thought of as a friendly conversation in which the interviewer makes explicit at the beginning the purposes of the discussion but offers additional explanation only as the conversation continues. This can be an important tactic because it educates the interviewee to his or her role in the process, especially the role of "guiding" the worker through a cultural setting that is unfamiliar.

This is a simple point but it is one that is sometimes missed, for several reasons. First, the social worker is supposed to be the expert, and it is hard for experts to say, "I really don't know much about you and where you live." Second, clients don't usually think of themselves as being experts, especially experts in a "problem." The role of clientship, as it is established in our society, is usually thought of as a dependent, even passive one. Yet in the model I am proposing, the client's perception that there is value in one's experiences, even those that are stigmatized, is the beginning of true empowerment. The message the worker must convey is: whatever you do or have done, I want to know more about it simply because it is your experience, it is worth understanding, and you can probably teach me something new I didn't understand before. This approach is not going to work with every client. But it will work with enough that you can gain insights that might otherwise be missed.

An example will help clarify this. Some years ago, I was interviewing West Indian men who were illegal immigrants to a United States territory (the Virgin Islands) (Green 1973). Most had limited job skills, were having difficulties reestablishing their family life, and out of anger and frustration were willing to talk about their experiences as aliens in a society that did not want them. Typically, I explained that the purpose of my interview was to learn more about the needs of immigrant West Indians and that I wanted to hear about each one's particular experiences since coming to a U.S. territory. Having a list of general questions in front of me, the interviews began. The explanation of my ethnographic purposes was offered in comments interspersed throughout the conversation: "I'm new to the Virgin Islands myself, and I want to know as much as I can about what 'down islanders' do in their first week here." "Tell me how people get fake green cards since I'm not familiar with how that is done." "I've never been to [the interviewee's home island] so tell me why you think people leave there to come to St. Croix." Those kinds of questions and the small self-confessionals they contained not only established what it was I was looking for but informed the hearer that I needed guidance myself in a world filled with hazards that they knew very well. The questions elevated each interviewee to the position of "expert on survival as an illegal alien" and put me in a temporarily dependent relationship, exactly where I wanted and needed to be.

Given that my culture guides were in the island illegally, it was critical that I explain my recording procedures because there were suspicions that I might be an Immigration agent. I showed people my notes so they could see that there were no names on them. I asked them to take the pencil and write or diagram something if that seemed to help. I took no notes if they preferred that. But I always made something of a fetish about getting things exactly right, which I soon discovered was important to them. Typically, I would say things like: "I want to write all this down, word for word, so I have it just right. Is that OK with you?" "Would you say that again? I want to get your exact words here, because I'm trying to understand your anger about this." "When you talk about this with other people from your island, do they say the same things?" Such questions were intended to keep the interviewee in the "knowledgeable insider" or "tour guide" role, as one who could speak authoritatively to my interests. The technique is simple and demonstrated that I took them seriously.

There is nothing magical or difficult about this interview style. It simply keeps the learning and information collecting purposes at the center of attention. It reinforces over and over again the message that the interviewee is the expert, the cultural guide; that everything said is important and must be recorded accurately; and that as the interviewer I have a clear purpose in mind, that of getting the client's perspective, the "native point of view," as explicitly and as fully as it can be articulated. This emphasis on guiding the interview, using cues supplied mostly by the respondent, can be most helpful with individuals who ramble, who are initially distrustful, or who feel they have nothing worthy to say. Simple as it is, the procedure makes the interviewer's communication with the client much more active and productive than do the usual bland injunctions to use paraphrasing, interpretation, and "minimal encouragers" (Ivey 1971, 1983) as devices to keep things moving.

There is a subtle but important shift that takes place in an interview that moves the client into the culture guide position. As the interviewer, you want the client to know that you regard him or her as a kind of spokesperson for others in the same situation. (That is the salience issue again.) To do that, questions can be phrased so that the answers reflect a sense of speaking about the experiences of others as well as oneself. In my West Indian work, for example, I would ask: "Tell me about the different ways you have heard some people get jobs without a green card." A less helpful way of asking that question would have been, "How did you get your job without a green card?"

Consider these two forms of that question. The first says to the interviewee: I don't know or care if you are in a U.S. territory illegally but I'm very interested in what you have heard from people who are; you probably could tell me some great stories about that. The latter question suggests that as the interviewer I am interested only in what happened to my listener, not the experiences of the many others he may know about. I learned that most men would eventually tell me about their personal heroics in avoiding Immigration officers but that it was easier for them to do that after they first described what they knew happened to others. Too frequent use of the word "you" forced the person being interviewed into a narrow vision of what they were guiding me through. Personal details will inevitably appear but it is the vantage point of "expert" that the interviewer wants to keep encouraging as the stories unfold.

Culture guide questions are an example of the efficiency I mentioned above. It is one thing to delve into the private life of one person. It is something larger when we ask them to take a longer look at why they have come to us and tell us about others with concerns like their own. Culture guide questions signal an adjustment in the power relationship between social worker and client. The worker is making it clear that the client's knowledge is worth something and that part of constructive intervention is allowing the client to feel that power, to know that there are important reciprocities in the culturally sensitive interview.

Cover Terms

Neither worker nor client can specify in advance everything that will emerge in an interview, particularly in its early, exploratory stages. It would be presumptuous to assume that one could know at the start which topics are important and which are not, although many interviews are conducted exactly that way. As the interview develops, however, certain phrases and words begin to stand out, either because they are unfamiliar to the cultural outsider or because they appear to have special meaning to the interviewee. Often these are words in the vernacular of the speaker, although they need not be. These special terms, words that the respondent uses casually and with familiarity, are called "cover terms." Cover terms literally "cover" a number of ideas, objects, concepts, or relationships that are part of the client's experience. They are linked features of the individual's mental lexicon. For example, if I were interviewing a former drug user who said something like: "I quit because I just got tired of being fried all the time," the word "fried" should be immediately recognized as a cover term. It refers to a special category of experience that is familiar to those in this subculture, and it has cultural significance and psychological reality to the speaker. In my example of West Indian labor migrants, a man might have said: "You can't get into this country legally without a green card, it's your ticket to security." The expression "green card" is part of the specialized knowledge both of labor immigrants and the law enforcement officials who have the power to deport them. It is, therefore, a cover term. I occasionally hear Japanese students speak of "the Issei" and Native American students refer to "bloods" and "skins." Local politicians are fond of speechifying about "welfare mothers," and an acquaintance once told me how he was "born again." All of these expressions are cover terms. Cover terms can appear in nearly every sentence uttered by a respondent, and it is critical that they be recorded exactly as the interviewer hears them. They are the basic ethnographic materials around which much of the rest of the interview will be built.

Cover terms are our windows onto the mental and experiential world of others. The collection and annotation of cover terms are central tasks in seeking to understand others from a cultural, holistic perspective. Their importance became apparent to me when, some years ago at a cultural awareness training session for nurses in the Southwest, I casually suggested that they might want to learn a few of the Spanish terms for diseases they commonly saw in their Hispanic patients. I added they might even want to make up a short list and circulate it among staff on the wards, or have a Latina nurse explain to them what the disease names meant and how, in some patients, folk illness categories were as real as the biomedical ones the doctors and nurses used all the time. This simple suggestion was met by surprise ("we never thought of that before") and outright hostility ("ours is an *English*-speaking hospital and it will stay that way"). Yet without a knowledge of how their Spanish-speaking patients conceptualize illness, it would be difficult to know how they understand the medical advice they are given or how they intend to act on it.

Why are cover terms such powerful devices for eliciting information about cultural matters? In the interview, they focus attention on what the client knows, on blocks of information that can be shared with someone else. The discussion, without a lot of "you" words, emphasizes subject matter and information—client expert knowledge—rather than immediate needs or personal failings. The client in particular has less reason to feel defensive if the topic for discussion is "Why I think men want to hit someone when they are mad" rather than "Why I hit my wife whenever I'm angry." The latter issue will certainly emerge over the course of the interview but it will do so within a context in which social worker and client cooperatively reconstruct the complex of values, behavior, and expectations that surround domestic violence. Men who hit their wives are "experts" on just that kind of behavior, and if we want to ameliorate the problem we need to understand wife battering in exactly the same way they do.

Another strength of the cover term approach is the way it structures the narrative flow of the interview. The social worker's power and control is in choosing to follow the cover terms that seem interesting and worth pursuing. This is especially useful, for example, in working with older adults who sometimes ramble or are repetitive. To recall a client's previous cover term or cover phrase can keep an interview on track by redirecting attention to an earlier point. The client's control is in offering words that are points for further exploration. Using this approach, even sensitive or volatile subjects can be cautiously but systematically addressed, and neither the worker's ego nor that of the client's need be threatened because what we are talking about is our words.

In this kind of interviewing, my preference has always been to accept any statement an interviewee makes as a potential cover term or cover phrase because, if the individual offers it, it is fair game for discussion. The veracity of the client has to be the starting point and, even when I have believed I was being given a "tall tale," I have accepted it as data. A falsehood cannot be forever maintained, especially over a series of intensive interviews. Further, embellishments are important as information because they tell us what the client wants us to believe about himself or herself. In addition, some people clearly want to test the listener, to see what will be accepted. Testing is not uncommon in initial cross-cultural interviews and a willingness to accept information at face value, combined with a vigorous strategy of pursuing its implications, usually conveys the idea that we are serious about what people have to say and that we intend to stay serious, right through to the end of the conversation.

Descriptors

Words and phrases are useful because they open windows onto the experiences and thoughts of others. Alone, however, they are simply collections, additions to our own lexical inventory. The value of cover terms is that they open topics for exploration that lead to eventual intervention and treatment of the problem. By exploring the meaning of cover terms, we develop ethnographic *descriptors*. For example, suppose that the social worker and client have been discussing family issues and that the word "family" has come up several times in the conversation. What, exactly, is being discussed? Most practitioners are aware that many people live in extended families, that the nuclear, monogamous family is the mythical ideal of the white middle class, and that single-parent and even same-sex-parent families are becoming more common. Similarly, we are all aware that "family issues" and the call for a return to "traditional family values" are potent political symbols, especially in controversies that surround abortion and welfare. So what is involved when a client refers to "family" and "family life" in a particular community?

It is simply not adequate to hear a client say that her family is an "extended" one and leave it at that. The ethnically sensitive worker needs to know what "extended" means and if the client can clarify its functioning among those she thinks of as ethnic compatriots. The "extended family" is probably something quite different among immigrant Vietnamese from what it is among the Amish, Louisiana Cajuns, or barrio residents of East Los Angeles. To accept that a client's family is "extended" without pursuing the meaning of that cover term is to accept a vagueness that is not acceptable in cross-cultural interviewing. One would want to know, for example, what portion of the client's community has extended families; what its norms are and what happens when people depart from those norms; expectations of adult men and women in extended households; how money is managed and arguments are settled; what children see, hear, and do that is different from the experience of those who do not live in extended families; how elders are regarded and what expectations and practice typify their treatment. This kind of list could go on at some length but the point is clear: we need the kind of descriptive information that only careful probing of a cover term will reveal.

Collecting that information takes effort and time. So where is the efficiency in it for the busy social worker? The value of the effort is in building a knowledge base, one small and manageable bit at a time, gathered with the cooperation of a number of clients, until a general picture of life in a given community and its many variations emerges. But the effort has to be systematic. Given the chance, every client can tell us something that is new. Descriptors should be written down in a log book and periodically reviewed to see what new areas can be explored with future clients.

The collection of cover terms and descriptors over a number of interview sessions can illuminate numerous areas in the life of a community, many of them normally hidden from outsiders. The worker who is familiar with the terminology, the rituals, and daily rounds in the lives of substance abusers, illegal labor migrants, runaways, or prisoners will not only be familiar with the rationales for behavior from their point of view but will recognize familiar sequences as they unfold in interviews with new clients. Perhaps one of the most startling and exciting things that can occur, as one's sensibility to the nuances of another culture is growing, is sudden recognition of previously hidden connections, even in the most mundane and casual activities. That is when the pieces begin to fit together, we see the sense of it all, and we "get it" just the way the client does. That knowledge marks the beginning of real communicative competence and it is one of the most satisfying growth experiences the cross-cultural social worker can know.

One result of all this effort ought to be some kind of personal guidebook or notebook, a place where you continually add to the data collected about your clients. When done systematically, this process can lead to a surprisingly sophisticated ethnographic document, one to which you can refer and which can be used in training new workers. The collection and organization of this data should have at least as high a priority as the all-too-numerous bureaucratic forms that social workers are already expected to complete. Carefully prepared information on client values, behavior, and preferences is essential for effective service delivery. Anything less means that social workers function in ignorance of what is really happening in the lives of the people they want to help. That should be professionally unacceptable. The accumulation and cultivation of ethnographic data and the shaping of such data to more accurately define the needs of clients constitutes one of the basic tasks of cross-cultural social work.

WORKING WITH A TRANSLATOR

Obviously, not all social work can be done in English. Nor is there any reason that it should be. Even individuals who have considerable facility in English as a second language often feel that the nuances of meaning that are important to them can be conveyed best in their first or "home" language. The ethnographic interviewing style I have been describing is particularly useful in this context. Any worker who is professionally active in, for example, a Spanish-speaking community, should probably consider learning enough Spanish to understand at least some of what is being said. But what of workers whose contact with Spanish speakers is only occasional, or the worker who regularly sees a few Chinese American clients but who perceives that learning Chinese is too much to ask? A logical solution is to collect cover terms and descriptors while working with a translator.

All languages contain an extensive vocabulary that is descriptive of physical and mental discomfort. But the goal cannot be compiling terms as though one were constructing a dictionary. What gives these terms particular power is (1) the context in which they are used and (2) their connotations within a vocabulary of suffering. That is where descriptors can be particularly useful. Descriptors are more than dictionary definitions; they are a kind of running commentary on the language of illness or pain. That commentary has to be collected over time, through the contributions of numerous social workers and clients, and it has to be written down and passed on to other workers as part of their preparation for working with clients. This process is very different from trying to learn a bit of Spanish or Japanese by signing up for classes at a local university. Cross-cultural language sensitivity for the worker is not a matter of grammar or even one of correct pronunciation. It is very much a matter of understanding contexts, especially those in which clients invoke the vocabulary of their distress.

When clients speak little or no English, a translator is essential. Glasser (1983), an anthropologist as well as social worker, has published guidelines for using interpreters. Her suggestions have the additional credibility that in her ethnographic and service work in soup kitchens in the Northeast (Glasser 1988), she learned Spanish in order to better understand the people she met. An overview of recommendations for working with a translator is shown in Figure 4.3.

Glasser notes that the social worker needs to understand the differences in power and affiliations (e.g., kin, class, or factions) that may characterize the translator and client. These issues can be especially important if the translator is someone who is simply available and is not trained or practiced in translation work. Novice translators can be expected to shield from the interviewer's "prying" unpleasant matters in their own and the client's community. Some translators may give the worker information that is so condensed (or even sanitized) that it cannot possibly convey all that the client intended.

Various suggestions for effective use of translators have been made (Phelan and Parkman, 1995). They include facing toward and speaking to your client directly rather than speaking to the translator; keeping the translator fully involved throughout the interview; asking the client for corrections to your understanding of what was said; staying with an issue until you understand it fully; emphasizing repetition; and avoiding use of family members of clients (especially children) as interpreters (Putsch 1985). Monolingualism is a handicap in any cross-cultural,

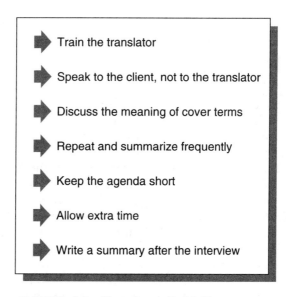

- Train the translator
- Speak to the client, not to the translator
- Discuss the meaning of cover terms
- Repeat and summarize frequently
- Keep the agenda short
- Allow extra time
- Write a summary after the interview

FIGURE 4.3   Translator Guidelines

(Based on Glasser 1983.)

cross-language encounter and, as the service professional, it is your responsibility, not that of the client, to take the lead in overcoming it.

Good translators are usually people who are practiced in the skill, who know well what the interviewer wants and why, and who appreciate the pressures on both the client and the social worker during an interview session. They are like good umpires or referees in a sporting event: they strive to be completely fair, to maintain the activity's smooth progress, to convey information promptly and accurately, and to remain unobtrusive. A good translator can signal to the worker the client's expectations and uncertainties. She or he can also convey to the client the worker's sense of confidentiality, desire to help, and trustworthiness. Workers with whom I have discussed this and who have had this kind of interview experience are usually very enthusiastic about "their" translator and the interesting nature of this kind of communication. That satisfaction usually overrides the inevitable frustrations of the slow pace of translated interviews and the natural difficulties of communicating complex ideas across language boundaries.

IS ETHNOGRAPHIC INTERVIEWING THERAPEUTIC?

Throughout this discussion, I have described the ethnographic interview as a learning device, something to benefit the service provider. But is there a sense in which ethnographic interviewing may have benefits for clients, benefits that could even be labeled therapeutic? I do not want to make any special claims for ethnographic interviewing because there is little research or discussion of its therapeutic potential. But I think the possibility is worth considering. I mention it, too, because if such benefits exist, I suspect it will be social workers, not social scientists, who will discover them.

An example is suggestive of these possibilities. Ortiz (1985) describes how, during her work among Cuban refugee women in Los Angeles, she followed standard anthropological interviewing procedures to collect life history narratives. She met regularly with a number of respondents to tape record interviews that she later transcribed for analysis. What was striking to her, however, were the effects of the interviews on these women. First, telling others in a systematic way what they had learned and felt over a lifetime gave a sense of validity to their experiences. Several older women expressed a profound satisfaction in having told a life story that only they could tell and that others around them found interesting and important.

Second, there was a cathartic effect. Ortiz notes that these women "had never had an opportunity to tell their entire stories to anyone, to have their pain acknowledged by an outsider, and to see their lives as a process over time" (1985:108). This was important because outsiders (including other Hispanics as well as Anglos) were prone to see refugee Cubans as people who had left their country for selfish reasons. The opportunity to explore the trauma of that experience, in a systematic and unobtrusive way, "was almost uniformly acknowledged as a welcome relief" (1985:109). Third, the interviews led to increased understanding among the women themselves and others around them. That was important because these women lived in large, multigeneration, extended families that were often squeezed into crowded apartments. Despite the intensity of their contact, family members often avoided or discounted communication of personal feelings or needs because it was potentially disruptive to family life overall.

How can we generalize from an example like this, to make it useful to social workers serving other clients in other communities? In a discussion of the universal features of therapeutic processes, Csordas and Kleinman (1990) suggest three healing aspects of communication, which I suggest are potential aspects of skillful cross-cultural interviewing as well. The first of these is transactional. The individual comes to perceive similarities between privatized experiences and those of some larger entity such as one's community, nation, race, or a religious figure or theme. The discovery and verbal articulation of that correspondence is a transactional event in which selfhood is linked, however briefly or imperfectly, to something larger, transcending, even universal. This connection between self and something universalizing may be somewhat indeterminant, but it is certainly not mystical or unusual. Dow (1986) describes in detail how those who seek healing for a variety of mental and physical conditions often come to terms with their illness by realizing that what has happened is part of some larger and more significant perspective. In encouraging the client or patient to explore the meaning implicit in experiences of pain, the culturally sensitive social worker is encouraging this kind of therapeutic transaction. Clearly, however, interviewing at this level is far removed from (and occurs much later than) the use of ethnographic techniques to simply gather background information.

The second aspect is social support. There is an extensive literature on the relationship of religious participation to the general health of individuals (Levin and Vanderpool 1987, for example). People who actively practice their religion tend to be healthier than those who practice none. But we do not need to confine ourselves to religion. Alcoholics Anonymous and similar organizations explicitly ask participants to forsake former ways, account for and confess behavior, and be absorbed by the group. Healing in these settings is thought to derive, in part, from the intense involvement of the participants. Although in social services such intensity in relationships between workers and clients can lead to problems in the termination phase of treatment, nevertheless the supportive aspect of the ethnographic approach is clear. Elevating the client to the honored position of "culture guide" creates an expectation that the client and worker have formed a small community of inquiry (as well as treatment) and that the client is valued, not just as the bearer of a problem, but also as someone who can contribute to the worker's professional capabilities. The positive mood that such a stance generates should not be underestimated.

Third, all storytelling, whether about oneself or what one knows about the neighbors, has a performative aspect. An interview is more than talk and information; it is a little play in which as dramatists we present ourselves to others in the way we would like them to see us, thereby making claims about the kind of person we are (Goffman 1959). These claims may be deeply held and thoroughly believed, or they may not. But in telling about ourselves, we all have the opportunity to elaborate and think about what we would like to be. Every culture comes with its own repertoire of expressive forms, in both spoken and body language. Our individualized use of these forms, bending them to suit the image we have of ourselves, is the aesthetic dimension of our selfhood. It is our style. Although we all respond to cultural imperatives, doing what we were taught to do, we are not automatons who respond unthinkingly. We are creative participants who find our unique ways for carrying out the role of bus driver, probation officer, or even town drunk. We are unique because we take what we have inherited from a history and a community and turn it to our private uses. In a sense, we are all good and earnest actors, drawing on the scripted idioms of our culture to create a satisfying persona for ourselves.

Is ethnographic interviewing therapeutic? Perhaps it can be if it is appropriately used by a skilled practitioner. It can help clients put their personal concerns in a larger, even ennobling perspective. It can help establish a relationship of trust between worker and client, a relationship that also links differing cultural communities. It allows people to describe, even invent, their persona, an essential life development task from the point of view of psychoanalyst Erik Erikson. The basic purpose of ethnographic interviewing is information gathering, but that does not mean it cannot have other consequences for both worker and client.

One of these consequences—one that apparently invokes ambivalence if not anxiety among many service providers—is the issue of spirituality. Social work originally grew out of ethical and religious concerns for the well-being of others, particularly the poor, children, and the elderly. Early on, however, as the endeavor became less a matter of charity and more one of professionalism, it also became more secular, taking its inspiration from emerging "scientific" theories of deviance, social disorganization, and personality. Freud's theories became popular in the field and, we need to remember, his views of religion were less than appreciative. Yet one aspect of things therapeutic, for many people in many cultural traditions, is a sense that the spiritual and the circumstances of their lives are linked. One need only think of the role and teachings of the African American church both before and after slavery, the significance of Catholicism in all its diversity in the Spanish-speaking world, and the proliferation of cults, sects, and nondenominational spiritual activities among Americans in general. Despite an overall decline in church attendance and affiliation since the 1960s, more Americans than ever describe themselves as "spiritual" even when they will not use the term "religious."

The importance of the spiritual, especially as it relates to how people respond to crises in their lives, seems obvious. Yet service providers and educators often say that, although they are respectful of religion in their own lives and those of their clients, they prefer not to "take it on" in their professional work. Nor is it often addressed in the curricula of schools of social work, nursing, or related areas. Unless service professionals work in hospices, with elders, or as grief counselors, they usually do not deal with religion, do not feel comfortable doing so, and prefer that it be left to the clergy.

This is an odd situation, since in an on-line search of social service data bases done in the summer of 1997, I used "spirituality" and "religion" as search terms and quickly found several hundred references, including many for recently completed doctoral dissertations. Apparently, among some social service professionals there is a real search for clarity about how the spiritual might relate to human services in a secular society.

I would argue that one way of incorporating the spiritual into professional work, in interviewing, assessment, and treatment, is to think of it as another aspect of an individual's ethnic identity. I have students in my classes who describe themselves as seekers, agnostics, born-again Christians, devotees of East Indian gurus, witches, and nature lovers. I also see people who say they are faithful Catholics, tepid Methodists, lapsed Baptists, questioning Mormons, and enthusiastic Pentecostals. Many have sworn off the faith of their childhood, and some are returning to it with a more sophisticated and critical eye. I suspect that for all of them, regardless of their age or background, their thinking about how they relate to ultimate things is one way they are self-consciously reconsidering who and what they are. Given that, it is not too difficult to think of individual spirituality as an aspect of identity construction, not a theological argument about the reality of spirit beings on which we as help providers are required to have an opinion.

To know one's client well, when spiritual concerns are part of a crisis, we need only use familiar skills. The work of Bullis (1996) is particularly impressive here. He covers a lot of territory in his recent book, including the historical dimensions of spirituality in social work, and he should be consulted for details. But I especially like his suggestions that spirituality is a normative aspect of many of the world's healing systems, that under appropriate circumstances a worker can take a "spiritual history" of a client just as he or she might take a family history, that clinical practice has spiritual dimensions whether we recognize them or not, and that religious experts are just as important as resources as are other kinds of professionals. As in any cross-cultural work, however, to be effective we have to know our own religious understandings and their limitations before we can be useful to others who may want to articulate and act on their beliefs.

NARRATIVE AS STORIED INSIGHT

Interviews are like mystery stories, a point made by Brown (1993), who studied seventy-five psychiatric intake interviews in a mental health center in the Northeast. No story told by a patient or a client is a historically accurate retelling, newspaper style, of events in the past. Our stories about ourselves are our current assemblage of experiences, feelings, and attributed motives, in addition to what we say "really happened." In the very telling, stories contain clues to hidden meanings, clues such as pauses, asides, slips of the tongue, narrative order, and what is included and what is left out. As good listeners, our job is like that of a detective, unscrambling the mixed messages and finding the clues that reveal hidden meanings. "Hence the clinical setting is set up like a detective story because the clinic is filled with people whose status is unclear and difficult to disentangle, and the intake interview resembles a mystery in its interrogation qualities" (Brown 1993:259).

But a narrative is more than a mystery, even though it is that too. The act of telling has a feedback quality for the narrator because it opens the possibility of retelling, or "reauthoring" as is sometimes said, in ways that can be helpful. In his discussion of working with narratives in counseling and psychotherapy, McLeod (1996:189) lists what he calls the "facilitative processes" that narrative makes possible. They include the opportunity to be heard, especially where secrets or painful recollections are part of the story; the chance to discover that any story has more than one possible telling and therefore more than one possible meaning; an occasion for finding a pattern in events that seem to be chaotic or unconnected; release of emotion through sharing an experience; discovery of a story ending that may be satisfying and creates closure; and learning that one's story is not unique and that others have endured comparable pains. The idea of "reauthoring," as many narrative therapists describe it, is finding the implicit threads that hold a story together and then connecting them to some larger structure of meaning so that, ultimately, one's experiences, however difficult or confusing, come to have "sense" in some new and liberating way.

How does this work in practice? An impressive example is that of Strickland (1994), writing in the *Clinical Social Work Journal,* an article that should be read in full to get a clear idea of how narrative interviewing and analysis is done. He provides an ethnographically rich autobiographical interview with a middle-aged woman being treated for alcoholism and who has a long history of drug use. The woman was using heroin in her early twenties, lived in Europe for a period of time where she was active in drug trafficking, returned to the United States when she suspected she was going to be murdered by fellow dealers, and had a series of unhappy relationships with men who had organized crime connections. In Strickland's account, she goes into these experiences in detail.

The analysis is organized around three principles. First, stories have plots, but the number of plot types are limited. With Strickland's client "Jill," her plot type is a heroic, almost romantic saga, for she tells her story as one of harrowing adventures and near escapes. But unlike traditional sagas, Jill's story does not rise to a single moment of triumph toward which all previous action has moved her. Nor is there a coda, an end to the action and final reflections on what was achieved and what it all meant. The story line is like a roller coaster, all action-packed ups and downs that lead her nowhere except back to the beginning of the ride. There is no sense of what it might mean, where it might be going, or where it might end. Jill reveals herself to be highly focused on events and actions, with relatively little thought for their consequences or awareness of their dulling repetition.

Second, episodes within a narrative have a number of distinctive features. They orient the listener to time and place, mood or expectation. They introduce complicating action and subplots that enrich and enliven the story line. Editorial asides and evaluations, verbal and nonverbal, a laughing snort or rolling back of the eyes, can be offered. Resolutions of the action can be suggested and justifications made of the course selected. The coda comments on what it all means and leaves it open to the listener to respond, if only with an appreciative "that's amazing!" In Jill's case, she embeds herself so deeply in her story that she cannot say something like "I might have been killed for doing that" (reflective) but offers instead "I lived on the edge" (descriptive). Says Strickland, "she stays inside the dramatic action and evaluates only from the point of view of the protagonist. She orients us minimally; she provides only what the listener needs to appreciate the dramatic nature of the action.... Her coda, in which the story teller returns to the present at the end of an episode, is limited to 'anyway,' and alerts the listener to what is coming: another action packed episode" (1994:33). There are important psychodynamic implications in this kind of episodic structure, for the client is telling us that she is independent, trusts no one, expects little from others, and sees the future as more of the same.

Third, a narrative is a joint enterprise between the teller and an audience. Stories we tell about ourselves come out slightly different every time, because the occasion of the telling and the appreciation of the audience are clues to what we should emphasize and what to keep in the background. In Strickland's example, the more he listened to Jill's story and commented on it, the more he came to see that there were really two voices speaking and they were poorly integrated. There was a protagonist-self who pushed the action along and took an almost perverse delight in the sheer adventure and risk of it all. But there also emerged, as the story unfolded, a narrator-self who was confused, even timid, and uncertain about what to do next. Inevitably, in predictable vacillation, the narrator-self capitulated to the protagonist-self and resolved each crisis by plunging into more action and a new adventure. "The more she acts without reflection, the more she must act. She repeatedly exhausts herself and checks in (to the hospital or drug program) or out (with drugs and alcohol)" (Strickland 1994:38). Jill is a woman who is impulsive, little able to abstract the implications of her experiences, and fixated on what is happening to her rather than on where it might lead her. Strickland concludes that her current treatment and participation in Alcoholics Anonymous may restrain her out-of-control protagonist-self and even offer solace to her tentative narrator-self.

The strengths of this kind of diagnostic approach, as Strickland sees them, are its humanistic orientation, its ease of use, its ethnographic richness in contrast to the relative sterility of checklist questions, and the quickness with which teller and listener establish rapport. The procedure is initially labor intensive, especially where tape recordings and transcriptions are used, but with practice one can learn to listen efficiently and effectively so that plot, episode features, and characteristics of voice are quickly identifiable. Narrative construction is one possible use of the ethnographic interview techniques described earlier in this chapter. The therapist begins with a global question to start a story sequence and then can use cover terms to gently and unobtrusively keep talk moving. The therapeutic enterprise begins immediately, flows smoothly and naturally, and replicates in accessible form the experiences of the help seeker.

CONSTRAINTS ON CROSS-CULTURAL COMMUNICATION

In the model of ethnic group relations discussed in the first chapter, I suggested that all communities seek to protect their distinctiveness by regulating the character and quality of intergroup contacts. I also suggested that the subculture of social work professionals is in some ways like an ethnic group, with its own values, knowledge, and patterns of organization. In the area of communication with ethnic or minority cultural "outsiders," that distinctiveness is forcefully, and sometimes painfully, evident.

Consider briefly the social setting in which many social work interviews take place. Interviews are usually held in offices, away from the more naturalistic settings where most clients are comfortable. They are highly structured events, both in terms of time (with specific, marked beginnings and ends) and the relative status (usually unequal) of the participants. Emphasis is placed on the immediate problem that has brought the participants together, and there is little time for informalities other than handshakes or cursory comments about the weather. The interview is expected to have an "outcome"—a verbal agreement, a signed document, a prod to some kind of action. This outcome is expected to be additive to the ongoing interviewer–interviewee relationship and the "work" the client is doing. Finally, the relationship is expected to terminate at some future point so that the social worker can go on to other, similarly structured encounters with other clients. In short, this style of interviewing suggests a certain type of culture: bureaucratic and corporate.

There would be nothing wrong with this as the prevailing style of worker–client communication if social workers, as members of bureaucratic organizations, only interviewed other office workers. But precisely because minority groups have been largely excluded from participation in the institutions of power, their communicative styles are adapted to cultural settings other than bureaucratic ones. Those settings are the home or the neighborhood tavern, the store-front church, or the nearby park. The people in these places have multiple interests in one another, not a single "problem" to discuss, and they are often of the same or similar status. A high value may be placed on the freedom to come and go, on entering and leaving conversations with no reference to clock time at all. In addition, personal contacts in these settings are considered interesting and valuable in their own right and do not require an "outcome" or a progression through stages toward an eventual termination. The imposition of an agency-oriented, "professional" communication style on a minority client could well be regarded, from the "native's point of view," as a highly aggressive and ethnocentric cross-cultural event.

Is there a solution to the dilemma of having to employ a bureaucratically styled form of communication when its appropriateness and utility are uncertain? One part of the answer is recognizing the limitations of all interviewing. The guided, intensive interview, with its emphasis on the client's ethnographic perspective, goes a long way toward overcoming rigidity and superficiality. But it is still a highly structured linguistic event that is intended in many ways to serve the information-gathering and people-processing interests of the bureaucratic culture.

The challenge to the culturally sensitive practitioner is to expand personal and professional capabilities beyond the superficiality of most cross-cultural service contacts. That takes effort, the effort of preparing global questions, of listening carefully for cover terms, and of systematically recording and reviewing new information. It takes the effort of playing with the model, trying out ways of adapting it to one's tasks, agency, and clients. It takes the kind of critical self-awareness that most good social workers have and redirecting it toward learning a new set of relationship-building skills. It requires a genuinely experimental attitude toward one's work and toward clients, an attitude that not all agencies are willing to support.

The other part of the solution is refusing to be content with building one's knowledge base through interviews alone. Consider the background of many minority group professionals. Whatever specific helping skills they may have learned in their formal education, they have been added to prior personal experience. As I have already noted, minority professionals often make commitments of time and energy to a home community far beyond that of their white colleagues. They do this because they are a resource to those communities. But they also do it because they know that they must be kept informed of the needs of those they serve. As professionals, they do not lose their home-grown communicative competence. White professionals, and minority professionals working in ethnic communities that are unfamiliar to them, can follow this example. They can inform themselves by seeking contacts and relationships outside their bureaucratically defined responsibilities. In that way, the limitations of interviewing can be partially overcome.

FOLLOW-UP

1. Considering Cases

Case 1: Interpreting a Narrative

Go back a few pages to Strickland's client, Jill. Read the summary of the case again or, better, go to the original article in the *Clinical Social Work Journal* (22:27–41, 1994) and read it through. When you are done, imagine that you are in Strickland's position. How would you respond if the following situations occur?

- After initial pleasantries about the weather and how she feels today, Jill looks out the window and says, "So, what do you want to know about me?" She seems quite willing to talk.
- Jill lived for a time in Paris where she was a small-time drug dealer. Occasionally she drops a French phrase into her narrative. You don't know what it means.
- Jill concludes all her stories about herself with little asides such as "things like that just happen to me" or "life's funny that way." You wonder if she can be more reflective about her experiences. What would you say to see if that is possible?

- After a long monolog about how most of the people she thought she could trust eventually turned against her, she looks at you and asks, "Has that happened to you too?"

Case 2: Language as a Key to Worldview

Not everyone who works in human services needs full command of a second language but sometimes it helps and sometimes it is critical to professional effectiveness. Irene Glasser, who is both a social worker and a medical anthropologist, has worked with women in prisons, spent time with the regulars at a soup kitchen in Connecticut (which led to two books, one on homelessness [1994] and one on the soup kitchen [1988]), and now works with the homeless in Montreal. With the latter, of course, she uses French, but before that, she found it was necessary to learn Spanish. In a statement prepared for this book, she tells how it happened:

> *I began working with a Puerto Rican social service agency in a small New England city in the 1970s. It was obvious to me that to understand and communicate one needed some Spanish. I had been a mediocre Spanish student in high school but had had some good experiences speaking whatever Spanish I knew a decade earlier in eastern Oklahoma at an Indian hospital. I had also traveled to Mexico fairly often.*
>
> *When I decided to learn Spanish again in the 1970s, I took some courses in my university where, at the time, I taught social work. I listened a lot to a Spanish radio station, especially the commercials, which greatly increased my understanding of what some would perceive as "rapid fire" Spanish. Ads are repetitious so they help with learning, and they tell you what is important in the popular culture. For example, I often heard "Compre sus ropas para su boda en Calle Park ahora"—buy your wedding clothes in Park Street now. The news, the public service announcements, the dedications of songs, all were excellent for accustoming myself to the sounds of this beautiful language. I also tutored ESL students, letting the class instructor know I was interested in an "intercambio"—an exchange of English lessons for Spanish. A factory worker who wanted to improve his English so he could preach in his church was a great help, and an excellent way to immerse myself in the language without leaving home.*
>
> *Gradually, I was able to practice social work in Spanish. I learned the polite things that people say to each other that makes interaction warm and respectful: "con mucho gusto" (with pleasure); "me alegre verte" (it's good to see you), "recuerdos a tu familia" (regards to your family). I became very impressed with the lack of social distance between social worker and client. Much that I would never have known was understandable to me because I had learned the language and used it with clients as often as I could. The lessons of cross-cultural living, as well as of language, have been important to all my professional work.*

You may not need the impressive level of second (and third) language proficiency that Glasser acquired. Yet increasingly we all come into contact with individuals for whom English is not their first language even though they may use it well. Typically, people under stress, or those attempting to communicate complicated or emotionally intensive ideas, prefer to use their first language whenever they can. They know its subtleties well. Interspersing English with words and phrases from another language is technically known as "code switching" and is one of the formal features of speech that any clinician can learn to work with effectively. It is a good place to start because it is salient to the counseling relationship. It may lead you as well to the skill level achieved by Glasser in her work.

Assuming you work or have an internship in an agency where more than one language is sometimes heard, you can do the following to strengthen your understanding of what people are saying:

- Make a list of unfamiliar words and phrases (essentially cover terms that are new to you) as you hear them in consultations. After each session, ask the client to translate these items for you and explain the circumstances when they are used. This is an additional opportunity to pick up new vocabulary on related topics.
- Ask the client (or someone else who is a native speaker) to help you pronounce the words and phrases until you get them about right. This can be tricky, and if it seems it might be embarrassing, set out to make it a fun and even humorous experience, perhaps at your expense. But emphasize your seriousness about getting meanings and pronunciations right. If people smile because of your mispronunciations, learn to smile with them and they will respect you for the effort you are making.
- Share your list with co-workers, asking them to add to it with additional material as it comes up in their own sessions with clients. Over time, you will have produced a small dictionary of key terms useful both in training and in expanding your own awareness.

Warning: be cautious and humble with your newly acquired vocabulary. Dropping foreign phrases casually into conversations can and will be perceived as presumptuous. Communicative competence means knowing vocabulary that can help you in consultations but, much more important, also knowing when and when not to use it. The latter is the more difficult skill.

2. Test Drive an Idea

Use of linguistic clues provided by respondents is one of the quickest, most efficient ways of acquiring ethnographic information. The technique, as I have outlined it, is a simple one, although it has been developed by Spradley (1979) as part of a larger and much more complex investigative process, and his publications should be consulted for more details. All that is required by the learner is a linguistic sample from a respondent. For instance, consider the following bit of conversation, taken from my own research notes of an interview with a child protective services worker:

> *I see all kinds of clients. Just recently I worked with a woman who was very disturbed; I'd say she had severe depression. Her child had a number of contusions on the head and arms and the X-rays showed subdural hematoma. I took that as evidence of the battered child syndrome and asked the judge for a preliminary hearing.*

Just this snippet of conversation contains enough cover terms to keep an interview going for an hour or more. Remember that I described a cover term as a word or expression, sometimes in a vernacular, that may be unfamiliar to the interviewer but seems to have particular meaning or importance for the respondent. In this sample, there are at least seven cover terms of interest: clients, disturbed, depression, contusions, subdural hematoma, battered child syndrome, and preliminary hearing. Each term stands for, or "covers," a block of information that is part of the shared subculture of protective service workers, the things they know as members of specialized and distinctive professional community. (Some of the terms, of course, are shared with other subcultures—other kinds of social workers, doctors, and lawyers, for example—and their meanings may shift somewhat from one professional culture to another.) These words are the emic labels of the professional subculture.

Using the cover terms as guides, we can begin to elicit descriptors which will help us define the cultural world of these social workers. Descriptors are identified by asking questions concerning kinds, qualities, features, characteristics, relationships, and the like. For instance, if this was our first of several interviews with this person, we might ask a global question: "How many kinds of clients are there? Can you list them for me?" For example, the respondent's comments suggest that there is a large category, *disturbed,* of which *depression* is a special case and *severe depression* is an even finer subdivision of the category. We might ask, therefore: "When you say *disturbed,* how many things does that include?" Or we could ask: "Can you tell me some of the characteristics of *depression* that you look for, and what distinguishes *severe* depression from that which is less severe?"

In short, we are asking: How do you know it when you see it? What to you are a category's descriptive characteristics? This same line of questioning can be applied to the other cover terms in the sample. Some terms may be precise, such as the legal or medical ones; others are more generalized. But it is having these terms defined as clearly as possible, and under conceptual control by the worker, that is our goal. Without that, how could we expect to have precision and accuracy in our assessments, diagnoses, and evaluations?

We do not demand full, exhaustive information from one respondent. Where the respondent's knowledge is unclear, that too provides important insight. For example, if the social worker's knowledge of the descriptors for *battered child* syndrome is vague, contradictory, or shifting, that in itself would be important to know since it would tell us that this worker is making decisions about intervention without a clear idea of what is involved. If interviews show that to be true of a number of workers, we would have hard data for making a case for better training. The data would have come to us through ethnographic interviewing.

It is clear that even a tiny fragment of linguistic information is a clue to a great deal of cultural knowledge. The worker need only find the clues, the cover terms, and pursue them in a systematic way. The possibilities for doing this are endless. Social workers who want to practice the technique can do so with other workers, focusing on the specialized tasks, skills, or client communities associated with their interview partners. Where willing clients are available, they might be interviewed on topics of interest to them.

3. More on the Issues

- Interviewing

There are many good books available on ethnographic interviewing skills. One good one is Herbert J. Rubin and Irene S. Rubin, *Qualitative Interviewing* (Thousand Oaks, CA: Sage, 1995). A book of exercises is Paul B. Pedersen and Daniel Hernandez, *Decisional Interviewing in a Cultural Context* (Thousand Oaks, CA: Sage, 1996).

- Names and Labels

What people are called, and what they want to be called, are sensitive and sometimes explosive topics. A good discussion of this in a social service framework is Yvonne Asamoah et al., "What We Call Ourselves: Implications for Resources, Policy, and Practice," *Journal of Multicultural Social Work* (1:7–21, 1991).

- Interpreters and Interpretation

Much of the literature in this area comes from medical settings. One example is Dedra Buchwald et al., "The Medical Interview Across Cultures," *Patient Care* (27:141–144). An especially interesting case of how subtle differences in understanding can be, even where everyone is using English, is Woolfson et al., "Mohawk English in the Medical Interview," *Medical Anthropology Quarterly* (9:503–509, 1995).

- Narrative Therapy

The journal *Family Process* (35:4, 1996) has a special section, entitled "Applications of Narrative Therapy," in which the articles deal with children's issues.

- Religious Dimensions

An overview of religious aspects of intervention is in David Lukoff, Francis G. Lu, and Robert Turner, "Cultural Considerations in the Assessment and Treatment of Religious and Spiritual Problems," *The Psychiatric Clinics of North America* (18:467–485, 1995). They propose adding spiritual issues to the *DSM-IV* system. Also of interest is Mary Sormanti and Judith August, "Parental Bereavement: Spiritual Connections with Deceased Children," *American Journal of Orthopsychiatry* (67:460–469, 1997). They discuss implications for clinical work.

CULTURAL COMPETENCE IN MULTICULTURAL CONTEXTS

Part 2 examines problem solving, why it is so complex in a pluralistic society, and how we can move beyond simplistic ethnic trait lists in our best efforts to understanding others. Individual chapters take up the unique experiences and needs of those in specific communities: African Americans, Native or First Americans, Asian Americans, and Spanish-speaking Americans. Historical information about these broad categories of people is supplied because, within their communities, their history is usually well known and meaningful. A distinctly comparative way for you to examine your own cultural background in relation to that of others is described within each chapter. The skill of comparative thinking, along with facts and information, is basic to cultural sensitivity.

5

CROSS-CULTURAL
PROBLEM RESOLUTION

Alicia Lieberman (1990), an expert on the mental health of very young children and a researcher on the child-rearing styles of Latina women in California, was asked to discuss cultural issues with a group of service professionals who worked with women with blind infants. These social workers complained that their Latina clients were emotionally suffocating the children by trying to do too much for them. For example, they carried them about instead of letting them learn to crawl. They bottle-fed them well into the years when "other" (meaning Anglo) women encouraged their children to eat on their own. The workers felt that all children need to learn self-reliance early, especially blind children, and they wanted Lieberman to give them some cultural "tips" on how to persuade their clients of the importance of autonomy for healthy children.

According to Lieberman, she refused to acquiesce in this request, and subsequent discussion in her training session became tense. She writes that "it dawned on me that we were actually unconsciously reenacting the struggle between workers and the resistant Latina mothers in their work together. I was identifying with the mothers, refusing to yield to the intervenors' demands to let go of the child and to foster the child's autonomy. The intervenors understandably perceived me as one more Latina mother who was opposing their efforts" (1990:110).

Was Lieberman being unreasonable in defending these apparently controlling mothers? Was the workers' request for her professional guidance culturally sensitive? Was the intended use of "cultural information" by the workers legitimate? What were the divergent, underlying cultural assumptions about child rearing and family life in the opposing positions of Lieberman and her trainee audience? How might those assumptions have been identified and resolved, or could they be resolved at all?

Some of the important ethnographic issues in this example include:

1. Latina child-rearing preferences that the workers apparently did not understand or recognize.

2. Anglo child-rearing preferences that Hispanic clients rejected, perceiving them as unreasonable.

3. The Latina mothers' ambivalence when encouraged by cultural outsiders to raise children in ways other than those they understood and commonly saw in their own community.

4. The Anglo workers' apparent lack of awareness of how their cultural (i.e., professional) assumptions were driving their intervention decisions, and their inability or unwillingness to articulate those assumptions.

5. The cross-cultural trainer's unwillingness to offer an insider's "tip list" that might enlarge the worker's impact on clients from an unfamiliar community.

6. The workers' and trainer's inability to generalize from specific clients to larger issues of cross-cultural social work. For example, they might have also asked: how are the child-rearing practices of other Spanish-speaking mothers with blind children, such as mothers from Panama, Colombia, or Puerto Rico, similar or different from those of the current clients, and what are the intervention implications of that diversity?

In terms of culturally competent practice, these issues point to at least three major problem areas: (1) the adequacy of the social workers' ethnographic knowledge of child rearing among their clients; (2) how the workers determined that a "problem" existed and whether their determination was, by some clearly articulated standard, a valid one; and (3) the workers' ability to know if they had made an appropriate "fit" between their diagnosis, assessment, and treatment plans and the perceived needs and expectations of their Spanish-speaking clients.

As I have discussed in previous chapters, in an explicitly cultural approach to problem resolution, the alert and responsive social worker has several tasks. They are not difficult but they do require a way of thinking about clients and about problem solving that is only now beginning to emerge in social services training. First is the importance of a *knowledge base* adequate to day-to-day work with clients. Second is the need to identify the cultural *salience* of specific client issues and make their behavioral dimensions explicit. Third, in developing treatment plans it is critical to think of how the client functions not only in a psychological sense but in a social *context* as well. Fourth is recognition of the meaning of *power* in service encounters, especially as it relates to treatment outcomes and evaluations of "what worked" and what did not. Fifth, good cross-cultural work depends on the ability to think *comparatively*, to see individual cases as both unique and as exemplars of community-wide processes and needs. Figure 5.1 identifies each of these features. None is more important than any other, and all must be considered significant in developing a holistic approach to working with clients and patients.

The five steps of cross-cultural learning should be read as preparation for the four ethnographic chapters that follow. They are your guide to interpreting and using the information in those chapters, and for appreciating the inevitable limita-

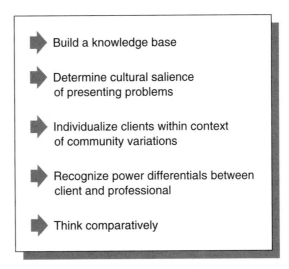

> Build a knowledge base
>
> Determine cultural salience
> of presenting problems
>
> Individualize clients within context
> of community variations
>
> Recognize power differentials between
> client and professional
>
> Think comparatively

FIGURE 5.1   Cross-Cultural Skills

tions of all such overviews. You can think of the steps as a road map for developing your cross-cultural skills and for evaluating your current strengths and weaknesses. Some of the steps emphasize information and others stress skills. But all are important for cultivating your own professional style.

STEP I: BUILDING THE CRITICAL KNOWLEDGE BASE

It is probably the general failure of American education to deal honestly and directly with the fact of cultural pluralism that leaves most of us uninformed about what cultural diversity really means for us, or how we can proceed to understand it in a useful way. Some social workers have felt they had to immerse themselves in the history, sociology, literature, music, and even the cuisine (*especially* the cuisine) of their client communities to gain enough knowledge to function effectively as service providers. Although I don't discourage that kind of academic industry for those who have the time and energy, I think that for busy professionals there is a more appropriate and more efficient way to go about it.

In a training workshop for state adult service workers several years ago, I was leading a discussion of why the names for ethnic groups are sometimes controversial and what the historical and sociological reasons might be for that. One participant, uneasy from the start, was visibly annoyed with me and the direction of the discussion. Finally, with great indignation, she announced that she was an American, nothing more and nothing less, and that we were all making too much out of something that was simple and settled long ago. She ended by emphatically asking the group, "Why can't we all just be Americans?"

Indeed. Why can't we?

In the discussion on language (Chapter 4), I described how the power to name is the power to control. It is important that what people are called, and what they want to be called, be considered carefully. Inappropriate and insensitive labeling is always the banana peel pratfall of cross-cultural communication. Those who are well intended but uninformed are soon on the floor, often without even knowing it. Part of the problem is that labels change, not because people are arbitrary, but because society, politics, and the distribution of power change. Labels reflect that. There is no final, correct list for what ethnic group members ought to be called or want to be called. But ethnic groups are the final source of authority for the designations that we all use. That is a volatile issue, and in commenting on it here, I do so with full acknowledgment that the terms in use in the 1990s may be "old stuff," even unappreciated old stuff, in later decades. (For an extended discussion of naming and why it is such a complex issue, see Asamoah et al. 1991.)

I will start my consideration of the meaning of names with whites, because they are the politically and socially dominant group at the present time. "White" and "Caucasian" are the two most common (of the polite) terms, "white" being the choice of the U.S. Census Bureau for the 1990 census. What do these two words mean? Physically, no one is really "white" unless they have no pigmentation at all (a condition that occurs in all populations including dark-skinned ones). All people are really brown, for that is the color of the melanin that tints our skin. The word "Caucasian" refers to the Caucasus Mountains, just north of Turkey, and was the name given to a prehistoric skull found there in the late 1700s and believed at that time to be archetypal for all Europeans. "Caucasian" is reflective of the state of the biological and archaeological sciences at the end of the eighteenth century. But now it is a term that has no scientific validity and, more to the point, it designates no one in particular. Spanish speakers sometimes refer to whites as "Anglos," and in certain contexts that is appropriate. "White" is probably the most acceptable term for the present and the one I use in this book. But I do not capitalize it as I do other labels for the reason that whites rarely think of themselves as "ethnic" except when they describe themselves as fractions of European nationalities (Thorne et al. 1983). Given the claims to distinctiveness and ethnic solidarity made by other ethnic communities in recent years, one of the problems posed for whites is just what their "ethnicity" might be anyway. For most, a diffuse idea that they are "generic American" apparently suffices.

The term "black" has its own complex history. For much of the colonial period in North and South America, the Spanish "negro" was the accepted term. During slavery, both in the United States and in the West Indies, there was an extensive and complex vocabulary for presumed degrees of Africanness in the blood. That vocabulary, with words like "octoroon" and "quadroon," was once common in everyday speech but is now so archaic that it can be found only in history books and dictionaries. A capitalized "Negro" and "Colored" were widely used after the Civil War, the word "black" considered at that time a slur. (Hence the continued use of "Colored" in the name of the NAACP, founded early in this century.) Black, first in lower case and then capitalized, became popular during the 1960s, as activists deliberately took on a stigmatized name and turned it into "Black is beautiful." Afro-American, first proposed in the late nineteenth century, and African-American, have been replaced by African American without the hyphen when used as a noun. Many in the black community do not feel they are "hyphenated Americans," and they find the newer usage more descriptive of their origins. African American and black, as of this writing, are used interchangeably by many people of African ancestry, although other terms may come into use in the future.

Native Americans were here first, of course, but there was no "America" for most of their 40,000 years of residence. The term "Indian" is a misnomer, from Columbus's mistaken belief that he had discovered India and the East Indies. (The term "West Indian" is equally erroneous, as the native peoples of the Caribbean were quickly exterminated by the Spanish and the region has been overwhelmingly African American since the late seventeenth century.) Generally, the terms Native American and American Indian are acceptable, although many Indian people prefer to identify themselves by their tribal affiliation as, for example, members of the Menominee or the Yakama nation. Many tribal names, now compromised by English or French spellings and pronunciation, originally expressed an idea such as "the people" or "the people of the mountain." As names for localities and for historical traditions, they remain important and will not disappear however acculturated some individuals or groups may appear to be.

Spanish speakers often identify themselves with their country of origin as well, as in "Mexican American" or "Puerto Rican." The term "Hispanic" has been widely used, and continues to be, but is losing out to "Latino," "Latina," "Chicano," and "Chicana" in some areas. "Hispanic" was a word originally coined by the Census Bureau, and so it has never had the sense of legitimacy many whites might assume. "Chicana" and "Chicano" came into vogue during the 1960s and 1970s, when some felt that the word "Mexican" conveyed an image of poverty and backwardness. Now even those terms are questioned by those who prefer to think of themselves using a national designation such as Cuban American. As with many of the terms discussed here, more precise designations are better than vague, all-encompassing ones, particularly as more and more ethnic groups assert their distinctiveness and their unique cultural identity.

The term "Asian American" is probably the most inclusive and the least descriptive in this list. "Oriental" is definitely out, but Asian American is only a slight improvement. The ethnographic diversity of people of Asian origins in America is staggering: China (with all its regional and ethnic diversity), Japan, Taiwan, Hong Kong, Viet Nam, Malaysia, Indonesia, the Philippines, Micronesia, Polynesia, American Samoa, Guam, Thailand, India, Pakistan, Sri Lanka, and Tibet. People from all these countries, and many more, call themselves Asians and insist, when they become resident here, that they are Asian Americans. Not only is there great national and ethnic diversity represented, but there are significant religious and racial variations too. The Asian American category really explodes the putative melting pot. As in the case of Spanish speakers, many Asian Americans prefer to be identified with a nationality. In all cross-cultural work, what individuals and families are called is *their* choice, and if the choices change with the political or economic climate, that is just what life is in a genuinely pluralistic society. We can't be "just Americans" because we are so much more than that.

What of the more recent expression, "people of color" and others like it, phrases that attempt to be inclusive almost without restriction? There seems to be little consensus about this kind of language. Some individuals like it because of its democratic emphasis on people and its implied claims of a universal opposition between white Europeans, their descendants, and their hegemonic cultures on the one hand and the peoples of Africa, Asia, and the Americas who were colonized and dominated on the other. Others reject the term as too vague, or for perpetuating simplistic ideas about ethnic diversity and the complexity of each ethnic community's historical experience. For this book, I do not use the term "people of color" because for me it belongs to a body of discourse that is essentially political. As a descriptive and analytical phrase, the usefulness of "people of color" must be determined by those interested in ethnic politics and historical patterns of dominance and subordination. In human services, where we work with personal and family needs, and try to individualize clients and patients within their specific cultural tradition, an expression like "people of color" is just too broad to be useful. That does *not* mean we can ignore issues of power and inequity in the way services are provided. I am simply suggesting that sweeping rhetorical forms belong in a forum other than client–worker consultations.

Finally, I want to suggest that in reality all these words of identification are a kind of shorthand, even a fiction. Race, ethnicity, and the language associated with them are constructs that we use for social convenience. They suggest a simple, neat, and orderly world where everyone is slotted into their proper place. But the truth is otherwise, profoundly so, and even well-meaning persons are misled by the vocabulary we all employ. Many of us in America, perhaps *most* of us, are ethnically and *racially* mixed in some sense. But our habits of language and thought do not allow us to perceive that at all. It was as recently as 1967 that the Supreme Court abolished antimiscegenation laws (then existing in fourteen states), some of which had stood for three centuries. The longevity of these laws is evidence that interracial marriage and mating was an old practice and, at least for the lawmakers and their constituencies, a deeply troubling one. But the laws were never enforced in a uniform way, nor could they be, and the evolving physical diversity of the American population is proof of that. Our labels help us deceive ourselves, preserving the fiction that all that mixing, mating, and marrying never went on, when in fact it did.

Consider this. It has been estimated that in terms of family history and genealogical lines, half or more of all African Americans are multiracial (Root 1992). So are almost all Hispanic people (Fernandez 1992), most Native Americans (Wilson 1992), and a significant proportion of whites (Alba and Chamlin 1983). Most whites, unless they have written genealogical records, cannot trace their ancestry further back than three or four generations. Yet the greater the duration of their family "line" in America, the greater the likelihood of interracial ties. (To imagine the possibilities, we have to think of the family "line" not as descent from a common ancestor. That is another fiction. Rather, it starts with oneself and branches out much like a tree, with the tree getting bushier with more connections the further back in time one traces the limbs.) Most of the people in my university classes identify themselves as white, and I believe that many of the students who will use this book are white. I also think that many of them have racially diverse family connections they do not even suspect. In hidden and even secretive ways, most of us are already multiracial because that is a fact of our biological past, although it is usually denied or not known. Whites commonly name multiple European national origins to identify their ethnicity without ever considering the possibility of African American racial or ethnic linkages (Alba 1990). Daniel (1992) argues that multiracialism was probably more common in our past than we realize and, further, it will be much more so in our future. He suggests that individuals who "call themselves 'mixed', 'biracial', 'interracial', or 'multiracial'" are the carriers of a new multiracial consciousness, representing "the next logical step in the progression of civil rights, the expansion of our notion of affirmative action" and especially the affirmation of nonhierarchical ways of constructing personal identity (Daniel 1992:334).

Multiracialism may well be the new frontier of American racial consciousness, an idea convincingly put forward by sociologist Maria P. P. Root (1992, 1996). She describes how, in the 1990 national census, the racial category "Other" was checked by almost ten million Americans, a 45 percent increase over the previous census and more than all those who identified themselves as Asian American. In addition, a quarter million people exercised their option to write in a racial or ethnic designation other than what was supplied on the Census Bureau form. They identified themselves as biracial and multiracial individuals in combinations of their own choosing. There are many reasons for this, including immigration, cross-ethnic and cross-racial marriages, and the fact that, at least at the Census Bureau, there are choices.

Beyond census figures, however, it is clear that the idea of biracialism is rapidly entering American popular consciousness. This is something new. There has always been in the African American community a sharp awareness of degrees of darkness and lightness in skin color, with lighter blacks distinguished from darker ones. And there is a tiny but recognizable segment of the Asian community, mostly Vietnamese Americans now in their twenties and thirties, who are the children of Vietnamese women and black or white American servicemen. Until now, discussion of these variations has largely been confined to the communities concerned. But that conversation has changed and is now much more open, partly because of the media prominence of golfer Tiger Woods. Woods' father is African American and his mother is Thai. In a *Time* (May 5, 1997) magazine article headlined "I'm Just Who I Am," he is described as "one-eighth Caucasian, one-fourth black, one-eighth American Indian, one-fourth Thai and one-fourth Chinese," and when he is asked to check a racial identity box he checks both African American and Asian (1997:34). The same article contains several vignettes, one on a California high school woman whose parents are African, Cherokee, and Irish on one side and German and Jewish on the other, and one of eight-year-old Jordan of Dade County, Florida. Shown in his Scout uniform alongside his parents, Jordan says "I'm American

Indian, African American, European, African American." But it took both his parents and the ACLU to force the school district to add a multiracial check off to the school registration form, something they still find unacceptable because they want to check three races, not one.

These examples are notable not just because they suggest something of what sociologists are calling the "browning of America," although that is significant, but because they were featured in a popular publication making the point to a national audience that the demographics of the future are on the side of multiracial people. That is going to mean huge changes in attitudes and behavior in the twenty-first century, and not just among whites either, about what an ethnic group is, what ethnic consciousness means, who the constituents of ethnic politics are, and how the economic pie is going to be divided up.

At the personal level, Root suggests this transition is not going to be easy, especially for those who are the pioneers of this future. She calls for a "bill of rights for racially mixed people" that includes the right not to have to justify one's existence, the right to identify oneself as one chooses independent of parents and siblings, the right to change one's identity over time, and the right to have loyalties to more than one group (1996:7). Preferences, not genes, will be the determinants of which box or boxes to check.

If our future is to include an unapologetic affirmation of multiracial diversity and nonhierarchical ways of thinking about difference, then it should be clear that we can't forget about labels, "just be Americans," and get on with business as usual. First, we have yet to settle what being an "American" means. Second, we have to acknowledge that for many people "being American" is synonymous with being white. Whites control the discourse about what America is. Acknowledging diversity as something more than ethnic holidays and special foods will require that we rethink some very old and pernicious ideas about what our collective experience means to us.

STEP II: CULTURAL SALIENCE IN PROBLEM SOLVING

If comparative sensitivity marks the beginning of knowledge about differences generally, the idea of salience focuses that sensitivity on a specific service issue. The word "salience" suggests something that is noticeable, prominent, or distinctive. My suggestion is that what may be salient for clients, their ways of comprehending and working with a problem, the "commonness" of their common sense, may not always be obvious to a counselor. In reference to psychotherapy, for example, it has been suggested that minority patients have to be approached as "knowers," that is, "individuals who shape their worlds and destinies through conceptual frameworks which they develop about the world and their lives" (Tyler, Sussewell, and Williams-McCoy 1985:311). As "knowers," their experience is rich in matters that I know little or nothing of, but about which I need greater familiarity so I can better meet their needs. How can that be done?

The help-seeking behavior model is our guide for this kind of inquiry. Recall that the model was made up of a number of components: the experience of a problem; naming of the problem through labeling; selection of healers, followed by treatment and some level of compliance with their suggestions; and determination that an acceptable outcome has been achieved. The steps of the model suggest a map for tracking and identifying the salient features of client problem identification and problem resolution. For example, once a problem is experienced, what are the rationales for assigning it a particular label? Given a decision about labeling, how does that influence choices about self-treatment or referral? How wide is the range of options for consultation, and why are some chosen in preference to others?

The range of possible decisions and behavior is enormous, and some choices are more salient to a given client than others. The matter of labeling is a good example. Dufort (1992) describes the management of physical disabilities among Papago Indian children and their families in Arizona. She was interested in how client–health worker communication styles, and Papago medical knowledge, influenced the quality of care available to those with severe disabilities. The Papago were not ignorant of contemporary treatment methods, and they wanted all the help they could get. But the way nurses, doctors, and social workers defined care made it difficult for Papago patients to work closely with these professionals. Papago families often concluded that decision making had been taken away from them, substituted by lists of "shoulds" on how treatment routines were to be followed. In addition, although the Papago accepted biomedical accounts of a specific disability as the proximate cause of the condition, they added another layer of explanation of their own. That layer included moral and personal factors that were important in their etiological accounts. Dufort was able to document these factors because of the way she listened to her respondents: Papago explained illness through long, personalized narratives that put the experience of illness in a dense context of meaning. They disliked the brief "patient histories" taken by the nurses and social workers, to them just bureaucratic conveniences reflecting a narrow, instrumental view of illness favored in the clinical subculture. Before they would respond to clinical suggestions favorably, they wanted their own accounts to be given a place alongside those of the biomedical specialists.

There is a second aspect of cultural salience suggested here, one more ephemeral and difficult to access than the knowledge base described in Phase I above. That is the meaning emotions and emotional experiences have within a particular ethnographic context. Most social workers understandably take pride in their "people work" skills and their ability to respond positively and helpfully to the pain, anger, or suffering their clients endure. I suggest, however, that those emotional states are not "pure" in the sense of being "natural" responses that any reasonable person might have in a crisis. Like knowledge, emotions too have their cultural dimension, and the sensitive worker will recognize that and want to understand them that way.

But how can emotions be thought of in cultural terms since it seems they are preeminently psychological manifestations? And what might that mean for someone who wants to intervene in a culturally responsive way? The argument is a complex but interesting one (see Lutz 1988:53–80) and it is best understood by considering how, in American culture, many of us routinely think of emotional states.

In the folk psychology of American middle-class culture, emotions are usually conceptualized in what could be called "essentialist" terms. That is, they are "things," "energies," or "forces" of which we each have some given quantity. Conceived this way, as a kind of internal stuff that sometimes seeps out even against our will, we "work with," "control," "manage," "hide," "cope with," "release," or otherwise regulate them as best we can. On permitted occasions, however, we are allowed to "vent" them. Emotions are perceived as a physics of sensibility. They are also thought of by most Americans as universal—everyone "has" them, although some people seem to "have" more of them than others, and sometimes they are even "lost" (as in "I lost my cool") so that people feel compelled to reclaim and "own" them. (The latter is an interesting metaphor in itself—the middle-class depiction of emotions as comparable to commodities or property, objects that can be "spent" or "wasted" on something unworthy, or rediscovered and "owned" because they have been stolen by someone else. Thus, some people speak of "owning" their experiences.) Emotions are also thought of as "natural," being intimately associated with the body and often described in medicalized terms. Thus people experience the "pain" of grief, or they have "butterflies in the stomach" when they are under stress. Emotions as essentialist, as characterological properties of the individual, are even genderized, women presumed to have a wider range of them but those of men under more explicit, rational control.

All the words I have put in quotes, along with many others like them, are commonly used in American middle-class culture to describe emotions. The language also suggests a particular cultural bias: emotions as universal, as naturally occurring "inner stuff," stuff that has dimension, that is privately claimed, that is gendered, and that may be dangerous. If you doubt me, just keep a mental list of the linguistic descriptors you hear in a five minute conversation as someone tells you how they felt about something. The folk psychology of middle-class Americans is a psychology of quantities and uneasily managed forces, moving precariously about within an imperfect, poorly constructed container. This essentialist folk theory forces us to think of emotions as things that are "deep," "buried," "hidden," or lurking underneath the surface, always interiorized and, like goods and commodities, privately possessed and rarely shared.

This is not, however, the only way to think about emotional experience and, for cross-cultural social work, it may not be the best way either. I say that deliberately and advisedly for I am always amazed at the presumptiveness of some participants in my workshops who genuinely believe that they can penetrate and comprehend the psyche of another, especially another who is culturally a world away from their own. Sometimes the language of "growth," "change," or even "empowerment" is used to convey that presumptiveness. But such careless use of language should remind us how difficult understanding others really can be.

Some brief examples will help illustrate this point. In her field research with a group of Eskimo, Jean Briggs (1986) discovered that any display of strong affect, or even discussion of feelings, was incomprehensible and unacceptable to her hosts. Hostility was never acknowledged and the discourse of anger was phrased in terms of protectiveness and great concern, as in a gentle advisory that "You can't come fishing with me because you'll hurt yourself on the sharp rocks" (Briggs 1986:39). Kleinman (1982) describes Chinese experiences of depression, usually somatized and expressed as vague physical complaints. Discussing Indonesians, Geertz (1975:49) says they seek an "inner world of stilled emotions" that, following a geographical metaphor, is like a flattened plane rather than variable and contoured hills and valleys. Csikszentmihalyi (1975, 1982) has identified a "new" emotion, one that is related to total mental concentration and that temporarily dissolves the boundaries between self and activity. What he calls "optimal experience" (Csikszentmihalyi and Csikszentmihalyi 1988) may be something all people can cultivate but few bother to label or describe. Cultures that value optimal experience will develop a vocabulary and explanatory apparatus to account for it; others will ignore it or treat it as an individual peculiarity. In either case, the point is that emotions, like language, are constructed by and responsive to situations. Emotions are cultural, temporal, geographical, and contingent, never something inevitable, universal, or natural.

One could usefully think about emotion, then, as a sociocultural as well as a psychodynamic event, specifically as a kind of "discourse" that is both pragmatic and communicative. It is pragmatic because it is a commentary about the relationships that prevail (or ought to) in certain circumstances. Emotional discourse can be seen as a form of behavior that makes an assertion about the state of the world and one's place in it. In that sense, it is a profound inner or psychological event and an ideological statement as well. Emotional discourse is also communicative. It challenges an audience to affirm or deny the appropriateness of the sufferer's current state of being. Emotional behavior may be verbal or nonverbal, but it always represents commentary within a community of those who understand the messages. It can only be prudent, then, for the cultural outsider to try to understand what that commentary is about. Attempting to mimic the inner state of another through a display of cultivated empathy, without knowing the pragmatic basis or the communicative codes of that experience, is not helpful and probably not possible.

STEP III: INDIVIDUALIZING THE CLIENT WITHIN CONTEXT

All that I have said so far about the ethnography of problem resolution should make clear that the individual exists within a cultural matrix, and the idea of the individual solely and purely as a unique entity makes no sense at all. The insistence, which I sometimes hear from social workers, that individualizing the client means stripping away all social or cultural "incidentals" in order to focus on the person as person is exactly comparable to a view in biomedicine that healing only involves repair of the patient's hydraulic, molecular, or biomechanical systems. It would be like filling a cavity in a tooth but ignoring the patient's eating and brushing habits. That model may work in some areas of medicine, but in human services individuals must be seen as more than damaged psychological mechanisms. Their complexity, and the complexity of their needs, derives precisely from the fact that both clients and professional helpers swim in their own cultural pond, and neither has much experience outside of it. Effectiveness in helping others must take experiential differences fully into account. How, then, can we begin individualizing others within a cultural context, one that for them is familiar but to us is a mystery?

A technique for doing this has emerged over the past decade or two and has become more common in cross-cultural training. But the way it is used is not always effective, partly because it is a variant of the trait list approach to ethnicity. To date, its most explicit use is in health care, especially nursing, although it appears in social services training as well.

Typically, cross-cultural training is built around lists of values, preferences, and cultural norms intended to be representative of specific ethnic groups. The lists are variously called profiles, fact files, cultural checklists, and other names suggestive of an abbreviated introduction to a community. Disclaimers about stereotyping, internal group diversity, and sensitivity to individual needs are usually included.

One example, better than most, is *Culture & Nursing Care: A Pocket Guide* (Lipson, Dibble, and Minarik 1996). It introduces cultural competence for nurses, states the limitations of the information contained in the guide's chapters, offers useful suggestions for working with an interpreter, and supplies general tips on conversational styles, eye contact, body touch, personal space, and time awareness. This is followed by 23 chapters, each on one ethnic group, of about ten pages in length. The chapters are simply lists of bulleted items, each item followed by a two- or three-sentence paragraph. Short bibliographies are included. Topics covered include history, communication styles, food preferences, symptom management, birth rituals and care, death rituals, family relationships, religious concerns, illness beliefs, and health practices. The chapters are prepared by one or more members of the groups described in the lists.

Two additional examples, ones with considerably more detail, are *Cross Cultural Caring, a Handbook for Health Professionals in Western Canada* (Waxler-Morrison, Anderson, and Richardson 1990) and *Caring for Patients from Different Cultures, Case Studies from American Hospitals* (Galanti 1991). Both are competent presentations, and the former is especially strong in its detailed case studies and ethnographic richness. It is not hard to imagine that nurses working with multicultural patients and, at the same time, absorbing the information offered by these and similar titles ought to feel well prepared for effective cross-cultural service. Yet some are beginning to suggest that that is not always the case and that overview type guides to cultural differences have limited usefulness and, worse, may even be counterproductive. What is the problem?

Working with focus groups at a London hospice serving families from the West Indies, Africa, the Middle East, and Pakistan and India, Yasmin Gunaratnam (1997) identified three areas where cultural checklists impeded real cultural sensitivity and performance. First, in "the factfile approach" as she calls it, professionals are admonished to learn to "read" cultural signals from their patients so they can respond "appropriately." Culture is viewed by the nurses as a "constant," something free standing and composed of discrete "things" that patients do or say. They express distinctive values through their actions and are seen by staff as carriers or exemplars of those values.

This "values" approach is quite old, in both the health and social services literature, and one can still see an occasional reference to Kluckhohn and Strodtbeck (1961) as the source. But, on the face of it, it is a fairly wooden concept of multiculturalism. All disclaimers aside, it still carries a potential for stereotyping. In addition, its practical limitation is that it promotes a checklist mentality as a way of responding to others: if patients of culture X, Y, or Z prefer certain foods, then making those foods available is multicultural because it meets their needs. The rhetoric of "needs," which is heavy in the cross-cultural service literature, is a substitute for the more difficult task of entering subjectively and practically into the lived experience of people in communities other than our own. Instead of the genuine empathy and shared knowledge that comes with comparative understanding, the checklist view of a culture directs us to cultivate task-centered competencies, our own menu of what we are willing or able to do. While there is nothing wrong with ensuring that dying people have the kinds of foods they like, and certainly nothing wrong with learning to say the things they appreciate rather than those they don't, such consideration is not cultural competence. Simply meeting needs tells us little about why the needs exist in the first place and less about the subjective realities behind them.

The second limitation, then, is that checklists offer no clue to the experiences and subjectivity of others. They imply that we are all cultural actors programmed to speak our lines and play our parts exactly as scripted and, further, that the script itself is an authentic and authoritative representation of a culture. There are several problems in this. One has to do with the notion of "authenticity," whether or not there is a singular and "true" form of a culture that everyone accepts as final. If that is so, it implies that there are also those who can speak authoritatively for everyone else. Yet few modern cultures, and especially those of immigrant origins, are so homogenous that one or two people can claim an authoritative role. Second, all cultures now are fractioned and factioned. One of the features of postmodernity is that even in closed communities people argue and struggle among themselves over whose behavior is consistent with authentic traditions and who has compromised, assimilated, or otherwise made themselves marginal to the rest of the group. These contests routinely challenge generational and gendered standards of propriety, often centering on language (what to speak at home and what in public), religion (how and even whether to observe), food preferences, traditional dress, parental control of children, the powerful American commitment to personal freedom and choice, expressive styles in speech and entertainment, and most especially choice of marriage partner. These contests may emerge in daily routines and allocations of responsibility and obligation. They are almost inevitable, dramatically so, in moments of crisis. One of the hospice nurses in Gunaratnam's focus groups is quoted as saying:

He was a young man who wanted to die in the hospice…and the friends he had said he should go home to die…. And I would always go with the patient choice, but I mean, it was partly difficult because sometimes he wasn't conscious to say that. But also feeling…that it was quite hard to disagree with these people who perceived themselves as being extremely helpful and knowing something that I didn't know. (1997:178)

In a second example, a nurse told Gunaratnam of an African woman who did not want her body returned to Africa, as tradition dictated, because she preferred the money be used for her children instead. Frustrated, the nurse added, "But the culture says the body must go back and so there's a huge wrangle going on within the family now, and the men will win because the men in the family always get their say. Um, but I was thinking how it touches me as a worker" (1997:178).

These statements—the nurses' perceptions of others "knowing something that I didn't know" and the emotional ambiguity of "how it touches me as a worker"—point directly to the limitations of checklist knowledge. Lists fail, Gunaratnam declares, because they "are constructed around the benign description of cultural and religious practices, [and] they overwhelmingly neglect to address such ambivalences and power relations which criss-cross and continually destabilise cultural practices" (1997:179). It is exactly that complexity with its "destabilizing" of cultural practices—what postmodernists call the "contested" nature of contemporary experience—that the effective multicultural professional needs most to know. Simplified lists of cultural prescriptions won't get us there.

A third limitation is that a listing of cultural features, the "baggage" that everyone brings with them when they see a professional, ignores the power dimensions of all service relationships. One of these dimensions is control, something that is always part of the professional's work site. Among other things, power involves expected codes of conduct, including the decorum of the service provider's setting, the privileging of professional recommendations, and compliance by the help recipient. Yet in Gunaratman's experience, the workers in the hospice, being properly British, had a hard time with the overt and sometimes noisy expressions of grief of their patient's families. Repeatedly, they used the words "raw" and "rawly" to describe extended wailing or a dramatic collapse to the floor. Said one, "And that is very frightening if it's different from what, what you perceive as normal" (1997:182). What is normal, apparently, and not frightening is control of the ward and racializing of its space so that those who want to grieve in foreign, exuberant ways are encouraged to do it at home.

So how can the limitations of checklist ethnicity be overcome? The lists I have discussed here all have one significant deficiency that leaves out you and me as participants in a relationship. They describe someone else's culture, the culture of an "other," as though we weren't there. They offer "insider tips," standing in well-regimented isolation and bulleted on the page. They are not wrong in and of themselves, but they miss the point that comparative understanding of a lived culture emerges only when we talk seriously one on one, make inferences about potential contrasts in our experiences, articulate those inferences, and test them against what others say in reply. It can't work any other way. The nurse who thought that the way some families grieve was "frightening" didn't need a cultural sensitivity workshop. He or she needed to talk with someone from the patient's community to learn about their norms for expressing grief, why the "frightening" emotional style was important to them, and how they would feel if they could not observe what they saw as honest and respectful. But, more than that, the nurses needed to discuss among themselves what their notions of the decorum of the ward and of British styles of grieving suggested about their authority vis-á-vis patients. That could lead to some useful discussions about hospice procedures that would be helpful to staff and patients alike.

The "selected cultural contrasts" in each of the following chapters have to be read in light of these criticisms. What are offered are *contrasts*, not traits. As contrasts, they do not nail down definitive features for any category of people, and if you read them as trait lists they will not get you very far. Rather, they point to areas of possible differences that may emerge in service encounters. In addition, the contrasts are made with what are presumed to be Anglo American norms. That choice would be arbitrary (why not African American/Hispanic contrasts instead?) were it not for the fact of the political and economic dominance of the white middle class in virtually all public policy, and Anglo dominance in the histories and ideologies of most service professions, including social work and health care. The best use of these lists is not as guides to specific cultural features but as a stimuli to discussions, in classes, in offices, and with clients, about where contrasts of substance really lie and how, together, we can do something useful with them.

STEP IV: CULTURAL COMPETENCE AND POWER

Clearly, individuals who have strong negative feelings about race should not be advising and counseling those who are different from themselves. Even though the Archie Bunker syndrome is now recognizable and generally considered tasteless, it is an unfortunate fact that racism persists as a malevolent and pervasive feature of American life. But what of those who do not consider themselves racists, who want to eliminate racism from their own lives and workplaces, and yet are perplexed by their inability to communicate effectively in cross-cultural encounters? And what of systemic power differentials, the hierarchical arrangements of the larger society that create inequalities of race, gender, and language to begin with?

Distressing as it is, it is not uncommon for individuals of genuine goodwill and honest intent to have difficulty communicating across racial and cultural boundaries. I want to suggest several reasons why that is so, reasons that come down to our difficulties with understanding power and the differential access to privilege that power represents. In a discussion of this problem in relations between black clients and white therapists, Jones and Seagull (1977) identify what they see as one important difficulty. As most social workers know, countertransference is projection onto the client of the therapist's feelings and experiences from previous relationships. These feelings may have resulted from prior frustrations or from a lifelong pattern of dislike of certain peoples. In the service encounter, they become part of the dynamics of the event and may be difficult to mask or control. Members of minority communities, usually more sensitive to the nuances of cross-racial transactions than many whites appreciate, quickly recognize countertransference when it is occurring, and most certainly have their own terms for describing it. Whites who do not understand that often become defensive, tentative, even hostile. Neither client nor therapist is anxious to continue the relationship any longer than necessary. This extreme individualizing of ambiguous feelings about power and difference is usually difficult to resolve and almost always a barrier to the comparative understanding of those we serve advocated here.

A second problem is guilt. Guilt is the response of social workers who, perhaps too anxious to "do right" for historically "wronged" people, overreact or overidentify with a client's problems. Zealousness, moral crusading, and ingratiation become substitutes for the reality testing that ethnic competence requires, and they limit the worker's potential effectiveness. A rhetoric of "concern" too often repeated, great shows of sympathy, and an "us against them" mentality are symptomatic of the problem. As in the case of countertransference, minority individuals are usually more sensitive to this overreaction than many whites realize. They often perceive it (correctly so, in my view) as patronizing, and they dismiss it. More importantly, it puts an agenda of expiation ahead of the process of learning about cultural differences. It becomes another impediment to the development of a genuinely helpful cross-cultural relationship.

The explicit need for control is a third area of difficulty. As I indicated in the discussion of cross-cultural interviewing (Chapter 4), managing the interview is viewed in the profession as one indication of the social worker's skill. Yet in cross-cultural work, the exercise of control is very complex. The line between control as therapeutic guidance and control as dominance is always problematic, whatever the worker's intentions. The issue is compounded by the client's own perceptions, stereotypes, and misinformation about the social worker, the agency, and service organizations generally.

It is the social worker, not the client, who will have to take the first steps in resolving these difficulties, and that is not easily done. Part of the effort involves self-knowledge and fairly explicit clarification of one's own values and desires. Knowledge of the culture of one's clients, and particularly of the hidden and quiet sources of their community's strengths, is also important. Perhaps part of the effort will require rethinking what "professionalism" means and how the values and practices of a professional subculture either help or confound relations with ethnic communities. If we can approach power that way, at least we can begin thinking about its reality in all cross-cultural encounters.

I have already suggested that service professions are a kind of culture and that service agencies, indeed, every office within a service agency, has its own local culture that more or less replicates that of the sponsoring organization. But these local service cultures have another dimension, which I will argue reproduces in localized form the relationship of the dominant society to specific ethnic groups. For example, the dominant, white, middle-class culture of America (and the many service organizations that function in it) can be thought of as a "host" society that contains within itself a large number of "guest" participants. Some of these "guests" came involuntarily, some were here before the first representatives of the host culture arrived, and some are desperately trying to get in through the host society's borders. But all have been engulfed, followed by varying efforts at absorption, dominance, and control.

STEP V: THINKING AND WORKING COMPARATIVELY

This host–guest metaphor can be a provocative one because in some ways service agencies and their personnel are always in host relationships with clients. The cultural formation of hosting tells us something about the implicit cultural features of the dominant group and the people who function as service providers in it. Citing the work of Boekestijn (1984), Furnham and Bochner (1989:230) see the following as some of the important cultural features of host relationships in cross-cultural encounters.

1. Hosts have rules of *territoriality* or "turf." Some of these rules involve competition among agencies for "ownership" of clients or public issues. Turf also involves protective routines and policies that exclude clients and patients from full knowledge of what the agency can or is willing to do for them. These policies and routines, especially those that are in some sense "unspoken," mark the territorial limits of the host agency's culture.

2. Hosts have multiple definitions of their clients. Official definitions are maintained in statutes and administrative directives. Unofficial ones, much richer and more varied, are maintained in shared understandings embedded in agency practice. These are the things that are commonly but privately discussed with co-workers during coffee breaks, between meetings, and in after-work gatherings.

3. Hosts vary in their commitment to their work, their profession, and even the mandate of their agency. Similarly, agency administrators vary in the kinds of reinforcement they give staff. These *identity issues* combine to create agency "morale," an elusive quality that nevertheless translates into service to clients.

4. Hosts vary in their expressions of ethnocentrism or intolerance. Guest outsiders are always sensitive to power differentials, which may be expressed subtly or overtly, by legal mandate or quiet implication. Mechanisms of control are sometimes so routine they are not visible to those who use and rely on them. Suggestions that control may be a response to racial, cultural, linguistic, or class differences often meet with sharp denials.

5. Hosts vary in their willingness to spend the necessary time to work with those who are "hard to reach." Because continuous interaction with others who are not like oneself is physically and psychologically demanding, fatigue is a factor. How well agencies help their workers cope with that fatigue, and how regularly they acknowledge the best efforts of their staff, is an additional measure of an organization's capacity and suitability for working with diverse clients.

None of these five aspects of agency culture is more important than any other, and all must be considered when thinking about how a professional or agency culture responds to the challenge that those who are "different" always represent. But examination of self and agency, as important as that is, cannot be the sole focus when we are considering issues of power. One of the criticisms commonly made of the social service profession and of cultural awareness approaches to ethnicity is that they ignore structural inequalities in the larger society. For example, McMahon and Allen-Meares (1992) reviewed 117 articles appearing in a ten-year run of four major journals, *Social Service Review, Social Casework, Child Welfare,* and *Social Work.* They wanted to assess how the literature deals with both individual and institutional racism. Their conclusion, not very flattering, was that "the literature portrays the social work profession as naive and superficial in its antiracist practice.... [O]ne of the main remedies proposed for the racism minorities suffer focuses, according to the literature, on *mere change in the awareness of social workers*" (1992:537, my italics).

Similarly, Longres (1991) holds that cultural models of ethnic-sensitive practice may be useful for work among immigrants and refugees, people whose social and historical backgrounds are obviously different from those of most Americans. But for individuals who are members of a long-standing minority group, issues of differential privilege, opportunity, and life chances are more important. He adds that, "If social workers are to be helpful, they need to spend less time thinking about differences in norms and values and more time in thinking about how to operate in encounters between high and low status people. Helping minority clients means changing stratification systems" (1991:55).

I am in basic agreement with these criticisms, but with this qualification. To the extent that cultural differences are seen only as differences in "norms and values," as Longres says, then cultural awareness will never be much more than an adventure into quaint customs and someone else's fun cuisine. The "norms and values" approach is the most superficial one I can imagine, but it is exactly the "safe" and narrow perspective that has driven cross-cultural thinking in social services and its research literature. McMahon and Allen-Meares are right: that kind of cultural awareness is incredibly naive, even damaging, because it distances people from their clients by making the latter objects of exotic otherness. It should be obvious that that is not what I advocate here. Yet there is much more that separates people than their status, be it high or low. Any culture is more than its hierarchical dimensions, and whatever stratification may exist, along lines of race, language, gender, or age, flows from a shared world view of what is acceptable and what is not. We cannot divorce norms and values from power, nor can we limit ourselves to thinking about one at the expense of the other. They always work in tandem.

Genuine cultural awareness must include a comparative, self-critical understanding of how, as a professional, one participates in a system of differential privilege and power (Gutiérrez 1990). The host–guest analogy identifies some of the ways hosts (social workers, nurses, doctors, teachers) are in a position to take advantage of those who need their services. The transactional view of ethnicity discussed earlier requires the social worker to see that helping services, "delivered" by a bureaucratic system, are never free of the encumbrances of privilege. Professionals who believe that displays of empathy or cultural "understanding" can overcome inherent inequalities delude themselves. When we see how the professional culture of an agency or an office includes the cultural meanings assigned to power, and their enactment in service relationships, we will be led directly into the heart of inequality, its justifications, and its rationale. Real cultural awareness exposes privilege and may deprive the comfortable of some of their sense of ease.

GETTING FROM HERE TO THERE

Is there a "fast track" for cross-cultural learning? Sadly, no. But there are ways to speed it up. The skilled use of language, especially in ethnographic interviewing, is one way of adding efficiencies to our work. Two more are important to mention: achieving small wins on a day-by-day basis, and turning to the right kind of people when expertise is needed.

I wish I could take credit for this idea of small wins, but it belongs to psychologist Karl Weick (1984). He analyzed strategies of social and personal change and found that small wins, not hard-fought battles against major foes, are more likely to lead to changes of real consequence. Modesty and quiet persistence often succeed. Heroic stands are gestures, and mostly only that. He cites several interesting examples of the principle, which I paraphrase here.

Over the last twenty years, the title "Ms." has come into common English usage. That is a direct result of feminist cultural lobbying spearheaded by the editors of the magazine of the same name. It is an impressive achievement because languages are normally resistant to change. The hope of the proponents was that a new language form, such as a term for address, would lead to new ways of thinking about gender. Yet the same activists failed to secure passage of the Equal Rights Amendment. That we should ignore marital status in forms of address now seems reasonable to most of us. But changing the United States Constitution, for any reason, is something monumental and even alarming for many. The Equal Rights Amendment, aside from its merits, was truly a grand gesture, and seems for now to be dead. But the use of "Ms." is now so common it is hardly noticeable.

Alcoholics Anonymous, and the many spin-off support groups that have adopted its model, does not promise its members a permanent cure. Instead, it asks that they follow a prescribed regimen one day at a time and, sometimes, for just a few hours at a time. In new or difficult cases, they ask for adherence only for as long as it takes to make a phone call for help. The AA time horizon for measuring success can be incredibly short, yet many people have gone for years without alcohol. Changes are incremental, not dramatic, and the ideology of AA says that is the way it must be.

Compared to passage of the ERA, the general use of "Ms." was a small win and, in time, we may hear "Mrs. (followed by husband's first and last name)" only in reruns of 1950s sitcoms. That may or may not change the world fundamentally but it is a change. So is avoiding a drink, one hour and one day at a time, especially in a culture that glamorizes youth, sex appeal, and links them both to alcohol consumption.

Weick defines a small win as "a concrete, complete, implemented outcome of moderate importance"; small wins are "controllable opportunities that produce visible results" (1984:43). More important, "Small wins provide information that facilitates learning and adaptation. Small wins are like miniature experiments that test implicit theories about resistance and opportunity and uncover both resources and barriers that were invisible before the situation was stirred up" (1984:44).

Small wins are always opportunistic, but they are *not* accidental. The people who get small wins have prepared themselves; they have both the mind-set and skills to take advantage of an occasion. They also know that successive small changes are more likely to result in long-term, bigger changes. Goals for change that are too easy or too hard, that do not build on incrementalism, and that do not have a small but noticeable effect, usually have no force.

In addition, small wins are often small pleasures, even when discomfort is present, because they create positive (even comic) relief in chaotic or uncontrollable situations. They define the structure of hope by creating a base for the next win, even if it is only a repetition of the last one, something the AA member would accept as central to recovering sobriety.

Seeking small wins, while a useful strategy in itself, is not enough for developing real cross-cultural interviewing and intervention skills. We think about service to clients in terms of cultural context, and we need to think about that in training as well. What kinds of contexts are most likely to generate high-quality professional learning? What contexts trivialize and even defeat real learning?

My second suggestion is that efficient, effective learning generally occurs when two things happen. First, individuals are assigned as apprentices to a person with recognized and validated skills in an area of mutual interest. The "master" in this master–apprentice relationship is qualified not by university degrees or an accumulation of workshop certificates but by "recognized and validated skills." Only that qualifies someone as an "expert." Who experts might be, what it is that they know, and how they can meet the learning needs of apprentices ought to be the only matters of importance.

Second, small groups of learners ought to focus on a limited number of issues and systematically review their success as they go along. (Small wins again.) Review should be done with the expert but also by the learners among themselves, conferring on a regular basis in a systematic way. That helps build learning into the job routine, rather than separating the occasions for learning from daily activities. Experts are important but, in my view, most people can effectively direct their own learning much of the time if it is clear that that is one of their responsibilities and that there are personal and professional benefits in doing so. Calling on experts for help in starting the process and for occasional consultations may be all that is needed from outsiders and specialists. Experts are in a position to validate the progress that has been made and they can legitimize the efforts of individual participants. They usually have useful knowledge to impart, but real change comes because of committed engagement by students and trainees working on issues among themselves.

Learning in a community of apprentices, be that the community of an agency, an office, or a classroom, is quite different from workshop-style training and it produces two effects that the usual kinds of staff training do not. First, apprenticeship learning creates an institutional memory about "how cases like X, Y, and Z are handled in our organization." That is an important administrative concern, especially when turnover of agency personnel is high.

Second, it institutionalizes a work style that generates enthusiasm for skills improvement. That is less likely to happen when workers take released time to go to a distant training site, returning to a job that continues just as it always has. For training "to take," to produce agency and client benefits, it must be part of work routines and everyone has to feel that it enhances their professional performance.

This model has been called "situated learning" by Lave and Wenger (1991). It emphasizes participation in expertly guided performances, not episodic accumulation of facts and skills that have no clear relationship to work tasks. Situated learning has a number of features that distinguish it from traditional classroom education and the cycle of in-service workshops that most of us have experienced (and endured) for most of our student and professional careers.

First, situated learning is democratically "decentered." It is not the property of experts and authorities but is the *experience* of the learning community. Lived learning experiences are what count, not lectures, video tapes, or contrived "role plays." Real learning that has detectable results is "embedded"; it is part of routine job assignments and is done every day. One advantage to thinking of learning as a job activity rather than as something done at a pleasant retreat far from the office is that it encourages a holistic view of what is really going on. One can see more clearly, through the tasks and the learning done with co-workers, the strengths and limits of an agency's goals and capabilities; the real skills of colleagues; the real needs of the community served; and clients' responses to small changes in intervention and practice.

A second and closely related point is that situated learning is always participatory. The "learning curriculum is a field of learning resources in everyday practice *viewed from the perspective of learners*" (Lave and Wenger 1991:97). That means that learning is necessarily opportunistic rather than logically sequential. Writing in the *Journal of Social Work Education*, Nakanishi and Rittner (1992) put it nicely:

> *Intercultural learning is never linear or orderly. It is a process that occurs in complex ways with increasing levels of* cultural self-knowledge *as an integral part of understanding how responses to culturally different persons are manifested.* (1992:29)

Only in formally organized classrooms and workshops is education thought of as a linear progression with a beginning, middle, and end. Everywhere else, when each one of us first learned to walk, talk, kiss, or drive a car, learning was opportunistic. Real learning happens when we have need for it. Lectures, training films, and role plays are at best anemic substitutes. They have their uses but by themselves they will never lead anyone to real cultural awareness or ethnic competence.

Third, decentered learning in a community of participation is *transparent*. Informed, critical, self-reflection on our responses to others, especially in challenging situations, is the bedrock of situated learning. That is far, far different from the generic "skills" and heightened "cultural awareness" so often promoted in lectures and training seminars. Through carefully examined cases in which we are a participant, we really begin to see the larger dimensions of our professional activity: the strengths and weakness of the delivery system; the fragility and complexity of human beings; and our personal effectiveness in assisting others. As learning proceeds in an experiential community, hidden personal and institutional agendas are harder to conceal because each learner grows "savvy," not only about how the service system really works but how client communities work as well. That kind of learning inevitably leads to professional maturity and competence.

Fourth, the experiential "discourse of practice," as Lave and Wenger call it, shifts our attention from the abstract to the concrete. We no longer work with "dysfunction families" or "co-dependent spouses." Instead our concern is with how members of the Jones family are managing violence or how the elderly Smiths are complying with a visiting nurse's suggestions for regular exercise and a better diet. In situated learning, office talk and folklore are less about the presumed characteristics of people in community X and more about stories of how things were done with specific clients having particular needs.

But more than just stories, in this model case accounts are used for explicit, systematic comparisons of those times when an intervention worked, those when it did not, and the reasons why. For case discussions to be more than office gossip, they must be analyzed in comparative terms, understood as Weick's "miniature experiments." Only then can the apparent mysteriousness of good cross-cultural intervention be made explicit and a piece of well-tested practice.

If this idea of "situated learning" sounds wildly idealistic, something hatched by an academic who seems innocent of the "real world" of service agencies, their bureaucracies, budget struggles, office politics, and angry clients, then let me put it in a context that ought to be familiar. What I have described here, following the suggestions of Lave and Wenger, is exactly what makes Alcoholics Anonymous and many other multiple-step, self-help, and group-support programs successful. They could never have succeeded any other way.

What AA pioneered was apprenticeship learning for people in trouble. In that model, newcomers were given access to full participation through "old timers" (the "experts") who initiated them into a relearning process. The newcomers learned as apprentices always do, one day at a time, opportunistically, with democratic review and consultation on specific, individual cases. An important part of their relearning was adopting a new style of discourse: a new vocabulary, new metaphors of affliction, and new stories illustrating their struggle, all told and retold publicly. No one was allowed secrets, the learning community was transparent, and the warts and strengths of everyone were revealed. From that kind of experience, new identities emerged and were maintained because lifelong relearning about alcohol control is what the community is about. Finally, the best recommendation that could be made for the method is that for many people, it works. It is not perfect but it is better than a lot of the alternatives.

Wins in learning most often occur in a community of practice, where committed people work together over a period of time and where cooperation and enthusiasm are institutionalized. This contrasts markedly with the usual methods for teaching skills in social services with their dependence on guest experts invited for one-shot presentations at staffings and workshops. Some states mandate a set number of hours for attendance at this kind of training, apparently in the hope that skilled workers will emerge, fired with eagerness and newly discovered capability. It is sometimes called a "training the trainers" model, the newly converted sent out to win over co-workers. But it is still a top-down approach and I seriously doubt its effectiveness, even though I have taught in many workshops and will probably do more. Its limitations are of two kinds.

First, in traditional methods of training the emphasis is on the guest presenter and the presenter's agenda, as though the trainees had little to offer. The trainer hopes to say something relevant; the trainees hope they will not be bored. Second, there are few opportunities for extended, deliberative engagement with other professionals, a condition that real cross-cultural learning requires. Time is given instead to role plays, responding to videos, and various "sensitizing" and self-disclosure activities. These are not bad in themselves, but they aren't very effective because they have little or no long-term consequence.

What is needed are not more workshops but an entirely different division of labor, one in which learning rather than training is the goal, and where a learning curriculum rather than a training curriculum is stressed. The difference between these is really very simple: learning begins with a small community of those who need and want to upgrade their capabilities. They are guided by someone who takes account of their experiences and limitations and helps move them toward a group-selected goal. The "learning effect" is the apprentice's progressive ability to make sense of specific cases and to demonstrate more complex understanding in work with increasingly difficult ones. Learning this way is *efficient*, both in a time management and administrative sense, because knowledge is always additive to what one already knows and new effort goes to acquiring only what one needs, on a case-by-case basis.

Training, by contrast, is hierarchical and authoritative, designed to transmit great principles and keen insights to the less knowledgeable, so that they may hear and go do likewise. It assumes that what the expert offers is identical to what learners need to know. Training is usually decontextualized, offering something for everyone, and it is long on generalities. It is not surprising, then, that training workshop evaluations stress the presenter's performance, not that of the learning community. How well participants "liked" the instructor and his or her teaching style is the measure of success, not whether new skills were acquired, or specifics on how they will be used on the job.

Small wins and the right kind of experts, linked in highly focused and administratively supported communities of learner-practitioners, could go a long way toward building the kind of cross-cultural effectiveness we all desire. Does that seem a bit utopian? It certainly does. All the more reason for us to review current practice and imagine what we would like it to become.

AMERICAN ETHNICITY

The next four chapters are overviews of African America, Asian America, Native or First America, and Spanish-speaking America. The rationale for this grouping is not particularly logical; it is simply an artifact of American history and, in the current political climate, reflects how we generally talk about race and ethnicity.

A friend who is a medical anthropologist, Dr. Sharyne Thornton, has used previous editions of this book in her teaching and she once suggested, only somewhat jokingly, that the categories represented by these ethnographic chapters are artificial but not meaningless. They are, she says, like the "five food groups." Not all starch is wheat, nor are all vegetables carrots, and what exists in nature are not food groups at all but individual wheat grains and carrot seedlings. Lumping them together as food and then splitting them off into distinctive "food groups" is our invention, not nature's. The chapter titles, then, are really a kind of sociological shorthand, devised in the past by people for whom these ways of lumping and dividing served a purpose. Of course, purposes change over time along with the meaning and importance of the labels. Given their ambiguities, then, why continue to refer to huge numbers of people this way?

First, I didn't choose the categories. Some existed well before any of us were born. Others have come into public consciousness more recently. But they all emerged from social, political, and bureaucratic struggles that are now part of our common history. They are categories of convenience, exploitation, enumeration, and celebration. Yet they are also important because they point to certain realities that are not always acknowledged, be they ancient cultural traditions once demeaned or brutalizing enslavement and labor endured over generations. We can't afford to lose that historical consciousness.

Second, each of the named categories serves a political interest. They have a constituency. Once federal and state governments started funding programs "aimed" at "targeted groups" (note the government's fondness for military metaphors), whole categories of people associated with diverse historical traditions became potential recipients for goods and services. They were the beneficiaries of "entitlements." (Only recently, with budgetary threats looming, have majority whites begun to notice that they too receive entitlements, lots of them.) Quite rightly, minority people care deeply about preserving what they have achieved through hard community organizing and American-style political lobbying. Ethnic consciousness is clearly more than traditions and values. It is also linked to power, political savvy, and struggles for a fairer share of the national bounty.

Finally, no assumptions are made here about the order of presentation. Suffice it to say that Native Americans were here first and may have been living in North America for 40,000 years before Columbus. Spanish colonizers occupied Florida, the Caribbean, Mexico, and the American Southwest well before the English and other Northern Europeans came along. Particularly in the Southwest and parts of California, Spanish communities were established and the people living there considered themselves long-time residents well before their land was incorporated by war into the current United States. Africans came to North America in bondage, almost with the first whites, and their fortunes have been intertwined with those of the dominant Euro-Americans from the beginning. Asians arrived later but were an "early" group in the sense that they joined whites in the pioneering of the western and Rocky Mountain states. As with African Americans, their lives were part of the white settlement of Native American–occupied lands. Each of these groups now has a lengthy and significant history in this country; they are no longer sojourners or recent arrivals.

FOLLOW-UP

1. Test Drive an Idea

Idea 1: Building Your Knowledge Base:
The Pros in the Office
The aim of the following activity is to help you clarify your own expectations about working with minority practitioners and clients—what you anticipate your knowledge and skill needs will be, and how you can expand your capabilities.

Before you can do this exercise, you need to arrange for a minority professional to meet with your group or class. The role of this professional is as a discussant, not a lecturer who will tell you what is right or wrong. Part of doing this exercise is locating the discussant, explaining to that person your learning needs, and clarifying how the person can assist you and others. Obviously, getting to that point is part of preparing yourself to work cross-culturally and it is much more than the logistics of simply arranging a meeting. So take your selection of someone seriously and think through the process and what you expect to learn from it. You may find some minority professionals who are willing to give their time to this, and some who are not. That is part of the learning curve, as well as the reality of race and ethnicity in America. They are busy professionals too and you will have to make a case for the importance of their commitment of time to your concerns.

This is a group discussion activity, with a minority professional available as a mentor, not a presentor. Someone needs to take the role of moderator and lead the discussion. Each participant is asked to respond to the statements below, either verbally or in written form. One rule is that everyone must take a stand of some kind. A polite "pass" on a given question is not acceptable because it defeats the goal of learning through honest engagement of the issue. Part of the moderator's job is to refuse to accept a "pass" and to encourage a response of some kind from everyone. There are no right or wrong answers, and each statement and individual reply are deserving of fair and open discussion.

Statements

a. It is generally best that clients and practitioners be of the same ethnic background if any successful counseling or therapy is to be transacted. Therefore, minority practitioners ought to assume primary responsibility for caseloads with ethnic minority clients, because they are better qualified to do so.

b. White practitioners experience fewer discontinuities between personal and professional values than do minority practitioners.

c. Learning the cultural values and norms of an ethnic minority client and having some facility in his or her language are absolutely necessary in providing services.

d. There are uniform, established procedures for learning counseling skills and for providing counseling services. These procedures should be taught and practiced without reference to the ethnicity of the social worker or client.

e. While cultural awareness training can provide important skills in handling a multi-ethnic client caseload, it is unrealistic to suppose that a white practitioner can do as well as a bicultural, bilingual practitioner in cross-cultural situations.

f. Minority professionals and dominant-group practitioners have different career paths, goals, and experiences. It is normal, therefore, for them to respond differently to the expectations of their jobs. Agency and personnel evaluations should take that into account.

g. While it is important for non-minority practitioners to work cooperatively with their minority colleagues, they should avoid interethnic counseling where they feel a lack of cultural knowledge about prospective clients.

h. Ethnic minority content should be widely dispersed in the social work curriculum, rather than concentrated in a few specialized courses or training programs.

Most minority professionals have special insights into the needs of the communities they serve. In addition, they are usually sensitive to the way social service organizations affect persons of minority background generally. What they know is "insider information," the emic perspective. White social workers can learn much from their minority colleagues if they choose to do so. This activity assumes you have the opportunity to meet with a minority professional to discuss his or her work. The questions listed below are examples of things that they might be asked. Other questions can and should be added to the list.

Relations with Clients of Minority Groups

a. What are the distinctive problems of the minority clients whom you see?

b. Are there things that minority clients might say to a minority worker that they would probably not tell a white social worker?

c. How do they describe these things to you? Is there any special language or terminology they use?

d. What do clients expect you as a minority professional to understand intuitively about them and their needs?

e. What do you think clients look for in you that they would not expect in a white social worker?

f. Are there any distinctive advantages that you as a minority professional have with your clients?

Relations with White Social Workers

a. In the relations of white social workers with minority clients, as you have seen them, is there anything that troubles you?

b. In your professional relations with white social workers, is there anything that troubles you? How could white social workers be more supportive of you as a minority professional?

c. What do you think white social workers could do or should know if they want to work more effectively with minority clients?

d. If a new social worker were assigned to your agency tomorrow, one who had never worked with minority clients before, and your task was to spend the day getting this worker started, specifically what would you do, and what would you want him or her to know by the end of the day?

Role of Education

a. What in your formal or informal education best prepared you for working with minority clients?

b. What else would have helped?

c. How do you keep up with research and other literature on minority communities and clients? What sources are important to you?

d. What advice would you give to a class of aspiring minority social work students?

Agency and Policy

a. Can you describe instances where you felt the needs of your clients were in conflict with the kind of services offered by your agency, or in conflict with its policies?

b. Can you give an instance where you felt that your agency had failed a minority client? Why do you think that happened?

c. If you could restructure your office, program, or the personnel in it to better serve minority clients, what would you do?

d. What are some of the treatment plans or intervention strategies most commonly used in the agency? Describe how an intervention plan is developed.

e. Are there any significant ways that these plans differ from those of other minority agencies or from those of agencies serving largely white clients?

f. Do the concerns that clients bring to the agency and the ways staff deal with them suggest norms or values that are typical of the client community? Can these be defined and described?

Adjusting to a New Agency

a. Are there some common errors of assessment, diagnosis, or treatment that a visitor or social worker unfamiliar with the agency or its clients might make? Can you describe an example?

b. Are there any special communication techniques or skills that a visitor or new social worker should know about?

c. Are there any special words or phrases used by clients or staff members that might have a special meaning in the agency or the community? If so, list some and define them.

Idea 2: Building Your Knowledge Base:
Visiting a Minority Agency

There are many minority-oriented and -operated social service agencies, and their number is growing. They serve every ethnic group and deal with most of the needs handled by professionals in other agencies. But they often have a special tone that sets them apart from more established organizations. Part of that is due to the backgrounds of the clients and social workers, and the distinctive ways in which they interact. Frequently, minority agencies work to emulate in their services some of the cultural characteristics of the communities they serve. They usually do this under serious financial limitations, limitations which are disruptive but which also increase the sense of urgency and importance about the work they do.

A visit to a minority social service agency can be an illuminating experience, not only for social work students but also for established professionals. I used the list of questions and statements below in a study in which white social workers made visits to minority agencies (Green and Wilson 1983). The list was used for training purposes, and it suggests some of the things that social workers can ask about and look for as participant observers.

A word of caution: for an activity like this, the staff of a minority agency must be approached with all the sensitivity that would be involved in any effort to enter an unfamiliar community. Minority professionals are overworked and underpaid, and they get more requests from whites for "resource" assistance than they can reasonably fulfill. White workers who are negotiating informational visits need to make clear what benefits, if any, will accrue to minority agencies for the time and effort they invest.

General Background

a. What is the recent history of minority social service organizations of this type in your area? How and when were they established, and what do they do?

b. What kind of training and experience is common for staff members in agencies of this type?

c. What kinds of relationships do minority agencies have with one another, with large state organizations, and with county and city organizations? What benefits derive from those relationships?

Working with Clients in Minority and Ethnic Group Agencies

a. What are some of the common problems or complaints that are brought by clients to the agency?

b. In making an assessment or diagnosis of some of these issues, what kinds of questions do staff members ask their clients? Are there questions you might not have thought of yourself? Give some examples.

c. Do staff members feel that any of their clients' needs are related to class or to the cultural characteristics of their community? If so, describe what these might be.

Idea 3: Building Your Knowledge Base: Mapping Your Service Area

This is an ideal exercise for beginning the work of communal learning, although it is really more of a long-term project than an exercise in the usual sense. It can be done in classes, agencies, and individually. It systematically explores the community an agency might serve and it can lead to specific agency benefits, especially where planning and community relations are involved. The various elements of this activity, listed below, could be assigned to "task forces" in a class that could then develop them as term projects.

In describing the concept of social mapping, Cochrane notes that "poverty is not merely a matter of not having things or access to them; it is also a matter of how people behave in particular cultural contexts" (Cochrane 1979:37). Social mapping is a way of learning about those contexts.

The task for the learner is to identify a community for study and become familiar with some of its cultural features in a general sense. The community can be a geographically coherent one or one that is dispersed but within which people experience similar problems and have common concerns. An example of the former would be an ethnically distinct neighborhood and the latter a group of single parents in a large city. The exercise requires collection and study of appropriate documents, including maps and census material; review of whatever sociological and anthropological studies of the community (or ones like it) that can be found; and development of a file of information to be used in training other social workers who may have clients from the community in question.

Following Cochrane's outline, and adapting it to the needs of social service workers, the exercise involves the following steps:

a. Define the community of interest and identify all relevant statistical and demographic information. On a map, draw the boundaries of the group and show any subdivisions that may be appropriate. Special attention should be given to subdivisions that are emically significant within the community. These would include the vernacular names for regions of the community and the significance of those designations. In addition, identify what might be called "local knowledge." For example, what streets do people there consider safe or unsafe? Which neighborhoods are desirable for home ownership and which not? Where do those who are employed or upwardly mobile live, and those who are not? Where are older people concentrated, and younger people? What institutions serve the area and what are their reputations?

b. Describe the social organization of the community. Where are resources located, and who controls them? What are the leadership roles, formal and informal, and who occupies them? What types of organizations operate and who is in the important positions in each one? Certain values will probably attach to these organizations, and those values should be made as explicit as possible. Where there are important informal patterns, such as personal networks and cliques or factions, these should be identified and their significance described.

c. Describe the prevailing belief system in the community. What are the predominant values? In what kinds of symbols, ceremonies, or community events are they expressed? What variations on prevailing values are permitted, tolerated, or disallowed? Where particular values seem important to the kinds of problems often handled by human service workers, those values should be defined in detail. Their bearing on intervention activities and outcomes should be made explicit. Topics for values analysis are almost endless, but examples include male–female relations, parent–child relations, patterns of sharing and reciprocity, generational differences, the use of wealth, beliefs about the larger society, attitudes toward social services, and the like. The ethnic contrast tables in each of the community chapters are useful for defining areas of interest.

d. Patterns of change, historical and recent, should be described. How has the community in question evolved? What shifts in wealth or political power have occurred? Can these be expected to continue, and what are their implications for social and health services?

e. How members of the community utilize social services should be described. Alternative sources of aid should be noted, and community preferences as well as complaints made explicit. The relationship of wealth, values, and community organization to the use of services is always a complex matter.

To pursue this study agenda in detail is a major task, one that should be broken into discrete pieces and assigned to different individuals for research. But the resulting information can be invaluable as an inventory of the community served and its needs and concerns. All information collected should be stored in a systematic way so that it is always available for training and consulting purposes. It can also serve as a basis for staff meetings and for planning new or revised services and policies.

2. More on the Issues

- Case Studies: More Is Better

Practice-relevant case studies are in short supply in the social work literature, and those that exist tend more to "thin description" than to "thick description." Why case studies are important in all kinds of social work research and what they ought to include to make them useful to practitioners are topics convincingly discussed in Jane F. Gilgun, "A Case for Case Studies in Social Work Research," *Social Work* (39:371–380, 1994).

- Reflective Practice

In a thoughtful discussion of how people learn and how self-reflection on what we learn can lead to skills enhancement in social services, the authors suggest a model for social work training and education generally. It is applicable, however, to cross-cultural work as well. Catherine P. Papell and Louise Skolnik, "The Reflective Practitioner: a Contemporary Paradigm's Relevance for Social Work Education," *Journal of Social Work Education* (28:18–26, 1992).

A second article, also in the *Journal of Social Work Education,* suggests a striking analogy between the pain of child abuse and how service professionals might better understand the pain of some of their clients, including minority clients. It is another "thought piece" and should be read in conjuction with Papell and Skolnik. See Mary A. Rodwell and Adell Blankebaker, "Strategies for Developing Cross-Cultural Sensitivity: Wounding as Metaphor" (28:153–165, 1992).

6

AFRICAN AMERICANS, DIASPORA, AND SURVIVAL

In 1976, Alex Haley published his monumental work, *Roots*, a national best-seller that also became a popular television series. That event was more important than many Americans may have realized, for it was not about literary success or a television special alone. What Haley achieved was permanent installation of an African-centered perspective at the heart of our national discourse on race and ethnicity. He was the historical successor of all those who had argued that there is a distinctively African way of seeing the world, one preserved and elaborated by contemporary African Americans. Earlier voices had made similar claims but were rarely heard outside small academic and literary circles. Haley touched cultural sensibilities on a national scale, perhaps the first African American writer since Frederick Douglass to do so.

As is true of most ethnic groups, the African American community is diverse, and that diversity has important implications. Most blacks did not come to America by choice, as is well known. Less appreciated is the diversity of ethnic affiliations in Africa and, even under the harsh regime of slavery, the diversity of their communities and activities throughout the Old South. Although most Africans brought to America were involved with the operation of plantations, many "freemen" who had been manumitted by slave owners lived in urban areas where they worked as artisans and small-scale entrepreneurs. These urban-based individuals were the nucleus of a small but growing black middle class. The Civil War ended slavery and the plantation economy but did not change the poverty or racial discrimination that would affect the former slaves and freemen for generations to come.

In the late nineteenth century, blacks began migrating north in significant numbers, usually occupying the poorest sections of large cities such as Chicago, Detroit, Philadelphia, and New York. The work they found—usually in service and domestic occupations—was poorly paid, required few skills, and led to nothing better. Nevertheless, it was for many an improvement over the rural poverty, sharecropping, and Jim Crow racism they left behind. Most migrants who went north improved their circumstances economically and socially but always within the confines of continued discrimination. Not only a revived black middle class but a tiny economic elite appeared. Many members of the latter were of urban Southern origins and had been well established before they migrated north. They were familiar with the operations of the white economic and political world and worked carefully and skillfully in it. After World War I, whole sections of some northern cities evolved complex and socially diversified black communities with their own businesses, newspapers, service organizations, churches, and, in the style of the day, their own political machines. Undoubtedly the most notable of these was Harlem in New York City, which became famous in the 1920s for the cultural florescence known as the "Harlem Renaissance." The success of these northern black enclaves was a terrific magnet to many in the South and migration north became a symbol of upward social mobility.

The Depression of the 1930s undercut the economic vitality of many of these communities as unemployment reached massive proportions. Undercapitalized businesses failed, and underfunded community agencies could not cope with the level of need. The policies of the New Deal, however, established a new relationship between the African American community and the dominant white society. Legislation friendly to collective bargaining made union participation easier for black workers. Government agencies hired many individuals for white collar positions, establishing government employment as a career option and placing some in positions where they could direct relief programs to their own communities. Jobs in war industries and the desegregation of the military following World War II created new opportunities and also moved workers around the country to areas where they had not had a large historical presence, particularly in the West. Within a hundred years of the termination of slavery, African Americans were so geographically dispersed that they had become a national rather than a regional ethnic minority.

By 1986, African Americans were approximately 12 percent of the U.S. population. Median income was about half that of whites although there were substantial numbers of blacks at all income levels, including a few at the highest. The gap between white and African American incomes narrowed only slightly during the 1980s. Yet improvements in black educational and occupational achievements were significant in comparison to previous generations, and in most cities and towns with a sizable black population there was a well-established middle (and sometimes upper) class. African Americans can now be found in the same occupations pursued by whites. Most never come to the attention of social workers nor do they seek out the kinds of professional help social service agencies typically offer.

That is not true of another group of African Americans who, for a variety of reasons, are trapped in circumstances they may never escape and for whom social services of some kind may be needed on a short-term or even long-term basis. In an important book, they have been called by black sociologist William Julius Wilson (1987; 1996) "the truly disadvantaged," an "underclass" of extremely impoverished individuals and families concentrated in inner cities where they are effectively isolated. They are, according to Wilson, the victims of two historical trends. First, growing joblessness during the 1970s and 1980s separated people from the workforce and from the acquisition of workforce skills. These individuals now lack the educational and technical preparedness that would serve them when employment conditions improve. Second, this group has been isolated by the withdrawal of other blacks into working-class and middle-class black neighborhoods and sometimes into predominantly white areas. Those left behind are substantially different from the "inner city" black residents of twenty or thirty years ago; they are more impoverished and they are much more isolated. Wilson refers to this isolation as a "concentration effect," where people "not only infrequently interact with those individuals and families who have had a stable working history and have had little involvement with welfare and public assistance, they also seldom have sustained contact with friends or relatives in more stable areas of the city or the suburbs" (1987:60). Wilson argues that this isolation is a new phenomenon, one of the 1970s and 1980s, and not a legacy of the poverty of the rural South. We can better understand their position, as well as that of other African Americans, by briefly considering the values and institutions that have characterized the black experience generally.

"ROOTS" AND AFRICAN AMERICAN ETHNICITY

The "roots" phenomenon that Haley created led to searches for an ennobling ancestry by African Americans and by members of other ethnic groups, including many whites. Yet a public sense of historical legitimacy is not the same as understanding how that history bears on the problems and conflicts of contemporary life. Billingsley (1968) has provided a useful overview of the African past, one that puts history in a cultural context.

He notes that in West Africa, from which most of the slaves came, family life had great strength and was complex in ways not appreciated by Europeans. Marriage was not a private arrangement between individuals but a community event, one in which permanent relations between lineages and across villages were established. Those relations had important economic and political significance for the families involved. Consequently, marriage ceremonies were marked by extensive public rituals. These customs had the authority of centuries of tradition and were linked to highly elaborate theological systems and well-defined principles of family organization. In a lineage system traced through the male line, typical of some groups, a man, his sons, their wives, and their children all shared a living area under the senior male's authority.

But the organization of the slave trade and of the slave-based plantation economy in North and South America and the West Indies made it difficult if not impossible for enslaved Africans to maintain an uninterrupted and secure domestic life. There were various reasons for this. Men were enslaved more often than women because slavery was primarily a labor-supply system; more could be gained by having men rather than women working on plantations. Unlike slavery in Catholic-Iberian areas such as Brazil, colonizers in Protestant and English areas of settlement placed little value on the family life of slaves. Individuals had the status of chattel property and could be sold according to economic need and their owner's sentiments. Family relationships were seen by whites as an impediment to efficient plantation operations. Reproduction and child rearing were expenses most plantation owners wanted to avoid. In addition, a slave's life was short, rarely more than a decade in slavery during the early years of slave trading. Older or sick individuals were a liability to an estate, and few were given care of any kind. Almost none lived to old age.

Given these characteristics of the plantation economy, the opportunities for maintaining any kind of family were very limited. The most outstanding characteristic of the slave family was its lack of autonomy. Legal marriage did not exist, and the remembered African marriage rituals that might have been practiced were not tolerated by whites. Whereas some planters encouraged marriage among their slaves, others had little interest in the matter, and none would allow a marriage relationship to interfere with the sale and transfer of a slave. Frequently owners simply assigned specific men and women to share a dwelling, with or without a marriage ceremony. This was done in order to minimize time spent on courting activities and to preserve a measure of domestic peace in the slave cabins. When one partner to the relationship died or was sold to settle an owner's debts, another was supplied as a replacement. Slaves were viewed as units of labor and their personal preferences had little to do with how that labor was exploited.

Instability in family life was inevitable. Nevertheless, certain patterns did emerge. Men asserted domestic authority when they were able to do so and established close and affectionate ties to their spouses and children within the limits imposed by plantation life. Women were attentive both to their children and to their husbands, and all adults played important roles in instructing children in the etiquette of race relations and physical survival. Often these supportive functions were carried out within a monogamous, nuclear family unit. Where individual planters permitted, older persons and single adults shared quarters with a family, creating an extended family unit. Estate owners generally avoided involvement in domestic relations in the slave quarters unless issues of plantation economics were involved. (The important exception, of course, was the sexual license of white men with female slaves.) Consequently, a small but very limited measure of household control was possible, and men and women could exert their authority within this sphere.

This very limited autonomy was always threatened by the selling of individuals and the dispersal of family members over many estates. Marriages or stabilized mating relationships were often ended this way. Yet the sense of kin ties and obligation, so important in the African homeland, persisted. Vigorous efforts were made by both men and women to be reunited with spouses, children, and other persons regarded as family friends or members. Consequently, kinship linkages and the sentiments of kinship often spanned several plantations. This created a network of communication and even clandestine economic support. It extended people's knowledge of the world beyond individual plantations, including the knowledge that in times of need, help might be available from a distant source. Thus the plantation regime with its stark sense of isolation and helplessness was moderated by an awareness of a larger community, one that could offer limited support in an economic as well as a moral sense.

Recent historical research has suggested that family patterns emerged in pre– and post–Civil War black communities that were distinctive to them and not simply imitations of the norms of Southern whites (Gutman 1976, 1984). These patterns, which initially appeared in the mid-1700s, included an emphasis on extended family networks, strong intergenerational ties, distinctive naming practices, emphasis on sibling loyalties as a model for other relationships, and nurturance of fictive kinship linkages. Fictive kin are unrelated individuals who are treated "as family" and may even have affectionate kinship titles such as "uncle" or "sister." The expansive and inclusive use of kinship terms helped socialize children into the larger community, not just the residential unit, and it enlarged an individual's protective network. It was this emphasis on *kin networks* and *kin-oriented values*, not simply "families" and individual households, that made these black family patterns unique.

VARIATIONS IN THE AFRICAN AMERICAN COMMUNITY

Many researchers, both black and white, have attempted to describe and summarize the diversity of the African American community (Green 1970, 1978; Dressler 1985; Dressler, Hoeppner, and Pitts 1985; McAdoo 1988; Williams 1981). In a recent discussion of the black aged, Stanford argues that "Black older persons should be viewed from the perspective of their own history, without having to suffer the indignity of being compared with those older persons who have, for the most part, had entirely different social, political, and economic experiences" (1990:41). He proposes the concept of "diverse life patterns," the "culmination of the multiple effects of the unique experiences of the black older person" (1990:42), as an important way of identifying the variability that exists among African Americans. Following Stanford's suggestion, I will review several researchers' efforts to describe that internal complexity. In doing so, it is important to recognize that diversity is to some degree a response to the crippling effects of racism and powerlessness over long periods of time, a point well made by Solomon (1976) in her important book on empowerment. But it is also reflective of an inherited tradition of West African origins.

Hill (1971) has identified some of the general social forms and cultural strategies that have been critical to that survival. They are themes that underlie the diversity of the black community and give it coherence. Briefly, they are:

1. Strong kinship bonds linking a variety of households.
2. A strong work orientation in support of family ties.
3. A high level of flexibility in family roles.

4. A marked achievement orientation, particularly in the areas of educational and occupational success.
5. Commitment to religious values and to the African American church as one of the defining and sustaining institutions of the community.
6. Commitment to a language tradition, black English, and appreciation of the skills and subtleties of bilingualism.

It is important if not critical to note that these themes are not associated with deficiency-oriented explanations of cultural difference. They are positive values, contributing to the strength and survival of individuals and families. In addition, however, there is a dimension that is more difficult to define. Solomon (1976:169) has argued that African American family patterns "for the most part are more humanistic and have greater validity than the hollow values of middle-class American society." She argues that there is a strong sense of hope and integrity that is linked to black religious belief and that this humanistic as well as religious orientation parallels and is different from the values of the dominant white community. If the traditional Puritan work ethic of the white community can be described as task oriented and motivated by economic success, then the African American community can be described in Solomon's terms as more person oriented, favoring the cultivation of relationships and expressive communication styles. This is a challenging hypothesis, one on which there has been relatively little rigorous comparative research. But it points to an important, perhaps pervasive cultural contrast, one that may distinguish large segments of the African American community from the politically and economically dominant white world.

In his study of a poor African American neighborhood in Pittsburgh, Williams (1981, 1992) emphasizes these expressive values as the "genuine" black culture of that community and, by implication, other urban black communities as well. He carefully documents the behavioral and value elements of an explicitly anti-white worldview. They include an emphasis on verbal and body communication that clearly signifies who is and who is not a "true" member of the community; social and economic reciprocity so intense that it significantly reduces the social distance among community members; a preference for public over private locales as sites for intense interaction; and hostility toward other blacks not seen as "genuine" in terms of these values. To enforce their codes, the people Williams studied creatively invented and enacted a variety of "degradation rituals" that mocked not only the values of mainstream American society but also the behavior of blacks who mixed with whites and presumably acquired "white" sensibilities. As sympathetic as Williams was to the problems of these terribly poor neighborhoods, he also saw the culture they generated as self-defeating in some ways, perpetuating an insularity and hostility to even occasional opportunities for economic improvement. Yet they replicated in local terms deeply held black values concerning separateness and self-identity despite the disapproval of the outside world.

In their studies of midwestern African American families, Martin and Martin (1978, 1985) looked at family issues as community members, not as outsiders. They defined the African American family as:

> *a multigenerational, interdependent kinship system which is welded together by a sense of obligation to relatives; is organized around a "family base" household; is generally guided by a "dominant family figure"; extends across geographical boundaries to connect family units to an extended family network; and has a built in mutual aid system for the welfare of its members and the maintenance of the family as a whole. (1978:1)*

In their research, the Martins found that a typical extended family network may include five or more households centered around a base unit, the family "home," where an informally recognized family leader resides. In this example, the emic view of "family" is a central household connected to satellite units. These units vary in their composition but they all look to the base household for leadership. That leadership is an important source of stability and direction for others in the family network. Satellite households can and do have relationships among themselves, but services and information are often routed through the base household. The base is usually the home of the family's founding couple who, as they age and become grandparents, become increasingly important and powerful in the affairs of the entire family network.

The flexibility of this system is the ease with which individuals are incorporated into households and, consequently, into the total family network. In poorer families, those who attach themselves to a unit may bring added burdens, stretching resources thinner than they already are, but they can also bring new opportunities —a regular paycheck, material goods, connections to other families, and useful knowledge or skills. Pooled resources make it possible for more people to survive, if only marginally better. In her work among very poor African American families, Stack (1975:6) found one case of fourteen individuals surviving on a yearly income of less than $5000. Family members were discouraged from leaving, and the additional wages even from part-time, low-paying work were critical to the survival of the entire unit.

Martin and Martin found that the senior male in the base household was typically the main provider, not only for his own unit but sometimes for several others. The female head was often responsible for distributing pooled resources among satellite units, caring for young children in them and making decisions affecting everyone in the family. That put her in a very powerful leadership position. When a dominant figure in the base household died, either the surviving spouse assumed the family's leadership position or another adult was informally eased into it. The new leader might be an eldest daughter or another adult child who was close to the family leaders. If no one assumed that position, the family network would be in danger of disintegrating.

This structure of the extended family illustrates Hill's argument that one of the strengths of African American families is their diversity and flexibility in kinship roles. This flexibility is part of the "social security" that the black family provides. Even when members of satellite units achieve a high level of economic achievement and stability, family traditions of reciprocity in goods, cash, and services often continue (McAdoo 1979). This mutual aid system is based on a moral imperative that the benefits that accrue to a few ought to be made available to others so that the entire family survives. Group interests are expected to predominate over individual ones. This pattern of sharing and the strong value of reciprocity are apparently widespread in African American communities as well (Zollar 1985).

African traditions are one source of the culture of the African American community. The values of the larger society, particularly those associated with educational and occupational attainment, are another. Pinderhughes (1979, 1982), however, argues that there is a third force to be considered. She suggests there is a "victim system," a set of self-reinforcing beliefs and practices contributing in some ways to the perpetuation of poverty and hopelessness. Those who possess the least and those whose opportunities are the most diminished, develop a distinctive, protective victim mentality. The victim system emphasizes a present (as against future or past) orientation; trust in religion, magic, or luck; personal impulsiveness and high emotional expressiveness; and manipulativeness in relationships (Pinderhughes 1979:26).

The implications of this argument, if there is in fact a "victim system" in the African American community, and if it is an indispensable part of being black in America, are enormous. It suggests that a culture is more than its historical backlog of strengths and assets, more than the flexibility and adaptability of its social forms. Each generation is faced with the need to find new responses to new forms of discrimination. What worked in the past may be maladaptive in the present and the celebrated strengths of the past may not ensure survival tomorrow. If Pinderhughes is correct, one can be victimized by an obvious and present oppressor, but one can also be victimized by the inappropriateness of old responses to new forms of danger.

The traits listed by Pinderhughes are difficult to interpret, and they may or may not be overstated (Foster and Perry 1982). But either as a set of heroic responses (too often subject to romanticization by outsiders who have not been victims themselves), or as an ideological and emotional trap (thus confirming the biases of those who would blame the victim anyway), they are certainly not characteristic of the whole of the African American community. Combining the notion of a "victim system," if that is an accurate description, with the diverse heritage of African cultural forms and the horrors of slavery, we get a picture of great cultural complexity. It also becomes apparent that development of cultural competence in social services for African Americans is more difficult and more fascinating than simplistic integrationist and assimilationist models could ever suggest.

AFRICAN AMERICANS AND SOCIAL SERVICES

In their recent history of social welfare, Axinn and Levin write of the charitable and settlement house movements of the early part of this century: "Neither the public nor the private sector was responsive to the needs of black families" (1997:13). This was due to racism, to an ideology that need was a consequence of personal failings, ignorance of the social sources of deprivation, and simple lack of exposure to black individuals by the leaders in these reform movements. The 1990 census shows that American blacks are a predominantly urban people concentrated in the twenty largest cities (U.S. Department of Commerce 1993a). Less than a quarter now live in rural areas. But in the early 1900s, the number of urban blacks was tiny and almost all African Americans lived in the South where relief and reform were not high on anyone's agenda.

With the emergence of the civil rights movement of the l960s, the helping professions were dramatically reminded of the needs of the African American community and of an unfortunate history of neglect in services to black clients. Indeed, not only was the adequacy of services a point of contention, but racism within social work itself became an issue. A landmark editorial in a 1964 issue of *Social Casework* announced that problems in the relationship of the profession to African Americans could no longer be ignored:

> *The relative dearth of literature on the racial factor in casework treatment,...and the conspicuous absence of research on the subject suggest that repressive psychological mechanisms may be at work. Perhaps it is difficult for a profession committed to humanistic tenets to engage in honest appraisal of possible disparities between its ideals and its accomplishments. (1964:155)*

That statement was a welcome one in that it recognized the potential for racism within an avowedly helping profession. But it was also a manifestation of the limited understanding of racial issues typical of many professionals at that time, particularly evident in the curious, now almost quaint way the source of the problem was described—"repressive psychological mechanisms may be at work." As a psychological (as against an environmental or sociological) view of the origins of the problem, racism within social services was attributed to ignorance, fear, and guilt. The question of institutional sources of racism, of racism as an endemic feature of the environment of both blacks and whites, was not addressed.

The *Social Casework* editorial did inspire, however, a proliferation of research activities and research reports on how racism might be a potential factor in human services. Typically, the center of this new interest was the client-practitioner relationship. The research literature analyzed, often in psychological terms, the complexities of cross-racial encounters between white workers and black clients (Fibush 1965, Bloch 1968, Simmons 1963); black workers and white clients (Curry 1964); and in racially mixed service settings (Lide 1971, Fibush and Turnquest 1970). The significance of race in interviewing (Kadushin 1972) and in clinical work was also discussed. These studies of the 1960s and 1970s launched a trend that, to some degree, continues. Most of them concluded that racism in some form did indeed exist in social services, that it created problems for communication and worker effectiveness in interracial encounters, and that some of the problems could be overcome when people learned to cope with their feelings about race.

But was that response, with its emphasis on interpersonal encounters and re-examining feelings, an adequate one for the profession? Is race simply a "factor" to be recognized and added to existing intervention formulas for working with clients?

Is it sufficient, as one commentator proposed, "to examine and loosen these 'repressive psychological mechanisms' by means of an honest appraisal" (Lide 1971:432)? The reply of some black social workers and of many black critics of social work has been a qualified if not negative one, and they have called for something more ambitious. Their concerns, then and now, focus on three issues.

First, some critics (Devore 1983, and Gwyn and Kilpatrick 1981, for example) have argued that traditional, individualistic approaches to problem solving can do little to improve the lot of many African American individuals. Intervention based on psychodynamic theories is at best palliative and, at worst, counterproductive to the advancement of blacks as a group. These critics have emphasized that solutions cannot be limited to assisting clients in resolving immediate personal problems; the helping agent must also act to change the system of control itself, a system that creates barriers to productive living for the majority of black people. Thus, an exclusive focus on the mental state of the minority client and the social worker's intellectual and emotional problems in relating to it diverts attention from the ecological sources of that client's problems. Solomon has put it bluntly and forcefully: "Powerlessness is a more virulent stressor than anxiety. Consequently, empowerment becomes a more important treatment goal than reduction of anxiety" (1982:166).

The Black Task Force Report of the Family Service Association of America (Delaney 1979) also illustrates the general critique of individualistic intervention based on psychodynamic models. That report stresses an ecological systems perspective, which "widens the scope of assessment to include the transactions between poor black individuals and the systems within and outside their neighborhoods" (1979:12). This suggestion, while it does not negate a psychodynamic approach, broadens the areas of concern to include structural factors that impinge on the lives of black communities.

A second criticism has been that the strengths of the African American family have been ignored (Jackson 1993). Years of research and more research dollars than probably can be accounted for have gone into demonstrating the supposed deficiencies of the black family, blaming it for many of the community's problems. These studies culminated in the infamous Moynihan report (1965), a document whose influence persists, despite its weaknesses and the criticisms made against it (Rainwater and Yancey 1967). Moynihan described the African American family as a "tangle of pathology...capable of perpetuating itself without assistance from the white world" (Moynihan 1965:47). This notion of minority families as the source of their own problems has been attractive to conservative interests, to whom it has been convenient to "blame the victim" (Ryan 1969). But the idea also held appeal for a number of liberal, humanistic, mostly white scholars and social workers who were attracted to the "culture of poverty" idea and who, despite a genuine concern for righting the inequalities of racism, were prone to romanticize pathology and find its causes largely in the very people who were being victimized. It is now apparent that these deficiency-oriented explanations and the catchphrases associated with them—"cultural deprivation," "multiple-problem families," "female-centered" family—were seriously misleading.

The ethnographic evidence demonstrates that African American families and households are often highly flexible and effective in coping with the problems of poverty, although there are conflicting theories as to why this is the case (Fine, Schwebel, and James-Myers 1987). Black values centering around children, elders, and the quality of interpersonal relations are more intense and subtle than outsiders have been willing to recognize. These features are all sources of strength and represent, according to Billingsley (1968), a "bundle of complexity" rather than a "tangle of pathology." What that cultural complexity means for the effective delivery of social services is a topic that is finally being addressed in the social work and social science literature (Dedmon and Saur 1983).

A third criticism of the social service system, one often made by African American social workers, is their profession's neglect of indigenous forms of assistance already in place. The black church has served a number of service functions for many years (Solomon 1985). Senior citizen services, day care, credit unions, housing developments, and education in survival skills are just a few services offered by this sometimes overlooked institution. Indeed, the black church in its various forms is probably the oldest helping institution in the African American community. One religious leader has described it as "the first welfare organization on earth" (Jemison 1982:40). Prior to the American Civil War, there were itinerant black ministers in much of the South, small and scattered congregations, and many mutual aid societies, some of which were the forerunners of contemporary denominations. These societies took care of their members in illness, handled the expenses of burials, and gave small amounts of money to orphans and widows. They were also leaders in literacy and education, using the Bible as a text. All of these groups and their activities constituted an "invisible church," linking black groups both before and after emancipation (Bullock 1967).

One result of this historical experience has been great variety in religious expression among African Americans up to the present time, a variety as great or greater than any other ethnic group. Baer and Singer (1981) have tried to summarize that diversity in what they call a "typology of black sectarianism." They see four major kinds of black religious institutions. Established or mainstream denominations such as the African Methodist Episcopal Church and the National Baptist Convention USA tend to adhere to the values of middle-class America. But they also pursue an agenda of social reform and community improvement. Messianic-nationalist groups repudiate white society and its religious practices while affirming the sovereignty of the black community. Their doctrines foresee a return to former positions of power and integrity, either in Africa or selected parts of America. Black "conversionist" groups often emphasize a strict, even puritanical, ideology, and encourage the spiritual conversion of their members through ecstatic experiences that include energetic singing and dancing. Although unstable in an institutional sense, conversionist groups flourish in most African American communities, and their combined membership makes up a substantial portion of all black church affiliation. Finally, there are "spiritualist" churches, mostly small and localized, which in addition to their ritual enthusiasm work to help their members solve very practical problems with employment, money, love, family matters, and health (Baer 1981).

Given this social diversity and its historical depth, it is apparent that the African American churches are a major institutional element of the African American world. They meet a variety of human needs and do so in incredibly diverse ways. They are a rich resource not only for those who affiliate with individual congregations but for those who might want to know more about their helping practices and the people who have quietly served for so long.

IDEOLOGY AND CARE

But the African American church is not the only source of care, aid, and support. The help-seeking model directs our attention to other, sometimes less visible, forms of community strength, especially forms that are ideological. One example of this is an ethnomedical system of belief and care that is important not only to a significant portion of the African American community in the United States but is found in some rural, largely white areas as well. This is a set of beliefs about health, illness, and general well-being derived from older European as well as African sources. The African origins of these beliefs are bodies of knowledge common to the west coast of Africa during the time of slave trading in the seventeenth and eighteenth centuries. The European origins are just as old and were brought to North America by the earliest immigrants. There is no generalized name for this system of knowledge, although terms like "witchcraft" and "spiritualism" have been used and there is a wide range of practitioners, from herbalists and "root-workers" to faith healers and midwives (Baer 1981). In its contemporary form in the African American community, it is a consistent, self-contained set of principles for accounting for the problems that beset individuals. It is associated with practitioners who, under some circumstances, provide effective assistance to those who seek it. It is not a set of beliefs typical of all African Americans and should not be regarded as such. But it is common in some parts of the United States and is an instructive example of how local belief and practice can coexist with so-called mainstream health institutions.

This ethnomedical system has been studied by a number of anthropologically oriented researchers, not only in this country but also in the West Indies and in Africa (Snow 1973, 1974, 1977, 1978; Whitten 1962; Wintrob 1973). It is thus very widespread and some of its elements appear in a number of communities. The system is based on a fundamental division of illness, mental as well as physical, into two kinds: that which is "natural" and that which is "unnatural." Natural illness results from failure of the individual to properly care for the body. It may also come about as divine punishment for one's misdeeds. In either event, a lack of wellness is due to an improper relationship with natural forces. Cold air, strong drafts, misuse of alcohol, or poor diet can all be responsible for illness and can signify the individual's inattention to basic health and hygiene requirements. Similarly, illness that is a consequence of God's displeasure results from failure to respect principles of decency and morality as they have been established by Biblical and church authorities.

By contrast, unnatural illness is the result of evil influence. Illness may range from obvious physical ailments to psychosomatic symptoms to problems commonly classified as mental health concerns. But they are all similar in that their origin is in the evil intentions and the evil actions of others. Unlike natural illnesses, unnatural ones are initiated by a human agent against a victim and fall outside the orderly domain of the universe established by God and nature. Various terms for this activity are "hexing," "rootwork," "fix," "mojo," and occasionally "witchcraft." It is believed that evil intentions and evil actions are efficacious because all events in the universe are interconnected, and if one knows the interconnections and how to use them, one can have a measure of influence and control over others. It is the wrongful use of this power, not the knowledge of occult things per se, that is evil. Thus, the individual who suffers an inexplicable physical or mental problem has reason to believe that someone else may be the cause of it. It is important, therefore, to find a specialist who can identify the source of the problem and deal with it.

Clearly, neither mental health specialists nor biomedically oriented professionals are in a position to respond to individual complaints based on this kind of conceptualization of illness and misfortune. But there are individuals in the African American community who are effective as far as they and many of their clients are concerned. These healers are variously known as psychics, rootworkers, counselors, and root doctors. Snow (1973, 1978) has described in detail the skills and procedures of a woman she calls a "voodoo practitioner." What is remarkable are the similarities of her techniques to those of some mental health professionals. The woman's practice was located in her home in the downtown section of a large southwestern American city. Her clients included blacks, whites, Native Americans, and Mexican Americans. Snow had difficulty locating her because she was known only by word of mouth. Yet her place of business was similar to that of many doctors, counselors, and other professionals. She had an office in which she kept nine-to-five hours, and patients met her in a waiting room. She was trained by her grandmother, who also possessed special healing powers and who was widely known in the local community for her skills. The training consisted of learning ways to utilize her "gift" in helping others, a gift with which she was born and which could not be obtained in any other way. Portions of her therapy involved touching and massage, but much of it involved talking through a problem. Using an idiom with which most black patients were intimately familiar, including the personalities and events of the Bible, she was able to illuminate the sources of personal difficulties and ways of coping with them.

Snow's practitioner made use of the critical distinction between natural and unnatural illnesses, claiming no special medical skills for those problems that were clearly within the domain of medical providers.

> *Now an unnatural sickness, well, that's a person that's sick in the mind. Mentally sick. Doctors can't find that. They Xray and they can't find it.... And yet they are sick, mentally sick in mind. And then, I'm a counselor, I counsel them.... I give 'em medicine you know, through their mind. I call that spiritual medicine. (Snow 1973:278)*

Judged by the enthusiasm of her patients and the size of her clientele, this practitioner was very successful in her community. She did not compete with established medical professionals, as both she and her patients recognized that she dealt with problems that such practitioners were not trained to handle. Furthermore, she had an intimate knowledge of the pressures of life in the African American community and of how poor people are vulnerable to forces they cannot control. Many of her clients came to her after having seen certified, mainstream counselors and social workers. These clients were disappointed with the kind of treatment they received and had concluded that professionally trained experts could not treat the kinds of problems that afflicted them.

It is especially important to note, as Snow does, that these beliefs in unnatural illness are not simply the legacy of prescientific superstitions. It would be a serious error to interpret them that way. Rather, unnatural illnesses "are those that have to do with the individual's position as a member of society.... Some arise from the tensions and anxieties of everyday living.... Hostility in interpersonal relationships, on the other hand, may cause the individual to become the target of witchcraft" (Snow 1973:272–273). Where social relationships are strained because of the problems of poverty, discrimination, and exclusion from full participation in the larger society, beliefs in the efficacy of evil influences are a reasonable response to the daily problems of living (Rainwater 1970). A remarkable discussion of this form of healing, rich with case material, can be found in Snow's latest book (1993), documenting the operation of this complex system of traditional belief and community-based care. She effectively makes the argument that it is alive and well in many parts of America.

Foster and Anderson (1978) have identified a number of characteristics of healers and curers, which they believe are the marks of healing individuals in many cultures. These include specialization, selection and training, certification, an aura of capability or professionalism, expectations of payment, and an ambivalent public image. Snow's practitioner fits all these criteria. She has a specialized store of knowledge—the treatment of unnatural mental and physical illness—and she was specially selected and trained for her task. That selection came about through the influence of her grandmother, but it was also a divine choice. "I was born just exactly with the gift," she said. Certification of competence was oral, in the testimony of patients, and did not require framed certificates issued by hallowed institutions. Further, she conducted her practice as a business, and, as she herself admitted, her public image was a mixed one. Some in the community accused her of manipulating dark and forbidden forces. Yet she responded that she was simply implementing the power, the "gift," that God had given her.

To the extent that Snow's respondent had success with her patients, it must be attributed not only to her personal skill in counseling others but also to the sense of legitimacy she enjoyed in her community. It is this legitimacy that strangers and outsiders, stationed in agencies that are themselves outposts of larger, alien bureaucracies, cannot hope to obtain simply through formal training and completion of specialized, degree-granting programs. Outsiders can acknowledge, however, the importance of indigenous help providers such as this practitioner and, to the extent feasible, attempt to learn something of their methods and the reasons for their success. Cultural awareness does not require imitation of the skills of knowledgeable insiders, however desirable that may sometimes be, so much as it presupposes an honest sensibility as to who and what is really helpful and how resources can best be utilized.

CULTURE CONTRASTS AND COMPETENT PRACTICE

This brief review of the African American experience and the institutions and ideologies that have emerged within it makes clear that there are major historical differences between blacks and whites. It is important to see those differences as creative and life-affirming responses to nearly four centuries of persecution and injustice. The differences have also led to a distinctive cultural configuration within the larger American society. The issue for intervention and for the ethnically competent worker is not simply that these differences exist, but that their meaning and significance be explicitly known in counseling relationships (Gwyn and Kilpatrick 1981).

It is worth repeating that *contrasts,* not just differences, are important in the ethnic competence approach. To identify and describe only difference is to assume an "us versus them" stance: "they" are different from "us"; "we" know what "their" differences mean. Clearly, that is the formula for stereotyping. By emphasizing contrast, however, the worker is put fully into the relationship as an engaged participant. The practitioner, after all, is "different" in the client's eyes, and the client's perceptions of contrast are at least as important to the dynamics of the event as the social worker's. By looking at contrasts rather than differences, everyone is required to evaluate the cultural baggage they bring to the conversation and what that means for quality service.

Table 6.1 on page 206 presents a series of contrasts in the form of brief statements. They represent a first step toward thinking about differences in legitimately comparative terms. I have brought these statements together from a variety of sources, including my reading, conversations with African American scholars and social workers, teaching, and years of training workshops. They are not the only items that could have been included in the table, nor are they comprehensive, but they are important statements and make a good starting point. Some of my sources for this overview include the publications of Barbara Solomon, the author of *Black Empowerment* (1976); Elmer and Joanne Martin, sociologists of the black family; Andrew Billingsley, a well-known historian of the African American experience; and Robert Hill, whose pioneering work with the Urban League identified critical issues confronting the community. But the table's form is not their responsibility. It is my own reading and interpretation of the issues they have said are important.

Among their many concerns, including those political and economic, I have chosen to highlight issues related to the family. My rationale is that myths about African American families are widespread in American society and in many social services agencies. Further, issues concerning the family and its functioning underlie much of what social services is all about.

TABLE 6.1   Selected Cultural Contrasts between the African American and Anglo American Communities

African American	Anglo American
Flexibility in family forms is considered normal; the word "family" sometimes refers to a household unit and sometimes to a network of households containing affiliated kin.	The single-household "nuclear" family is the preferred form, although numerous variations occur and the perceived strengths and/or weaknesses of these variations are topics of discussion and sometimes controversy.
Extended family networks are common, usually centered on a "base" household with specific links to satellite households. Satellites may be newly married couples, single adults with children, or individuals living alone. The term "family" often includes these units.	Extended families in regular contact are believed to be uncommon although they occur in many communities. Individuals linked by kinship have limited obligations to one another and are expected to show loyalty to members of their own household first.
One individual in the base household commonly takes on a leadership role on behalf of all members of the family and their households. This individual is often an older woman, occasionally an older man. She may make day-to-day decisions affecting the welfare of others in the family network, and that leadership provides centrality and stability to the family as an extended unit.	Each household is its own base, a resident adult (often male) its real or nominal head. Adult decisions affect the members of the household, not kin in other units. Interference in the affairs of other units, even when well intended, is viewed as a transgression.
A mutual aid system is typical of extended family networks, and the welfare of others in the network is a primary obligation. Mutual aid is strongly linked to person-centered (in contrast to object-centered) values and to a diffuse sense of humanitarianism, assistance, and sharing.	The primary obligations of adults are to their own children, secondarily to the children of kin or to aged parents. Care of persons outside the nuclear family is a special task, sometimes seen as a hardship, that can intrude on responsibilities to one's immediate family, on one's personal needs, or on career aspirations.
Flexibility of roles is highly valued. Wives may work, older children may supervise younger ones, and children may be informally adopted as the needs of households vary. Relations between men and women are ideally egalitarian. Flexibility is viewed as critical to the survival of households and families.	Although men's and women's roles traditionally have been defined as separate and distinct, role clarity is sometimes difficult to maintain as economic expectations lead to two-career families.
Older persons are often held in high esteem, their experience in surviving in a hostile world viewed as evidence of skill and wisdom. A strong religious orientation is sometimes associated with aging and authority. Deference to elders sometimes demanded.	Older persons often retain their separateness and independence from the households of their adult children. They sometimes worry about "becoming a burden" on others and are expected to maintain their independence as long as possible.

My emphasis on contrast rather than difference also suggests that the objective truth of cultural differences may be less important than beliefs about what that truth might be. For example, some blacks and some whites may look at specific items in the table and object: "That isn't me and the people I know!" That may be so and, in fact, in some cases it ought to be. The issue, from the perspective of the cultural competence model, is: what kind of *generalizable statement* would be *more* true for a specific service population. Statements of cultural contrast are only starting points, *always* provisional and hypothetical. They are to be used for thinking about potential contrasts in values, beliefs, behavior, and social context, exactly the kinds of things social workers refer to when they speak of "individualizing the client." The only legitimate use of the table is in locating areas of potential contrasts, determining their salience for the service to be provided, and revising them as necessary in order to improve service outcomes with individual clients. I want to be as emphatic as I can that the statements are not "insider tips" that tell us what the people in any community are "really" like. They are generalizations, suggested in part by minority scholars and social workers, to help us think comparatively, both about others and about ourselves.

The reader is cautioned, then, that any set of generalizations in this book about a given community may or may not apply to specific individuals. We all vary in our commitment to the norms of our own community and in how we observe them. The contrast statements in the table refer only to general tendencies within groups, not to the attributes of individuals. It is the social worker's responsibility to determine if and how clients approximate those tendencies, and how they might be salient to resolving specific social service issues.

Clearly, the contrasts suggested in Table 6.1 show a strong orientation in the African American community toward a rich and diverse family life, popular stereotypes notwithstanding. For instance, the concept of "family" is more open and flexible than that commonly used by whites. There is heavy reliance on others within a large network and, because of that, social services are "not necessarily the first and only place poor blacks turn to for help" (Neighbors and Taylor 1985:266). Within the family network there is often a strong sense of obligation and a value orientation that favors group needs over individual preferences. Jones (1983:423) has written that "the sense of 'we-ness', the need for interdependence, and cooperation are major humanistic themes permeating the motivational and behavioral system within black communities." This is not to say that this system of values and behavior always works the way individuals expect it to. Rather, it is a culturally recognizable standard used to judge the correctness of one's own behavior and that of others. It is also a standard for making comparisons, favorable and unfavorable, with the dominant white society. A culturally sensitive assessment, diagnosis, or treatment of African American clients would have to take these standards, and especially their local and family variations, into account.

In their study of helping traditions within the African American community, Martin and Martin (1985) identified general areas where inquiry into black family life can usefully begin. Questions they consider important include: How often do family members come to one another's aid? What are the relationships between those family members who are well established financially and those who are struggling? What is the nature of male/female relationships and how do men and women work to advance their joint interests? What are the values adults instill in children and how do they use spiritual resources in family life? How are institutions and networks used to secure aid when it is needed? And finally, "How race conscious are family members, and to what extent is racial consciousness a source of inspiration, pride, therapy, and commitment to black liberation and social change?" (Martin and Martin 1985:86). These are important questions that complement the topics suggested in Table 6.1. Any one of them could be the starting point for a culturally sensitive analysis of a family's needs and for planning appropriate intervention.

DEVELOPING SKILLS FOR SERVICE

Typically, whites (and sometimes members of other ethnic groups) are relatively inexperienced in working with African American clients. This inexperience can lead to awkwardness and an occasional gaffe. Hunt (1987) has documented some of the most common ones, including pretenses to familiarity with street slang; self-effacement and apologetics for being white or privileged; and promotion of an "us versus the system" stance that the social worker hopes will find favor with minority clients. Name dropping (usually sports or entertainment figures) is only one step removed from the now discredited "some of my best friends are" comment. These errors, as well as others, are quickly recognized by minority persons who are sensitive to how whites respond to their presence (Davis 1984). Sykes (1987) has commented that in cross-racial social work, white counselors often fail to use even the normal interpersonal skills they routinely bring to their work with same-race clients, believing they must make heroic and even theatrical efforts to prove they are trustworthy.

One of the few models of counseling interaction between African Americans and whites is that developed by Gibbs (1981). She notes that there are important ethnic differences in the expectations African Americans and whites bring to a counseling relationship and that these differences have consequences for the encounter's outcome. She argues that "Blacks typically evaluate professional interactions in terms of the *interpersonal* skills demonstrated in initial encounters, while Whites typically evaluate similar interactions in terms of the *instrumental* skills demonstrated" (1981:166–167). Participants who focus on interpersonal skills are most attentive to moods and responses. The emphasis is on the dynamics or flow of the event, especially the flow of language. Those who focus on instrumental skills place more value on the results of the encounter. They are more oriented toward tasks and goal achievement, and language is a secondary device for achieving some desired or remote end.

This does not mean that blacks and whites inhabit entirely different linguistic worlds, or that they are incapable of understanding one another. It means that emphases vary according to cultural traditions and expectations. In her own interactions with schoolteachers during a research project, Gibbs found that blacks and whites each used interpersonal and instrumental ways of responding to others. But she also found that the sequencing varied: "Black teachers tended to respond to us in a very personal, non–task-oriented way in the initial phase of the consultation and became task-oriented much later in the project; while White teachers tended to be very task-oriented initially and developed personal relations with us much later in the project, if at all" (1981:176).

In Gibbs's model, from a black perspective there are five stages and sets of behavior in a consultative relationship. These stages are the "cultural lens" through which African American clients interpret their meeting with a white counselor. These stages derive from a cultural preference for emphasizing, at least initially, the interpersonal over the instrumental.

In Stage I, which Gibbs calls the "appraisal stage," the client "sizes up" the counselor and minimizes the intensity of the interaction. Whites may interpret this as aloofness, reserve, hostility, or the stereotyped "inability to verbalize." But such distancing gives the client an opportunity to evaluate the counselor for honesty, genuineness, and the potential for trust later on.

Stage II involves the client's more assertive investigation of who and what the counselor is about. The client may ask questions about the counselor's personal life, experiences, and beliefs. He or she is trying to determine how willing the counselor is to go beyond stereotypes, power, or dominance. The search for egalitarianism as a personal (as against professional) quality is being explored.

This stage may be an opportunity to determine if and how race is a factor in a consultation. Jones and Seagull (1977), in their research on black–white interactions, suggest that "the issue of color difference should be brought up early in the relationship, certainly not later than the second session, but preferably in the first…. The white therapist should model such openness by examining his or her own feelings if they are relevant to the relationship" (p. 854–855).

Needless to say, this is a potentially explosive moment in counseling. Workers often dread it, may evade it, and always risk a disruptive faux pas. But to pretend that race is not an issue may be as damaging (and preposterous) as to launch into apologetics for being white, neither being a useful response and both indicating that a social worker is still struggling to get some sense of genuineness and understanding in handling cultural or racial differences. The cultural competence model calls for veracity, a simple and straightforward statement that race, ethnicity, or general background may be an issue and it should be clarified.

At Stage III, the client "may make overtures to the consultant to establish a personal relationship characterized by the exchange of information, personal favors, [and] mutual obligations" (Gibbs 1981:169–170). Whereas white clients usually prefer to keep the exchange at a strictly professional level, black individuals may place greater emphasis on the willingness of the social worker to identify with the client personally as well as professionally.

Stage IV is the client's commitment to entering into a service plan. The client's language may still be that of personalism (such as expressing personal regard for the counselor), but the client may now be willing to consider the counselor's professional recommendations. Gibbs argues that at this stage white clients may also accept the counselor's program but will express that acceptance more in terms of commitment to the program goals than in terms of their interest in the counselor as a person.

In the last stage, Stage V, the client engages the counselor's program. Again, Gibbs notes the differing cultural agendas that may emerge. "While black persons will make this commitment as a result of their evaluation of the consultant's *interpersonal competence* in the first four stages, white persons will make this commitment in terms of the *instrumental competence* shown by the consultant up to this time" (Gibbs 1981:170).

While the cultural contrasts outlined in Table 6.1 are the beginnings of the social worker's knowledge base, Gibbs's intervention model suggests something of the interpersonal "style" that goes with using and expressing that knowledge. It is important to note that this notion of "style" contrasts dramatically with some of the standard operating procedures of health and social service organizations. While an organization's emphasis is on data gathering for administrative convenience or for short-term, highly focused intervention, the culturally competent worker will need to find ways of accommodating both agency requirements and the expectations of clients. That in itself may be one of the more difficult tasks in acquiring cultural competence.

African American social workers and researchers have often been critical of their profession, especially as it relates to the members of their community. One target of that criticism has been the discipline's emphasis on the intrapsychic state of clients as a way of resolving problems, an approach that too often ignores the need for changes in the social and physical environment. "Talking therapies" are an example. Devore (1983) has called attention instead to the stressful experiences of black families, noting that problem resolution must also take account of the hostile environment in which they live. Similarly, Gwyn and Kilpatrick (1981) question traditional forms of family treatment, urging that it is an "ecological perspective, which treats environmental as well as emotional problems in a cultural framework, that can be most effective" for low-income African American people (1981:265). They call for greater use of short-term therapy, cooperation with nonprofessional, indigenous counselors, frequent home visits, and careful planning of family tasks. The model proposed by Gibbs, and the knowledge base to be built through comparative understanding, are beginning points for addressing these issues in compassionate and culturally appropriate ways.

OTHER BLACK COMMUNITIES

Many African Americans born and resident in the United States have family ties to the West Indies. The islands of the Caribbean were settled earlier than the eastern seaboard of this country, and it was in the Caribbean that the system of slave-based plantations began. The original Indian inhabitants of the region were virtually exterminated within a century of Columbus's landfall, and African labor and European capital combined to create the system that turned once forested islands into sugar-producing slave societies. The economies of the early North American colonies were closely linked with those of the Caribbean. For several hundred years, ships left European ports with cheap trade goods to exchange for human cargo in West Africa. The infamous "middle passage" was the cross-Atlantic link that carried Africans first to the islands and Brazil and later to the Gulf and south-eastern American colonies. Ships carried slaves, raw sugar, molasses, and rum from the Caribbean to southern and New England ports before returning home across the north Atlantic. Slavers from the West Indies and their cargos were a common sight all along the eastern seaboard for more than two hundred years.

It would be a mistake, however, to assume that the island cultures of the Caribbean are identical to their African American counterparts in North America. Slavery ended throughout the West Indies a full generation earlier than it did in the United States. Whites were a tiny minority in the islands, and in the latter part of the nineteenth century their numbers diminished even further. In the past fifty years, most of the former colonies have become independent countries and, although they may be affiliated with their former colonizers, as is true of many of the British and the French islands, they run their own affairs. The islands are also people-exporting countries, economically dependent on the remittances of massive numbers of labor migrants, men and women, living in the eastern United States, eastern Canada, and the larger cities of England and France. There were well over a million English-speaking West Indians living in this country in 1980; now their number is probably twice that.

These migrants represent a distinctive group even within their home countries. They tend to be young, many are educated, they are highly motivated to succeed, and they have a view of race and race relations that is their own. They are aware of the bipolar black–white distinction that dominates racial thinking in this country, but their own experience is more complex. Brice (1982) puts it this way:

> *A light-skinned British West Indian who comes to the United States is in a dilemma. In the islands, he or she has a certain amount of status, at least more than a Black person. In the United States, however, Whites reject the British West Indian as "another Black," while Blacks may reject or look down on the West Indian because of his or her refusal to identify with other blacks. (1982:126–127)*

But the issue goes beyond race alone. Most West Indians, including those who become U.S. citizens, continue to assert their ethnic identity as one distinctive from that of North American blacks. They maintain ties with their island of origin, send money home to mothers, often retire to the islands, and continue to use their island patois in addition to the British standard of English they learned in school. They are proud of Caribbean cultural exports, especially calypso and reggae. They may observe island-based forms of Christianity along with African religious creeds, and they often have a "Commonwealth" point of view in matters of politics, soccer pools, and especially cricket.

There is an extensive social science literature on West Indian family patterns (Smith 1988), and the term "matrifocal" comes from an early phase of that research (Clarke 1957). Families of upper-class origins (often of light complexion) tend to adhere to European models of the patriarchal family. Men are expected to be dominant and children quiet and obedient. Great emphasis is placed on formal education, correct English, thrift, ownership of property, fidelity in marriage, and participation in mainstream churches. But most West Indians are not upper class, and it is common for a man and woman of modest origins to live together for many years, have children, and marry only when there is enough money to purchase a house. For them, as for other West Indians, hard work is valued because in the islands the acquisition of property is critical to improving one's status. Also valued is a knowledge of West Indian herbal medicines, use of West-Indian folk healers, and beliefs and rituals associated with *obeah*. Pentecostal churches are common in West Indian communities, both in this country and in England and Canada.

There have been few studies of West Indians in social service settings. Several important ones are those by Thrasher and Anderson (1988), Sewell-Coker, Hamilton-Collins, and Fein (1985), and Watts-Jones (1992). Caribbean migrants tend to come from rural backgrounds, and even those who lived in larger cities such as Port of Spain, Trinidad and Kingston, Jamaica often have important ties to country villages. Consequently, the culture shock of adjusting to life in New York City or Miami is often part of what brings islanders to the attention of social workers. (The study by Watts-Jones, cited above, of a Jamaican women suffering panic disorders is a good example.) West Indian families usually follow a pattern of chain migration in which one member finds a job and a place to live and sends for others as resources permit. Family life, therefore, is very fluid, with new members arriving as they can. Through informal patterns of sharing or "child-minding," children may live with grandmothers, aunts, or other women for years before joining one or both parents in the United States or in England. Given these long separations, family life never picks up where it "left off," and conflicts between children and parents are common.

It is important to note that West Indian migration to this country is often more a matter of women than of men. The "feminization" of Caribbean migration means that kinship and family life are really matters of maintaining long-distance, international networks. West Indian family life cannot be thought of in terms of discrete, localized, small household units. It is not that, even for those who remain home in the islands. Men but also women follow economic and educational opportunities where they can, and they utilize far-flung friends and relatives to help them care for their children and to channel economic resources. Balancing job and family demands over distances of thousands of miles is costly and exhausting. But those who do it become skilled administrators of their time, money, and energy. Many of the stresses they face, quite apart from racism and adjusting to cultural differences, are the result of heroic efforts to achieve some balance in their obligations to distant people who are dependent on them.

Perhaps as a historical residue of slavery, corporal punishment is common in the Caribbean (Payne 1989). There is also a great emphasis on seniority, with elders as important decision makers on behalf of children. But decision making is not the same for boys and girls. Boys are given much more freedom, whereas there is great concern that girls may "get into trouble" (Sewell-Coker, Hamilton-Collins, and Fein 1985:564), usually meaning teenage pregnancy. There is also a great concern with propriety and its opposite, "rudeness." A rich oral and performative tradition surrounds "rudeness," from inspired calypso lyrics to the verbal stylistics of male–female verbal bantering. But rudeness is not acceptable in children or youth and is often handled by ritualized strapping (Payne 1989:397) or "giving licks." Adults, who place great emphasis on the privacy of family life, are dismayed when what they see as legitimate discipline brings them into contact with protective service workers. In their study of a Brooklyn area population, Thrasher and Anderson (1988) found a high incidence of suspected child abuse and high use (83 percent) of corporal punishment. They noted that "these parents expressed anger and confusion that their belief in physical punishment as an appropriate method of child rearing was in conflict with the dominant society.... [and that] it may lead to allegations of child abuse by non–West Indian observers" (1988:175). The same researchers found little in the vast child abuse literature that was applicable or helpful in their attempts to understand West Indian disciplinary practices.

Sewell-Coker, Hamilton-Collins, and Fein (1985) and their associates found that West Indians are neither familiar with nor greatly interested in family therapy counseling models as these have been developed for use with middle-class whites. Their recommendations are for more concrete, short-term forms of intervention such as organizing activities for youth and academic advising. Thrasher and Anderson (1988:176) describe West Indian clients as "formal and distant when interacting with authority figures and professionals," a feature that probably derives from British models of social class hierarchy and elitism that still dominate Caribbean societies. Sewell-Coker, Hamilton-Collins, and Fein (1985:565) go on to argue that "West Indians, a conservative people, do not readily express emotion.... [and] say little." Frankly, I find this very surprising. My two years of researching interisland migration in St. Croix taught me that West-Indians are exceptionally gregarious, often wonderfully so. Behind their formal, European-style class consciousness is a remarkable sense of individualism and personal animation. Our differing perspectives point to the necessity, I believe, of meeting and knowing West Indians or any ethnic group outside of institutional settings. Clearly, the West Indian community is growing in North America, and there remains a need for "identification of relevant cultural variables and family patterns that influence the[se] immigrants' ability to adapt to their new environment" (Thrasher and Anderson 1988:172).

Fortunately, such information has recently become available. Gopaul-McNicol (1993) has published a major study on West Indian families and she is eminently qualified to do so, having grown up in Trinidad and Tobago. She presents a detailed discussion of West Indian family values and makes an explicit contrast between them and comparable family values in the United States. Her chapter on counseling West Indians and the uses of language in counseling ought to be mandatory reading for professionals working with clients from the islands. Her book also provides assessment, self-concept, and attitude scales that any social worker could use, scales that are sensitive to the cultural distinctiveness of West Indians. The research she reports is an important addition to the social services literature, a literature that for too long has neglected the people of the Caribbean.

Finally, American social workers who have contact with West Indian families should familiarize themselves with the British social work journals. Along with Africans, Indians, and Pakistanis, West Indians have greater visibility within British social work than they do in North America. Consequently, somewhat more research and journal attention is devoted to their concerns (Atkin and Rollings 1992).

FOLLOW-UP

1. Considering Cases: Cultural Competence Demonstrated

The literature of the helping professions does not have enough lengthy, well-developed, ethnographically grounded cases studies. For cross-cultural purposes, good examples are even rarer. That is one reason this sensitively presented case, from clinical social worker and family therapist Lynn Pearlmutter, is so special. (Her full presentation appears in the *Clinical Social Work Journal* [24:4:1996] and is summarized here by permission.) The case involves a middle-aged, working-class African American couple. Pearlmutter describes herself as white, Jewish, and highly educated, and early in the counseling sessions that contrast between herself and her clients was openly acknowledged and discussed. The couple came to counseling because the wife complained her husband had a history of passivity in his relations with her and their daughters. She was exasperated and, as she described it, at the point of "giving up" even though a divorce did not seem imminent. The husband's view was that he had always done the best he could, his wife expected too much from him, and at this point in the marriage he didn't intend to change the way he lived.

Pearlmutter proposed a plan for improved communication and social skills that initially worked very well. The husband became more outgoing and was increasingly talkative in their sessions. The couple practiced problem-solving techniques that seemed to take care of some of the irritants of daily life. But the wife's response to these experiences was less than enthusiastic. In her view, he was becoming more skilled at presenting his side of the story, but it was still the same story of why he felt his way of doing things was adequate. Pearlmutter was frustrated and wondered why her usual psychotherapy techniques did not work and how she could move the process toward an agreeable resolution.

At this point, because she knew something of African American history, she asked the couple to develop a three-generation genogram and to view it in the context of that history. "My goal was to reframe this problem and find a way to promote a 'cognitive shift' with the goal of helping Ms. A. to see herself and Mr. A. through a new pair of lenses" (1996:393). With the aid of the genogram, the couple began discussing their relationship in terms of several male role models that had developed historically in the local black community. In a follow-up meeting, the couple spontaneously informed Pearlmutter that history discussions had continued at home and they were better able to understand each other's personal style, both strengths and weaknesses, by talking about it in terms of historical and community leadership imagery. They also reflected on their home lives when growing up and how their respective parental images were learned. While not all their domestic problems were resolved, the issues that had brought them to Pearlmutter had indeed been reframed and they could talk about them in a more creative and less confrontational way.

But that is not the end of the case. In the article, in a section entitled "My Own Story," Pearlmutter discusses her own ethnic background and how her explicit and articulate understanding of it led her into the culturally responsive clinical style she now uses. Self-evaluation made it easier for her to talk about racial and cultural differences with this couple and to comfortably use cultural resources such as the genogram later in their sessions. One of her key points is that although she had always tried to be culturally sensitive with clients as a matter of engagement, that would not have been sufficient in this case. It was her knowledge of African American cultural history that made the use of cultural resources in the psychotherapy with this couple so effective. Cultural competence as skill, a more sophisticated matter than mere "sensitivity," was critical to her clinical success.

She concludes, "cultural responsiveness does not end with the engagement and assessment of clients. The culture of the clients and the culture of the therapist provides the therapist with powerful metaphors and rich resources with which to introduce change possibilities. When this is combined with an appreciation of the intersubjective meanings for both clients and therapist, culturally responsive and effective therapy indeed becomes possible" (1996:400).

- In addition to a genogram, what other things might Pearlmutter have tried as a result of her knowledge of African American history and experience?
- This couple looked at parental role models in the context of their community's history and linked that to their own family practices. Speculate what some of those models might have been and why they might be distinctive to this community. How might you use that information to work with these clients?
- If you knew nothing of this couple's background and the African American experience generally, what kind of questions would you ask them so you could be better informed?
- Pearlmutter says she was "up front" with this couple about racial and ethnic differences and how that might affect their counseling sessions. What would you say to someone very different from yourself to introduce that topic into a planned course of therapy, and what would tell you the appropriate time for doing that?

2. Test Drive an Idea

Idea 1: What Do We See in a Client?

An ingenious experiment was carried out by Gibbs and Huang (1989) that can be easily replicated in any classroom or training session. They presented two clinical cases, of a child and an adolescent, to an ethnically varied group of practitioners. The facts of each case were always the same, but each practitioner was asked to assume that the client was of the same ethnic identity as himself or herself. Thus, an angry and disruptive nine-year-old boy was alternatively presented as Native American, African American, and Japanese American to comparable-ethnicity clinicians. The clinicians were asked to do an assessment, recommend treatment, and state what kinds of information they would need to fully evaluate the case from a cultural perspective. While the resulting analysis and treatment recommendations showed some similarities across this ethnically varied professional group, there were important differences of emphasis as well.

To try out Gibbs and Huang's experiment, a case can be extracted from virtually anywhere, from either the social work literature or the practice experience of those around you. Gibbs and Huang separated their respondents by ethnicity (individuals who, incidentally, did not have opportunities to discuss the two cases among themselves), and that is a good strategy although it may not always be possible to do so. Instead, small groups could be asked to study the cultural contrast tables in each of the four ethnographic chapters of this book and use the information they contain along with the text as guides to assessment, evaluation, and treatment. Individuals or small groups could each present their findings but also be asked to justify their conclusions in terms of the ethnographic data presented in the relevant chapters.

Gibbs and Huang make a strong case for the relevance of cultural data to intervention, including such topics as the meaning of the presenting problem, family attitudes toward it, existing strategies for working with it, patterns of help-seeking behavior, identity conflicts in stressful environments, appropriateness of recommended treatment, "and applying, with caution, the conventional differential diagnostic criteria. Consequently, ethnic factors should be seriously and carefully considered in every phase of the assessment and treatment process" (1989:374). Their discussion of this exercise is revealing and should be read in full. It is in the chapter entitled "Multicultural Perspectives on Two Clinical Cases" in their book, *Children of Color* (1989).

Idea 2: What Does a Client See in Us?

Those who insist they are ideologically color blind usually believe that their client's appearance is irrelevant to what they do because, they claim, they treat an illness, not a culture. Others argue that body language and nonverbal communications are so easily and so commonly misread that we cannot ignore them as a potential source of tension if not as an outright faux pas. How real are body language differences between cultures and are they important as anything other than individual mannerisms?

In a carefully argued and documented black perspective on psychology and social work, Lena Robinson (1995) says gestures are very important: "we need to examine impression formation from a black perspective, as white social workers working with black people may make judgments about them unaware that the behaviour they are observing has a cultural bias that they are misinterpreting" (1995:30). In her book, she describes a number of culture-specific black communication styles, things familiar to black observers but usually mystifying to whites. She writes of handshakes, walk and stance, hairstyles, dress, eye contact and "gaze behaviour," touch, personal space, and volume levels in speech. These are things that signal who is an insider and who is not, and, as she points out, they have evolved both as individual proclamations and culturally generated defensive maneuvers. They are also, as everyone knows, the fodder of ethnic jokes and mimicry.

Nonverbal behavior can be provocative stuff, and while noticing it in others is commonplace in a pluralistic society, recognizing it in ourselves is more complicated. Again, the comparative approach, and a little ethnographic data, can be enlightening. You can observe nonverbal behavior and body language anywhere, in public or in private. I see it in students in the cafeteria, on the bus I ride to work, and especially on busy downtown streets. In television sitcoms, so-called ethnic (and gender) mannerisms are routinely exaggerated for comic effect. I have asked students to write descriptions of what they see in these settings, the more subtle the behavior described the better, and then to establish that what they have seen is not simply idiosyncratic by noting its appearance in more than one individual.

The real exercise begins, however, back in the class. I ask the students to describe comparable behavior in themselves (walk, voice modulation, touch, gaze, spatial distancing) and explicitly state how they think they were "read" by the people they saw in public places. Some individuals are uncomfortable with this—and they should be—because body response is one of the subtle areas where our protestations of color blindness and egalitarianism are easily undermined. The point of the exercise is to turn the controlling gaze back on ourselves, to make ourselves objects of inspection, and to explore the ideological implications of even the most innocent gestures. This is a real post-modernist activity, if you like to think of it that way, and ethnic and gendered presuppositions can quickly, and explosively, surface. To do the activity well requires maturity and self-comfort that not everyone has, so proceed with caution.

3. More on the Issues

- Building from within

An Afrocentric approach to social work—and critique of the discipline—is developed by Jerome H. Schiele. In a provocative discussion, he calls for more emphasis on building from community strengths and from community-based individual insight and spirituality. His position is powerfully argued and ought to initiate active discussion. It is titled "The Contour and Meaning of Afrocentric Social Work" and appears in the *Journal of Black Studies* (27:800–819, 1997). A related article,

"Afrocentricity: An Emerging Paradigm in Social Work Practice," is in *Social Work* (41:284–295, 1996).

- Working for Children

Two explicitly cultural presentations on the needs and well-being of black children appear in a special issue (January/February 1997) of *Child Welfare* that is exceptional for its coverage on this topic. The entire issue is mandatory reading for those working with black families, but do see Sheryl Brissett-Chapman, "Child Protection Risk Assessment and African American Children: Cultural Ramifications for Families and Communities" (45–64), and Ruth G. McRoy, Zena Oglesby, and Helen Grape, "Achieving Same-Race Adoptive Placements for African American Children: Culturally Sensitive Practice Approaches" (85–106).

- Ethnicity, Women of Color, and Eating Disorders

Identity conflict, media-generated Euro-American body imagery, and their linkage to eating disorders are the subject of this impressive article on ethnomedical problem solving. Treatment procedures are discussed. Diane J. Harris and Sue A. Kuba, "Ethnocultural Identity and Eating Disorders in Women of Color," *Professional Psychology: Research and Practice* (28:341–347, 1997).

- Engaging the Community

The Rutgers Family Project is an innovative program of family support that makes extensive use of community resources, especially black churches. How it was put together is described by Nancy Boyd-Franklin, Tawn Smith Morris, and Brenna H. Bry, "Parent and Family Support Groups with African American Families: The Process of Family and Community Empowerment," *Cultural Diversity and Mental Health* (3:83–92, 1997).

- Help-Seeking Behavior

There are many useful books on social services and African American families. One good one is Sadye L. Logan, ed., *The Black Family, Strengths, Self-Help and Positive Change* (1996). See especially her Epilogue on help-seeking behavior and empowerment.

- Diversity in the Black Community

The recent history of the black middle class and its struggles to achieve identity in a hostile surrounding culture is a subject much overlooked. A very readable introduction is Charles T. Banner-Haley, *The Fruits of Integration, Black Middle-Class Ideology and Culture, 1960–1990* (1994). Included is a discussion of popular culture icons, an important topic since media personalities are often seen by whites as "typical" of their community of origin. Banner-Haley's book provides solid background information that service professionals ought to know.

- Therapy and West Indians

An excellent case study of therapy with a Jamaican woman is reported by Darielle Watts-Jones in *Family Process* (31:105–113, 1992). Watts-Jones's own family comes from the islands so she is familiar with the issues in her client's life and is able to interpret them both as a professional and as someone who has lived the culture. She is explicit about her counseling procedures, one of the solid ethnographic strengths of her article.

- Getting Connected

Looking for on-line access to the African American community? Check into *The African American Network* by Crawford B. Bunkley (1996). He has a huge listing of names, organizations, addresses, and web sites. Included are foundations, charitable organizations, civil rights and political action groups, businesses, churches, and sources for grants and scholarships.

7

NATIVE AMERICANS
IN A NEW WORLD

Forced relocation is not a new experience for most Native or First Americans. There was an Indian Removal Act in 1830 and an Indian Relocation Program in the 1850s. Many elders can recall their childhood, or that of their parents, as an unhappy and confusing time of submission to the discipline of boarding and missionary schools. Two thirds of all contemporary Native Americans live away from reservations—most of them not original homelands anyway. Now, some modern Navajo are being relocated, again with the predictable consequence of high rates of depression, suicides, alcoholism, and various mental health symptoms (Benedek 1993).

The reasons for the current removal are old, another instance of misguided judgment and legalism. In 1882, an executive order of President Arthur gave land around certain mesas in Arizona for the exclusive use of the Hopi and "such other Indians as the Secretary of the Interior may see fit to settle thereon," virtually ignoring the fact that many Navajos lived within the boundaries of the new reservation. Inevitably, conflicts over land (for herding and homes sites) quickly escalated into long-running and expensive legal battles, the Hopi and Navajo each asserting their own claims. The Navajo-Hopi Land Settlement Act of 1974 mandated the partition of 1.8 million acres of the 1882 reservation and the relocation of all members of either tribe living in the area awarded to the other. Over 10,000 Navajo and about 100 Hopi were to be relocated. Numerous Navajo slated for relocation resisted, and legal battles continued until passage of the Navajo-Hopi Land Settlement Act of 1996, whereby Navajo families remaining in the Hopi Partitioned Land were given the option either to sign up for relocation or to sign a seventy-five-year lease with the Hopi. Representatives from all but five resisting Navajo homesites have complied. The legal stirrings of this battle may be over for now, but the personal and familial ones are not. That is why many Navajo, those who must move from homes they have occupied for generations, are seeing counselors and making more use of the Indian Health Services. Others, equally distraught, grieve in more traditional ways not subject to administrative count. The imagery the relocated Navajo use for describing their pain is distinctive and a clue to why land separation is so devastating to them personally. By knowing something of that imagery, we can begin to appreciate some of what they are experiencing.

Maureen Schwarz (1997a) gives a sensitive rendering of a Navajo emic perspective on self, personhood, land, and place and explains how they are linked:

> *This attachment to place—first established during the prenatal stage of life and reaffirmed at every step on the path to full Navajo personhood—is solidified shortly after birth through burial of the umbilical cord. This act anchors an individual to a particular place. This sense of anchoring, and the spiritual and historical nature of the connection to one's home, is implicitly understood in the Navajo world.... [W]hether they are politicians seeking reelection or people facing relocation[,] Navajo men and women...frequently refer to the places where their umbilical cords are buried as "home." (1997a:43)*

The implications of this are developed fully in her book, *Molded in the Image of Changing Woman* (1997b), where Schwarz explains why an umbilical burial literally "screws" or permanently attaches a person to a physical place. Breaking that connection, by abandoning the spot or failing to visit it on a regular basis, is quite literally an unnatural act. Loss of access to the site is "unnerving" in a physical and spiritual sense because it destroys one's referent to the homesite where one is a whole person and it undermines faith in the design of the cosmos that guarantees the validity of that wholeness. As Schwarz points out, Navajo personhood is attenuated by separation from the land. Navajo understanding, captured in lengthy narratives of distress and illness, reveals that many Navajo attribute their community's problems with gangs, drugs, alcohol, and violence to uprootedness. Their views of the causes of their distress are practical, such as the loss of homesites and the expense of rebuilding. But their accounts are also explicitly spiritual, and trauma was explained by reference to supernatural beings, the original plan of the cosmos, and the continued interaction of matter with human purpose.

Not all Native Americans are Navajo; the Hopi of course have their own side of the story, and many Native people who live in urban areas and rarely visit reservations develop their own distinctive narratives to account for the frustrations they feel. My point here is simply that in their narratives many Native Americans foreground images, metaphors, and events that to most outsiders seem "exotic" and certainly not clinical. Theirs is not the language of "relationships" common to pop psychology and the tabloids or of the syndromes reported in *DSM-IV.* Nor are all Native Americans inclined to voice their conceptions of the cosmological since that is not what passes for evidentiary truth in meetings with clinicians. The culturally sensitive care provider need only be aware that powerful and complex beliefs about what a person is, what causes things to go wrong, and the agency of things unknown and unseen may be embedded in narratives of distress. Each community and each client will shape and present his or her understandings as he or she sees fit and may occasionally offer them to us, as the Navajo did for Schwarz, if we are open to taking them seriously.

WHO IS A NATIVE AMERICAN?

The 1990 census counted almost two million Native Americans in the United States, a dramatic increase of 65 percent in the decade since 1980. Although their total number is less than 1 percent of the overall population, their rate of growth is one of the fastest in the country. That is significant because, at the time of European contact, there was an estimated one million people living in North America. By 1920, their numbers had been reduced by war, disease, and poverty to less than 240,000. There may be more Native Americans alive now than at any time in their history. But these statistics are deceptive. They hide a complex political and demographic past, one in which it is not always obvious who is an Indian, or what constitutes Indianness. Through intermarriage with whites, African Americans, and other ethnic communities, through government and tribal labeling (usually based on percentages of "blood" in one's ancestry), and through personal choice and opportunity, some people with Indian ancestry do not think of themselves as Indian. Many others do. For some, their Indianness is an identity they can situationally invoke. For others, it is a permanent affirmation. For many, it is a challenge that raises fundamental questions about self and community.

Over half of all those who identify themselves as Indian are married to non-Indians (Greenbaum 1991:107). Degrees of Indian "blood," used as a measure of Indianness, vary widely. Groups in the Southwest, being more isolated, tend to marry out less whereas those in the South, East, and Midwest have long histories of intermarriage with whites and African Americans. Some groups in the Northwest intermarried with Filipinos and other Asian immigrants. Contemporary Native Americans tend to be younger than the general population and to have higher fertility rates, although these may have declined somewhat in recent years (John 1988). The composition of Native American households is varied, as would be expected among people affiliated with hundreds of ethnic communities, speaking many languages, and exploiting the ecological diversity of an entire continent. But this cultural variation between tribes is not a "problem" for most Native Americans; local and regional differences between Native American communities are expected and, for most people, are a point of interest and discussion.

If cultural variation is expected and normal, the question of who and what "an Indian" is remains contentious. As mentioned, "degrees" of blood are a common measure of Indianness. But it is a measure that was imposed by the dominant white society and, although widely used by Native Americans themselves, it is not indigenous to Native American cultures. (Nor does it have any scientific basis. There is no naturally occurring entity identifiable as "Indian blood" any more than there is "American blood" or "Chinese blood." Interestingly, many white and black Americans describe themselves as having Indian ancestry or "blood" even though they know little or nothing of the specific genealogical connections. Apparently the popularity of "Indian" values has prestige among non-Indians.) Labeling individuals on the basis of "blood quantum" derives from older racial taxonomies formerly used to classify blacks during slavery. Because there was intermarriage among Native Americans and Africans, especially in territories bordering on early colonies and slave states, Native Americans were included in this pernicious form of categorization (Wilson 1992). Porter (1986, cited in Wilson) has argued that far from resulting in ethnic extinction, however, intermarriage with both whites and Africans was a way for Native Americans to preserve their cultural identity. Native American men and women took mates and lived in "marginal environments," adopting features of the dominant society that made them appear non-Indian while in fact Indian ways of living and thinking persisted (Wilson 1992:113). That may account for the difficulty experienced by some tribes, especially those in the East, of establishing that they are in fact Indians and deserving of recognition by governmental authorities.

Because "degrees of blood" are now significant for claiming entitlements through a tribe, and because tribes set their own standards for what constitutes an appropriate degree of authenticity, the "quantum blood" view of Indianness sets the stage for the divisive struggles between "traditionals" and "moderns" in some Native American communities. It is significant that virtually all contemporary Native American novelists, of which there are many, explore the meaning of this conflict in their writings. "This is not surprising, as most of the writers are mixed bloods and utilize mixed-blood protagonists to deconstruct the tensions of modern Native Americans gingerly negotiating life strongly influenced by the majority culture" (Wilson 1992:124). It is a struggle that persists among Native Americans whether they live on reservations or in urban areas. It continues to be discussed, and to be contentious, in virtually all Native American communities and, sometimes, even within families.

Where do contemporary Native American people live? Despite romanticized images suggesting that Native Americans live more in tune with nature than everyone else, only about one third of all Native American, Eskimo, and Aleut people currently live on reservations or on Indian-designated lands. Most live away from reservations, and a substantial number live in cities and towns. Location is important, for John (1985) has noted that "the deprivation experienced by reservation Indians is substantially greater than urban Indians. In general, the reservation group is poorer, supports more people on its income, has fewer social contacts, lower life satisfaction, and poorer health" (237). Nationally, Native Americans tend to be concentrated in the West, especially California, Arizona, and New Mexico, some areas of the South (notably North Carolina), Oklahoma, and the states of the upper Midwest, although they are located in virtually all parts of the country and can be found in wealthy suburbs and middle-class neighborhoods as well. Many Native Americans live in groups that have never been legally recognized as "tribes," yet they keep their sense of ethnic affiliation through their families, community organizations, occupational choices, and residential stability. "It is perhaps remarkable that so many of these groups have retained, in some cases for as many as ten generations, a sense of Indian identity and distinct community organization in spite of the fact that the government has effectively denied their status as Indians" (Greenbaum 1985:362). As with Indian history generally, Indian demography is a picture of geographical dispersion and enormous cultural diversity.

Yet that diversity was neither appreciated by Columbus five hundred years ago or by most of those who came after him. An almost cultivated legacy of ignorance has led to a history of stereotypes that seem truly designed by Hollywood central casting (Bataille and Silet 1980), stereotypes of savages, warriors, cannibals, and humorless stoics. Yet the original peoples of the "new" world were as different among themselves, perhaps even more so, as the peoples, languages, cuisines, and religions of "old" Europe. Many lived a hunting and gathering way of life that was exquisitely attuned to the landscape. Others lived in small, bandlike groups in arid regions that supported only a minimal population. Still others were committed to agriculture and permanent urban settlements. Several major civilizations flourished and they, like civilizations elsewhere, occupied themselves with defense, administration, tax collection, and pursuit of higher scientific and religious knowledge. Freebooting his way among a few small, remote islands in the Caribbean, Columbus was grandly ignorant of the complex world he claimed to have discovered. What lay unseen before him were multiple peoples, languages, religions, and economic adaptations. To speak of "the" American Indian or even "American Indians" generically is one of our most long-standing historical fictions.

The real "discovery," if it can be called that, preceded Columbus by tens of thousands of years. During the last great ice age, a vast amount of seawater was stored on the landmass of North America and Asia in the form of ice sheets and glaciers, significantly lowering ocean levels around the world. That exposed a land bridge nearly 1,000 miles wide, connecting Siberia and Alaska. At the time, no people lived in North America, but hunting and gathering populations were common in eastern Asia and its far north. It would be a mistake, however, to assume that people on the Siberian side of the bridge decided one bright morning to set off and "discover" the Western Hemisphere. Small groups simply hunted game and collected available foods as they always had, moving with the seasons and the animals, until over the centuries they followed their food supply all the way to the tip of South America. The habitation of an entire hemisphere occurred relatively fast, by people known to us from archaeology as Paleo-Indians.

In their thousands of years in the Americas, Paleo-Indians and their descendants pioneered the cultivation of corn, potatoes, pumpkins, squash, beans, sunflowers, peanuts, cotton, tobacco, turkeys, guinea pigs, and llamas. (It is estimated that one-third of all the plant species used to feed people and animals in the world today were first cultivated in the Americas.) They gathered rubber, cocoa, vanilla, and hundreds of pharmaceutical products (including ipecac and quinine) from wild plants. Trade and travel routes were established over which freeways and railroads now run. The confederate government of the Six Nations was a model for the English colonists, and the practice of speaking publicly, but only in turn, was a North American invention, one that we now teach as politeness in children and expect as civility from senators and congressmen. (Contrast our Native American–derived practice of taking turns with the rhetorical styles of the Canadian and British parliaments, with their interruptive shouts and loud table slapping during speeches.) Nor should we omit what may be the ultimate contribution of Native American people to general human knowledge and to the ultimate fate of us all, Vine Deloria's suggestion (tongue in cheek?) that in all likelihood *God is Red* (Deloria 1973).

The earliest indigenous people in North America lived by hunting and gathering, a way of life in which large game animals and seasonally available plant foods were important. Of necessity, their bands were highly mobile, their political organization egalitarian, and their numbers small. About 6,000 years ago, however, the archaeological record shows a transition to greater emphasis on foraging and an increased reliance on plants, fish, and smaller animals. There was nothing simple or "primitive" about these early economies, for they required a high level of cooperation between men and women and between children and adults, and an encyclopedic knowledge of animal habits, plant species, ground and water conditions, seasonal variations, weather, geography, and the nearness and movements of other groups of people. Nor was their lithic or stone tool technology in any sense "simple," for it required great skill in manufacture and use. The archaeological evidence also suggests the existence of extensive, almost transcontinental trade routes, for stone tools are commonly found far from where they were quarried and manufactured. The foraging economies of the people of that time were highly varied, as one would expect for a huge continent with a range of ecological niches. They included the sea-oriented fishing of the Northwest, the very difficult small animal and root and seed gathering of the Great Basin, and the game forests and lake and river fishing of the Midwest and the East coast. Buffalo hunting was practiced on the Great Plains, but not until the introduction of horses and guns by the Spanish did it become the wholesale slaughter subsequently indulged by whites and Native Americans alike.

Agriculture emerged in a number of areas, including the central valley of Mexico and in Peru. In North America, the early phases of plant production appeared both in the Southwest and among some groups east of the Mississippi about 5,000 years ago. Sophisticated farming techniques were common in these areas, including field rotation and irrigation. When Europeans arrived in the late 1600s, they found complex farming communities in the Northeast (the Mohawks, for example) and in the Southeast (the Creeks, Cherokees, and others).

Like their economies and their various histories, the religious beliefs of the native North Americans were diverse. Olson and Wilson (1984) note that polytheism was common, there being a multitude of deities and many levels of religious hierarchy. One widespread element (which may or may not have been universal) was a belief in a singular, permeating creator spirit. But this spirit is probably not comparable to that of the monotheistic god of the Europeans. Rather, it was explicitly pantheistic; "a fusion of matter, spirit, time, and life, a divine energy unifying all the universe. It was not at all a personal being presiding omnipotently over the salvation or damnation of individual people" (Olson and Wilson 1984:11). Beyond that, however, there was a remarkable profusion of ideas about the spiritual realm, including spirits of animals and natural entities, witches and sorcery, the prophetic power of dreams, individual spirit quests, and a complex organization of the spiritual realm and the afterlife. Similarly, religious rituals varied from place to place, with a wide range of "world renewal" ceremonies, winter ceremonials, cleansing and curing rites, and vision quests. Although most Americans, and some contemporary Native Americans, tend to lump all these beliefs and practices together, creating a pan-Indian homogeneity and a singular "great spirit," in fact there was probably far more religious variability among Indian peoples than there was among all the Europeans who arrived after Columbus.

As a part of the homogenizing and romanticizing of native peoples, early Europeans and Americans evolved a popular fiction, more recently abetted by films and the media, suggesting that Native Americans lived "closer to nature" and were more "natural" and spiritual than whites. This belief, counterposed to one which held that Native Americans were only savages and wild animals, led to a mystique, still favored by some, that Native Americans are more ecologically sensitive. There may be a general truth in this but it has to be seen as an ethnographic and historical one, not as a sentimental or romantic imposition. The Europeans who came to North America viewed the continent as a place for a new beginning, one partly spiritual (as expressed by some of the earliest New England colonists) but mostly economic. It had development potential and unclaimed squatter's rights.

By contrast, many Native Americans viewed the land as a locale, the place where human and spiritual agencies intermingled. Where Europeans perceived opportunity through modification and use, Native Americans cultivated rootedness and religiously inspired loyalties to the world as it was. Early generations of Americans acted individualistically, with an "open frontier" and "raw land to be claimed and tamed" mentality. Native American views were more communal, with a strong historical sense of interconnectedness among people, animals, ancestors, and physical places steeped with mythic associations. Their rites and beliefs, in all their diversity, were intended to reinforce that sense of communal purpose and linkage.

The introduction of industrial trade goods (along with literacy, alcohol, diseases, and assimilationist policies) exaggerated and distorted many features of traditional Native American cultures. Guns and horses made hunting, once done entirely on foot, more efficient and ecologically more devastating. Westward expansion by Euroamericans crowded people off of familiar lands, disrupting economic life and contributing to inter-Indian warfare and conflict. While trade goods displaced traditional crafts and skills, Christian missionaries and boarding schools undermined ancient faiths. Despite these impositions, however, the fundamental world view of many Native Americans was always at great variance from that of Euroamericans, and in many quarters that variance continues with surprising vigor despite superficial appearances of assimilation.

CONTEMPORARY ASPECTS OF NATIVE AMERICAN LIFE

The history of Native Americans is much too complex to pursue in detail here, but we must note some of the major events that have influenced the lives of contemporary Native American people. This is important because many Native American people know these events well and discuss them regularly. Unlike whites, Native Americans generally do not view their history as a boring academic exercise. The allotment acts, the Indian Reorganization Act, the drive for reservation termination, a recently revived Indian militancy, and "self-governing" relations with the Bureau of Indian Affairs are all major concerns for them, worth noting for what they reveal about the fundamental difficulties that have marked relations between Native Americans and whites. We can usefully think about these events in terms of assimilation and nativism, opposing values that are evident throughout the long and painful history of Native American–white contact.

As noted above, some Native American groups were practicing agriculture when Europeans began arriving in North America. But Native Americans usually thought of their farming as a communal activity, something done to feed everyone as needed. It was never a "job" intended to produce a surplus for sale and profit. Farming as a "business" was a view that motivated Congressional and other reformers who, after the Civil War, believed the solution to the "Indian problem" was the conversion of Native Americans into small-scale, entrepreneurial farmers. Militarily defeated by the U.S. Army, Native Americans were moved onto reservations, and the idea was to transform these reservations into family farms, integrated into the prevailing capitalist agricultural economy. These "allotments" were the subject of legislative actions throughout the 1880s, of which the most important was the Dawes Act. It authorized the President, through the Department of the Interior, to create allotments for family farms, usually 160 acres each. Other laws permitted Native Americans to lease or sell their allotments to non-Indians, who often turned out to be speculators who sold the land to white settlers. The Dawes Act was predictably disastrous. Millions of acres of reservation land were lost by Native Americans to whites, thousands of Native American families were left without land resources of any kind, and many who did retain titles owned worthless tracts that they could neither farm nor sell.

Following the period of allotments, the U.S. government became more active in regulating Native American affairs. It established a system of boarding schools and the Bureau of Indian Affairs took control of existing tribal schools. The Bureau established a curriculum, some of it modeled after the new schools for freed slaves in the American South, with an emphasis on trades, domestic management or "home economics," and agriculture. In the Indian schools, native languages were prohibited, often brutally so, and Christianity and nineteenth-century notions of industry, thrift, and Victorian propriety were imposed with a militaristic ruthlessness and efficiency. The explicit goal of the system was to obliterate traditional Native American cultures within one generation, two or three generations if necessary. While assimilation was the stated goal of this policy, its effect was not assimilation into the mainstream of the American economy but into subservient, marginal positions at its edges. This was especially so for young Native American women, subjected to an extreme regime of boarding school discipline and drudgery that passed as "training." "Habituation to simple labor clearly superseded any truly vocational goals—that is, training for employment—for Indian girls" (Lomawaima 1993: 230). The Bureau of Indian Affairs was not accountable to Indians nor interested in determining their views or their self-determined concerns. "Charged with guarding Indians interests, the BIA also largely determined what those interests were.... [Its] supervision was tutelary, intended to break down indigenous social relations and cultural practices and replace them with the sociocultural patterns of Euro-American society" (Cornell 1984:45).

In the 1920s, however, a reaction set in against the abuses surrounding allotments and Native American education. A new generation of reformers, many of them whites, called for a revived tribalism as a way of reinvigorating Native American communities, and for a new role by the federal government in safeguarding Native American rights. The Indian Reorganization Act of 1934 stopped the selling of Native American lands, in recognition of the failure of the Dawes Act to assimilate Native Americans and improve the economic life of their communities. Under New Deal legislation, tribes were encouraged to set up tribal governments, and a small amount of land was returned to Native American ownership.

But those who administered the reforms for the federal government underestimated the strength of the opposition to the 1934 Reorganization Act, especially from western congressmen who feared that large tracts of land would be lost to potential development. The reformers also underestimated the uneven response of the various tribes. While some took advantage of the opportunities the act provided, others were severely divided on what they wanted for the future of their communities. The factionalism that was prevalent among so many tribal groups not only forestalled much of what the New Deal planners hoped could be done, but it also contributed to growing Congressional sentiment to "terminate" the tribes and the reservation system altogether.

The desire to terminate all special claims and relationships Native Americans might have with the federal government had always been favored by some politicians. Termination of reservations was seen as an opportunity to "resolve" the "Indian problem" permanently. During the postwar Communist baiting scares of the 1950s and the national paranoia of McCarthyism, any expression of ethnic independence was seen as a threat to the holy task of containing international Communism. Calls for Indian separateness and tribal revitalization were seen as politically suspect, even treasonous. (This despite the fact that many Native Americans served honorably in the military during World War II.) In addition, there was no sympathy for allocating funds to Native American interests when so much of the government's financial resources were committed to the emerging military-industrial complex. A demand arose from some politicians to "get the government out of the Indian business," as they described it, an issue that periodically reappears in conservative political circles to this day. Plans for termination called for the dissolution of tribal governments; transfer of tribal civil and criminal jurisdiction to state and county governments; transfer of Native American health and education services to the states; political subordination of reservations to local jurisdictions; and cash inducements to individual Native Americans who would agree to relinquish all their claims and privileges as Native Americans.

Predictably, termination proposals were divisive in virtually all Native American communities. Traditionalists and "full bloods," usually resident on reservations, resisted termination of the benefits they had come to expect under the reservation system. (For some tribes, those benefits were and remain the very lucrative sponsorship of bingo and, more recently, multimillion dollar casinos, especially in states where gambling is prohibited.) Some less traditional Native Americans, living off reservations, found the government's offer of a "buy-out" to their personal advantage. Many of these latter individuals were poor and termination promised them, quite literally, a once-in-a-lifetime windfall. But the federal government's efforts at termination were so confounded by economic, jurisdictional, and intraethnic complexities and contradictions that the issue finally died in the early 1960s. However, it did not die before nineteen tribes lost all of their federal support and nearly three million acres of Native American land were sold to outsiders.

During the period of national turmoil marked by the Vietnam war and the rise of ethnic militancy in the 1960s, Native American groups were planning and debating a new phase of pan-Indian activism, with an emphasis on tribal self-determination. They confronted the assimilationist policies of allotment and termination directly. The most dramatic examples of this challenge were the much publicized seizure of Alcatraz in San Francisco Bay by a group of Native American militants and armed resistance to the federal government by members of AIM, the American Indian Movement, at the Pine Ridge Reservation in South Dakota. In the Pacific Northwest, Native American "fish-ins" attracted sympathetic celebrities from the entertainment industry and challenged state game departments and white dominance of commercial fisheries. These events, as well as many smaller and less publicized ones, were indicative of a new mood in many Native American communities, a determination to protect local, tribal autonomy and eliminate federal policies restricting the sovereignty of tribes. Assimilation was explicitly rejected. As a troublesome relic from pre–Civil War times (when it was part of the old War Department), the Bureau of Indian Affairs also came under attack. Its usefulness was debated (and continues to be) by Indians and non-Indians alike.

One of the important legacies of the activists of that time was the Indian Self-Determination and Education Assistance Act of 1975. The act declared that:

> *The Congress hereby recognizes the obligation of the United States to respond to the strong expression of the Indian people for self-determination by assuring maximum Indian participation in the direction of educational as well as other Federal services to Indian communities so as to render such services more responsive to the needs and desires of those communities. (Quoted from Olson and Wilson 1984:205)*

Under the act, tribal governments now contract with the Bureau of Indian Affairs and the Department of Health and Human Services for educational, health, and other services. The implementation of social services is generally left to local initiative. Other laws have attempted to maximize Indian control so that the preservation of ethnic identity is both policy and practice. For example, the Indian Child Welfare Act of 1978 restricts the removal of Native American children from Native American families, although there are circumstances under which this regulation has been controversial among both Native Americans and non–Native Americans. Differing tribal communities, of course, have their own understandings of the act and sometimes there are conflicts over the interpretation of the laws and regulations that continue to emanate from Washington, D.C. Native Americans, like anyone else, have differing views of what they want for themselves, their families, or their tribes. Some groups are essentially closed communities, guarding their ethnic distinctiveness with seclusion and social distance, while others work actively with a multitude of local and state agencies. In either case, the preservation of distinctiveness is now the law of the land and that policy is reflected in social services, health, education, and housing.

Paralleling the local implementation of federal policies, Indian people are also working toward preservation of traditional cultural forms. While English is common on most reservations, Native American languages still persist in surprising number. The fact that whites do not often hear them does not mean they are not there. In addition, Native American religions, in their enormous variation, continue to be important. Sweat lodges and winter ceremonials are common, especially among some groups in western states. In recent years public celebrations have become more inclusive, not less so, and there is hardly a weekend where there is not, somewhere, a powwow attracting people from all over the United States. Some ceremonials are open only to Native Americans or by special invitation. But many are public, and interested outsiders are welcomed and treated graciously. Hospitality, nonintrusiveness, and sharing have been important values in Native American communities literally for millennia. In contemporary America, that is still true.

NATIVE AMERICANS AND SOCIAL SERVICES

As with any underserved community, the range of social service and mental health needs among Native Americans is daunting. But there are special challenges facing social workers who serve Native American communities. Meketon (1983) has listed some of them. First is the basic issue of language. Most Native Americans know and use English, but many do not, and many do not use it comfortably. There are more than 300 dialects and separate languages in use in contemporary Indian communities and, given the current political mood of ethnic distinctiveness, those languages are valued in a way they were not just a few years ago. One result is that even communication with outsiders who want to be helpful can be awkward and, on occasions, difficult. There is no reason to believe that monolingual social service personnel would be willing or able to learn languages that are complex and pho-netically unfamiliar, hence the importance of the word-centered ethnographic interviewing styles described earlier in this book (see Chapter 4). But good inter-viewing skills are no substitute for second language proficiency. Even skilled workers will be at a disadvantage if they do not show at least a minimal interest in local language preferences.

Second, there is enormous cultural diversity among Native Americans, far more than among any other ethnic community in America. How can service pro-fessionals begin to appreciate how great that diversity is? Anthropologists have often thought of cultural variations in traditional North America in terms of "cul-ture areas." Culture areas are large regions within which more or less similar lan-guages, community organization, religious beliefs, and economic adaptations can be found (Driver 1969). In pre-Columbian times such areas included the Southeast, Midwestern Woodlands, Great Basin, High Plains, Central and Southern Califor-nia, and the Northwest Coast. While many Indians are highly mobile, and many now live in cities, these large divisions demarcate known and remembered differ-ences that Native American people recognize and respect. However, within these regions, localized diversity is common, a diversity that is made even more complex by urban–rural and reservation–off reservation distinctions (Ross and Moore 1987).

Third, many Native American communities are geographically isolated, which contributes to their cultural uniqueness and has an impact on how services are used. People who live in remote areas find a trip to a clinic or a store a major effort, both in time and money. Old cars, bad roads and weather, nonexistent or unreliable public transportation, and cost are all obstacles to getting help. Home visits by social workers are expensive, and costs per client visit may be more than many agencies are willing or able to pay. Those concerns are a reminder that many of our social services are really designed for urban people and for maximizing cli-ent contact within an eight-hour day. Some Native American communities may require innovative and time-generous ways of delivering services to those who need them, ways that may not always be cost-effective compared with those in urban areas.

Fourth, there are numerous local, state, and federal jurisdictional issues that get in the way of providing effective services to Native American people. They range from overlapping and contradictory laws and policies to turf wars within agencies and between community groups. Resolving some of these obstacles to effective service delivery may be the most important and culturally responsible service some social workers can provide.

In addition to these points, there are complex variations in family life among Native American people, and most social workers serving Native Americans prob-ably do not know enough about them. Traditionally, "family" has meant not only household but also extended networks, lineages, and clans. It is rare for individu-als, including urbanized ones, to think of family in the narrow sense of the nuclear unit. Particularly in rural areas, where intimate face-to-face relations are common, one's kin are many. Childhood naming ceremonies often establish lifelong linkages between the infant and adults who will share in the responsibilities of child rearing along with biological parents (Shomaker 1989, 1990). In addition, lineage and clan membership may be an important basis for affiliations, cooperation, even marriage choices in later life.

Nor are these variations restricted to rural or reservation life. Red Horse and his associates (1981) documented important differences among Native American urban families in Minneapolis. They found that some families were "traditional," continuing to use the Ojibway language in the home. While they participated in some of the sports and cultural activities of the larger society, their real loyalties were to powwows and traditional religious observances. "Bicultural" Native American families used English at home, were members of mainstream (usually Catholic) congregations, and saw themselves as highly integrated into the dominant society. In "pantraditional" families, the entertainments and social life of the dominant culture were explicitly rejected; both Ojibway and English were used in the home, and everyone was involved in self-conscious reidentification and re-creation of Native American belief systems drawn from a variety of tribal sources. These diverse family patterns add complexity to the task of understanding Native American communities, both rural and urban. They suggest a world generally hidden from the scrutiny of the larger society, one with which social service personnel need to be more familiar if they are to deliver services in culturally acceptable ways. As Red Horse puts it, "each [family] pattern is legitimate within its own relational field and contributes to a family sense of selfhood" (1981:59). The task of the social worker is to discover why that is so among the Native American clients he or she serves.

THE SPECIAL CASE OF ALCOHOL

Alcohol is perhaps the most serious challenge facing modern Native American people as well as the health and service professionals who work with them. Generally, alcohol use and misuse is more common among minorities than among whites, but for Native Americans its prevalence is devastating (U.S. Department of Health and Human Services 1985). Compared with the general population, rates of alcoholism among Native Americans are higher, death rates due to alcohol-related causes are eight times higher, and Native Americans as a group tend to die younger, often from alcohol and alcohol-aggravated conditions (Christian, Dufour, and Bertolucci 1989).

That said, it is equally important to note that patterns of alcohol consumption are, like Native American cultures, highly variable. Drinking, even problem drinking, among Native Americans is a culturally constructed phenomenon, its expression indicative of historical as well as current social circumstances. "Drinking" as a customary practice cannot be treated as a unitary pathology for which a singular treatment modality is recommended. Drinking may also be linked to other conditions, such as depression and suicide, in what some researchers are now calling combinations of "comorbidity" (Maser and Dinges 1992; O'Nell 1992). That is, drinking, depression, and suicide may be linked in ways that are community and culturally specific, their interrelationships undetectable using the decontextualized diagnostic categories of the *DSM-IV* manual. The possibility of comorbidity enormously complicates any kind of problem assessment. It may be culturally myopic, as a Native American social worker once suggested to me, for anyone to speak of a "treatment of choice" for Native Americans or their drinking. In this section, I want to suggest some of the reasons for that, and review what the multiplicity of Native American drinking styles suggests for planning and intervention. I also want to affirm, as a necessary and preliminary caution to any generalizations made here, that not all Native Americans drink, and abstainers as well as moderate users can be found in all Native American communities.

A number of theories of Native American drinking have been proposed, three of which I will discuss briefly following the work of Weisner, Weibel-Orlando, and Long (1984). First, sociological theories emphasize the history of repression and economic marginalization of Native Americans over nearly 500 years of European occupation and dominance. Those theories argue that whether Native Americans are on reservations or in urban areas, they respond to their experiences as do members of poorer or lower-class communities generally. Stress underlies the misuse of alcohol and that, in turn, leads to violence, family disintegration, and all the problems that beset an underclass regardless of its ethnicity. In this perspective, there is nothing culturally unique to excessive drinking among Native Americans; drinking is what oppressed people do, and their unfortunate personal choices in the matter are compounded by society's habit of blaming the victim.

Cultural theories usually begin with the cultural history of a specific community, in addition to experiences of repression and dislocation, looking to the distinctive ways that drinking behavior traditionally have been interpreted. The argument here is that variations in worldview and social organization will correlate with variations in drinking experience. Thus societies with a tradition of the vision quest, or where psychoactive substances were part of religious rituals, will attach less opprobrium to heavy drinking, at least under some circumstances. The "ecstatic" nature of certain patterns of drinking may fit into preexisting explanatory frameworks, making drinking in public and excessive drinking more difficult to control. According to this viewpoint, groups such as the Navajo and Sioux will not have sanctions against destructive drinking. By contrast, Native American societies that are more hierarchical might be expected to place greater sanctions on drinking since outbursts of "deviant" behavior violate strong community norms of order. In these instances, problem drinking could be hypothesized to be a more privatized, secretive activity, one that isolates the individual from the community at large. Eastern Oklahoma Indians (Cherokee, Creek, Choctaw, Chickasaw), for instance, were predominantly horticulturalists rather than nomadic hunters. They used fermented beverages in ceremonies well before white contact and have had longer exposure and experience with European-style alcohol products. Historically, they may have had more institutionalized controls on drinking and, since they reside in what is now the Southern "Bible belt," they have acquired traditional Protestant objections to drinking of any kind. Drinking for them would be a different kind of experience with a differing set of meanings and controls.

As Weisner, Weibel-Orlando, and Long (1984:240) point out, there may be more recent cultural models for Native American drinking as well. California Indians, and perhaps some in other parts of the West, may have adopted a lumberjack or frontiersman model. That model stresses hard, episodic, binge drinking as found in male-centered communities of ranch hands and prospectors. It would be less common among the farmers and merchants who represented the second wave of white encroachment on the frontiers. As "work ethic" types, these second wave Euro-Americans had more privatized drinking styles, which would have been less visible to Native Americans.

Another variant of the cultural approach has been suggested by Morinis (1982) in his work among "skidrow" Indians. He sees alcohol less as a drug than as a symbol of exchange in an urban setting, one that deliberately inverts the standards of the larger society. Thus, urban drinking is bar oriented with intense social interaction. It is episodic rather than ongoing, with heavy consumption tied to brief stints of work and the availability of cash. It is followed by a period of abstention until more money is at hand. Morinis found that police, social workers, and aid car attendants reported Native Americans to be noncompliant, hostile, poor at communication, and uncooperative when efforts were made to provide them with simple medical care. He argues that the urban Native Americans he studied in Vancouver, British Columbia, "did not require much alcohol to begin *acting* very drunk" (1982:205), that their offenses were usually alcohol related and not against property or persons, and that display, especially that which was antisocial, was typical of their drunken behavior. If these findings prove to be typical of Native American drinking in urban areas generally, then it is clear that addressing the subcultural meaning of drinking, especially its rejection of the values of the larger society, is as important as understanding clinical symptomotology. Further, intervention techniques that urge compliance with "respectable" standards of work and family life may have little meaning for these clients.

A third set of explanations for Native American drinking are psychological. These theories look to intrapsychic stress, family experiences, life history, role models, peer group attachments, and acculturation difficulties as explanations of alcohol and substance abuse. Studies of "locus of control" are typical of work in this area (Mariano et al. 1989). Researchers often find problem drinkers, including Native American drinkers, to have more "external expectancies" and "perceptions of less personal control" over their drinking (1989:336). That is, their behavior is a response to suggestion and opportunity, and they are unable to control themselves. But from a cultural perspective, interpreting the meaning of "expectancies" and "personal control" among Native Americans has to be viewed as a conceptual minefield, especially where the analyst has limited understanding of the history and cultural configurations of the specific communities in which Native American drinkers live. Recommendations for relief through social skills training or other standardized modes of clinical intervention are, from an ethnographic perspective, an admission that the analyst does not know how to integrate cultural variables into clinical technique or how to devise a culturally responsive service.

Alcoholism is one of the most vexing problems in Native American communities and, as indicated, there are many theories about it. But the fact is that for all the research on drinking among Native Americans, and there has been an enormous amount, very little is known about what "works" to change people's behavior, or under what circumstances a given intervention "works" for the long term. There are, however, some interesting clues.

Based on her analysis of more than fifty Native American alcohol and substance abuse programs in recent years, Weibel-Orlando (1989:153) made the following observations and recommendations. She found that successful efforts to resolve problem drinking involved at least one of several features. They included:

1. Self-generated and self-directed actions by the community that were community rather than individual oriented. Court-directed intervention, and standardized clinical models such as one-on-one and family "ecological" approaches did not usually have a long-term impact.

2. A charismatic individual who served as a focus for action. That person could be a shaman, tribal leader, or other high-ranking individual who, as a recovering alcoholic, could make extraordinary demands on the behavior of others.

3. A healing community with historically established values, procedures, apprentice-like relationships, and narrative styles. Explicitly oriented toward healing as a group process, this activity offered a substitute to the values and relationships of local subcommunities of drinking and drinkers.

Weibel-Orlando adds that abstinence and doctrines of the "recovered alcoholic" typical of the Alcoholics Anonymous model did not need to be the operational goals for these healing communities, although they could be. Controlled or moderate drinking could be a legitimate aim, with an emphasis on reducing risks from interpersonal violence, car accidents, and hunting and drowning accidents. Her point, however, is that in successful programs all these activities were locally generated and legitimized. It may be, then, that the most important efforts of social and health care professionals are those that facilitate, in whatever way necessary, the creation of healing communities and the provision of technical assistance only to the extent that its need is recognized by Native American beneficiaries.

One population with special needs in this area is that of Native American adolescents. For them, the teen years can be a turbulent if not deadly time. Alcohol and drug use, in some communities, is well above national averages. What may be most important, however, is that experimentation with alcohol, drugs, and toxic inhalants such as glue and gasoline begins among some at an early age. Beauvais and LaBoueff (1985) found that on the seven reservations they sampled, fully one-third of all children between ages 9 and 12 had used either alcohol or drugs or both. Their sampling was of students in schools; had they reached those not in schools the percentage probably would have been higher. They observe that "Indian alcoholism has usually been seen as an adult problem. The majority of treatment efforts have been slanted toward the adult population, with detox facilities, halfway houses, Alcoholics Anonymous, and one-to-one counseling being the typical responses on the reservation" (1985:149). Where children are involved, prevention and intervention have to be thought of differently.

It is important to note that drug usage has never been typical of Native American peoples historically. Where psychoactive substances such as peyote have been common, they have always been part of religious and ritual activities in which their availability was regulated and their use was related to the acquisition of supernatural power. Drugs for recreation were never sanctioned. Casual use of drugs is an invention of the dominant white society. The fact is that many if not most adult Native Americans use alcohol very little and drugs not at all.

The reasons for drug use by Native Americans vary, of course, but they may not be entirely due to generalized problems of "acculturation," at least as that is normally understood. Oetting (1980, quoted in Beauvais and LaBoueff 1985) went beyond the usual research formulas by dividing sample subjects into three categories: "traditional," "acculturated," and "bicultural." Survey results showed that the highest rates of drug abuse were among the "acculturated," those who identified least with Native American values of any kind; the next highest group of users were those described as "traditional." The lowest usage was among "bicultural" individuals, those who were effective in both the white and Native American worlds and moved comfortably between them.

How does that relate to younger people? Edwards and Egbert-Edwards argue that "many Indian adolescents have lived with drinking/drug behavior to the extent that they see them as 'Indian' behaviors" (1990:287). Further, they claim that many adults and tribes do not acknowledge that such usage is a problem. "In some situations, substance use and abuse are seen as components of Indian life-styles. A myth is perpetuated that 'everyone' participates in substance abuse" (Edwards and Egbert-Edwards 1990:287–288). Confrontation with drug and alcohol use among teenagers usually occurs when professionals from outside the community demand that "something be done" and bring solutions of their own. The list of programs that have been proposed and tried is impressive and most, according to Edwards and Egbert-Edwards, do not work. They argue that,

> *(1) a simple program aimed at improving self-esteem will fail; (2) a program based on the idea that alcohol is used as a substitute for social acceptance will fail; (3) a program based on the idea that alcohol is taken by depressed, anxious, and otherwise emotionally disturbed youth will fail; (4) a program that uses "socially acceptable" people to reach deviant youth will fail; (5) a program that provides cultural ceremonies and doesn't follow through to ultimately change peer clusters will fail; (6) recreational and social activities that do not actively and completely exclude alcohol will fail (1990:286).*

So what will work? Edwards and Egbert-Edwards (1990) offer overviews of a number of programs that do work, and the interested reader should examine their sources. They include the Soaring Eagles program in Minneapolis, the Native American Youth "Drug Busters" in Colorado, and the Chevak Village Youth Association in Alaska. All of these programs began as community prevention efforts. Their core was a group of local, concerned people, including tribal leaders and elders. As a group, they systematically studied the problem in their own locality through self-identified task groups that included membership from across the community. Outside experts were involved when the task forces felt they needed them, not before, and their assistance was advisory rather than managerial. Schools were the focus of activity—for discussions, planning, implementation— because that is where young people and the drugs are. Because family life and family values are central to Native American communities, whole families, extended and otherwise, were recruited into programs. Family units, not individuals, were the object of "intervention," and counseling, by locals, was on matters of behavior and behavior control, not feelings. Ceremonial and recreational events were frequent, and strong community expectations that everyone participate were made explicit.

A communal approach is not always easy to implement. New research to accurately define the extent of a problem will probably arouse old suspicions because for too long Native Americans have seen research projects come through their communities with no benefits as a result. Public gatherings and discussions can become difficult if they are not kept on task, especially where there are factions and cliques with their own agendas. But most important, predetermined solutions must be avoided, and local responses must take precedence. Enthusiastic outsiders, however well intentioned, usually lack the knowledge of local history or internal conflicts to comment authoritatively on what Native American people ought to do. Their most important contribution may be encouraging families and groups to invest their time and energy in devising solutions that they can support after all the social workers, applied anthropologists, and health professionals have gone away.

NATIVE AMERICAN SUICIDE

Alcohol is only one part of a large set of complex issues affecting Native Americans, another being exceptional rates of suicide in some Native American populations. Rates and patterns of self-destructive behavior vary by tribe, of course, but nationally the figures are alarming. Native Americans have the highest suicide rate of all U.S. ethnic groups and Native American adolescents have a rate about twice that of their peers in other racial and ethnic communities. (An important document, *The State of Native American Youth Health* [*Division of General Pediatrics and Adolescent Health* 1992] summarizes the current information in this area.) Manson et al. (1989a) found that among a cohort of youth who attended a Native American boarding school, fully 23 percent had attempted suicide. By one estimate, for every achieved suicide eight others are attempted (Rosenberg et al. 1987). Among adolescents, significant risk factors included alcohol and suicide attempts by friends or family members. Suicides among Native American youth tend to occur in clusters among people who know one another, several occurring within a short period of time. In some instances alcohol, especially "hard" liquor taken in lethal doses, is the mechanism of death (Grossman, Milligan, and Deyo 1991). The picture that emerges is one of loss of life at near epidemic proportions.

How, from a cross-cultural perspective, can we begin to understand high rates of suicide in any particular Native American population? Recall that in Chapter 2, I suggested that a social problem, and the way a people experience and define it, is in some sense culturally constructed. Each suicide or hunting accident is a distinctive event, but each also invokes a set of implicit cultural themes. The task in culturally sensitive intervention is to find these themes so we can understand better the role they play in how people define and act on their needs. Only then will we be in a position to plan intervention that will make sense to clients. Suicide is an instructive example.

Most whites and many Native Americans believe that the prevalence of suicide is a consequence of forced and incomplete acculturation. In some instances this is probably true in a general sense, but it is not universally true. It is merely an assumption. The story is more complicated. Levy and Kunitz (1987), an anthropologist and a physician, respectively, looked at the history of suicides in Hopi communities and the prevention programs designed to control them. While many Hopi, especially Hopi elders, attribute increased suicide to the influence of white culture, Levy and Kunitz could not find that suicide rates had changed significantly over many years in these relatively isolated and self-contained communities. They did find, however, that suicide victims were people who occupied a predictable place in the traditional Hopi social order.

Hopi communities are matrilineal. A man marries into the lineage of his wife, and his wife's brothers have considerable influence in their sister's marriage and her household. Although unfamiliar to most white Americans, matrilocal residence is not that rare, and the powerful role of a woman's brothers in her marriage and domestic life is normal in matrilineal societies around the world. Where it occurs, this arrangement is not a problem since everyone expects that the interests of the group, here the matrilineage, take precedence over the wishes of individuals. Further, the Hopi, like many Native American groups, prefer endogamy, marriage within a clan line close to one's own. By marrying within an affiliated line, it is more likely that personal and clan loyalties will coincide and conflict will be reduced. In addition to these expectations, the public ideology of Hopi society is egalitarianism; differences of wealth or rank are said to be slight. However, everyone knows that not all family lines are of equal social status. Some families have control of productive lands while others have access only to marginal areas. Some lineages own important religious ceremonies and songs that only they can use and the ownership of these symbolic goods is very important in most Native American communities. Clearly, despite professed ideology, not all lineages and clans are equal, and that can generate conflicts.

When considering the effects of demography on marriage patterns—births, sex ratios, residence patterns, and emigration and return—Levy and Kunitz found that some marriages will inevitably be "deviant." They are marriages that link socially unequal clans, lineages, or communities that did not customarily intermarry. "Deviant" marriages challenge the moral differences that distinguish historically distinctive marriage units. They also put at risk the men and women, especially the men, who enter into them since their actions will be heavily scrutinized by the wife's brothers and any disgruntled members of her lineage or clan group. Levy and Kunitz found that individuals in "deviant" marriage relationships, and especially their children, were most exposed to community stigmatizing and were at highest risk for alcoholism and suicide. Not only were these individuals exposed to unusual stresses, but their marriages and subsequent behavior were subject to negative labeling, a highly charged feature of life in small, predominantly face-to-face communities.

The lesson here is that clinical factors alone, and epidemiological factors alone, could not predict who was at risk among the Hopi. A knowledge of community culture and history, especially the history of marriages, was crucial. Levy and Kunitz found the sources of the twin demons of alcoholism and suicide far more elusive than models of "failed" acculturation or clinically defined pathology could predict. In fact, it could be argued on the basis of their evidence that explanations of Native American suicide that rely on acculturation theories or psychological variables alone are essentially ethnocentric. These models originated in the white community, yet they are accepted by whites and Hopi alike. That is because as explanatory models they serve the ideological needs of both groups. For whites, failed acculturation and psychological deficits justify continued efforts to assimilate Native Americans and treat their deficiencies with individualizing interventions. For Hopi, the models blame the victims and relieve others of having to confront the destructive effects of community-generated labeling and the contradiction of egalitarian beliefs created by historical variations in lineage power.

The Levy and Kunitz analysis is specific to the Hopi situation, but it has a general implication for intervention that is important. Social change, traditional patterns of community organization, local history, and the current activities of service providers and external agencies are complex and intertwined. Models of causation and intervention based on the presumptive importance of specific clinical, diagnostic, or other singular features may not be accurate or adequate. Further, any model of therapeutic intervention carries with it implicit values and preferences, including values about which data are important for an assessment and which are not. So-called treatments of choice are always "someone's choice," and that someone's preferences may or may not be appropriate to small, closed groups where community sentiments have powerful effects on the behavior of others.

Successful suicide prevention may require something exceptional and innovative, perhaps activity that is outside the established institutions of health and benevolence. Levy and Kunitz argue that "an essential task for prevention programs is the identification of community strengths rather than deficits or weaknesses" (1987: 938). In the Hopi case, they recommended programs for youth such as wilderness adventures. Those kinds of preventive activities draw upon valued experiences in the community, mix individuals who are and are not "at risk," have explicit goals that do not identify participants as "deviants," and put advisees and counselors in relations that do not carry the stigmata of "client" or "patient." They are also low in cost and have the advantage of reaching individuals before a crisis develops. The disadvantage of their proposal is that it implicitly challenges the assumptions and practices of those whose institutional services are already in place—health and social service agencies, staff, and sometimes funding sources. They also challenge the therapeutic models of many who work in established programs.

CULTURAL CONTRASTS AND CULTURAL COMPETENCE

This brief overview of the Native American experience and several of the health and service issues that concern Native people identifies some of the complexities professional workers in this area face. Native Americans have the oldest cultural traditions on the continent, yet in some ways theirs are the most fragile of any ethnic group. Engulfed by an industrial consumer culture built on unapologetic exploitation of human and natural resources, they have faced everything that is the antithesis of their history and traditions. Exposed to genocidal rates of population loss, Native Americans have preserved a sense of identity through individual flexibility and high regard for communal traditions. Many Native Americans, especially those who live on reservations and in rural areas, think of themselves as Indians rather than as members of a "minority" group (Neumann et al. 1991). Their sense of cultural distinctiveness may be greater than that of other ethnic peoples, suggesting that social workers who serve Indians will need to make special efforts to understand the rationale of their clients' responses to offers of support and assistance.

In reviewing some of the practices and preferences that distinguish many Native American peoples from those in the dominant culture, it is worth mentioning again that it is cultural *contrasts*, not just differences, that are important in the ethnic competence approach. An emphasis on difference alone presupposes an "us versus them" relationship; it is essentially adversarial. Clearly, that is not helpful in providing services and it abets the process of stereotyping. In emphasizing contrast, the social worker must put himself or herself into the relationship. The service provider, after all, is "different" too, and the client's perceptions of difference are at least as important. Professionals must examine the cultural baggage they bring from both their institutional and personal backgrounds.

In Table 7.1 on page 240, a series of very generalized Native American–white American cultural features are contrasted. They represent an initial effort to think about differences in legitimately comparative terms. I have brought them together from a variety of sources, mostly prominent Native American scholars and service providers. But I have also had the advantage of drawing on the tradition of anthropological field research in Native American communities. Because of the historical presence of anthropologists among Indians and on Indian reservations, a comment on that is useful here, perhaps as a short cautionary tale for social and health service workers.

TABLE 7.1   Selected Cultural Contrasts, Native American and White American Communities*

Native American	White American
Family structure is varied from tribe to tribe and rural to urban areas, but extended units in various forms are common.	Nuclear families are assumed to be the norm although there is great variability and experimentation.
Children often have multiple care givers and live with various relatives as is convenient.	Children are expected to live with biological parents and, in cases of conflict, preference is given to the mother.
Cooperation and sharing are highly valued; individualism, assertiveness, and impulse are discouraged.	Early displays of individualism and lifelong care for the needs of the self are considered normal and even healthy.
Noninterference and respect for the rights and choices of others are highly valued. Confrontation is rarely appropriate.	Assertive (but not aggressive) speech and behavioral styles are favored. Leadership and individual achievement are honored.
Pacing activities according to the needs and expectations of others is more important than observing clock time and abstract schedules.	Punctuality, promptness, and adherence to abstract time schedules are critical to success.
Elders have important ceremonial and sometimes political roles; their views count.	Elders usually live apart and are not expected to exercise political, ceremonial, or financial control over others.
Religious values and ritual practices infuse Native American life and are regarded as critical components in preserving Native American identity and in promoting healing.	Religious and ritual practice is a matter of personal preference with little stigma attached to either participation or avoidance.

*As with all the cultural contrast charts in this book, this list of statements may or may not apply to any specific individual. *These contrasts refer only to general tendencies within groups, not to the attributes of persons.* Individuals vary widely in their commitment to the values of their own culture and to how they choose to observe them in their daily affairs.

The love–hate relationship between anthropologists and Native Americans goes back well over a century to a time when the federal government first began financing research expeditions into Indian territories. The goal was ethnographic information that would lead to enlightened administration, pacification, and speedy assimilation. It was also seen as "pure research" into the disappearing customs of dying cultures, saving for the record whatever could be found before it was gone. Anthropologists and anthropology graduate students inundated Native American settlements until very recent times, their notebooks, tape recorders, and cameras poised and ready. Almost all Native American readers of this book will know that "the anthropologist" is a stock character in their community's history, one more often derided than welcomed. There is good reason for their suspicion and distaste.

Much of American anthropology as an academic discipline was built on Native American studies, yet for the most part anthropology's success has not benefited Native Americans. But some of it clearly has: many anthropologists have assisted Native American groups with their legal claims for recovery of traditional lands and natural resources and preservation of sacred sites. Some researchers have investigated Indian schools and made recommendations for enlightened teaching and educational policies. Others have studied traditional curing and health beliefs, bringing to the attention of biomedical practitioners the needs of Native American communities and ways these professionals can work with patients more effectively. They have also documented the success of many traditional healing activities. Anthropologists have worked with Native Americans in developing tribal museums and, through repatriation programs now underway, are helping remove Indian artifacts and skeletons from government and university museums and returning them to their owners. Much of what we now know about the history and diversity of Native Americans in North America is due to anthropologists who quietly studied and documented changing cultures, religions, and languages. Perhaps the ultimate compliment to those efforts is that some Native Americans are now anthropologists themselves, reviewing and revising our understanding of their cultures from their own, special perspective. Native Americans have made the anthropologists learn the meaning of cultural sensitivity; it is appropriate that health and social service professionals be co-partners in the process.

Indian scholars (and scholars of Indians) on whom I have relied include but are not limited to John Red Horse and colleagues (1981), Carolyn Attneave (1982), Spero Manson (1989a, 1989b), Joseph Trimble and associates (1983), Robert John (1985, 1988), and Lou Matheson (1986). They, of course, have nothing to do with the table I have constructed here nor with the interpretations I have made about Indian–white contrasts. As with the other chapters, I have chosen to emphasize family relationships since those are the areas that most concern health and social service personnel. But this table is shorter than other summaries of ethnic group contrasts in this book, and there is a good reason for that. Native Americans are far too diverse for anyone to summarize their cultures in any meaningful way. The suggestions given here can only be thought of as the most tentative of generalizations, features that each worker in contact with Native American clients will be required to refine and refocus for the community concerned.

As with a listing such as this, its value is not in providing "formulas" for instant understanding of any Native American person or group. That would be absurd, as the discussion of Native American diversity ought to make clear. The proper use of the table is in pointing to areas of contrast and posing questions, such as: If these descriptive contrasts are not true of the community or individuals served, then what contrasts *are* true? What kinds of generalizable characterizations would be *more accurate* for a given situation? Clearly, that approach is a strength for the worker willing to use the table that way. Statements of contrast are not lists of cultural features; they are provisional hypotheses whose accuracy must be explored and examined in every professional encounter. That is especially important since no Native American community is exactly like any other. It is critical for the user to locate potential cultural contrasts in service relationships, assess their salience for the service offered, and revise them in order to improve the cultural meaningfulness and acceptability of the work done. That is the only way clients can be individualized, and it is the only way the cultural context of client experiences can be recognized and respected.

DEVELOPING SKILLS FOR SERVICE

As values, contrasts like these frequently emerge in discussions of Native American cultures. An older body of anthropological literature referred to values such as strength, self-control, obedience, tranquility, cooperation, and protectiveness among the Hopi (Aberle 1951), and conservatism, persistence, generosity, and deference to elders among some groups of Dakotas (Schusky 1970). As reported by Trimble (1981:71), Zintz (1963) adds an interesting value contrast: while whites prefer to win, as much as possible and all the time if they can, Native Americans prefer to "win once, but let others win also." Trimble (1981) has his own list of traits that appear repeatedly in descriptions of Native American communities, and he wonders if they might not be quite widespread: a strong present-time orientation; time consciousness defined socially rather than by the clock; sharing combined with avoidance of personal acquisitiveness; respect for age and for elders; a preference for cooperation over competition; and an ethical concern for the natural world (Trimble 1981).

While probably valid for large numbers of Native Americans, these value stances may not be valid for many others. We need to consider that as a possibility rather than taking lists like these as eternal truths. Further, individual adherence to a value such as "noninterference" or "generosity" is certainly not wooden. Values and choices are always situational; individuals act on values, when they choose to, in their own way and with reference to a specific circumstance. Knowing the situation —in Indian terms—is absolutely essential to knowing what the values even mean.

Consider, for examples, the meaning of the terms "family" and "family values" in Native American communities. First of all, there is little consensus. Yet families of some kind have always been at the center of Native American life, and they remain so. Many Native Americans live in nuclear family units, many others in extended households, and perhaps most in three-generation arrangements of some kind. But knowing the composition of a household is not enough; lineages and clans are also an important part of Native American ideas about family, even among those for whom a lineage may not be operative. A lineage is a group of people related by descent from a common ancestor. The means of tracing those relationships can be through either the male (patrilineal) or female (matrilineal) linkages. Clans are even larger units, containing more than one lineage and often traced far back in time to an ancestor (sometimes an animal) with founder or mythological significance. Lineages and clans create enormous systems of kinship ties and loyalties, and in smaller communities those loyalties will be critical for who does what with whom. So-called family "ecological" perspectives in contemporary social services usually refer to the immediate, nuclear family, sometimes even to extended units. But in many Native American communities, the social worker will also have to learn of local clan and lineage affiliations to more fully understand the values that motivate and govern behavior. Clan and lineage ties are background information in the life of any Native American community, things that may not often be commented on but that everyone implicitly understands. The worker who wants to appreciate the local meaning of "traditional family values," therefore, will have to be alert to the significance of these larger kinship ties, in the organization of community life, in ritual activities, and in patterns of sharing and cooperation.

How can that be done? In a useful discussion of family therapy with Native Americans, Ho (1987) also begins with a list of presumed, all-Indian values. They include themes we have come to expect: harmony with nature, cooperativeness, a present-time orientation (1987:71), and others. However, Ho does not limit himself to this rather narrow list. He takes it simply as a starting point for moving on to the meaning of cultural relevance in intervention and family therapy with Native American clients. He analyzes cases to help illustrate how values underlie choices and action, offering his own suggestions for service practice as he goes. For example, he remarks on the need to be alert to "American Indian communicative pragmatics" and suggests that "a therapist needs to be attentive, talk less, observe more, and listen actively" (1987:95). He also notes that group interdependence usually takes precedence over personal needs (another value) and that reestablishing harmony within families requires less of psychodynamics and more of group consensus on what needs to be done:

> *As can be expected, group consensus in goal-setting is time consuming, but an American Indian family has a flexible time orientation. The family can wait patiently for a group decision and will experience no urgency in completing certain tasks required of each family member for change. Hence, the time-limited and goal-directed mentality of the therapist may need modification when working with a Native American family (Ho 1987:97–98).*

Of particular interest is Ho's suggestion for using a "genogram" as an aid to understanding family dynamics. Genograms are graphic devices for mapping family relations but, unlike traditional genealogies that start with a remote ancestor, a genogram begins with oneself. Relations are pictorially mapped out from the point of view of the individual, with other significant data added to the chart as it becomes available: residences and dispersion of kin, household membership, exchange relationships and visiting patterns, types of informal support, and stresses and conflicts. The genogram gives a pictorial representation of an individual's family situation, one that can be added to over time and that gives the reader a quick overview of the resources of individuals and families. Genograms speed up the worker's understanding, not only of the client and his or her family but of relationships and activities (including those based on lineages) that may extend throughout the community.

But knowing about families, lineages, networks, and the values that underlie them is only one area where the social worker needs information and understanding. Another is the relationship of social service and health institutions to indigenous helping patterns and what that means for interpersonal behavior in cross-cultural settings. Several years ago Kahn and associates (1981) helped establish a psychotherapy service for the Papago Indians of the Southwest and they listed what they saw as critical issues in developing a successful Indian-oriented mental health program. Their list included not only the things outside professionals needed to know about the Papago but, just as important, the things service professionals ought to be willing to support in their work. First, service providers needed to respect "the spirit of the clinic" (1981:92), that is, the style and procedures that exemplify a Native American point of view in program management. A suggestion like that may seem obvious enough, except that sometimes that spirit clashed with the canons of administrative practice and efficiency taught in schools of social work and expected by remote state agencies. Yet just because organizations have their own cultures, a genuine cultural awareness would involve learning the style or "spirit" of a local agency and working with it to further the services goals that everyone agrees are important.

Second, the Kahn team noted the importance of appreciating the distinctive work patterns of indigenous service providers. While these individuals often do not have professional degrees, they do have experience that is finely tuned to the needs and expectations of their clients. Professional standards of service, although important, should not be used to challenge local procedures that outsiders do not fully understand.

Third, and following logically from the second point, a good share of any new service provider's time must be spent as a student. A period of sustained learning is critical; later the service specialist will be expected to act as a translator between the standards for service set by outside organizations and the expectations of local staff and clients. Obviously, effective translation of ideas, procedures and expectations, and an ability to find common working agreements, requires commitment to learning not only the culture of the local community but also that of local agencies. That knowledge puts the social worker in a position to recommend locally acceptable ways of carrying out service mandates.

Finally, Kahn concluded that "in working with this particular culture and Indian group [the Papago], a relationship style that is low-key, accepting, and open to input is important. Assertive, pedantic directing styles, especially in any forceful and loud way, would be disastrous in this setting" (1981:94). Obviously, those recommendations cannot be said to apply to all Native American mental-health sites. They are insights that Kahn and his team reached only after careful, patient learning among the Papago. The same, slow procedure would be necessary at any other site before a social worker could come to conclusions appropriate to local clients, indigenous service providers, and a specific Native American community.

WHO IS A NATIVE AMERICAN?—AGAIN

Amid all this gloomy discussion of personal pathology and cultural threat, it is important to conclude by noting some of the things that are right about contemporary Native American communities and the people whose lives are satisfying just because they are Native Americans. Neumann and associates (1991) surveyed a sample of Southern Cheyenne and Arapaho respondents in Oklahoma. They were interested in those who felt they had been successful and who were proud of their heritage and their achievements.

Individuals who rated high on the numerous scales the researchers used had a number of characteristics in common. All were effectively bicultural, meaning they had significant commitments to activities in both Native American and white communities. They grew up in caring families, were educated at least as far as high school, some had college, and they felt they knew how to navigate the institutional structures of the white world. They participated in Native American community events and some practiced the Native American

religion their parents had taught them. Others declared themselves Christians. But all considered Native American ways superior to those of whites. They did not want Native American tribes to change and believed it was important that both they and their children know about their Native American heritage. Rejecting acculturation models, few viewed schooling as a first step toward losing their cultural heritage. Tribal identity, maintenance of the tribal community, and the importance of elders were all rated highly. "Respondents did not agree that the popular public image of an Indian defined them as Indians; that is, they did not define their Indianness by singing and dancing, by using the language, or by dressing in Indian attire. In addition, they did not feel that their degree of Indian identity was defined by their tribe" but was a feature of their observance of Native American ways as they understood and interpreted them (Neumann et al. 1991:109).

So I return to the question raised earlier in this chapter. What is a Native American? Clearly it has much to do with self-identity, commitment to a tradition, and observation of Native American ways in some areas of one's life. It may have something to do with language, ritual, and participation in tribal affairs. It has less to do with how people look or what they do for a living. The relationship of Indianness to the larger society, and to the health and social service programs it offers, is always open-ended, always local, and always problematic. But that is a good place for any service professional to start.

FOLLOW-UP

1. Considering Cases

Few issues involving Native Americans and social service authorities are as contentious as those involving children. There is a long and sad history of removal of Native

American children from their homes and placement with whites (Mannes 1993). As tribal governments have acted to assert their sovereignty in recent years, child removal practices have come under strict surveillance and control. Yet, they remain a politically and emotionally charged issue in most Native American communities.

Comparable to out-of-tribe adoption in its effects—at least from the point of view of many Native Americans—is the intervention of child-protective service (CPS) workers. Allegations of child abuse or neglect are amplified because of the history of forced relocations, removals, boarding school separations, and the fact that many Native American children, once placed with outsiders, never return to their homes. CPS investigation is also complicated by local circumstances. As a group, Native Americans are younger than the rest of the American population, and many Native American women have their first child at a relatively early age. They may or may not have all the child-rearing skills they need, they may be raising one or more children without the aid of an adult male, and they are very likely to be living below government definitions of poverty. Nevertheless, they are often part of an extended family. Children grow up using kin terms that identify a number of people as "mother" and "father," and parental responsibilities are expected to be shared by multiple adults. Many of these adults, for good and sufficient reason, have an intense distrust of government representatives, including courts, police, and social workers. To make things more complicated, Horejsi, Craig, and Pablo (1992) note that

> *Life in a tribal community is much like living in a very small town where everybody knows everybody else and their "business." The lives of people in a Native American community are even more interwoven because so many are related by blood, marriage, or long-time associations; privacy and confidentiality are nearly nonexistent. (1992:339)*

When families are investigated on charges of neglect or abuse, rumors travel quickly, provoking an enormous sense of humiliation. Some individuals "disappear" rather than live among their neighbors with such embarrassment. Most Native American communities are normatively egalitarian, although in fact some families have more power and prestige than others. How one responds to a CPS investigation, or even the rumor of one, is partly dependent on local kinship and political connections. Who does one know, what are one's marriage and lineage connections, to whom does one owe favors, and what favors are due in return? One's cultural capital, or lack of it—measured in vulnerablity, protection, and support—becomes crucial when a threat is imminent. These internal complications are invisible to outside observers and are kept that way. Many whites know and work with Native Americans; very few really know how Native American communities operate.

Kathleen Ann Long (1986) describes the case of an eight-year-old girl living in an isolated area of a reservation in the Northwest. The girl, who rarely attended school and had few contacts outside her home, was frequently beaten by her alcoholic mother. A neighbor contacted the local Family Services office after seeing a particularly violent incident and was promised by the social worker that her complaint against the woman would be kept confidential. However, when the matter went to a tribal court, the mother demanded to know her accuser and was given the neighbor's name by a court official who was of the same clan as the defendant. Later, other clan members of the mother harassed and intimidated the neighbor who had initiated the complaint. The Family Services workers lost enormous credibility in this small, tight community and were no longer effective in cases involving family violence.

- If you were a CPS worker newly assigned to this agency shortly after the incident described by Long, what would be your priorities for the first few weeks on the job?
- If after a month in your position you were given the name and address of someone accused by a neighbor of mistreating a child, how would you introduce yourself to the family in question, how would you explain your purposes, and what might you do to establish your own credibility?
- Suppose one of your colleagues in this office were a member of the tribe. What would you want to learn if he or she agreed to "mentor" you for a week?

2. Test Drive an Idea

A number of psychiatrists, physicians, and medical anthropologists interested in Native American issues (some of them Native Americans themselves) are attempting to develop what they call "cultural formulations" that add salient cultural data to standardized psychiatric categories. Some of their work is represented by the cultural amendments to the *DSM-IV* program, discussed in Chapter 1. One of the leaders in this area is Spero M. Manson. A prolific scholar and researcher, he has published a clinical case history entitled "The Wounded Spirit: A Cultural Formulation of Post Traumatic Stress Disorder," in *Culture, Medicine and Psychiatry* (20:489–498, 1996), which illustrates the procedure and is a model for cultural formulations with clients from any culture. The model is useful because it can lead to a culturally appropriate assessment in a systematic way.

Manson describes a 45-year-old Indian male, referred to a Veterans Administration (VA) hospital, who is alcohol dependent, alienated, hypervigilant, preoccupied with dying, beset by unexpected flashbacks of his Vietnam experience, and unable to sleep because of frightening dreams from which he awakes drenched in sweat. A standard personal, family, and psychiatric history is provided as well as citation of the appropriate *DSM-IV* categories of his condition.

The cultural formulation as Manson develops it for this case includes the following categories of information (pages 492–497, listed below in his words). Each category is presented in the article as one or two paragraphs of material (omitted here), which, in its totality, presents a clinically useful and culturally accurate overview of this man's situation.

A. *Cultural Identity*

1. Reference group
2. Language preferences
3. Cultural factors in personal development
4. Involvement with culture of origin
5. Involvement with the dominant culture

B. *Cultural Explanations of the Illness*

1. Predominant idioms of distress and local illness categories
2. Meaning and severity of symptoms in relation to cultural norms
3. Perceived causes and explanatory models
4. Help-seeking experiences and plans

C. *Cultural Factors Related to Psychosocial Environment and Levels of Functioning*

1. Social stressors
2. Social supports
3. Levels of functioning and disability

D. *Cultural Elements of the Clinician–Patient Relationship*

E. *Overall Cultural Assessment*

The final item, Overall Cultural Assessment, reviews Manson's findings and includes his recommendation that the man continue working with his VA counselors, draw on the resources of a Native American Veterans support group, involve himself in his extended family in culturally appropriate ways, and participate in tribal ceremonials that address issues of loss and grief in Native American men. Behind Manson's recommendations is a carefully constructed cultural history or "cultural formulation" for this man that leaves us feeling we know something about him, something well beyond usual clinical accounts.

To try out Manson's idea of a cultural formulation, select a partner who will work with you over several sessions of an hour or two each. You need to select some topic each of you is comfortable pursuing for the exercise. Identify the cultural contrasts between you and your partner—race, ethnicity, gender, sexual preference, and age cohort, are examples—at the beginning of the process and make them a part of the record of the interview. You also need to agree on a set of presenting symptoms, which should not be "faked" but should be real experiences in the life of the individual. To keep it simple, you can limit your presenting problem to a situation where the individual was uncomfortable and had to make some effort to adjust or to change the situation. Full-scale psychiatric issues do not have to be explored, and you and your partner should agree whether you want to observe limits before the exercise starts. Use Manson's list of categories as presented above, develop your own Global Questions for each topic as explained in the chapter on language, and begin your interview.

This project can easily be done as a course paper, your findings presented orally at the end of the term, or as part of a two-day workshop that allows you the time to do some in-depth interviewing. It should not be done as part of a single class-period exercise because you need more time than that. The exercise works best if you take detailed notes and use them extensively in your final write-up of the interview. If you and your partner find yourself "chatting" during the interview on peripheral issues (it sometimes happens!), you should recognize that you have dropped out of the model of ethnographic interviewing. When the focus leaves, so does the data.

More on the Issues

- Alcoholism

The most comprehensive single study to date of alcohol use in any Native American community is Stephen J. Kunitz and Jerrold E. Levy, *Drinking Careers: A Twenty-Five-Year Study of Three Navajo Populations* (1994). Although the focus is on the Navajo, the study has useful information for anyone interested in any tribe. Styles of drinking, male/female differences, historical variations, contrasts with Anglo drinking, cohort experiences, logitudinal effects, the demographics of drinking, and more are included in this comprehensive work. They also describe how changes are being made in traditional healing systems as they are integrated into bureaucratized health care. This book is basic to knowing about Native American alcohol use.

- Bicultural Competence and Biculturalism

Many Native Americans are bicultural, functioning in two or more cultures selectively by tuning in and tuning off situationally. The details of how young people do that in Boston, New York City, and several other areas in the Northeast are described by Hilary N. Weaver, "Social Work with American Indian Youth Using the Orthogonal Model of Cultural Identification," *The Journal of Contemporary Human Services* (77:98–107, 1996).

If you are interested in demographics, take a look at the study by Karl Eschbach on Indian–non-Indian intermarriages. Where those marriages occur, children tend to take the identity of the non-Indian parent. Nationally, Indian–Indian marriage is most common in Alaska, Arizona, and New Mexico. In all other regions, Indian out-marriage is high. Yet people can remain "Indians" dependent on variable tribal definitions of who gets on the tribal role and who does not. Eschbach's article is "The Enduring and Vanishing American Indian: American Indian Population Growth and Intermarriage in 1990," *Ethnic and Racial Studies* (18:89–108, 1995).

- Spirituality

Little has been written on Native American spirituality in the context of social services. But in recent years, Native American prisoners have lobbied for and sometimes been allowed to practice traditional religions within prisons. A good discussion of that is James B. Waldram, "Aboriginal Spirituality in Corrections: A Canadian Case Study in Religion and Therapy," *American Indians Quarterly* (18:197–214, 1994).

- Social Work Practice

A solid overview, "Social Work Practice with Native Americans," by Mary Blount, appears as Chapter 10 of Dianne Harrison et al., *Cultural Diversity and Social Work Practice,* second edition (Springfield, IL: Charles C. Thomas, 1996). Virtually all current issues are covered, although some of them briefly, and the bibliography is excellent. Strongly recommended is Blount's discussion of therapeutic approaches near the end of the chapter.

- Additional Sources

Less is published on Native Americans than on any other ethnic group, especially in the human services. One source that is useful for social workers, however, is *American Indian and Alaska Native Mental Health Research,* from the National Center for American Indian and Alaska Native Mental Health Research at The University of Colorado Health Sciences Center. Those working with Native people will want to be familiar with it and the range of practice as well as research issues it addresses.

8

LATINO CULTURES
AND THEIR CONTINUITY

José Antonio Burciaga is an artist, writer, founder of a comedy group, and Resident Fellow at Stanford. He grew up in El Paso, Texas, in a pious Catholic family, living in the basement of a Jewish synagogue where his father was the caretaker. After a B'nai B'rith meeting or a Bat Mitzvah, the senior Burciaga would gather up unused food and he, young José, and the other children would make deliveries to local Catholic and Baptist orphanages. In the same way, flowers used in Jewish weddings got a ritual recycling at St. Patrick's church and at the convent school. At the elder Burciaga's funeral, a priest said the mass in English, songs were sung in Spanish accompanied by a mandolin, and a representative of the synagogue gave a prayer in Hebrew. Members of Jewish, Catholic, and Baptist congregations sat among one another in the pews and no one thought that particularly unusual since they all knew of Mr. Burciaga's generous way of living. Commenting on that in his recent book of humorous essays, *Drink Cultura: Chicanismo,* son José writes that "I once had the opportunity to describe father's life to the late, great Jewish American writer Bernard Malamud. His only comment was, 'Only in America'!" (1993:118).

The unhappy counterpoint to one man's life of dignified and respectful ecumenicalism is the recent emergence of a new form of cultural chauvinism, the English-Only Movement. Historically, America has never had a national language policy, and restrictive language laws are something new in our political experience. But by 1991, eighteen states had declared English their "official" language: Arizona, Alabama, Arkansas, California, Colorado, Florida, Georgia, Hawaii (with two official languages, English and Hawaiian), Illinois, Indiana, Kentucky, Mississippi, Nebraska, North Carolina, South Carolina, North Dakota, Tennessee, and Virginia. (Crawford [1992] provides a valuable overview of the official English movement.)

Is the driving force behind all this ballot box nativism just a heightened linguistic appreciation of the distinctive sounds of English vowels and consonants, an aural aesthetic newly evolved among native English speakers? Or are there extra-linguistic concerns at work here? Hurtado and Rodriguez (1989) think that language, unlike skin color and national heritage, is perceived by some Anglo Americans as the one mutable feature of ethnic groups and therefore the place to begin with encouraging, even demanding, their assimilation to an Anglo norm. The nativist's rationale is that if they can't look like Americans, at least they can learn to talk like them. English-only promoters really have very little interest in language or language learning as such. In a report to the American Psychological Association, Padilla, Lindholm, and Chen (1991) found clear evidence of explicit political agendas in the English-Only Movement. For example, activist individuals and coalitions within it have "close connections to restrictionist, anti-immigration organizations" (1991:120). As propagandists, their appeals are aimed at those Americans who, for whatever reason, have vague, poorly defined grievances and who see in immigrant and ethnic groups the "cause" of various personal and social problems.

Whatever the political outcome of this sometimes noisy debate, in health and social services the simplistic and denigrating opinions of the pro-English zealots are not an option. Meeting the client "where he or she is at" means taking full account of each individual's speech preferences in useful and positive ways. That does not mean that service professionals are required to achieve fluency in a foreign language as a condition of providing quality services. But it does mean having some sense of the importance of language in people's lives and how they use language to describe and analyze their concerns. As I emphasized in Chapter 4, language is not a neutral tool for communicating information. It is one of the ways people preserve their identity. Social service professionals, therefore, need to be sensitive to the role of language in their work, both as a communicative device and as a signifier of ethnic and communal participation.

After English, Spanish is the most widely spoken language in the United States. According to the 1990 census, over 17,000,000 Americans use Spanish at home. Some cities, counties, and even states are de facto bilingual (even trilingual and more!) and that is likely to become more true rather than less so in the future. In some areas, especially in the Southwest, Spanish has more claim than English to being the historical, traditional language of the region. But not all Spanish speakers use their language the same way or with the same degree of comfort. There are significant dialectic differences between the Spanish of Mexico, Puerto Rico, parts of South America, and the various regions of Spain. More important, not everyone in the United States who identifies with the Spanish language has the same level of proficiency. In studying bilingual communities, linguists commonly distinguish between "communicative" and "symbolic" language (Edwards 1985). Communicative use is that which goes on everyday in routine transactions. It requires a high degree of "performative competence," the ability to speak and understand with fluency. Symbolic attachment to a language is a matter of community affirmation and affiliation, regardless of how well one uses the language of symbolic preference.

While most North American Spanish speakers are fully fluent in their preferred language, some (perhaps many) are not. Eastman (1984) argues that in multilingual nations, including the United States, the link between language and ethnicity is often one of "association" rather than performative competence. She suggests that "a particular 'associated language' is a necessary component of ethnic identity but the language we associate ourselves with need not be the one we use in our day-to-day lives" (1984:259). In fact, an "associated" language may be used only in limited contexts, even imperfectly in the grammatical or lexical sense. That is often true for second and third generation descendants of original immigrants. For them, fluency is less a concern than is loyalty to their community, its traditions, and the associated language. The alert and sympathetic service professional will see that such a stance is not necessarily an anti-assimilation stubbornness (although that is certainly possible) but rather a way for individuals to create an acceptable balance between communal loyalties and participation in a conventionally monolingual society (Keefe and Padilla 1987).

But language habits and choices are more than a matter of communal loyalty, even though that is significant. Espin (1987) has described some of the cognitive and affective issues that surround language use by her Latina clients. Language has a psychodynamic dimension, and in her practice, "even for those Latinas who are fluent in English, Spanish remains the language of emotions because it was in Spanish that affective meanings were originally encoded.... To try to decode those affective meanings through the use of another language may be problematic at best" (Espin 1987:496). For most health and social service professionals, the use of English in a consultation is simply a given, but the possibility that clients may want to switch into Spanish (or any other language) must be regarded as therapeutically important, especially where intimate subjects cannot otherwise be well described (Sciarra and Ponterotto 1991). Not only clients but Latino practitioners know that Spanish can convey nuances of therapeutic significance (Zuniga 1991). Language choice is not just a political or a communal issue. It is a treatment one as well and requires great flexibility, patience, and a willingness to do what is necessary to further the goals of intervention.

LATINO DIVERSITY

Within the Spanish-speaking population in the United States there is considerable diversity of cultural, racial, ethnic, and national origins. This makes it difficult, if not impossible, to speak of Latinos as a "consolidated minority." Rather, the situation is one of "a group-in-formation whose boundaries and self definitions are still in a state of flux" (Portes and Truelove 1987:359). That should not be interpreted to mean, however, that Latinos are beginning to "melt" into the larger American pot. Marín (1993) points out that "recently arrived Latinos, contrary to the experiences of other immigrant groups, seem intent on maintaining their language, cultural values, and other group-specific characteristics, requiring that attention be given to the group's characteristics whenever community interventions are designed and implemented" (149). Indeed, in some cases whole communities explicitly defend and actively preserve a distinctive cultural identity, a situation that was typical, for example, of the Chilean political refugees who came to this country after the 1973 coup in their homeland (Eastmond 1993; Gonsalves 1990). The cultural tenacity shown by Latinos in North America is remarkable, and it points again to the fact that they, like others, do not abandon their traditions and assimilate but selectively use their cultural background to redefine a sense of identity (Saenz and Aguirre 1991). Each community does that in a way that uniquely suits individual and collective needs. (Keefe and Padilla [1987:211–219] use a 136-item Cultural Awareness and Ethnic Loyalty Scale to measure Chicano ethnicity. Almost half of their questions concern Spanish language use.)

Those who are self-identified as Spanish speakers generally affiliate with one of four major regions of origin: Mexico, Puerto Rico, Latin America, or Cuba. (Many South Americans, however, identify historically with Italy and Germany rather than Spain, and those in Brazil, of course, with Portugal. Others stress their Indian heritage rather than that of the colonizing Spanish.) The cultural as well as dialectic differences among these groups are considerable and so too is their geographical distribution within the United States. Yet despite their internal diversity, the terms "Hispanic" and "Latino" have united many Spanish speakers in common political causes. As umbrella terms, they have come into general usage. Latino will be used here, although not without certain qualifications (Giménez, Lopez, and Munoz 1992).

"Hispanic" is not a term invented by the people it identifies. Its general familiarity is the result of a decision made by the U.S. government's Office of Management and Budget in 1978, a decision to help census takers who needed a term for whites (and others) who claimed some degree of Spanish language or cultural affiliation. A definition appeared in the *Federal Register:* a Hispanic is "a person of Mexican, Puerto Rican, Cuban, Central or South American or other Spanish culture or origin, regardless of race" (1978:19269). Like all ethnic definitions and labels, this one is awkward and incomplete. For example, are immigrants from Spain also Hispanics? What of Brazilians who speak Portuguese, or Indians whose Spanish is really just an overlay on a native South American language? What of Spanish speakers from the Philippines or the Dominican Republic? Do those in some parts of the Southwest, whose family lines in the region precede U.S. sovereignty there, think of themselves as Hispanic? And how do any of these people feel about accepting an ethnic label promulgated for them by statisticians and door-to-door head counters?

Some favor the term "Latino" (Hayes-Bautista and Chapa 1987; Pérez-Stable 1987). It has the advantage of both a linguistic association and a geographical referent. But it omits the significant number of South Americans who speak English (Belize, the Guyanas) and those whose family roots extend to Italy, Germany, and some areas of the Mediterranean. The names "Chicano" and "La Raza" have been proposed as well, but they have more limited reference. Chicanos are Mexican Americans north of the border, not Mexicans as such. La Raza, "the race," brings into the labeling a "racial" motif that has not won general acceptance. As identifiers, both Chicano and La Raza were associated with the cultural activism of the 1960s and 1970s, and, whatever the merits of the issues that were addressed then,

La Raza is now somewhat dated. So too may be the nominally masculine noun endings of some of the labels proposed, a feature that may be more troublesome for some sensitive whites than for Spanish speakers, but it nevertheless creates an obstacle to universal applicability.

Marín and Marín (1991:24) suggest that when using labels for a population this diverse, primary attention ought to go to people's own affirmations of their ancestry (usually a country of origin) and their preference for whatever cultural features they choose to emphasize. Working in Chicago on the meaning of ethnic labels, Padilla (1985) discovered that what people chose to call themselves was highly situational. While Padilla's research respondents had a generalized "sentimental and ideological identification with a language group," many saw themselves as Latino at one time and Puerto Rican, Mexican American, Cuban, or some other national identity at others (1985:336). Names and labels are always shifting and often controversial, and the discussion that surrounds them is a critical part of the ethnic identity process of both individuals and groups (see especially Giménez, López, and Muñoz [1992] on the politics of ethnic names). The point is that in work with Spanish-speaking clients, as in all cross-cultural activities, labels differ among individuals, families, and communities, even according to who is doing what with whom. If that seems confusing, it is, at least to outsiders. Insiders understand it perfectly well. Therefore the general rule for service providers is: preferences vary, so when you don't know, ask.

There are over 17 million Latinos in the United States, certainly more if the number of residents without official documentation could be known. At current rates of growth, they will be the largest minority in the country within thirty years, about 15 percent of the U.S. population by 2020 (Davis, Haub, and Willette 1988). Before 1950, most Latinos in North America were of Mexican origin and, while Mexican Americans are still the largest group among Spanish speakers, their proportion has declined. The second largest group is that of people from Central and South American countries. Their growth has greatly increased cultural diversity within the Latino population generally. Puerto Ricans are the third largest group, their presence in the United States facilitated by the commonwealth status of their island and freedom of movement to the mainland. Many Puerto Ricans virtually commute, at least on a seasonal basis, between San Juan and the major cities of the East Coast and Midwest. Cubans make up a small and specialized population that is quite distinctive demographically (about 6 percent of all Hispanics) and politically. Concentrated in Florida, many fled the Castro regime and are more properly considered political refugees than labor immigrants. Because of their urban and suburban concentration as well as their business success, they have exerted a powerful influence, relative to their numbers, especially in conservative political circles.

Demographically, Latinos in the United States are relatively young, due to immigration by younger people seeking work and to their high fertility rate. The Hispanic population is on average eight years younger than that of whites and two years younger than blacks, and fully one-third of all North American Hispanics are under the age of fifteen. The image of Spanish speakers as a predominantly rural, farm-oriented people is prevalent in many western states, but on the East Coast, urban residence for Spanish speakers is the norm. In fact, nearly 85 percent of all Spanish speakers in the United States live in urban areas (U.S. Department of Commerce 1993b).

Although Anglo Americans tend to think of all Spanish speakers as "immigrants" and "refugees," the Spanish were well established as colonists in this hemisphere long before the nations of northern Europe. Huge areas of what is now the United States were explored and settled by Spaniards. Mexico once included all of the Southwest, from Texas to California and as far north as Colorado, Utah, and Wyoming. In addition, Spanish attitudes toward commingling socially and sexually with Native Americans and, later, with slaves taken from Africa, were such that racial mixing (*mestizaje*) was common. (This was in marked contrast to practices in the American colonies established by northern Europeans where mixing, while it certainly happened, was prohibited in law and condemned in practice.) Many of the islands of the Caribbean, the northern coast of South America, and all of Central America were Spanish possessions. Spanish explorers were active in Florida, the Mississippi valley, northern California, and far up the Northwest coast. Native peoples were "pacified" and missionized and, when they resisted, ruthlessly exterminated so that settlements and trading centers could be established. Many of these once tiny centers still stand, known by their original names: Santa Fe, San Diego, Los Angeles, El Paso.

Mexican sheep and cattle ranchers who called themselves *californios* moved from Mexico northward in the early 1800s, about the same time small-scale cattle entrepreneurs were working their way into what would become Texas, Arizona, and New Mexico (Acosta-Belen and Sjostrom 1988). In addition to founding settlements, the Spanish were active in the American Revolutionary War. Siding with the American colonists, a large *mestizo* army held off the British in the lower Mississippi valley, keeping Gulf ports open for supplies intended for the American colonies (Acosta-Belen and Sjostrom 1988:88). Their contribution is not usually mentioned in American history books although it was critical to the success of the war.

Not until the beginning of the nineteenth century did Anglo Americans begin moving into Texas and the Southwest as colonists, competing politically, economically, and militarily with Latinos who had been resident in the region for nearly two centuries. A short war with Mexico in 1846 and 1847 added a huge landmass to the United States. Spain was forced to give up an empire spreading from Texas and Oklahoma to California, Wyoming, and Kansas, establishing the U.S.–Mexican border at about its present location. The *hispanos* who had long family traditions in this massive territory faced then, as now, laws and practices putting them at a disadvantage to the new Anglo occupiers.

Late in the nineteenth century, the U.S. government again became involved with other Spanish colonies. The final decades of that century were the great period of American imperial expansion. Now that the United States was a continental nation and a major trading and military power, politicians and military strategists wanted a canal linking the Pacific and Atlantic oceans. In concert with this was an interest in annexing Puerto Rico and Cuba (and later the Virgin Islands, owned by Denmark) in order to defend the proposed canal. The bombing of a U.S. ship in the Havana harbor in 1898 served as the pretext for the Spanish–American war. The United States seized not only the territories needed to police the Caribbean basin but also the remnants of the Spanish empire in the Pacific: the Philippines, the Hawaiian islands, and Guam. Almost 500 years of Spanish hegemony were replaced by an American political and military presence.

This very brief historical overview suggests something important not only about the diversity of Spanish speakers in North America but also about their durability. Many predominantly Spanish communities and families have a long and distinguished presence in what was once the European's "New World," a presence of greater historical depth than that of the English speakers who currently dominate. That fact raises a familiar but contentious question: what and who is an "American?" It also puts into a larger and more challenging context the claims of the English-only advocates that English is properly the "official" language of the country. The implication that English and the northern European cultural preferences associated with it are somehow "original" and therefore fundamental to American identity is simply not supportable. The Spanish language and Iberian traditions have been here much longer. The idea of a shared cultural ancestry may be difficult for the cultural nativists to accept. But for the rest of us it has to be the starting point in thinking about what it means to be a citizen and what is implied for social and health services in a historically varied population.

SPANISH-SPEAKING COMMUNITIES AND SOCIAL SERVICES

As would be true of any ethnic or minority community, the cultural variability among Spanish speakers challenges us to think about how we might implement an idea like "cultural awareness" in order to better meet their health and social service needs. It is not always obvious what should be done and how. López and Hernandez (1986) surveyed mental health practitioners in California, asking them to describe cases from their clientele where they explicitly used cultural features as an aid to diagnosis and treatment. Most of the cases reported to them involved marital counseling, psychotic symptoms, problems with male adolescents, hospitalization issues, and drinking. While "culture" as a factor was mentioned with some frequency, there was no evidence that the practitioners surveyed had a set of criteria by which to determine that cultural factors were important, or that the cultural features they chose as the basis for interpreting presenting problems were in fact the "right" ones from among the many possibilities. López and Hernandez (1986) suggest that in many of these cases, the therapist may have been relying primarily on commonsense understanding of Latino persons generally.

An important contribution to the cultural awareness issue has been made by Rogler and associates (1987) in a classic paper on defining culturally appropriate interventions. Lloyd Rogler has an especially rich background in research on

Puerto Ricans and mental health in New York City, and he has helped develop innovative approaches to serving second-generation Spanish-speaking children there. (Rogler's various publications [1984, 1985, 1987] would be useful to anyone who works with Puerto Ricans and his use of *cuento* therapy would interest those who work with children in any community.) Rogler and colleagues suggest that cultural sensitivity be thought of as a pyramidal structure, professional services becoming more creatively and elaborately cross-cultural the higher one rises on the pyramid. There are three levels to the Rogler model, and I will follow his lead in discussing its applicability to health and social services for Spanish-speaking communities.

Rogler sees the base of the pyramid, level 1, as a historical product of the civil rights movements of the 1960s and 1970s and the rise of community mental health programs on a national scale. The issue at that time, and the one that characterizes level 1, is accessibility. To make services culturally "sensitive," one must first make them available. Consequently there has been, from that time to today, a large and still growing literature on utilization and access barriers. The list of impediments to utilization and their effects on consumers is much too long to summarize here. But for Latino communities, important areas identified for improvement have been (1) a closer match between the client's and professional's understanding of needs and what can be done about them; (2) recognition of alternative forms of help and the skills and procedures of the individuals who offer assistance outside established institutions; (3) surveys and assessments of "needs" as they are articulated by the client community; and (4) recognition of the importance of language in providing services to multilingual populations. The latter issue has led to the rise of numerous referral and service agencies targeting specific ethnic communities and making use of native and bilingual speakers and translators. Individuals working in these agencies have become available as consultants to other organizations and are able to activate community-based networks simply because, as cultural compatriots, they are familiar with them.

One rigorous and theoretically well-grounded study of access issues for Hispanics is that of Rodriguez (1987), who looked at how Hispanics in the South Bronx seek help from a variety of social service agencies. That study looked at utilization of mental health, services for the elderly, the disabled, and women heads of households. Not surprisingly, in that area of New York City needs were high and so was utilization. One particularly important finding of the study was that the size of an individual's social network correlates well with service use. Networks are important channels for diffusing information. People with smaller networks, or who relied exclusively on family members for information, were less likely to know of and use services that had potential value for them. It is sometimes thought that large networks are likely to lead clients to alternative help providers. Sometimes that is true, but networks were also important for transmitting information about services from mainstream organizations. Further, Rodriguez's study found that those more familiar with American life, that is, more acculturated, were more likely to use services. Thus, cultural differences, and especially language differences, were significantly related to people's ability to find and use organizations expressly designed to help them.

Rogler identified the level 2 of the pyramid as any effort by service providers to utilize a perceived feature of Latino culture in furtherance of an intervention outcome. It is at this level that we meet again the familiar debate about the appropriateness to minority clients of therapeutic styles originally devised for upper middle class, Victorian-minded, urbanized European and American whites. Is insight therapy really useful for someone needing a job, a house, or vocational training? Does learning to "cope" with one's rage do anything to challenge racism, change divisive public policies, or bring about economic justice?

In general, the answers to these questions, at least as they relate to Latinos, have been negative. Sandoval and De La Roza (1986) examine the clinical implications of Latino cultural features and conclude:

> *Cultural differences in perceptions of health and illness, etiology and treatment, are also reasons why Hispanics do not adequately use mental health services.... Cultural differences in personality perceptions might render [insight-oriented] therapeutic modalities as useless. Hispanic perception of personality in general is that of a fixed entity. This leaves little room for therapeutic modalities that solely deal in intrapsychic process and are aimed at promoting personality change, growth and awareness. (161)*

To illustrate their point, they look at a number of generalized Hispanic values, including values concerning the family, personalism, individualism, authority, paternalism, machismo, and fatalism, and conclude that in general they are not congruent with the assumptions and treatment styles of most mental health practitioners. Their discussion of individualism is interesting in this regard since that is a value common to many Anglo Americans as well. For them, the Hispanic sense of individualism is distinctive. They cite a popular idiom, "Soy feo pero simpatico" —I am ugly but engaging—to illustrate the subtle difference. For whites, individualism suggests competitiveness, getting ahead, standing out as number one (or "numero uno" to those who know no other Spanish but that). Anglo individualism means being first or the best in a field of like-minded competitors. But the Latino idea of individualism suggests distinctiveness, true difference, including the things that could make someone ugly but charming at the same time. It also implies participation rather than separateness, in the sense that because of differences we all have something unique to offer and for which we can be respected.

In clinical relationships, Sandoval and De La Roza advise the therapist "to overtly accept a client's peculiarities," especially when they are presented as charming features of the individual (1986:170). They cite the example of a young man, Julio, who had repeated encounters with the police because of drinking and who believed that belligerence was one of his unique and valued personality traits. He rejected psychiatric and medical treatment but participated in discussions, apparently informational, about the nature of personality and how behavior could be changed under certain circumstances. The starting point for these talks was his uniqueness, and how belligerence was a distinctive feature of his personality. Once he was able to accept the view that he could modify and even control personality traits, including angry outbursts, and once he had practice in doing so, he was able to bring some stability to his everyday life.

This case is a more sophisticated example of cultural awareness. It requires the identification of a cultural feature—Latino beliefs about personality and this client's commitment to them—and the therapist's willingness to use a feature of Hispanic ethnopsychology as the starting point for intervention. The case illustrates Rogler's point that once we are beyond the first level, that of opening the doors and making access easier, we need to know what kind of background cultural material the client brings to the encounter and how we can use that as part of a helping relationship.

Marín (1993) has discussed this issue at length, especially in relation to community intervention efforts other than those related to mental health. He argues that a culturally appropriate intervention must be based on the cultural values of the group of interest, must adopt strategies that "reflect the subjective cultural characteristics" of the group, and must take account of their behavioral preferences (1993:155). Otherwise outreach and community information programs will have little credibility with those they seek to influence. He cites as an example his own work in anti-smoking campaigns. He found that where whites were more responsive to cessation messages that stressed personal improvement, such as no more coughing, bad breath, or burned clothes (Anglo individualism again), Latinos tended to identify with messages that emphasized family values (smoking as a bad example for one's children, the health risk of "passive" smoke for others in the household). It is widely reported in the literature that familialism is a powerful cultural value among Hispanics, so the family was a logical and culturally correct focus for health improvement messages. It also made good cultural sense to train nonsmoking family members to support smokers who wanted to quit, a technique that was more effective than the less family-oriented workshops and clinics widely promoted by hospitals and others. Success in this area really began with an understanding of Latino culture and how it might be integrated into the solution of a problem. Shortcuts such as translating into Spanish anti-smoking messages originally written in English, with their cultural assumptions still built in, simply were not as effective and would not qualify as cultural sensitivity.

On level 3 of the Rogler pyramid, the level most fully cognizant of cultural differences and their meaning for therapy, appropriate cultural materials are integrated into whatever intervention is proposed. This raises some interesting and challenging issues: which cultural traits are "appropriate," who is to decide that, and how will they be used? Since communities are not homogeneous, how do we know that a cultural feature is "appropriate" for use with a specific client? Most important, are we to assume that because some value or practice is a feature of the client's culture, it is necessarily a good or useful one that ought to be replicated in therapy? There is, for example, some discussion in the research literature about the power and powerlessness of Mexican-American (Vasquez 1984; Palacios and Franco 1986), Puerto-Rican (Rogler and Cooney 1984), and Cuban women (Ortiz 1985). Some view the position of Latina women vis-à-vis men as submissive and weak. Others claim women's power within the family is much greater than is known or appreciated and that the real disadvantages women face are in the marketplace, not with their husbands. Clearly, this is a complex issue, one that varies among communities, within them, and perhaps within specific families. Before a "trait" can be plucked for use in a treatment regimen, the therapist needs to know a lot not only about the client's community generally but about the needs and interests of individuals and families within it.

One way to prepare for that level of service delivery is to familiarize oneself with the research and ethnographic literature of the community in question. The material below, on health and illness beliefs and what they have to do with help seeking, is only an introduction to a vast literature on Spanish-speaking Americans. But it does indicate the range of issues one must consider when working with Hispanic clients and patients and where one can begin if a more intensive learning effort is required.

Because Latinos preserve some very old Iberian traditions, as well as others deriving from a lengthy colonial experience quite different from that of Anglo Americans, their views of health, mental health, and healing strategies are distinctive. Some of the values and beliefs described below have been dropped, at least by some Latinos in the United States, and others have been preserved or modified. I cannot stress too much, as I have elsewhere in this book, that the persistence and strengths of beliefs like those described below are highly variable. They cannot be used as infallible guides to the preferences or practices of specific individuals or families. But many of these beliefs are widely recognized ideas related to well-being, and they are topics that the culturally sensitive social worker will want to know something about. My discussion of them here is just an introduction, and those who will be working with Latino clients and patients will need to do much more study and analysis in this area.

HEALTH, ILLNESS, AND BELIEF SYSTEMS

Given the institutional and ideological predominance of scientific biomedicine and corollary fields such as psychiatry, physical therapy, and even chiropractic medicine, alternative forms of health belief and practice are usually below the horizon of awareness of most Americans. Yet embedded within the Latino community is a large and ancient system of health and mental health practices, derived from Greek, Roman, and Arabic sources and transmitted to this hemisphere in a distinctively Iberian form. In Chapter 2, I briefly described several Latino disease categories, *empacho, mal ojo,* and *susto,* to illustrate aspects of the help-seeking behavior model. In this section, I will expand on that information, adding other elements of the system to the list. I want it to be clear, however, why this material is here. In presenting it, I am *not* making a case that all Spanish speakers in the United States, or anywhere else, endorse the illness categories, diagnoses, or interventions described. Many do not and, as I have tried to show in the historical overview, there is enormous variation in matters like these as in all areas of life. Aside from the issue of whether people do or do not "believe in" these folk illnesses, most Spanish speakers have heard of them, know something about them, or know of people who accept them as important.

The real concern for social service and health professionals is not *whether* people believe in specific, culturally defined illness syndromes, but rather *how* they believe. The important clinical issue is knowing the circumstances under which a folk illness such as *mal ojo* is regarded as "merely superstition," or as a possible but unlikely diagnosis, or as something clients say "others" believe in but members of their family do not, or as evidence of real forces of maliciousness at loose in the world. People generally do not "believe" in illnesses abstractly. Rather, they know about them in reference to an individual who suffers with one. Similarly, the culturally sensitive practitioner does not have to personally "believe" in a folk illness or diagnosis to appreciate that other people do, and that their beliefs have consequences for their recovery. My claim, simply, is that attention to culturally specific categories of illness is a vital piece of ethnically competent social work and health care. Whether any health or illness belief is "true" in some fundamental, objectifiable sense, as those who rely on *DSM-IV* might suggest, is only marginally significant.

Why should popular illness categories and variations in local belief be so important to care providers and helpful in intervention? Using participant observation and life history interviews, medical anthropologist Laurie Price (1987) recorded illness narratives from a sample of Ecuadorian patients, most of them women. What is of interest here is not the details of the narratives themselves but rather what she discovered about the importance of naturally occurring discourse about illness as a means for understanding folk beliefs. First, she found that conversations about illness are an occasion for transmitting technical information about symptoms, diagnostic categories, local names, favored remedies, and appropriate helpers. Seemingly casual conversations had an important educational function.

Second, participants in illness narratives often explored and enlarged their theories of illness causation and treatment, building an increasingly global reservoir of information from which to interpret personal experiences. Their theories were not consistent nor scientifically verifiable, but they functioned as all theories do: they generated explanations. Third, narratives often validated treatment actions already taken. They presented the sufferer as someone who had tried to act positively; they helped legitimate the sick role. Finally, narratives intensified social relations and bonds of support. They helped build a small community of sympathizers whose advice and help would be needed before the illness episode was terminated. Recognizing that illness narratives can focus attention this way in any cultural context, we are in a better position to understand the culturally specific illness beliefs that patients and clients present.

In the section that follows, I will examine several categories of popular illness, all of which have varying degrees of explanatory appeal in Spanish-loyal communities. This is not a catalogue of what Latinos "believe" about illnesses, however. Rather, I want to suggest something of the complexity of these cultural themes and note how they supply the material from which patient and client narrative explanations are sometimes built.

The criticism has sometimes been made (Longres 1991, for example) that illness beliefs like those described here are "exotic" and that a cultural approach to social services exaggerates obscure and unusual features of ethnic communities. Yet a 1991 survey conducted at a health clinic for Mexican American farm workers in central Florida showed that folk illnesses were self-medicated by 53 percent of those in the sample (Baer and Bustillo 1993). Probably many more individuals had knowledge of these health beliefs and may have self-diagnosed as well but still went to a physician. What appears "exotic" to outsiders, or to biomedical and social service professionals, may or may not be unusual to patients and clients, and the task of culturally sensitive service providers is to be alert to all the possibilities.

Ataques de Nervios

The cross-cultural psychiatric literature has documented a condition called *ataques de nervios*, or "attack of nerves," for many years, in clinical studies, through epidemiological work, and in research on people's responses to natural disasters. Ataques de nervios is well known, not as a "disease" itself but as a culturally specific "idiom of distress" (Oquendo 1994; Guarnaccia et al. 1996) The literature on this syndrome is extensive (see especially the various chapters in Davis and Low 1989). Guarnaccia (1993) describes the classic features of an attack as:

> *a culturally sanctioned response to acute stressful experiences, particularly relating to grief, threat, and family conflict.* Ataque de nervios *is characterized by shouting uncontrollably, trembling, heart palpitations, a sense of heat in the chest rising to the head, fainting, and seizure-like episodes. Typical* ataques *occur at culturally appropriate times such as funerals, at the scene of an accident, or during a family argument or fight.* Ataques *mobilize the person's social network. The person usually regains consciousness rapidly and does not remember the* ataque. *(158)*

This collection of symptoms, however, is only a culturally naked trait list until we locate it within some larger system of meaning. Guarnaccia notes that an attack occurs only in conjunction with social circumstances that are stressful, that it is not the result of something physiological or of anything "mental." Attacks are responses to distress, to conditions that are social in origin, and for which neither pills nor psychodynamic analysis is necessarily helpful or appropriate. An attack is embedded in a system of culturally specific meanings, and resolution requires that those meanings be unraveled and given credence during treatment.

Ataques de nervios were first described in the medical literature in the 1950s, based on studies of Puerto Rican men inducted into the U.S. military. Some of these men were characterized by Army physicians as suicidal, psychopathic, and hysterical, and their condition was attributed to personality flaws, child-rearing and weaning practices, and an inability to adapt to the authoritarian structure and competitive values of American military life. Once known (somewhat pejoratively) as the "Puerto Rican syndrome," the condition was later identified by Latino and

Anglo mental health researchers as a folk illness also found among Dominicans, Costa Ricans, and some Latin American immigrants in North America. Guarnaccia, De La Cancela, and Carrillo (1989) describe it as a culturally recognized "expression of anger and grief resulting from the disruption of family systems, the process of migration, and concerns about family members in people's country of origin" (47). They describe four sample cases, all women, who illustrate variant expressions of the syndrome and point to its social origins.

In each case, the patient's attention centers on rage and anger connected to failures in key personal relationships. One elderly woman living in the Northeast had been "abandoned" by her adult children, all of whom had succeeded by American standards of careerism and were not available to her at times of distress. Her narrative description of her *nervios* attacks included references to cutting and self-mutilation. Another woman related an extensive history of physical privation and isolation from important men in her life, including her husband and adult son. Her pronounced fears of being alone often initiated an attack. A third client presented a quieter pattern of attacks, describing intense feelings of anger and overwhelming heat and pressure in her chest. She would have trouble breathing and speaking and could not move her hands. Her fear of losing control when she was with friends or neighbors kept her at home, further isolating her from all contact except with the staff of a local clinic who treated her somatic complaints. A fourth case was that of a younger woman, only a few months in the United States, who felt threatened by her hard-drinking husband and extremely isolated from family and friends in Central America who could help her. She had seen a priest and a physician, the latter prescribing Valium for her attacks. (Valium and other tranquillizers are widely used by patients suffering from *ataques* and commonly prescribed by physicians both Anglo and Hispanic.) As with many sufferers, this woman recognized that her seizures were associated with anger, but she did not associate that anger with specific people or events in her life.

In each of these cases, grief and rage (and a subsequent attack) were connected to personal isolation, fear that one might not see friends and relatives in a distant country again, an ongoing crisis in relationships such as marriage or with adult children, and a profound sense that there was nothing that one could do to change anything. Typically, these are conditions symptomatic of immigrants, especially women, who find that in North America they are cut off from traditional supports and that the (ideal) protective functions of male family leadership have collapsed (Espin 1987). In brief, *ataques de nervios* communicate distress, especially powerlessness and anger. "The relationship of these experiences to previous life events in childhood and adulthood shape the individual's current responses in culturally meaningful ways" (Guarnaccia, De La Cancela, and Carrillo 1989:50). *Ataques*, then, cannot be understood as a list of symptoms alone; their significance and amenability to treatment are completely embedded in a culture-specific system of meaning. Outside of that system, the illness is diagnostically incomprehensible, whether it occurs among young Puerto Rican men or older Central American immigrant women.

The idea that emotions are, to a significant degree, cultural products (as well as psychological experiences) is so important to cross-cultural social work that I want to emphasize it again here. In the Follow-Up section at the end of this chapter is a model adapted from Guarnaccia, Rivera, Franco, and Neighbors (1996) for investigating emotions and understanding them in a cultural sense, rather than the conventional but more narrow psychological one. That is a challenging idea partly because many middle-class Anglo Americans are attuned to a rhetoric of the interiorized self—a rhetoric of their emotional responses to others, perceived psychic needs, and urges to healing and "growth" through internalized, self-changing "work." Consequently, it is hard for them to appreciate that people unlike themselves may both feel and know the world in quite different ways. To engage others, however, especially around issues of suffering and pain, we cannot ignore the cultural dimensions of their emotional lives or we will miss much of what concerns them.

Embrujado

All cultures have folk syndromes, what cross-cultural researchers recognize as locally defined conditions of distress, sets of diagnostic categories, and appropriate intervention techniques. They are "exotic" only to those who do not use or understand them. *Embrujado* is a disorder that, like many in the Spanish-speaking world, employs religious ideology and language in its conceptualization. *Embrujado* hallucinations, paranoid reactions, anxiety, spirit possession, and witchcraft often involve communication with supernatural beings, be they good or evil, and with the dead. Sufferers sometimes invoke the symbolism and ideology of formal religion, which is not surprising given the historical importance of religion and the Catholic church in Iberian cultures. As with *ataques*, the issue is not whether *embrujado* beliefs are "true" in some objective sense but "how" they are true for those who rely on them to frame and narrate their afflictions.

The contrasts between *embrujado* and standard psychiatric categories in understanding mental illness are described by Koss-Chioino and Canive (1993:181). In the former, individuals believe they are powerless to manage daily affairs because an external force, a witch, has overwhelmed their inherent capabilities. The affected individual manifests inappropriate behavior and verbalization including frequent references to the pervasiveness of evil, communication with God and various saints, and fear of future witchcraft attacks. Bodily pains and deviant sexual behavior (if present) are attributed to the hostile attentions of a witch. Failure in a job or in relationships is likewise blamed on evil forces, often many of them converging on the patient in such numbers and strength that they cannot be fought off. Finally, after much struggle and anguish, the individual lapses into apathy and can no longer function in daily activities.

Viewed psychiatrically, the same individual is believed to suffer from a lack of ego strength or a damaged or regressive personality. The problem is generally due to an early life trauma. Anger, hostility, suspiciousness, paranoia, religious ideation, and deviant sexuality all typify the patient's condition, variously diagnosed as paranoid schizophrenia, depression, neurosis, even organic brain dysfunction. Sexual preoccupation is evidence of doubts about one's sexual identity and capability. Obsessions with good and evil, God and the devil, and the pervasiveness of malicious intent in the world at large suggest psychopathological mechanisms at work. Any evident somatizing is an expression of deep psychological conflicts as well as avoidance of the task of resolving them. The individual's energy is consumed by internal conflicts that finally lead to apathy and deep depression. Organic as well as psychological causes may be present.

Koss-Chioino and Canive (1993) studied a sample of Latino patients in a large mental health clinic in New Mexico, patients who believed themselves bewitched. All the patients were men who frequently complained about having been rejected by spouses or spouses-to-be. These women, and sometimes a mother-in-law, were suspected of the bewitching behavior. The men also complained of physical symptoms including tics, temporary paralysis, and back pains. They reported themselves to be filled with evil spirits and often spoke of violence and rage. Religious imagery pervaded much of their talk and they blamed evil forces for leading them away from the kind of life God intended for them. Some of the patients had been taken by their families to a *curendera* but the efforts of these healers had not been helpful. One patient exemplified the condition:

> He said that he wanted help [at the Psychiatric Emergency Unit] because, "my wife advised me to do it if I want to stay married." On further inquiry P.R. revealed that he had lost control and beat his wife. This was the latest in a series of aggressive behaviors that coincided with financial pressures stemming from P.R.'s attempt to run his own business. He felt that a devil had possessed him and "put bad thoughts" into his mind. P.R. appeared somewhat confused to the interviewers, who described his affect as "flat," and showed thought disorder (thought blocking and thought insertion). (Koss-Chioino and Canive 1993:178)

This individual was diagnosed as schizophrenic and treated with antipsychotic medications. His case had a two-year history at the clinic but, following treatment and discharge, his symptoms periodically reappeared. A number of other patients, similarly diagnosed and treated, also had a recurrence of symptoms on an irregular basis.

What is important to note in this study is the differing set of assumptions made in the folk model of *embrujado* and in the medical model of the clinic's staff. For the latter, a patient's talk about evil spirits was likely to be labeled "hallucinatory" or as grandiose religious "ideations." Difficulties in relating intimately with women were prominent in diagnoses and seen as evidence of childhood failures that required reexamination and "resolution." Most important, the clinical diagnoses assumed a flawed intrapsychic state, one that must be identified, labeled, treated (chemically or with counseling or both), and changed, with favorable outcomes expected within a given range of certainty. For their part, the patients were expected to do some kind of healing "work," something that would transform a damaged ego or low sense of self-esteem. That work would be undertaken with a specially trained therapist, not of the patient's culture, and failure of the treatment, if that occurred, would be blamed on insufficient effort on the part of the patient himself or, less likely, an incorrect diagnosis or ineffective therapist. Further, labels such as "schizophrenia" and "depression" suggested to the patient a chronic condition subject to recidivism, and the probability of a lifelong, individual struggle to overcome a very personal failure.

By contrast, a "bewitched" diagnosis would have assumed that the causes of the situation are external to the individual, located in a problematic set of relationships rather than a faulty psychic or organic condition. Issues of intrafamily conflict, power, and control, especially involving wives and mothers-in-law, would have been invoked. Questions of jealousy, spite, and anger over previous slights and hurts would be central to the counseling. Similarly, failures in the job market and expectations of economic success would have been linked to specific work skills and capabilities, with specific plans made for improvement where possible and appropriate. An *embrujado* diagnosis carries with it the implication that, unlike a ruined psyche, a supernatural hex or an external cause can be removed and something of a new start begun.

In addition, a folk diagnosis usually requires that an appropriate healer be found to help treat the condition, one who is willing to work in tandem with clinicians. A dual approach in these matters makes sense because it offers more alternatives for problem resolution (Koss-Chioino 1992). A folk diagnosis also invokes a potentially useful cultural ally, "extended family networks composed of consanguines, affines, and fictive kin acquired through *compadrazgo*" (Koss-Chioino and Canive 1993:184). The individual is absolved of having to bear full responsibility for his or her condition, and those who are emotionally closer than a professional therapist can be part of the treatment. While the *embrujado* strategy has its risks—especially where family networks do not function well and cannot assist the patient—at least as a diagnostic category it affirms that there are stresses in the lives of minority individuals that are not their responsibility alone and that there are acceptable, culturally tested and legitimated ways of dealing with them.

CULTURAL CONTRASTS AND CULTURAL COMPETENCE

The diversity of the Spanish-speaking population in North America makes it very difficult to offer generalizations. In this section, I have relied on scholars from various Hispanic groups for their views of the commonalities, as well as differences, they feel are important (Table 8.1, page 270). As in all the cultural contrast discussions of ethnic communities in this book, the information is most explicitly not intended to provide a trait list for any of the groups in question nor a shortcut to the real effort necessary for learning about an ethnic community. The value of the information is only in highlighting contrasts. Even when the suggested contrasts do not seem to fit exactly, their appearance here is intended to activate more detailed examination of specific clients, families, or a local area, so that a higher

TABLE 8.1   Selected Cultural Contrasts in Latino and Anglo American Communities*

Latino	Anglo American
Commitment to the Spanish language as a marker of ethnic identity is very high, even though not all persons of Latino descent use Spanish regularly.	Language is less important than income, education, occupation, or place of residence as a marker of social class and identity. "Ethnic" identity is sometimes uncertain and national origins may be used as ethnic labels.
Family matters command the individual's loyalty. Other institutions or activities are clearly of secondary importance. Families are thought of in an extended sense and include not only kin but sometimes fictive kin (friends of the family).	Family life is highly valued but sometimes competes with loyalties to career or "outside" interests and activities. Children are encouraged to develop interests and activities outside the home and their involvement in extrafamilial matters is interpreted as evidence of maturation and normal development.
Personalism in relations with others is a culturally recognized style and individuals are judged in terms of their behavior with family and friends, less on their roles or position in formal institutions. Strong personal commitment to others and a warm feeling tone in relationships are favored.	Many relationships are expected to be instrumental and utilitarian, especially the important relationships of jobs and community involvement. Competence, knowledge, and skill are highly valued and relations with others are expected to be fair and evenhanded.
Individualism is valued in the sense that the uniqueness and specialness of persons are in what they specifically do and in their relationships with others, for example, as someone's mother, father, brother, or child. Individualism in this sense is an aspect of one's personality.	Individualism is valued in terms of abstract qualities—skills, knowledge, capability, frugality, for example—that make each person stand out as distinctive in some objective way. Personal desires and "needs" are sometimes contrasted with obligations to others, the latter occasionally seen as impediments to meeting highly valued individual needs.
Respect for hierarchy and authority is important, especially when it is seen as an extension of family relations and values. By contrast, authoritarianism in extrafamilial contexts is subject to challenge and negotiation, especially if it conflicts with family values of hierarchy and clear role structure.	Emphasis is on egalitarianism to the extent that circumstances allow. Children are encouraged to offer their opinions and, ideally, the needs of all are attended to equally.
Machismo refers to male leadership (and female complementarity) as an extension of hierarchy and authority. Machismo is most properly associated with concepts of honor, trustworthiness, moral courage, and responsibility, only secondarily with sexual prowess. The honor of women for whom a man is responsible—wife, daughters, sisters, mother—is particularly important.	Male leadership is in providing socially and economically secure circumstances for a family. Changing definitions of male and female roles emphasize egalitarianism in decision making, providing opportunities for personal expression and "growth." Individual needs receive high priority.
Some Latino individuals and families exhibit a philosophy of fatalism, not as a negative or passive view of the world, but as an appreciation of human frailty and limitations. Wisdom is in recognizing limitations but also in the courage to cope with and endure them. Religious belief may support this sense of struggle as a normal part of the human condition.	Change and improvement are desired and problems, properly understood, are less obstacles than they are opportunities. One struggles to achieve and to improve oneself and one's family. Discontent with the status quo and willingness to meet the challenges of everyday life are evidence of a vigorous, positive attitude toward living.

*The contrasted items listed here may or may not apply to individuals. *The contrasts refer only to general tendencies within groups, not to characteristics of specific individuals.* In any culture, people differ in their commitment to approved values and practices.

level of understanding can be achieved. As usual, when we think in terms of contrasts we are forced to put ourselves into the equation. We come to see that differences as well as similarities are *transactional* features of relationships, not ascribed characteristics of persons different from ourselves.

Marín and Marín (1991) have described what they see as "basic Hispanic cultural values." Their selection is interesting because they are explicitly concerned with culturally sensitive research protocols and their translation into social science practice. They consider seven values which, they note, may not be everyone's choice but for which there is probably general agreement.

Collectivism (or "allocentrism") is a very broad contrast to individualism; it includes the willingness of individuals to seek mutual empathy, to sacrifice self-chosen goals in favor of the interests of the group, to conform to expectations, and to generally trust members of one's own family and community. In these emphases, "Hispanic culture differs in important ways from the individualistic, competitive, achievement-oriented cultures of the non-minority groups in the United States" (Marín and Marín 1991:11). Deference to the group is not always automatic nor painless, but it does confer prestige and respect on those who consistently put the interests of others ahead of their own.

Simpatia is part of a strong group orientation and is both a value and a style. Pleasantness and dignity are important in the presentation of self, and respect is reciprocated. Agreeableness is especially valued, and confrontations and negativism are avoided and discouraged. *Simpatia* requires simple courtesies, time to establish rapport, and small exchanges of gifts or favors. "La platica" or small talk is also important and is a polite way of beginning and ending a conversation. The Anglo value of "getting to the point" and the bureaucratic emphasis on "staying on task" do not inspire *simpatia.*

Not surprising, familialism or familiso rates very high as do loyalty, solidarity, and respectfulness. Loyalty creates obligations that often extend well beyond individual households to include others, both persons more distantly related and compadres or "fictive kin" who are treated "as family." Fictive kin include close friends and especially godparents, the latter a once-common relationship throughout Europe but now more important in southern Europe and South and Central America, areas where the Catholic church has been historically prominent.

Marín and Marín (1991) suggest that these complex ties of affiliation and kinship are not egalitarian but rest on a clear age and gender division of labor and a frank recognition of power differences. In Latino cultures, hierarchy and deference count. So do the native intelligence, education, and wealth that make some individuals more powerful than others. There is nothing inherently wrong in that. Those who enjoy advantages deserve whatever respect and obedience they can command. Teachers, healers, priests, males, and the aged rank high, and those lower in the hierarchy usually see that it is in their own interest to show deference as required. These are values that are hard for some other Americans to accept, however, especially if they are committed to liberal political and social agendas. In an officially egalitarian society, these values are almost too easy to stereotype as regressive, undemocratic, or even archaic. But their functioning in daily personal behavior is more complex than is apparent; moreover, millions of people find satisfaction and meaning in them. Whether they appear autocratic or enabling may be less a matter of objective fact and more one of perspective.

Two other distinctive Latino values mentioned by Marín and Marín (1991) are sensibilities related to space and time. They see Latinos as more "contact" oriented than Anglos, comfortable standing close to one another and with body touch. They also view time, as do many minority communities (and most of the rest of the world, I might add), in a flexible way. Time is always with and for people, it is not an abstraction established by clocks, schedules, and appointment calendars. "Quality time," apparently a recent discovery for some Anglos, is the norm in Latino and other communities all the time.

Finally, gender roles have a particular configuration in Latino cultures, one that we need to address since at least for Anglos stereotypes on the matter abound. Amaro and Russo (1987) note that the study of Latina women's issues is a relatively new field, one in which there is more stereotyping than reliable information. We know relatively little about migration, immigration, and Latina women's activities in the job market. Most research has been done on the traditional roles of women, not on changes that affect them as they move beyond the sphere of the home. These topics are important to mental health professionals since women who migrate and those who seek education and jobs are at higher risk than are Latino men for depressive symptoms and a variety of health threats (Vega, Kolody, Valle, and Weir 1991; Canino et al. 1987). Women are also exposed to the double jeopardy of gender and ethnicity in jobs and careers.

Gender roles in many Latino communities are carefully defined, even rigidly so by middle-class Anglo standards and by those of some Latina feminists (Comas-Diaz 1987). The code of male honor, well known as *machismo*, defines a man as the provider, protector, and head of his household. He represents the family within the community and, to ensure its honor, he enforces communal standards of respectability. While the association of machismo with drinking, fighting, and sexuality is sometimes made, these are not its essential features, although they figure prominently in folklore and stereotypes. It is more appropriate to say that a man with machismo is a man with honor, dignity, and pride, all expressed in the orderly, hierarchical relationships of the household (De La Cancela 1986). The female equivalent, especially in Puerto Rican culture, is *marianismo*, so named after the Blessed Virgin Mary, of Catholic veneration. Women are often seen as spiritually more sensitive than men, even superior to them on this dimension, and part of that superiority involves a martyr complex, their willingness to take on suffering and self-sacrifice for the good of husband and children. That willingness is the mark of a good mother, a highly prestigious role that is virtually sacred. Women may enjoy certain kinds of power because of that position, but it is a power that is usually exercised quietly and that does not draw attention to itself. Outwardly at least, women are expected to be dependent and docile with men, yet a reliable, capable manager in the home. Comas-Diaz notes that, "on the surface, these traditional sexual codes seem to condone the oppression of one group (female) by another (male);…relationships are intricate and complex, and power relationships between the sexes are not straightforward" (1987:463).

For women immigrants, diverse and sometimes contradictory gender-role expectations can combine with early marriage and child rearing to create severe physical and psychological stresses. To cope with these, the newly emerging field of feminist therapy for Latinas emphasizes integrating cultural content into treatment. Comas-Diaz is explicit about including a sociocultural perspective in her work (1987:468). Such an approach can include techniques as diverse as all-female support groups; assertiveness training built around themes and examples taken from Latina daily life; cognitive reframing of female gender and mothering roles; opportunities to discuss the relationship of traumatic experiences to somatization; and couple counseling on shared problems of migration, acculturation, language, and new expectations in a host country.

Work in this and related areas is just beginning, and a useful bibliography on gender values and issues concerning Latino families in North America can be found in Amaro, Russo, and Pares-Avila (1987) as well as in recent issues of the *Hispanic Journal of Behavioral Sciences*. Of particular value is the overview article of Fabrega (1990) on the cultural basis of Hispanic mental health research.

FAMILY LIFE

The value of "familialism" and its greater intensity among Latinos in comparison to Anglos has been well documented in the research literature (Rogler and Cooney 1984). That orientation, argue Rodriguez and Zayas (1990), has important prosocial implications: "Such solidarity implies that Hispanic families may create patterns of conventional behavior even when other factors may dispose adolescents toward deviance" (Rodriguez and Zayas 1990:156).

Juarez (1985) describes some of the clinical issues that are generated by Hispanic values and cultural features and suggests ways of working with them. I have already mentioned the importance of somatization as a means of expressing hostile or dangerous emotions. Juarez notes that this is especially true for women and children: "For example, Hispanic children suffering separation anxiety would present a variety of symptoms expressed through somatization (vomiting, stomachaches, headaches, etc.) and would more likely be taken to a physician" than to a mental health provider (1985:446). This is consistent with a Latino and Iberian view that "good" families do not have "disturbed" children and that if they do it may be related to "bad blood" and other inherited moral conditions.

The linkage of physical and mental states to moral imperatives is not unique to the Latin tradition but it is strongly held there. The importance of "blood" derives in part from medieval humoral theories that depict the body and its moral state as admixtures of four basic elements. These old beliefs are the cultural matrix for some kinds of contemporary behavior and expectation. Thus a child's problems may be attributed to "blood" passed on from parents and grandparents or from others in the family line. Juarez suggests the example of a child separated from its mother because the latter has serious mental health or somatization problems of her own. In such a case, if the child displays depression or mood shifts, they are not likely to be attributed to adjustment problems in a new environment. Rather, "grandparents would feel terrified and helpless that the child is going to 'turn the mother's way.' Thus parents get preoccupied with their child's future behavior which seems to have a destiny of its own beyond the realm of the family's control" (Juarez 1985:447). Destiny and control are linked to beliefs about fatalism, which should be read not as helplessness or acceptance of whatever comes along but rather as vigilance and care in managing what one has in a universe that is not always friendly. Fatalism is not necessarily an arcane viewpoint; it may make sense where the realities of power and especially powerlessness are fully appreciated.

Finally, Juarez mentions adult perceptions of children within the household. One component of Latino familialism is authority, especially that of the father. Anglo stereotypes of "machismo" usually suggest swagger and domination, but Hispanic male authority in the family can more correctly be thought of as economic and moral leadership, protection for women and children, personal and family honor and honorableness, and quiet persistence in overcoming obstacles. Complementary values expressed by women are those of obedience to the husband and nurturance and respect with children. Children, in turn, are expected to defer to siblings who are older. It is clear that within this framework of traditional family values it is hierarchy, not egalitarianism, that is prominent. Hierarchy is associated with unity and especially strength. That has serious implications for family intervention:

> *Children are perceived by many Hispanic parents as extensions of themselves and as objects or property without rights. Typically, they are not allowed to challenge or question their elders, nor do they have the right to voice their opinions. Basically, their behavior revolves around adult feelings. (Juarez 1985:447)*

Parents are at liberty to discipline children as they feel is appropriate, since it is they, not the child, who take independent moral action. Similarly, parents are in the best position to plan and make decisions for the child, including long-term ones, and loyalty and self-sacrifice are expected in return. One interesting implication of this value of hierarchy, especially when linked to fatalism, is that children who are disabled in some way may be indulged, for they are seen as less capable, perhaps much less so, than their "normal" siblings. Indulgence does not encourage them to change. The emphasis on "personal growth" and taking control and "ownership" of one's experiences, common among middle-class Anglos, does not appear here. The protection that goes with indulgence is more important. In matters of family intervention, therefore, the culturally sensitive social worker would want to be alert to the presence of these kinds of values and behavior, and especially of their relative strength in differing family units.

Family values carry an aura of sacredness in many Spanish-speaking communities. The Catholic church is an important adjunct to that value, and it remains a force even for those who are not regular church attenders. Yet debilitating family crises do occur, especially in the poorest of neighborhoods. For them, there are options when the protective family life that is so highly prized is not available. Despite unfavorable media treatment, most Latino youth are not involved in gangs precisely because children in strong, hierarchical families do not perceive them as attractive. Yet gang activities are clearly present in most large cities, sometimes lethally so.

Hispanic youth gangs have been studied in detail by Vigil (1983, 1988a, 1988b), who sees in them an alternative to the disrupted family life some barrio teenagers experience. Not surprisingly, generalized Latino values are expressed in gang culture but in exaggerated or destructive ways. (In fact, they are expressed in a very simplified form, a circumstance that has implications for acculturation, to be discussed below.) Likely recruits for gang life are those with few significant family connections and for whom street skills are essential to personal survival. "Gang members are usually reared in poorer homes, mother-centered family situations with more siblings, and marginal, unstable economic conditions" (1988b:425–426). For them, life on the street begins with an extended period of socialization by *veteranos* (veterans) and *carnales* (real and fictive brothers), some of whom are *locos* or "crazies," individuals renowned for outrageous acts of heedless, high-risk behavior. Life on the street is dangerous but also exciting, and it produces intense feelings of camaraderie, much like those that develops among soldiers in war zones. As a full-time gang member, the individual is part of a *klika* (clique), a subunit of the gang, and his primary activity is "protection" of neighborhood territory. Vigil quotes one gang member as saying:

> *If any intruder enters, we get panicked because we feel our community is being threatened. The only way is with violence. We can't talk because of our pride and their pride. No Chicano's going to lay his pride on the line so another can suck it up and make his pride bigger. (1988b:428)*

What is interesting about this individual's remark is that it parallels a community value reported by anthropologists who have studied poor, rural villages in Mexico. Known in the research literature as the "image of limited good" (Foster 1965), it asserts that where people have no hope of improvement in their lives, they perceive the availability of the good things they would like as absolutely limited. There is no thought to expanding the size of the pie so that everyone can have a larger slice. Therefore, any improvement in what one has (in goods, luck, or prestige) must come at the expense of someone else. Their slice will be proportionally reduced; others must lose for me to win. So, too, anyone who improves his lot must have done so at my expense. As Vigil's gang member very correctly notes, no one is going to put his pride up for talk and risk its being sucked up and lost. Violence will settle the matter immediately.

For boys and young men active in gangs, masculine identity is closely linked to success in street life and that creates a *cholo* cultural style. In parts of South America the term "cholo" refers to those who are neither metropolitan nor Indian but somewhere in between, that is, marginal to several major cultural communities. Vigil notes that barrio gangs were originally created by second-generation Mexican Americans, beginning in the 1920s in southern California. Later gangs sported the dramatic *pachuco* dress style that came to national attention in the 1940s. Like earlier gangs, modern *cholo* culture adapts some traditional Latin values—*palomilla* (age cohorts) and *camarada* (comradeship)—to the harsh economic conditions of barrio life.

> *The subculture in part is a reforged combination of traditional Mexican palomilla customs of adolescent age cohorts and the complex of cultural values known as machismo. There are many positive machismo traits (strong work ethic, responsibility for family and friends, and patient courage against seemingly insurmountable obstacles) but street life has especially nurtured an emphasis on masculine aggressiveness, dominance, and boastful assertion of individual and group pride.* (Vigil 1983:59)

Daily life in gangs is not all fights, however. Since gang members are not usually in school or working at jobs, casual and recreational activities take up much of their time. Pick-up ball games, drinking, gossiping, riding in cars, and watching over one's territory are important areas for learning gang etiquette, developing street skills, and establishing one's own role and style in the *klika*. Nicknames are also important, often denoting some trait of the individual and sanctioning his peculiarities and preferences. *Placas* or graffiti mark gang territory, sending warnings to others. Dress codes distinguish gangs and are matters of personal pride and presentation. The easy availability of guns and the profitability of drugs add to the risks but also the excitement of street living. Gang life creates a semblance of meaningfulness, however thin and temporary. It reproduces hierarchy, offers camaraderie, and creates opportunities to show one's individuality and prowess. In barrios, gangs are *familia*.

Chavez and Roney (1990) suggest that the risks faced by Latino youth, including the risks associated with gang culture, are due to a process of "deculturation." Deculturated individuals and groups are those that are out of contact with both the culture of their heritage and that of the larger, encasing society. *Cholo* describes them accurately: they are people who are set apart, not just in a spatial sense but also in a social and psychological one. They are literally rootless except for the small patch of territory they claim is theirs to defend. With "decultured" individuals, where would the culturally alert social service provider begin?

Individualistic approaches probably would not work, according to Rodriguez and Zayas (1990). They favor instead a program that builds on historical community values and reunites individuals with a tradition. The object of treatment has to be the family, and work with it probably should be undertaken by bilingual therapists. In counseling and planning sessions, the values of family hierarchy, deference of children to adults and younger children to older ones, gender obligations, and the priority of the family over the wishes of individuals ought to be preeminent. Differences in apparent acculturation between children and adults, and between children of different ages, may be important sources of conflict and should be explored comprehensively. Rebuilding intergenerational ties and especially obligations is a high priority, and specific tasks for doing that must be devised and monitored.

Further, community-based interventions should be launched. Schools are one of the most favorable sites for that since social workers can monitor performance both in the home and on school grounds. Recruiting paraprofessionals, "role models" in the parlance of some, ought to be encouraged since they not only add to the available personnel but are another form of community linkage and mentoring. Seniors can be important because they can be asked to share with more acculturated youth traditions that were once important and whose loss is painful. Rogler's *cuento* or folktale therapy, mentioned earlier, has been used with young children, but there is no reason it could not be adapted to work involving elders as living embodiments of valued Hispanic traditions.

Obviously, an effort such as this requires knowledge of a specific neighborhood, a city, and a distant home country. Those are topics as important to effective cross-cultural work as the traditional therapies and interviewing skills more commonly taught to social service professionals. As skills the latter can be useful, but their effectiveness is limited if they are not adapted to the cultural realities of a community's everyday experience.

ACCULTURATION—IS IT FOR EVERYBODY?

In a statistical study of life satisfaction among Cuban Americans in New Jersey, Gómez (1990) found positive correlations of high self-esteem, job satisfaction, and marital adjustment with biculturalism. The latter was measured using a 45-item questionnaire that distinguished individuals who were effectively monocultural (either fully acculturated or not acculturated to any significant degree) from those who were bicultural and saw themselves participating selectively in two valued traditions. He notes that one implication of his study is that "a culturally sensitive mental health service that supports the establishment and development of biculturalism is better equipped to help those with mental problems than a service that neglects the bicultural dimension" (Gómez 1990:387).

Gómez's findings are part of an emerging theme in Latino studies—melting pot enthusiasm was always misplaced and bicultural adjustment is not only possible but desirable. Further, multiculturalism should be the goal of health and social service programs and policies generally.

Several years ago Buriel (1984) emphasized the same theme, arguing in favor of "the seemingly paradoxical hypothesis that integration with traditional Mexican-American culture fosters healthy sociocultural adjustment to mainstream American society" (95). His thesis was that where maladjustment, deviance, or violence occurs, it is because individuals have drifted away from sustaining cultural traditions without having replaced them with mainstream American ones. Thus they are vulnerable to the situational effects of poverty, urban decay, and unrelieved personal stress.

Buriel reviewed a large number of studies on Mexican Americans completed by sociologists, psychologists, and educators over a number of years. He gave special attention to differences between generations as it was measured in the various studies. The first generation normally included individuals and families who migrated from Mexico, people who could be expected to retain a strong Mexican cultural orientation. Second-generation individuals were those born in this country but reared in traditional households by their Mexican-born parents. The third generation included all those born in this country and raised by parents also born in North America. According to standard acculturation expectations, later, more acculturated generations should have a mainstream American orientation, having sloughed off their traditional Mexicanness. By contrast, earlier, more traditional generations should show less acculturation and more evidence of difficulty in adapting to American life. It is the "traditionals," in the first and second generations, who would be expected to show the highest incidence of personal and family pathology. Buriel looked carefully at data on use of Spanish, education levels, income, job status, family size, religiosity, and other variables. The outcomes predicted in the acculturation hypothesis were not what the data showed.

Instead, there was a consistent pattern of high levels of achievement and adjustment in the first and especially second generations. The second generation did very well in terms of educational and economic success and general participation in American life. But they also preferred traditional Mexican institutions and practices in their family affairs, their religious participation, and the continued use of Spanish. It was the third generation that displayed the highest levels of personal and family maladjustment. This cohort also showed the least participation in either Mexican or mainstream American cultural values and institutions.

Several examples illustrate what Buriel (1984) found. In numerous studies of educational achievement, second generation Mexican Americans were much more likely to complete high school and college than were their third-generation counterparts. In fact, in some studies first-generation cohorts did better, significantly so, than did third-generation ones. In the workplace, second-generation Mexican Americans consistently had better paying, more professionally oriented jobs than did third-generation samples in the studies reviewed. Although Mexican Catholicism is often compared unfavorably with American Protestantism in terms of its support of a strong work ethic, most of the studies that included religion as a variable showed a high level of church participation in the occupationally successful second generation. Even with gender roles, one of the most stereotyped features of Latino cultures, many studies concluded that women participated in the workforce at almost the same rate as their Anglo sisters. Further, these women were generally practicing Catholics, had large families, were bilingual who spoke mostly Spanish at home, were very achievement oriented, and were little assimilated to mainstream Anglo values.

Buriel concludes, as have researchers and helping professionals since, that those Hispanic Americans who are most successful are those who are effectively bicultural. And those who have the most difficulties are the least integrated into either traditional Mexican or American cultures.

> [I]ntegration with traditional Mexican-American culture represents a highly adaptive strategy for satisfactorily adjusting to Anglo-American society.... Securely embedded in the reinforcing structure of the ancestral culture, these individuals are free to explore new cultural avenues without any threat to their sense of identity, and to adopt the skills, roles, and standards of behavior that are necessary to translate their native ability into conventional forms of success within Anglo-American society. In essence, such individuals are bicultural, which means that they are capable of interacting successfully in both the Mexican-American and the Anglo-American cultural worlds. (Buriel 1984:126)

Señor Burciaga, living and working among his Jewish, Catholic, and Baptist neighbors in El Paso, probably would have agreed.

FOLLOW-UP

1. Considering Cases

Case 1: "Dichos" Therapy

Dichos are proverbs, sayings, and idiomatic expressions, short and sometimes poetic, used by Spanish speakers to comment on work, family, love, and the human condition generally. Like jokes and song lyrics, they are a type of folklore that is sensitive to cultural context; those who don't know the culture will miss the point. As with any oral tradition, *dichos* are open to multiple interpretations, carry hidden as well as obvious meanings, and are devices for initiating commentary on why things are as they are.

Using *dichos* in clinical work is not a new idea (Zuniga 1991, 1992). But Aaron Aviera (1996) discovered that in therapy sessions with individuals diagnosed with chronic schizophrenia, *dichos* were an effective way to cut through communications problems. His patients had long histories of hospitalization and were frequently withdrawn, were hallucinatory, had difficulty maintaining a conversation, and lacked supportive networks outside their California hospital. Most were monolingual Spanish speakers who had migrated to the United States many years earlier.

Aviera organized a "dichos group" for these patients. For one hour each week, they met to discuss with each other what they understood a particular *dicho* to mean, occasions when it might be used, and any memories it recalled for them. Aviera led off the discussion with one *dicho* and then allowed the conversation to develop and flow as individuals offered their commentary. "Arbol que crece torcido nunca su tronco endereza" (A tree that grows crooked will never straighten its trunk) led to a discussion of being born with limited mental or physical capacities and fewer chances for the pleasures other people take for granted. "Caras vemos, corazones no sabemos" (Faces we see, hearts we don't know) was one suspicious individual's way of beginning a conversation about her fears of being in proximity to strangers.

More than picturesque phrases or clichés, *dichos* functioned as powerful devices for connecting Aviera's patients conversationally with one another. In addition, they became opportunities for people to make statements about their personal experiences and occasions to reconnect with familiar traditions, something difficult to do in an institutional setting. The *dichos* "immediately construct a bridge to [the patient's] past, identity, family and heritage. Because they can relate to the material, it facilitates more natural and relaxed interactions. Patients usually enjoy this group, and consider working with the dichos to be like solving puzzles" (Aviera 1996:79). The dichos helped build rapport and participation, reduced defensiveness, focused attention, enabled articulation, and led to personal insight. Many in the group thanked Aviera for the weekly meetings, and he came to see the *dichos* as useful for informally assessing cognitive skills and emotional states.

- Aviera's technique need not be limited to deeply disturbed patients, or to Spanish speakers. It is easy to imagine using the technique with other patients, those with Alzheimer's or other forms of age-related dementia, for example. If you were to set up a discussion group in an assisted-care setting, what are some English "dichos" you might use and why would they be appropriate?

Case 2: Bilingual, Bicultural Services

Thousands of infants and children from South America, Korea, China, and India have been adopted into American families. Adoption of foreign children is a legal procedure that is lengthy, costly, and handled for the most part by several well-known and reputable agencies in this country. Many of these children arrive with their first language well established. For them, American customs and English are foreign, leading to problems of adjustment—a new language to learn, unfamiliar food to eat, family members who are strangers, a different kind of schooling, and behavioral expectations that are occasionally subtle and almost always baffling.

De Verthelyi (1996) describes the case of a ten-year-old Central American boy, "Pedro," adopted by a white family in rural Virginia. The family already had two adopted children (siblings) from Latin America and wanted a third. While negotiations were going on, the husband died unexpectedly but the wife wanted to continue with the adoption anyway. Pedro arrived but did not adjust easily to his new life. After several months his new mother called de Verthelyi about the boy's mood swings, bed wetting, "and his intense oppositional behavior both at home and at school. She described him as very demanding, extremely stubborn and uncooperative, and not respectful of any authority or rules" (1996:59).

After interviews with the mother and the two siblings, de Verthelyi arranged a series of bilingual therapy sessions, something she could do since she was fluent in Spanish. Much of the discussion concerned the impact of the new adoption on their lives. The older children, now teen-agers, were encouraged to talk about their anxieties about Pedro. Throughout the discussions, Pedro was given opportunities to state his own views about what he felt was happening in the family.

Second, de Verthelyi did an assessment of Pedro's cognitive and language skills and used that information to counsel both his mother and teacher. Finally, in play therapy conducted in Spanish and using drawings, puppets, and games, Pedro was able to dramatize his feelings about his new life. Through continuous interaction with the therapist, he began to feel more comfortable and assured with the family and school. Not only did he respond to others both in Spanish and English, but also the older siblings, who had lost much of their original language, began Spanish classes in their high school. After a time, Pedro himself emerged as something of a hero on his grade school soccer team.

- While this case has a happy ending, de Verthelyi does not tell us specifically what she did in the bilingual family therapy sessions. If she had asked you to help her run those sessions, what topics would you want to raise with the family as a whole, with the older siblings, and with Pedro alone?
- In this instance, Pedro entered the fourth grade. If he had arrived in this country as a teen-ager, what different problems might he experience, and how would you work with him?
- What difference would it make if your client were not a teen-age Pedro but a Maria instead, and how might you assist her?
- Since the husband in this family died before the adoption could be completed, would you have recommended a delay or canceling the adoption altogether? If not, how might you have worked with the mother and the two siblings (who presumably were still grieving) to prepare them for receiving Pedro?
- In a discussion of negative outcomes in adoptions of Mexican American children by white parents, Bausch and Serpe (1997) argue that potential problems are always present: (1) Children may experience an identity conflict; (2) they may forget their Latino heritage; (3) opportunities for participation in Latino culture are limited; and (4) adopted children may not learn to cope with racism. Reviewing the case of Pedro, set up an intervention plan for him that would anticipate each of these problems and state what you would do to alleviate them.

2. Test Drive an Idea

Ataques de nervios is a well-known example of a culturally formed explanatory model of emotional experience. It fits neatly into the help-seeking behavior model as a feature of client problem recognition and labeling. Research on this syndrome is part of a much larger enterprise variously known as "cultural psychology," the "anthropology of emotions," and "ethnopsychiatry," in which the emotional lives of people in many cultures are being studied. Guarnaccia et al. (1996) state that "A central feature of these approaches is to study emotion as lived experience with a cultural context rather than as an internal experience of an individual, as emotion is studied in American psychology, or as a symptom of disorder, as emotion is often studied in American psychiatry" (1996:343).

To develop their understanding of *ataques* as "lived experience" in the Puerto Rican context, Guarnaccia and his team interviewed a sample of people who had suffered through floods and mudslides on their home island. They also interviewed samples of individuals who had experienced panic attacks not identified as *ataques,* and those who had had no panic attacks at all. From the interviews, they developed a "core image" or prototype of *ataques,* recognizing that each person experienced the condition in a somewhat idiosyncratic way. Listed below are the elements of the prototype. I have adapted these from Guarnaccia; in the original article they are described in much more detail.

- Loss of Control

The individual feels a loss of control of the body, a sense of not being in charge of what is going on, and is helpless to do anything about it. This idea runs through all the other elements of the prototype.

- An Initiating Social Context

Something provokes the crisis, and it may be anything that threatens to rupture family bonds: news of a death, a divorce, violence, leaving home, isolation in a foreign place, or children who are disrespectful or involved in illegal activities. The loss of control motif is apparent.

- Powerful Emotional Experiences

Sadness and/or rage are common in *ataques.* It may be expressed verbally but often it overwhelms the individual, who responds by crying, screaming, and rage. Those who experience it say they cannot control their responses. They are literally "overwhelmed" and "not themselves."

- Body Sensations

Trembling and irregular heart beat are common, and seizures may occur. Somatization is dramatic and demonstrates loss of control.

- Action

Aggressiveness is common; individuals show unexpected and surprising physical strength and may be dangerous to themselves or to those who are the objects of their rage. Women are sometimes "permitted" to act inappropriately because it is understood they are not in control of themselves anymore.

- Altered Consciousness

Individuals report dissociation, time slowing down, or inability to remember what happened at some points in the episode.

This list was developed from a study of *ataques*. But the general areas of emotional experience it describes can be adapted to any cultural setting to work up a culturally based description. This is another opportunity to test your ethnographic interviewing skills. Below is a short list of events, some of which we all have or will experience. The list is brief, so add additional items if you like since the specific topic of the interview is less important than the practice of working up a culturally based model of an emotion.

Select a partner and a topic from the list and, using the ethnographic interviewing techniques described in Chapter 4, explore each of the six dimensions listed above. It may be useful to start with item two, an initiating social context. Following the cover terms, develop your descriptors from the interviewee's narrative in as much detail as possible. The interview should take about twenty minutes to be effective.

Here is a word of caution: *you must write extensively and continuously throughout the interview.* If you stop writing and just listen, or if you cease tracking cover terms, you have fallen out of the model since you are not recording the narrative data you need both to consult with your partner later and to prepare your statement of the prototypical features of the experience. Novices typically get so involved in what is being said that they forget why they are doing the interview in the first place and consequently come up short in their final descriptions.

My list of events that may initiate an emotional experience is as follows. Choose others if they seem more appropriate.

Failing a course for the first time
Humiliation on a date
Falsely accused of something
First experience of homesickness
Loss of a job you needed
Robbery and a vandalized home
Coming out
A life-threatening medical condition
A terminal condition in someone close to you
Combat or some violent experience
The death of someone near to you
A life-changing spiritual event

Once you have finished the formal part of the interview, go over your notes with your respondent. Let your respondent change, add, or adjust as he or she desires. Throughout, be as accurate and specific as you can. This is an important follow-through procedure because it is one of the ways in which you show the interviewee that you are committed to understanding the experience and getting his or her words on paper exactly as preferred. It is part of the confidence building that is critical to good cross-cultural work.

When you are finished discussing your notes, write up your results as follows:

- Summarize in a page or two what your respondent said, along with quotes from his or her narrative as illustrative examples. Give your respondent "voice."
- Describe the conditions under which the experience occurred.
- State which features of the experience you think are unique to the individual you interviewed and which ones may be generalizable (and therefore diagnostic) to others.
- State who those "others" might be so that in future interviews you can confirm whether or not your respondent reported a culturally typical or purely personal response.
- Give the emotional experience its prototypical name.

You have now produced a culturally based description of an emotional experience. If you like, you can compare your findings to descriptions in the *DSM-IV* that might be applicable. You should note the differences in language, conceptualization, and ethnographic richness between your own account and that of the manual. If the interview was done well, your own example should give you a more sensitive and nuanced appreciation of the interviewee's emotional experience.

While the time spent doing a single interview this way may seem extravagant, in fact it is not. I argued in Chapter 4 that ethnographic interviewing is really quite efficient. Once you have a prototype of an experience clearly worked out—something that will take more than one interview to do—you will quickly recognize future instances of it and be better prepared to work with those clients. That is a major step in sensitizing yourself to the felt realities of people in different communities.

3. More on the Issues

- Narratives

If the case involving *dichos* interests you as an example of a narrative approach to intervention, look at Concha Delgado-Gaitan, "*Consejos:* The Power of Cultural Narratives," *Anthropology and Education Quarterly* (25:298–316, 1994). *Consejos* refers to nurturing advice and Delgado-Gaitan describes how these discourses in family life impart values to children, especially values about education. Those working with Latino children and teen-agers would find this article useful.

- Latino Values

Values and values contrasts are important aspects of comparative understanding. On these topics, see two articles in the *Journal of Multicultural Social Work,* 4:3, 1996. They are Maricela Ordaz and Diane de Anda, "Cultural Legacies: Operationalizing Chicano Cultural Values" (4:57–68) and Yolanda C. Padilla, "Incorporating Social Science Concepts in the Analysis of Ethnic Issues in Social Work: The Case of Latinos," (4:1–12). A third article in the same issue, by Warren Dana Holman, links Puerto Rican poetry to cultural sensitivity issues in practice.

- Health

Maternal health and care giving are critical issues in immigrant communities, and grandmothers may be critical actors in the well-being of Latino families. Two articles that address this topic are Denise Burnette, "Grandmother Caregivers in Inner-City Latino Families: A Descriptive Profile and Informal Social Supports," *Journal of Multicultural Social Work* (5:121–138, 1997), and Luis H. Zayas and Nancy A. Busch-Rossnagel, "Pregnant Hispanic Women: a Mental Health Study," *Families in Society* (73:515–521, 1992).

- Curanderismo

Recent research shows that *curanderismo*, folk healing, is widely known among elderly Latinos. While they often use standard medical institutions and practitioners, they consider *curanderismo* a significant alternative that is available when they need it, something gerontologists working with them would need to know. See Steven Lozano Applewhite, "*Curanderismo:* Demystifying the Health Beliefs and Practices of Elderly Mexican Americans," *Health and Social Work* (20:247–253, 1995).

- Alcohol, Treatment, and Community Context

In the middle of this long, passionately argued, and sometimes theoretical article is "The Case of Juan Garcia," a Puerto Rican immigrant with a history of alcoholism. The discussion of the historical and contemporary role of alcohol in Garcia's life and that of his community is excellent. This is demanding reading but worth it. Merrill Singer, Freddie Valentin, Hans Baer, and Zhongke Jia, "Why Does Juan Garcia Have a Drinking Problem? The Perspective of Critical Medical Anthropology," *Medical Anthropology* (14:77–108, 1992).

- Family Research

An excellent overview of current family research is Ruth E. Zambrana, ed., *Understanding Latino Families* (1995). The three chapters in "Part II: Program and Practice" are especially good on ways of including the community in building effective programs. Also useful is Amado M. Padilla, ed., *Hispanic Psychology* (1995), with articles on acculturation, ethnic identity, health, gender, and education.

9

ASIANS AND PACIFIC ISLANDERS

Sam Sue is a Chinese American who grew up in a small town in rural Mississippi. Today he is a lawyer in New York City. His story (in Lee 1991) is uniquely his own, but it contains themes that would be recognized by many Asian Americans and recent Asian immigrants and refugees. His father came to the United States in the 1930s at age sixteen and worked in a San Francisco restaurant to earn enough money to bring his wife to America. Eventually, he settled in a rural Mississippi town where he would raise his family and run a small general store for the next thirty years.

Why Mississippi? Much of the rural South at that time was impoverished, land and housing were much cheaper than in California, the town of Clarksdale already had a small number of Chinese families, and a Chinese hardware and grocery man could find an economic niche that no one else filled: selling goods to poor whites and even poorer blacks on credit.

Sue's family lived in the back of the store that was kept open every day of the week, including Christmas, and everyone worked as many hours as was required. Sam's father learned just enough English to get along with his customers; it came out as rural black English with a Chinese accent. Most whites could never understand him. When the family moved out of the store and into a house, it was in the poorer, black part of town because an anonymous caller warned that if they bought in the white area their home would be torched. The elder Sue closed his store in 1978, just two months before his wife died. He still lives in Clarksdale, although he has no affection for the place, because he has no idea where else he might go.

Sam no longer lives in the South, but he is bitter about much that happened to him there. In the rigid, paranoid world of rural Mississippi in the 1950s and 1960s, where separation of blacks and whites was enforced with stunning violence, no Asian found an easy place to alight. Sue recalls that when he went to movies, "I didn't know where I was supposed to sit, so I sat in the white section, and nobody said anything" (Lee 1991:3). He went to a white high school but never dated white girls—they always had a reason not to go to a dance with him. Dating Asian girls was not much of an option since there were few of them and taking one out was, from Sue's point of view, like dating a cousin. His sense of alienation was compounded by his parents' commitment to their store. As he puts it, "One common thread that runs through many Asian lives is that parents spend so much time working for the future needs of their children, that they don't devote enough time to emotional needs. Either the parents are working and can't be there, or if they are at home, they are so tired they can't devote themselves to the children" (Lee 1991:7).

When Sam left the South he went to college in Ohio. But his dilemmas did not end there. He recalls his first visit to a Chinese restaurant, in Cleveland, and his embarrassment at not being able to use chopsticks or read the Chinese portion of the menu. As a monolingual American who cultivated a northern accent by watching television, he resented being treated by both whites and Asians as though he ought to be thoroughly Asian, too. "I don't feel Chinese, and I am not. I identify myself as Asian American. I feel Chinese to some extent, but not necessarily to the extent of knowing much about Chinese culture and tradition" (Lee 1991:8). Just as his father would never return to China, Sam Sue will not return to Mississippi, and just as his father puts up with Clarksdale because he doesn't know where else he might go, Sam tolerates New York City because he feels he doesn't have many other choices.

Sam Sue's life is like that of many Asian Americans—an immigrant family history, the exhausting struggle of his parents' generation to do well financially, their exploitation of a marginal economic niche, a general sense of alienation from their country of origin and America as well, resentment of racism, and the need to survive in a sometimes hostile, sometimes open, but always ambiguous social environment. Those are some of the themes that social and health service workers will see in the lives of many of their clients and patients.

A HISTORICAL OVERVIEW

Asian emigration to the United States is somewhat recent, at least in comparison with other ethnic groups. There are several good histories on the topic but one of the best is that of Chan (1991), whose approach I follow here. She describes how emigration began in the mid and late nineteenth century; five major communities entered the western United States and Canada in three distinctive sequences. The Chinese came first, attracted by the possibility of finding gold and lucrative jobs in the settlement of the American West. Japanese, Korean, and Filipino emigrants came later, usually by way of the sugar plantations in Hawaii. South Asians, primarily Sikhs but Muslims and Hindus as well, represent a smaller but significant migration stream, mostly to limited areas of California and British Columbia. More recently, Vietnamese entered the United States following the Vietnam war, some of them as refugees from settlement camps scattered throughout Southeast Asia, others as immigrants who could not stay in their home country because of their close affiliation with the Americans during that conflict. While many Asians emigrated because of the economic opportunities available in the American and Canadian West, many, like the Vietnamese, left their homes because they had little choice. Local wars, poverty, colonialism, and the worldwide spread of capitalist institutions all combined to move huge numbers of people throughout the world in the latter half of the nineteenth century and the early decades of this one. The Asian migration to the United States was part of that global event.

Who migrates and why is always important to understanding human relocation. Migration is usually selective, and those who leave their homes are rarely representative of anything but themselves. For example, almost all the Chinese who came to the United States originated in three small regions, each with its own dialect, within one province, Guangdong, in southeastern China. Mostly peasants and landless laborers, they had endured fifteen years of the Taiping Rebellion as well as intense interethnic conflict, and their towns and economies were decimated by it. Similarly, the Meiji Restoration in late nineteenth-century Japan abolished the feudal land system as part of an effort to modernize and industrialize. But it also drove almost half a million peasants off their land because of high taxes and almost uncontrollable inflation. While the government was slow to permit emigration, it finally allowed contract laborers to go to Hawaii to work on sugar plantations. Most came from just seven prefectures in southern Japan.

During the late nineteenth and early twentieth centuries, the United States government and especially private citizens actively promoted migration from Asia. Missionaries, for example, had worked in China for many years, although without much success, and they believed that sending Chinese to live in Christian America would speed up conversions. In Japan, just a handful of American and Japanese businessmen running import/export companies promoted shipments of laborers to Hawaii. An American diplomat in Korea arranged with the government there for Koreans to join the Hawaiian labor flow, which they did for several years. When the United States took possession of the Philippines after the Spanish-American war, Filipino laborers also came to Hawaii, almost all of them from the three most northern provinces of their homeland. Because they had American passports and could travel to the mainland as well, a pattern of chain migration emerged, funneling thousands of Filipinos into the Hawaiian islands and then on to California, Oregon, and Washington State. The experience of Indian Punjabis was selective in its way as well, indicative of the worldwide reach of colonial and capitalist institutions. Punjabis, mostly Sikhs from that North Indian state, had been the police force and soldiers of the British empire and were famed for their willingness to travel in service to the Crown. When opportunities for farming and railroad work appeared in western Canada, small numbers of Punjabi families moved into that region from all over the British empire. But racial hostility toward them quickly grew violent and they moved south to claim and work some of the poorest lands in California and other western states. Through hard labor and quiet persistence, they made their farms productive and highly profitable.

The Vietnamese experience is, of course, the most recent and perhaps the most traumatic. Beginning in April 1975, following the chaotic American exodus from Saigon, over 130,000 Vietnamese were hastily escorted to the United States. The refugees in this initial wave were different from later refugees in that they had had close ties to the American military presence in their country, they were familiar with American customs, they were well educated, they knew English and were lifelong Catholics, and they even had other family members resident in the United States. Later refugees were very different. Many were from that country's minority groups—Cham, Hmong, Khmer, Chinese—and were distrusted and disliked by the Vietnamese who preceded them. Often peasants and laborers, they and their families had fled to huge holding camps late in the war, first in Thailand and Malaysia, and later Indonesia, Hong Kong, and the Philippines. Many waited and wasted for years, until permits for entry into the United States arrived. They were traumatized, poorly educated, and had few job skills when they finally stepped out on American soil. Unlike the first wave, they were not welcome and their resettlement was more difficult. Ultimately, nearly a million Vietnamese came to this country, almost half of them settling on the West Coast and many others in the upper Midwest, Texas, and New York.

ADAPTATIONS TO AMERICAN LIFE

The first large-scale Asian immigration to the United States was that of the Chinese in California, a response to the Gold Rush of the 1850s and the arrival of the railroads. The earliest who came worked as miners, but many others set up businesses to cater to the needs of their countrymen. Chinese importers, merchants, and cooks supplied Chinese laborers with familiar foods, clothing, and medicines. But the opportunities that attracted both Asians and Europeans did not last. Creeks and rivers were soon panned out and the rail tracks laid. Those who had saved money leased small plots of land and began their own fruit and vegetable farms, labor-intensive forms of agriculture that can be profitable with minimal investment. In urban areas such as San Francisco, many Chinese worked in sweatshops where boots, blankets, cigars, and household items were manufactured. The conditions in these factories were as oppressive and brutal as the better-known sweatshops of the East Coast but they offered the new immigrants jobs where none other were available.

The familiar stereotypes of Chinese laundries and restaurants come from this period of early settling in. Chan (1991:33) suggests that these were niche occupations for the Chinese since on the frontier there was a shortage of laundry workers of any kind (at one time laundry was sent from California to Honolulu and back!). In addition, only Chinese cooks could meet the culinary preferences of the immigrant miners and rail and sweatshop workers. Laundry and restaurant work enabled Chinese entrepreneurs to create their own opportunities, not only in California but in the Midwest and the East as well. Chan describes how these businesses were common in blue collar neighborhoods filled with ethnic whites, many of whom lived in boardinghouses and cheap apartments. Restaurants and laundries were low-profile occupations, neither dependent on large numbers of other Asians nor in competition with immigrants from Europe. Very much family businesses, their labor costs were not high and overhead was low. Typically, a few Chinese families could settle into a largely white community and quietly develop their business without arousing nativist fears. Some became prosperous, serving the needs of nineteenth-century corporate America's factory workers and clerks. By keeping to themselves and not advertising their success, only their bankers knew how well they were doing.

Unlike the Chinese, many of the Japanese, Koreans, and Filipinos who came at the beginning of this century did so by way of Hawaii and the white-owned sugar plantations there. The history of sugar in the Western hemisphere is a sordid one; the Hawaiian planters needed cheap contract labor as much as their predecessors in the American South needed slaves. Living conditions for the laborers in Hawaii were only marginally better than those in the Old South and many Japanese and Koreans returned home as soon as they could afford passage. Others, however, went on to California, leaving plantation agriculture for migrant harvesting of fruit and vegetable crops instead. Most of the Japanese in California, Oregon, and Washington State through the 1930s were migratory farm laborers who, with their families, did the kinds of work that postwar Americans associate with Mexican labor. But because land was more available in the 1920s and 1930s, in a way it never would be for the Mexicans who came later, many Asians were able to purchase small acreages and establish themselves as truck farmers. Highly dependent on intensive family labor, they supplied fresh produce to nearby urban markets. Some families were very successful and became wealthy, although they risked becoming targets of hate groups because of it. Like the Chinese, many Japanese and Filipinos worked in restaurants and hotels or as domestic servants and gardeners in white households. Some Filipinos in migrant agriculture came in contact with Native Americans who were similarly employed and one of the little known stories of American ethnicity is the frequency of Filipino–Native American marriages, especially in parts of the Northwest.

The presence of large numbers of Asians on the West Coast, while filling a labor demand created by the corporatizing of agriculture and the growth of western cities, also generated nativist and racist demands for their containment and even exclusion. Laws were passed to limit Asian wage rates, control buying or leasing of land, impose discriminatory taxes on Asian-owned businesses, and limit naturalization. The Immigration Act of 1924 effectively ended Japanese immigration by, among other things, denying passports to "picture brides," a practice whites disliked intensely. Lacking voting power and due process protections, Asians had almost no ability to influence legislative or judicial actions directed against them. Anti-Chinese race riots were common in the West in the 1880s, both in small towns and virtually all the big coastal cities. Troops were often called up to control mobs because local police neither could nor would. In addition, many states passed laws prohibiting interracial marriage, laws which persisted in some jurisdictions until as late as 1967. While interracial marriage laws had little practical effect, they nevertheless expressed the anti-Asian xenophobia common at the time.

In all the resident Asian communities so affected, mutual aid and beneficial societies of many kinds quickly emerged. These were groups organized to represent various Asian interests, to act as power brokers with the institutions of the larger society and even the government of the home country, and to settle disputes among their own membership. Each Asian community followed its own pattern but the historical importance of these organizations is the precedent they set for communal associations still active and important up to the present. Among the Chinese, organizations based on family names or on common dialects were headed by local entrepreneurs and merchants, people who had demonstrated their ability to work with hostile governments and racist business groups. These benefit societies established Chinese language schools, hired white lawyers to fight discriminatory legislation, created rotating credit associations, and arranged for funerals, an especially important function in a community that honors the elderly. Some associations were modeled after trade guilds or unions; others were fraternal bodies complete with secret rites and codes of brotherhood. A few of the latter, known as "tongs," carved up territories and were infamous for the "tong wars" that protected turf and illegal activities in West Coast Chinatowns.

Japanese benefit associations were based on prefects (counties) of origin, and they had special powers and financial support because, through agreement with the Foreign Ministry of Japan, they helped regulate the issuance of visitor certificates for Japanese returning to their home country for personal or commercial visits. Because agriculture was so important in the Japanese immigrant community, some benefit societies were organized as agricultural cooperatives and trade groups. Chan describes how these operations enabled some "to gain vertical control over their own sector of California's agribusiness: Japanese growers out in the countryside or suburbs sold their produce to Japanese commission merchants, who in turn sold it to wholesalers, who then supplied the numerous Japanese retail fruit and produce stores in the city" (1991:70). Like the Chinese, Japanese associations had their criminal counterparts whose activities, in no way typical of the Japanese community, were fodder for sensational journalism aimed at whipping up white fears of the "yellow peril" and other imagined threats to white control in the recently settled West. It is difficult now for whites to imagine the virulence of anti-Japanese racism in the American West for the half century prior to 1941, but it was part of the freebooting individualism and "America first" xenophobia of the time. The oldest Japanese Americans, of course, remember it well, for it had devastating consequences for them after the attack on Pearl Harbor in December, 1941.

In addition to benefit societies and guilds, Christian churches were focal points of Asian community organization. Protestants had long been active as evangelists in China, although the Jesuits got there first in the late 1500s, and they continued their efforts among Asians in the United States. Presbyterians, Methodists, and Baptists aggressively recruited among the Chinese and Japanese, and consequently those denominations are well represented in contemporary Chinatowns and Asian residential areas. For Koreans and Filipinos, Christian churches are a primary form of communal association. Most Christian Filipinos are Catholic due to the colonial presence of Spain in their homeland over several hundred years, and most of their fraternal groups have a religious tone in their statements of purpose and the kinds of activities they encourage. But many Asians are not Christian at all and are firmly committed to other religious traditions. Buddhist temples (sometimes renamed "churches") and their monks are especially important in the Vietnamese community. Among Sikhs, of course, religion defines their ethnicity, as it does for the Hindus and Muslims who also came from South Asia. Sometimes non-Christian immigrants have adapted their religions in superficial ways to meet American expectations. Rutledge (1992:52) describes a group of Vietnamese children in a Port Arthur, Texas, temple singing "Buddha loves me, this I know, for the sutras tell me so"! Despite superficialities such as this, most immigrants are firmly committed to the religious preferences they brought with them and have no intention or desire to give them up. Nor should they be expected to, for their own institutions are usually the best first defense against health and social problems that can afflict immigrant communities.

One of the significant features of the older Asian communities, especially in the years leading up to World War II, was their peculiar demographic shape, a historical circumstance that is very important in the Asian American experience. Sugar plantations, railroads, and corporate agricultural enterprises were not interested in families. They only wanted younger men willing to work hard, accept minimal pay, and not complain about shoddy and dangerous living conditions. Women were discouraged and at times even prohibited by immigration laws. Chan points out that at the turn of the century the sex ratio among the Chinese in America was 27 men to 1 woman (1991:106). It was only slightly better among the Japanese who, at least at that time, had fewer legal restrictions placed on them.

To resolve this problem, many young Japanese men worked through their parents to arrange for a "picture bride," a woman formally married in Japan to an absentia groom resident in America. The bride then joined her unseen (and often unknown) husband in this country. From the Japanese point of view, this was a simple and logical extension of arranged marriage as they knew it in their own culture. The number of these emigrating brides was controlled and limited largely by the Japanese government, but this pattern of trans-Pacific marriage allowed for the growth of more normal family life in the Japanese community in America until the practice was ended in 1920. White Americans, asserting the 1920s equivalent of the 1990s "traditional family values" argument, opposed picture bride weddings on "moral" grounds and used their objections to fuel anti-Japanese sentiment and racial hysteria.

Beginning in the 1920s and continuing into the 1930s, a first generation of Japanese Americans was born, creating what Chan calls the "second generation dilemma." Because most Asian societies are patriarchal and kinship oriented, generational placement is very important in defining privileges and responsibilities. In some ways, the Japanese are more observant of this than other groups, and their generations in this country are explicitly named. The first immigrants were *Issei;* their children, generally born between the war years, are *Nisei*. The first postwar generation are the *Sansei*. The Issei were migrants; their Nisei children were citizens, and that was a significant source of tension. The Nisei were Americanized in a way their parents were not, even though they were often sent to Japanese language schools, and deliberate efforts were made to instruct them in the culture of their parents' homeland. Nisei expected to make more of their own decisions about the use of free time, money they earned, choice of friends, and especially choice of marriage partner. The latter was often a flash point within families since the more traditional Issei expected to make marriage arrangements for their children as had been done for them. Inculcated in the American ideals of personal freedom and choice, Nisei children and young adults were further frustrated by racism and restrictions on job opportunities. Many had a good education and expected to do professional work. Instead, they went into occupations not significantly different from that of their parents: farming, small stores, restaurants, and service occupations. Whatever ambivalence they felt about this, and it was considerable, was overtaken by events following the bombing of Pearl Harbor.

The Camps

Executive Order 9066, signed by President Roosevelt in February 1942, was partly the result of FBI and military scrutiny of the Japanese community that had begun as early as 1918. Under the Order, much of the West Coast, including Alaska, was declared a security zone and arrangements were made to ship all resident Japanese to inland "internment" camps. Arrests of community leaders, teachers, priests, important merchants, benevolent association officers, and others began almost immediately. Within months, thousands of families, many of them including native-born American citizens, were rounded up, searched, tagged, put on trains, and taken to remote desert camps in Nevada, Utah, and as far away as Arkansas. Stores, farms, homes, and personal property were stolen, lost, or sold at such deflated values that even their sale was virtually theft. Liquid assets were frozen, in many cases for the duration of the war, and prosperous households were made destitute almost overnight. Nativist groups demanded the abrogation of American citizenship and deportation of all Japanese back to Japan once the war was over. (Significantly, American citizens of Japanese ancestry who happened to be in Japan when the war began were also treated as potential subversives and were detained and isolated by the Japanese government until hostilities ended.) Japanese living in the Midwest and on the East Coast were not subject to incarceration as were their West Coast compatriots, but they nevertheless suffered the stigma directed against all Japanese at that time.

One effect of the camp experience was to exaggerate the differences already separating Issei and Nisei generations. Nisei insisted on their loyalty to America since it was the only country they knew. Issei insisted on loyalty to family and family traditions, but their argument had little moral force since the senior men had been deprived of property and livelihood. Further, many of these men were separated from their families because of legal charges brought against them, and they spent the war years in separate facilities, often without their wives or children even knowing where they were. Some Nisei chose to demonstrate their loyalty by joining the 442nd Regimental Combat Team, one of the most highly decorated in the Army for its battlefield performance in Italy and France. Others fought lonely personal battles, insisting on their constitutional rights as American citizens, or organizing others and leading protests at the camps. The camp experience remains one of the most vivid among the oldest Japanese still living, and it is a powerful image and memory among their adult children.

The "Model Minority" Stereotype

Following the war, many Japanese returned to their homes, or what was left of them, and began rebuilding. Their hard work and eventual economic success led to a new stereotype, that of the "model minority." The image of a model minority was an appealing one for whites in the 1950s and 1960s, for it suggested that there really were no good reasons for other ethnic groups, blacks and Chicanos in particular, to be protesting in the streets when Asian Americans (called "Orientals" then) had "proved" that through perseverance the system "works." Japanese Americans were notable for having achieved, on average, higher educational levels than whites and, presumably, the higher incomes that go with them. Further, many whites perceived Asians as "deferential" and "polite" and unlikely candidates for noisy street demonstrations. The isolation of Asians in Chinatowns, and in their own businesses and churches, seemed to confirm that they were a minority quietly going about their own business, getting themselves educated, and lifting themselves up by their bootstraps. It was the all-American way.

The fact is that many Asians did surprisingly well, given the economic handicaps and vicious prejudice they faced in 1945. But many did not. Their apparent success, for which whites have been prone to credit "the system" rather than the efforts of the Japanese and Chinese themselves, has to be considered in the context of how it was achieved and how much was actually gained. By some counts, unemployment among Asian Americans seems low. Yet this is due in part to their high representation in low-paying service jobs, one of the growing sectors of the economy in recent years, and their participation in what is essentially cheap family labor in small businesses. For many Asians there is even a preference for underemployment rather than acceptance of government unemployment compensation and the appearance of being "on welfare." Thus, many individuals are not counted in unemployment statistics. While many Asian women are in the workplace, especially Filipinas, their presence there is as much a measure of their need to work as their willingness to do it. Asians tend to have high educational attainments as a group, yet many are underemployed if one compares their job category or income to the amount of education they have acquired.

Finally, regardless of educational and vocational capabilities, Asians tend to cluster in certain occupations. Chan (1991:169) notes that professionals tend to be in engineering, dentistry, and accounting, but not in law, administration, or social services. Asian managers are more likely to be self-employed than working in large corporations. Women tend to be in the garment industry, and few Asians are employed in construction, paper, or chemical operations. The workings of a "model economic system" cannot be seen in the employment patterns of those held to be model citizens.

Recognizing that there are indeed human as well as economic costs associated with membership in a model minority, Asian American activists began working for social change in the 1960s and the 1970s. They did so within the context of a lengthy history of Asian dissent against racism and inequality (Foner and Rosenberg 1993). Espiritu (1992) has documented the politics of this activism in a number of areas, including Asian-oriented social service programs. She notes that as part of the general protest against American cultural institutions and the Vietnam war, Asian activists challenged the traditional power of their own community's historic benevolent associations. They sought to create grassroots, "power to the people" coalitions that would address racism and poverty. Asian students were especially active in these new organizations, launching communal newspapers and setting up local action groups. But when enthusiasm overreached finances, many of these new organizations disappeared. Some of their members gravitated to social work and into governmental positions, hoping to pursue their original interests. Others studied for advanced degrees in public policy, health, and social work. The professionalization of this activist group meant that the influence of the old community elites, as well as that of some of the older organizers, was eclipsed. Those who had the desire to work in large bureaucracies and social service agencies, and who had the skills of grant writing and organizational management, came to prominence.

The institutionalization of Asian activism produced its own set of problems, however. Because of their education, Japanese Americans were often in the best position for leadership roles in Asian-oriented service bureaus and counseling and referral organizations. They were familiar with government funding practices and cultivated the skills of grantsmanship and fund raising. Smaller organizations, and those working with smaller communities such as Samoans or Koreans, found that they needed to ally themselves with government bureaucracies and major funding sources if they wanted to survive. Pan-Asian coalitions emerged, partly because it was less divisive for granting agencies to make awards to multi-ethnic umbrella groups rather than to agencies serving specific, narrowly defined communities. But this also led to friction. Smaller groups resented the power of larger ones; more recently arrived peoples were subject to the procedures and preferences of longer-resident ones. Charges of favoritism arose and some, Filipinos in particular, felt they could do better within their own organizations; they were especially vocal in their criticism of Pan-Asian groups and ideology (Espiritu 1992:103).

Some of these conflicts were ethnic in origin but others clearly related to differences in social class, styles of acculturation, and differences in how people chose to preserve their ethnic identity in a pluralistic society. Consequently, there is no single voice in the Asian community, just as there is no single homeland or historical tradition for Asian Americans. Their diversity is enormous and will become more so as political and especially economic relations among Pacific Rim countries expand.

SOCIAL SERVICE NEEDS AMONG ASIAN AMERICANS

Model minority images notwithstanding, there are serious health and mental health issues among Asian Americans just as there are in other ethnic populations.

Uba and Sue (1991) provide a useful overview of needs and services for those they describe as "APIAs," Asian and Pacific-Islander Americans. They note that mental health problems in particular are underestimated and overlooked when they occur in this population. Typically, problems arise from conflicts due to differential acculturation to American practices within families; intergenerational disagreements; trauma due to extreme conditions experienced prior to arrival in this country, especially among Vietnamese and those who spent time in refugee camps; and presumptions of ethnic foreignness by whites, especially toward Asians whose families have lived in America for many generations. These experiences, in addition to exposure to subtle and blatant forms of racism, result in high levels of stress but low levels of service utilization.

Uba and Sue (1991:6–12) list some of the reasons for underutilization. Perhaps most important, many Asian Americans stigmatize mental health problems to an extreme degree. Concealment is preferable to the shame associated with seeking out a professional service provider or to the humiliation that would result from public knowledge that an individual suffers with a condition that is "psychological." Thus many Asian clients and patients somatize emotional stresses. They report physical rather than mental illnesses, things that can be treated by medicines, acupuncture, or a physician. Sicknesses in a physical sense—generalized aches and pains, stomach upsets, headaches, insomnia—are more acceptable than psychic afflictions. Under certain conditions, mental problems may also be viewed as spiritual ones, requiring the intervention of a spiritual healer of some kind. Differing Asian traditions have different kinds of beliefs and helpers for this kind of service, beliefs usually unfamiliar to Western practitioners who are likely to dismiss them as fantasies and superstitions, or as something to be "overcome" as part of the helping enterprise.

There are also interethnic differences in the value placed on self-control during suffering of any kind. In some communities it is best not to think too much about one's difficulties because to do so may only make them worse. "Indeed, Asians are more likely than whites to believe that one should avoid morbid thinking to maintain mental health.... Since treatment often requires self-disclosure of personal and intimate problems (i.e., focusing on morbid thoughts), many APIA clients do not believe that treatment is helpful" (Uba and Sue 1991:10). Formal treatment may even be contraindicated, especially when endurance, quiet patience, and a will to prevail are highly valued as personal characteristics. Pride is at stake, not only for oneself, but for one's family. This is a difficult issue when social services are provided to those unable to pay for them. The stigma of "public welfare" is added to that of mental incapacity. Any suspicions that the sufferer was not able to exert enough self-control to contain and overcome a stressful situation only adds to the burden of admitting to a mental health "problem."

Language differences are also important in underutilization. Pain, physical or mental, is never easy to describe even when the patient and professional are users of the same language. Working across linguistic boundaries adds to the frustrations both client and social worker experience. While interpreters can be helpful, reliance on them always slows any interview and, more important, limits the quality as well as the amount of information that can be gathered. The nuances of language carry much of the emotional and informational weight of a counseling exchange, and they do not usually come through in an interpreted interview. When interpreters cannot be found, the common but problematic alternative is dependence on a bilingual youngster, often a member of the client's family. But that stopgap effort usually adds to everyone's frustration, since children may not fully understand what is expected of them, or may want to shield an adult from full disclosure for reasons of family loyalty. In addition, many clients would be understandably reluctant to burden or embarrass children or teenagers with the intimate details of their own problems.

Gender differences are another issue that may influence utilization and the receptiveness of clients to professional suggestions. Song-Kim (1992) suggests that wife battering may be one of the most common forms of family dysfunction among Korean immigrants but that women are unlikely to complain, either to other women or to social service providers. Given the strongly patriarchal organization of Korean households and the belief that beatings are deserved, women are not inclined to "confess" to violence in their own homes. Nor is the problem limited to Koreans. Furuto (1991) describes similar problems among Samoans and Hawaiians and argues strongly for devising culturally appropriate means of helping families adapt to their new circumstances before family violence becomes an issue.

But not all underutilization can be attributed to cultural differences alone. Simple inequities are part of the problem. Murase (1992:102) attributes these to inadequate funding, which shunts Asian patients into lower-cost services, wider use of paraprofessionals for Asian patients and clients, and greater use of public rather than private facilities by Asians. These are not problems that can be changed quickly given a national environment of financial constraint, but they are real and need to be corrected.

CULTURAL CONTRASTS AND CULTURAL COMPETENCE

Clearly, the cultural diversity among Asians in the United States is enormous, both between groups and within them. Generalizations are almost impossible to apply, yet there is a need for a starting point for the serious learner. However, I want to state as emphatically as I can that a starting point is only that; anyone who is content to practice social services on the basis of general guidelines has not even begun to move in the direction of cultural competence. It is also worth repeating, as I have in all the chapters on cultural communities, that the issue is not one of looking at a list of cultural features and concluding that it represents a summary of what a group of people is "really like." To use tables that are essentially overviews as a kind of laundry list for sizing up clients would be a perversion of their purpose.

What is at issue in the approach taken here is *cultural contrast*—how the social worker sees himself or herself as the "different" one in the helping relationship. The burden of making that mental and emotional readjustment is on the professional, not the client. In engaging cultural differences, the worker is really required to evaluate self-image and self-understanding as part of a caring work style. Cross-cultural empathy, if it is genuine, can proceed only in that way. By thinking in terms of contrasts, rather than differences alone, one can begin to appreciate the role of culture in shaping the dynamics of an interracial or interethnic encounter. That will be true whatever the racial or ethnic affiliations of both worker and client.

Table 9.1 lists a series of contrasts in the form of brief statements. I have pulled these statements together from a variety of sources, all made by prominent Asian scholars in several disciplines. I have been particularly dependent on the work of Kitano (1988), Chung (1992), Shon and Ja (1982), and Sue and Sue (1990). They are not responsible in any way for the interpretation I have made of their materials. It

TABLE 9.1   Selected Cultural Contrasts of Asian American and Anglo American Communities

Asian American	Anglo American
Strong mutual support, including cooperation, interdependence, and harmony are expected within the family and community.	Individualism, independence, and assertive behavior, which causes individual attributes to stand out and be noticed, are often favored.
A strongly hierarchical, stable pattern of family and community relations is the setting for mutual support, expressed through a strong sense of obligation and duty to others. This duty overrides individual preferences.	Efforts to minimize status and rank differences, to treat individuals equally or on par with one another, expressed through an ideology of growth and development of individual talents.
Relations with those outside the family are an extension of family interests expressed most pointedly in family influence in the choice of friends or a mate.	Relations with those outside the family are a matter of individual preference and limited family control.
Problems are solved within the family and a code of family pride and honor limits the degree to which internal problems should be known outside the family or shared with professional helpers such as counselors.	Problems are solved within the family but a wide range of professional help providers are available and used when needed.
There is great family pressure to succeed, especially through education. Failure is a failure of obligation to one's family.	There is family pressure to succeed, primarily in those areas where one has already shown distinctive talent. Failure is attributed to lack of individual effort and reflects primarily on personal or moral characteristics, secondarily on other members of the family.
Ambiguity in social relations is a source of anxiety.	Lack of structure, informality or "looseness" in social relations is seen as an expression of American egalitarianism. It also creates opportunity for personal and professional growth or advancement.

is gratifying, nevertheless, that the help-seeking behavior model, proposed in the earlier edition of this book, is seen as useful by some of these scholars and practitioners.

As with the tables of cultural features found in other chapters, the reader is cautioned that any generalization offered anywhere in this book may or may not apply to a specific individual or family. "Individualizing the client" means, in part, estimating any individual's commitment and involvement in the norms, values, and practices of his or her cultural tradition. The statements in the tables are only general tendencies, not "facts" in any objective sense. Honing one's skill in ethnic competence means knowing when the statements apply, when they do not, and, always, why that is the case.

The sections that follow give a brief overview of some of the significant health and social service issues for the various groups discussed in this chapter. I emphasize the word "brief" because in communities as varied as these, from so many parts of Asia, an overview is all that can be done. Each of these communities and their human service needs could easily be the subject of an entire book, as most of them are. It is critical, therefore, that students and social workers involved with members of one of these communities actively seek additional information. All the sources I have cited here contain more references and will lead you to additional authors. My intent has been to be suggestive, not exhaustive, and the best use of these sections is as a guide to additional information.

THE CHINESE

Chinese Americans tend to live on the West and East coasts, mostly in California and New York, but significant numbers reside in Hawaii, Illinois, and Texas as well. Huang (1991:82) notes that a high percentage, almost two-thirds, of all Chinese in the United States are foreign-born. Most of them speak something other than English at home. Their graduation rates from high schools and colleges, for both men and women, are higher than the national average. Yet like other Asians they tend to be underemployed for the amount of education they have, and their incomes lag behind those of similarly educated whites. They tend to cluster in technical and professional fields and in poorly paid service jobs. Poorer Chinese often live in Chinatowns, frequently in substandard housing, while those who can do so live in suburbs.

In the mid-1960s, the United States changed its immigration policies, encouraging whole families to migrate rather than single individuals. Since that time, many Chinese from Hong Kong and other areas have come into the country following the familiar pattern of chain migration (Wong and Hirschman 1983). There are several kinds of families involved in this process, however. "Chinatown Chinese," according to Huang (1988), are working-class families who cluster in Chinatowns where language, shopping, and services are familiar. Both husband and wife take low-paying, low-skilled, service-sector jobs. Their work schedules may or may not overlap, and they may see little of each other or their children except on weekends. Their jobs as cooks, dishwashers, and janitors have no integral relationship to family life, as they might if they were doing the same tasks in a family business. Family values are traditionally hierarchical, which may become a source of conflict where wives earn their own money and children are free to seek their own friendships and entertainments. By contrast, middle-class and professional families seek housing in suburbs or gentrified in-town neighborhoods. They see themselves as more American than Chinatown Chinese. Yet they sometimes replicate traditional extended family patterns, with grandparents living in nearby neighborhoods or even in the same apartment building.

In both family types, however, some traditional values remain important. Divorce is rare, and women are expected to accede to the wishes of their husbands, even if that means remaining in an unhappy marriage. Fathers express their authority by maintaining an emotional distance, and mothers expect children to react promptly to commands. Wong suggests that while "Chinese parents may be more indulgent with their young children than parents of the white American culture, discipline is much more strict than that which the typical American child receives" and that punishment, which is immediate, "involves withdrawal from the social life of the family or the deprivation of special privileges or objects rather than physical punishment" (1988:249). Overt expressions of emotion are discouraged; early independence, responsibility, and cooperation are stressed. Older children are expected to help with the younger ones. Sibling rivalry and aggression are not tolerated.

The often-cited central role of the father and the values of hierarchy and respect for age lead one to presume that elders are well taken care of in Chinese families. That is probably the case, especially for families that are financially able to do so, although supporting data for that is rare. Chinese Americans make little use of social services; other family members are the primary sources of support for the aged. Nursing homes in particular do not appeal to most Chinese since placing one's parents in an institution is seen as an admission that one cannot or will not care for them in the expected way.

The circumstances and needs of the Chinese elderly are a useful illustration of a number of issues affecting Asian elders generally. Their adjustment to life in the United States can be particularly traumatic because there is little in American culture that supports their expectations. Their view of the aging process, for example, is considerably different from that of most whites and white elders, and even in leisure activities many Chinese American elderly actively maintain their ethnic affiliations (Allison and Geiger 1993). Cheung (1989) lists several beliefs about old age held by these elderly, including their conviction that age is a source of prestige, that their life-knowledge has value and gives them authority, that growing old is pleasant and leads to greater solidarity with one's family, and that they can and should be active as workers and contributors to their family. Clearly, however, the American values of individualism, careerism, and the nuclear family challenge and undermine these traditional expectations. Language differences, problems with literacy, inappropriate work skills, physical immobility, inability to manage public transportation systems, and lack of familiarity with everyday routines such as banking may hinder an elder's ability to act authoritatively or to contribute directly to family welfare. For some of their adult children, especially those with strong career aspirations, a separate residence for an immigrant senior may be preferable to a shared residence as is common in Asia. This may not be an unreasonable choice since suburbs can be as isolating to an elder as an institutional confinement. But it does not relieve the sense of lost power and diluted authority that is typical of the elderly in American society.

Clearly, services directed toward the elderly, as well as to Chinese women and to struggling, low-income families, are important. The special strains experienced by Asian immigrants are well documented in the social work and social science literature (Lee, Patchner, and Balgopal 1991; Dhooper 1991; Le-Doux and Stephens 1992). What is needed is a framework for working with Chinese clients and planning services that will meet their needs in acceptable ways.

Huang (1991:89–93) suggests a number of "principles of practice" for working with Chinese clients and patients. First, most Chinese do not come to the attention of a professional until a problem, be it physical or psychological, is so serious that normal activities cannot be continued. The goal of treatment is symptom relief, and the client expects the social service provider to take charge in naming the malady and suggesting solutions. Both intrusive and indirect questioning may be resisted since the client expects a rapid diagnosis and prompt intervention. (Traditional healers, according to Huang, simply take the patient's pulse and then state what needs to be done.) The ability to quickly assess and name the problem is seen as a sign of the practitioner's competence. Making a reasonable guess about the source of a difficulty and what must be done to correct it is far more acceptable than attempting to access the client's feelings and display empathy by so doing.

Second, competence is displayed when the practitioner reveals a firm but comfortable sense of authority. Since relations in Chinese families tend to be hierarchical, the professional is judged according to how well he or she models hierarchical behavior in the therapeutic relationship. This is a very subtle but critical matter, and it has consequences for the client's willingness to comply with a treatment regimen. Many white social service workers (health services are probably different) prefer an egalitarian style, a friendly openness, and a casualness in the early phases of the relationship. To them "breaking the ice" is a style that shows mutual regard. But to many Chinese it is insulting, even a dereliction of duty, as though the social worker were not taking the problem seriously. A casual manner may make Chinese clients retreat into polite silence, and the therapeutic alliance will never really begin.

Third, many Chinese-American clients see the need to ask for professional advice on personal problems as potentially shameful, and their concern about this should be addressed as soon as is appropriate. They need to be reassured that they are not "crazy" and that the social worker understands that coming in for a counseling session is itself a difficult step. Respect for the client's circumstance can and should be verbalized, but concrete actions are more important. Huang feels that seemingly nonclinical tasks, such as helping a client fill out forms or calling someone in another agency to facilitate an appointment, are much more important as displays of respect than verbal reassurances. The directness of action not only shows the professional's willingness to help but is another sign of authority and competence.

Fourth, personal questions made to the social worker are not out of place, and an honest, straightforward response is a sign that the relationship is a positive one. Some whites view personal inquisitiveness as intrusive, as no one else's business, and not part of the job description. For Chinese clients, however, it is simply another sign that the level of trust is improving.

Fifth, what Huang calls "meta-rules" operate in Chinese communications. These rules govern the appropriate level of disclosure between speakers of different social rank. For example, fathers, physicians, and teachers occupy positions of respect; communicating unpleasant things to them is considered inappropriate, even a faux pas. These meta-rules are exquisitely nuanced in Chinese culture. Outsiders have ignorantly characterized such behavior as "inscrutable" but the culturally sensitive social worker will learn about these matters and recognize them for the finely honed sense of decorum they represent. Such recognition is a skill that takes time and practice; it is probably learnable only through careful mentoring with a sympathetic cultural guide. But it is critical for the professional who sees Chinese clients on a regular basis.

Asian American mental health professionals generally warn against insight-oriented therapies for Asian clients. Tung (1984, 1991), however, a Chinese American psychotherapist, disagrees. Her observations are especially interesting from a comparative cultural-awareness perspective because she is sensitive to the differences in her work style with white and Asian clients. She finds that Asians are not indifferent to insight and self-revelation therapies, but the focus must be different for them than for whites. Cognitive, didactic discussions of current symptoms and grievances are more important than identification of emotional distortions rooted in the past. It is useful for the therapist to directly teach the client about correct role behavior within the extended family. Asian clients, she feels, are not much concerned with transference issues nor do they need long periods of time to resolve old issues from early family life. Rather, they want to discuss what is culturally proper in Chinese family life and what they can do to return to a state of equilibrium. Typically, fewer treatment sessions are needed with Asian than with white clients because in Tung's practice their task is one of cognitive relearning rather than emotional resolution and redirection. This is consistent with the observation of Shon and Ja (1982) that a good therapeutic alliance with Asian families requires a prompt and firmly directed approach, one in which the therapist proceeds from both a solid ethnographic understanding of Asian family patterns and a genuine empathy for the needs of Asian individuals.

THE JAPANESE

What many Japanese and Japanese Americans think of as their "traditional" family pattern originally came from the *samurai* class of feudal Japan (Tamura and Lau

1992). There the system was one of three-generational families, the eldest son residing with his wife and children in his parents' household. The senior males, a married son and his father, would manage the household and its holdings while younger sons and daughters went elsewhere to start their own families. While relations between fathers and sons were somewhat formal, those between a mother and her children were expected to be emotionally intense. In these stem or multigenerational families, the lowest-ranking adult in the household was the daughter-in-law. She was subservient to all other resident adults and, in daily household chores, answered directly to her mother-in-law. This system, with local variants, was and still is common in much of Asia. It created a distinctive sense of family unity and obligation, one that contrasts markedly with the Western family model. Tamura and Lau define that contrast as one of connectedness versus separateness:

> *In British [and American] culture, the importance of the separateness of individuals takes precedence in value over connectedness among the members of a system.... [Personal growth] is a process of progressive differentiation of self from an attachment figure.... Japanese relate with others on the premise that they are mutually connected. It is like an identity whereby one belongs to a group that can consist of family members, classmates, or company colleagues. (1992:332, 334)*

This contrast differentiates Japanese and Westerners in a general sense, but there are other important distinguishing features as well. A number of specific, complex, "traditional" values operate within the modern Japanese American community. They include *amae*, the emphasis on interdependence in preference to individualism; a marked sense of hierarchical order that is important in personal relations; well-defined obligations that attach to one's position in the family and the culture; and *enryo*, respectfulness and modesty. There is also a concern with controlling emotions, doing the best one can in adverse circumstances, and appreciating that there may be limits to what one can do in difficult situations (Fugita et al. 1991:67–70). How this plays out in individual relationships can be complex and subtle.

These values are expressed in an intergenerational structure that emphasizes connectedness and continuity rather than the individualization and separation that is preferred by many whites. In fact, generational marking is so important that each generation is named and its distinctive experiences define the shape of the community. Mass (1981:319) notes that Japanese immigrants were the only ethnic community in America who named their generations and that it is virtually impossible to discuss their history or their personal experiences without knowledge of that. Kitano describes the situation as follows:

> *The Issei generally understood that their own participation in the American mainstream would be limited, but high hopes were placed on their American-born Nisei children. They saw the Nisei as American citizens with the advantage of American education.... Issei often thought of themselves as a sacrificial generation; their own lives were to be secondary to the advancement of their children;...and it was*

*a familiar sight to see parents in old clothes buying newer clothes for their children
and the larger and choicer portions of food going to their sons, with leftovers for
the mother. (1988:263–264)*

Yanagisako (1985) further argues that not only are there significant differences
between Issei and Nisei generations but that to describe them as simply differences
in "acculturation" is to miss (and even dismiss) much of their importance. A cultural understanding requires that we know something of the normative rules operating within each generational cohort and that we recognize how those rules have
consequences for individuals and for the harmonious functioning of their families.

A major component of the Issei/Nisei intergenerational dynamic is that of
family representation (Yanagisako 1985:174). It is generally the case that one individual among the adult Nisei siblings must represent the family and its multiple
households, taking leadership on decisions that affect everyone. That is usually the
responsibility of the eldest male, who is expected to deal with matters as varied as
his Issei parents' health care, maintenance of their home, and general comfort and
well-being. He also has important ritual functions connected with the *koden* or
mortuary offerings at their funerals.

A second component is the financial responsibility the elder son will assume.
Given the strong value of self-sufficiency among Japanese Americans, any form of
aid from outside the family (except for Social Security) is not acceptable. Elders
who must accept "welfare" of any kind are pitied and their adult children scorned,
especially if the latter are in a position to offer support and do not. The level of support does not have to be high, but it has to be sufficient to keep older parents
healthy and comfortable. Younger sons are expected to contribute their financial
share as well, leaving it to the eldest to see that funds are properly used. Daughters,
by contrast, are not expected to give money toward the financial support of their
parents since to do so would mean drawing on the funds their husbands need for
support of their own parents.

Third, three-generation households are not considered desirable, even though
they may be necessary in some circumstances. It is certainly better to keep an ailing
parent in one's own home than to send him or her to an institution. Although in
recent years Japanese-owned and -operated nursing homes have been built, the
need for them is far greater than their availability, and many families fear that institutions staffed by non-Japanese may not be truly sensitive to their elder parents'
needs. When living with adult children, elder Issei generally prefer to live with
daughters rather than sons. Since older Issei women outnumber older men, they
are most likely to be the resident elder in a household. Aside from demographics,
however, the cultural rationale for this is that mothers and daughters are assumed
to have a closer emotional relationship and to be more familiar and comfortable
with one another's housekeeping style, thereby reducing the likelihood of friction.
These arrangements also add to the solidarity of women within their homes and
their ability to exert managerial control even though male elders have titular
authority. In addition, daughters, not daughters-in-law or sons, are felt to be better
able to provide personal care to an older or disabled parent.

This intergenerational mix of expectations has an additional complicating ingredient. According to Yanagisako, Japanese American families are marked by very distinctive male and female domains. Especially in the Issei generation, a sharp line is drawn between matters "inside" (*uchi no koto*) and "outside" (*soto no koto*) the family, and these matters are gender marked. Women's actions are defined as "inside," serving the well-being of other family members. Even if a woman works in an office or a store, her work is "inside" in the sense that it is done in behalf of the family. Men, too, work to support their families but they are also committed to gaining recognition in the extradomestic world, "outside," and that may require giving energy and attention to corporate, professional, or social concerns. Further, given the hierarchical framing of family values and practices, male and female domains are not equal, at least among the Issei, for that which is thought of as "outside" and male encompasses what is "inside" and female. This distinction can have consequences for the harmony that is expected to prevail between men and women:

> *A common theme that runs through the women's accounts of their conjugal relationships is resentment of their husband's interests outside the family. In these complaints, they portray the family and the outside social world as competing for limited resources...even respectable interests outside the family were sometimes resented. (Yanagisako 1985:103)*

It is worth remembering that many Issei men are and were considerably older than their wives due to the contingencies of earlier immigration laws. Not only their gender but their greater age gave them enormous authority. Yanagisako found that many of the widows she interviewed regarded their husband's death as a personal loss but also as something of a release from their obligations to serve him and from the distractions and expenses of his outside interests.

The Nisei generation has a different sensibility. Nisei downplay but do not deny the importance of *giri* or duty, which motivated their parents and created a powerful sense of obligation. Along with the Sansei, or third generation, they value what they perceive as the more egalitarian nature of "American" marriages. A "Japanese versus American" contrast is common in their descriptions of their own families and how they believe they are different from their parents. Whereas Yanagisako's Issei respondents rarely talked of "love" in reference to their marriages, Nisei and Sansei marriage partners stressed love, intimacy, and communication. Their preference for the conjugal bond over that between parents and children is seen in their strong feeling that older parents should stay in their own homes as long as possible. Yet the clear division of labor based on gender is as characteristic of many Nisei homes as it is of their parents'. Nisei women place high value on working at home or in support of the home if they must work outside it. Like their fathers, men are expected to be good providers through their jobs. But they are not generally expected to share in housework, and at least one Nisei interviewee told Yanagisako that she thought it wasn't "normal" for men to do housework even though she knew that some white women expected that of their husbands. While most Nisei disavowed the rigid gender hierarchy of their parents' generation, they also felt that it was "natural" for men to "lead" the family and act in its behalf (Yanagisako 1985:118).

From this very brief overview of one part of Yanagisako's extensive research, we can identify a number of potential areas in which social service professionals might become involved. First, intergenerational conflicts are possible, not only because of differences in cohort experiences in America, but because conflicts are typical of three-generation families in Japan and other cultures where they occur as well. Fathers and sons may have conflicting expectations of how family resources are to be used, and younger sons may resent the authority of eldest sons in managing what is, after all, common family property. If money is needed to support elderly parents in their own home, wives of junior sons sometimes resent the competition that that creates with the needs of their own households.

Second, female alliances may undercut, or at least modify, the titular authority of men. Older men are increasingly confined to their own homes which are, after all, the "inside" domain. Women can and do make important decisions about money and other resources and those can include decisions about health care. Since mental health conditions are so highly stigmatized in Asian communities, an older man suffering with a disability such as Alzheimer's disease would be especially vulnerable to decisions to keep him away from public awareness or scrutiny, including the awareness of professionals who could help.

Other issues that can be sources of conflict include language, especially when grandchildren cannot communicate well with grandparents; intermarriage between Japanese and white Americans; the necessary mobility of sons who are on career and corporate fast tracks; and divorce, which is particularly shameful and is unfortunately associated with high rates of suicide among women (Ho 1987).

In a valuable review article, Marsella (1993) summarizes the state of knowledge about counseling and psychotherapy with Japanese Americans. Like Yanagisako and Mass, he asserts that ethnic identity among Japanese Americans is not a linear process of movement from traditional-minded immigrants to fully acculturated Americans. The complexity of intergenerational ties and the modification of values derived from Japan make that experience far more complex. Nor can a social service provider be very effective without first knowing how those factors enter into problem identification and resolution.

> *The assumption that a Japanese American client is acculturated or bicultural simply because of English-language fluency and appearance can result in problems. A thorough assessment must be made of ethnic identity to determine the appropriateness and applicability of different therapeutic styles and approaches. (Marsella 1993:201)*

To that end, he suggests that a useful client–therapist relationship must acknowledge and utilize a number of elements that Japanese Americans are likely to bring to the encounter. He lists and discusses the following: a preference to understate or indirectly express a powerful emotion such as grief or anxiety; reference to physical symptoms as metaphors for troubled mental states; conflicts and confusion around ethnic identity and normative expectations; ritualized self-depreciation as a way of emphasizing the primacy of the group over the individual; a willingness to endure and persevere even though suffering may be involved; use of idioms that are unfamiliar to Westerners (ancestors, unusual physical states or appearances) which are not delusional but metaphorical; and careful avoidance of tabooed topics such as alcoholism, family violence, sexual violations, and family finances. These latter are not matters of psychological denial but of loyalty and responsibility to one's family and kin.

Finally, Marsella provides a useful caution on the management of language in therapeutic relationships with Japanese Americans. The practices of verbalization, "venting," and self-disclosure that are sometimes encouraged as an adjunct to therapy, as though universally efficacious with troubled individuals, may be culturally inappropriate with some Japanese Americans. Many of them have high regard for the thoughtful silence, the brief and insightful comment. In their view that is not just a communicative event, it is an emotional one as well. Language establishes the feeling tone of the relationship. A competent counselor will be able to intuit that feeling tone and respond in like manner, without hiding behind a verbal barrage. Instead of talking, he or she will act quickly and authoritatively, quietly and with a clear focus, practically rather than abstractly, in an effort to rebuild family harmony rather than urge personal growth. The worker who can do that will be seen by clients as capable and skilled, and will have given a genuinely professional service.

FILIPINOS

It is unfortunate that there is so little in the social service literature on Filipinos, for they are a sizable community in this country. The Philippines came under American control in 1898 following the Spanish-American war, giving Filipinos access (with limitations) to the United States. Most went initially to Hawaii, where they were recruited by sugar plantation owners and their agents. Generally these were young men from rural areas who had little education and few economic prospects. Their hope was to save enough money to return to their homeland to buy a plot of land and marry.

Many Filipinos also came to California, either by way of Hawaii or directly. Most were not literate, few spoke English, and the only work many could find was "stoop labor" on farms. Others went into domestic service and some into the fishing and canning industries. (Filipinos are still heavily represented in Alaskan fish canneries, some of which provide less than ideal work conditions and have a history of corruption and violence.) Many went into what was to become a "traditional" industry for their community, hotel and restaurant work. As happened to other Asians, Filipinos were the targets of race riots in the 1920s for allegedly competing unfairly with white workers, socializing with white women, and for their presumed "unassimilability." And like other Asians, Filipinos were slow to establish families in this country; labor recruitment favored males and resulted in a severe shortage of Filipino women. After 1965, however, immigration laws were changed, and families and professionals typify the more recent migration stream. These later arrivals provide much of the current leadership in their communities.

Filipinos are concentrated in urban areas, especially Los Angeles, San Francisco, and Honolulu. There are also sizable communities in New York, New Jersey, Illinois, and Washington State. It is noteworthy that Filipinos are heavily involved in the workforce on the mainland. Not only do they experience relatively little unemployment, but an exceptionally high percentage of Filipina women work outside their homes. As a group, they are not poor and both men and women have high rates of graduation from high schools and universities.

Yet in Hawaii, Filipinos are one of that state's poorest groups. They are overrepresented in low-income, low-skill jobs and have low levels of educational training and background. They are different from their mainland counterparts in that most are immigrants, not American born, and come from poorer areas of their home country. Like the Vietnamese, those among them who are well educated are often employed well below their skill levels. They suffer "occupational downgrading"; former business owners work as clerks and teachers as teacher's aides. Their resentment is not directed against whites, however, but against Japanese Hawaiians whom they perceive as dominating government and industry to their own advantage.

Filipino families tend to be egalitarian and, in contrast to some other Asian groups, women have a powerful and prominent role in family life. Cordova (1983) makes much of this contrast between "pinay" (or Filipina women) and those from other Asian countries. Pinays, especially in the early years of immigration, were often more highly educated than their husbands, were active in the public life of churches, schools, and businesses, and often controlled family finances. Many were entrepreneurs and many were professionals, working as teachers and nurses. In Cordova's view:

> *The heart and soul of the development of the Filipino American experience were personified in Pinays—particularly first generation women, including those separated from their men, and their second-generation daughters, who tried to emulate their mothers. Pinays have been the yeast that set the men and children rising and the leaven that got their communities producing. (1983:153)*

As previously mentioned, there is almost no social service literature on Filipinos, and it would be an error to assume that what applies to Chinese Americans or Japanese Americans will work with Filipinos as well. Like other Asians, however, Filipinos respect the authority of the help provider and expect that person to show leadership in providing solutions. Age confers an advantage since it is presumed that age also leads to greater wisdom. Cross-gender counseling relationships, however, may be difficult to establish since one would not normally confide in someone of the opposite gender. While it is also true that most Filipinos are fluent in English, many use other languages in their homes, and the social worker seeing

Filipino clients on a regular basis will need to make at least some effort to become familiar with common phrases and any technical terminology associated with illness or personal distress. At a minimum, such knowledge can open doors and lines of communication in a way that few other activities can.

Being very family oriented, Filipinos may be more comfortable with practical suggestions and prompt guidance than with lengthy, individualized, ongoing sessions emphasizing personal growth and development. Some Filipinos attribute personal or mental distresses to hostile forces in the environment, not to character flaws or personal failings. Thus, the kind of advice they would expect and that they would be likely to act on would be that which focuses on immediate as well as underlying issues: discrimination at work, youth gangs in the neighborhood, disagreements over control of family finances, or a family member's drinking.

There are now over one million Filipinos in the United States, yet relatively little is known about them ethnographically and even less is known about their health and social service needs. One solution to that is greater recruitment and training of Filipino social service professionals. Because many Filipinos are church-oriented, ministers and priests are potential allies in working with social service professionals. Many Filipinos also feel that the larger society's sometimes faddish interest in ethnicity has overlooked them in favor of other Asians and other ethnic groups. Given their substantial numbers in this country, however, they will probably get more attention in the future.

THE VIETNAMESE

The end of the American government's costly and disastrous war in Vietnam in April 1975 was the beginning of a long period of suffering and transition for many Vietnamese and their families. As noted earlier in this chapter, the two waves of Vietnamese who fled the chaos were different. Those in the first group were well educated and well connected. They had had close ties with the American military, generally spoke English, and had professional and technical skills. The second wave, beginning about 1977, was composed mainly of ethnic groups who fled persecution by the Communist government that took control in the south as well as north. Among these were the "boat people" whose plight was made known to the world by television newscasts over several years. The end of the war generated a complex movement of refugees who fanned out into surrounding countries, disrupting lives, economies, and the precarious political stability of the region for over a decade (Rutledge 1992). Ultimately, almost a quarter million Vietnamese came to this country, although many remained in other parts of Southeast Asia as well.

In the United States, decisions were made at the Federal level that resettlement should involve private and voluntary organizations and that the refugees should be as widely scattered throughout the country as possible. No geographical or cultural "ghettos" were to be encouraged. Once dispersed, they were to be given short-term training in English and occupational self-sufficiency in the expectation that this would help them assimilate, melting pot style, into the larger society. While critics of this policy argued that such a plan would dilute the Vietnamese sense of cultural integrity, proponents replied that no other refugee group was ever given as generous a start-up for their Americanization. They were to be supplied with whatever they needed as they prepared for citizenship and eventual movement into the labor force (Matsuoka 1991). The hope was that quick assimilation would heal memories of Vietnam, both for the Vietnamese themselves and for Americans still troubled by the failed war.

The dispersion of the Vietnamese throughout the country, a policy based on administrative convenience and melting pot simplicities, has been modified both by secondary internal migration and the politics of the Vietnamese community itself. To reestablish old family and friendship ties, many Vietnamese have moved from the point of their original settlement, creating distinctive enclaves in many larger cities. This process began almost immediately after the initial settling in, and for some families it was a major sacrifice since they had to move to communities where they lacked governmental or private sponsors.

Equally important and difficult, some families sought an Asian enclave but were cautious about which Vietnamese they chose as neighbors. There are good historical reasons for this. As indicated, the class and economic differences between original and later wave refugees were considerable. Old hostilities and grievances from the war were not forgotten. In addition, there were significant internal distinctions and stereotypes among the refugees themselves. Rutledge (1992:109) describes the intraethnic competition, even discrimination and stereotyping, that differentiates those from the north of Vietnam, the central areas, and the south. Matters of dialect, religion, previous occupation, and family standing are as important to the Vietnamese as they are to people in other communities and, when combined with the war experience, they can make group solidarity and cooperation difficult. That is a political and ethnographic fact but it is also one with social service implications. No individual Vietnamese can be presumed to speak for others, and outsiders who wish to help promote community institutions need a good sense of the local political landscape before they venture into unfamiliar territory.

Several decades after the war, a number of social service needs remain, and they are typical of those associated with refugee communities. Matsuoka (1991) lists some of them, noting that among the Vietnamese hierarchical views of the family and personal relationships are as important for them as they are for some other Asian groups. I will discuss briefly several of the issues that Matsuoka presents and how they affect delivery of professional services.

Most Vietnamese are Buddhists; others are adherents of Confucianism, Taoism, and, more recently, Catholicism, since the country was once part of the former French colony of Indochina. Confucianism in particular prescribes a mode of social and ethical responsibility that emphasizes the family and the obligations owed to it according to one's age and gender. Filial piety is central to this hierarchical ethos: "son to father, wife to husband, younger brother to elder brother, servant to master, citizen to emperor" (Rutledge 1992:48–49). Elders, especially elder men who are heads of households (called *truong toc*), are senior in moral authority and expect deference from others. Even where they are "incapacitated" by American standards, through sickness, feebleness, or apparent senility, their voice is important in all family decision making. The sensitive social worker will want to be sure that voice is heeded and respected regardless of the seeming inability of an older man to contribute to a discussion. In America, these elders suffer not only the disabilities of normal aging but often increasing isolation as other members of their family adopt American preferences and behavior. Language is often a problem for them since learning any new language is generally a challenge for older persons. They also know that the quality of deference and respect they showed their own parents means little in American culture and that they may be accorded less in the way of family honors than they would like. As Tran (1988:283) points out, in America there is no patrimonial land to dispense nor ancestral graves to maintain. Without other claims to power and authority, older men lose the moral force their age once assured them.

The position of older women is even more precarious in the American context. They have their authority and standing largely through their husbands, not in their own right. Children, who are often under enormous pressure to do well in school and careers, find that their success requires them to leave home, thereby isolating older parents further. Isolation contributes to depression, apathy, and serious illness. Working with senior Vietnamese can be a difficult and challenging task for the health or social service provider. Lappin and Scott (1982) describe their work with a widowed and struggling Vietnamese woman as very slow and based on small, incremental, and very concrete steps. Among other things, she had to be helped with her command of English so as to reduce her dependence on her children as interpreters. She also needed to find others outside the family to whom she could talk confidentially about her concerns. All her needs—English skills, managing grief and depression, and dealing with isolation from friends—had to be dealt with one issue at a time so that she was not overwhelmed with the sheer weight of all that had to be done. In a community of ethnic compatriots that was small and dispersed to begin with, helping her find and use the resources she needed took enormous patience and persistence by the workers. Matsuoka (1993) suggests that Vietnamese women have more negative attitudes toward acculturation than men, partly because they are more closely tied to female kinship networks focused on domestic life. If that is the case, culturally sensitive family therapy techniques may be useful with these clients.

All Vietnamese adults face problems of adjustment. In addition to language skills, employment is a major concern. Many of those in the first wave of refugees took jobs for which they were overeducated. Doctors worked as janitors, and former military officers drove taxis or fried hamburgers. They did this because their tradition emphasizes hard work and self-sufficiency in whatever job one does. This same work ethic prompted many to open their own small businesses, many of which flourished due to the availability of low-cost family labor and the willingness to take entrepreneurial risks. Rutledge (1992:81) notes that "Vietnamese plazas and mini-malls.... are becoming somewhat commonplace" in Dallas, Houston, Kansas City, and parts of California. He describes how the Vietnamese prefer to work with other Vietnamese and that in some plants and businesses they are the majority of the workforce.

In their drive to succeed economically, Vietnamese parents place great pressure on children to do well in school. The success of Vietnamese students in business schools and technical programs such as computers and electronics is rapidly becoming a new stereotype on some university campuses. But the fit of student expectations and teacher demands is not always a happy one. In their home country, children (and their parents) learned that teachers were authority figures, their knowledge was not to be questioned, and the preferred style of learning was memorization and repetition. The American practice of classroom discussion and critique, with its democratic emphasis on the worth of everyone's opinion and the disconcerting possibility that no one, including the teacher, has a final, authoritative answer to every question, does not fit with traditional experiences. For many Vietnamese university students, the humanities and social sciences are educational mine fields where disaster lurks in every quiz and test. Reporting disappointing grades to parents is more than some students can handle. When this is added to the American emphasis on peer group association and individualism, both competitors for family loyalty and control, the possibilities for conflict at home are great.

Mention also should be made of a special group of young Vietnamese, many now about college age. They are the *haafus*, children and young adults whose parents were Vietnamese and either black or white American. Many of these children were conceived during the Vietnam war, some later in this country. Those with black parentage would have faced insurmountable discrimination and stigmatizing had they remained in Vietnam. They were held back from education in Vietnam because they were a visible reminder of the former American military presence and they were subject to ostracism and discrimination by other Vietnamese. In an excellent historical overview, Valverde (1992) writes that "Amerasians have the dual burden of the Vietnamese refugee experience and the marginal multiracial experience. Therefore, their needs are different than those of 'standard' refugees. Uncomfortable in a new land, still without a voice, they continue to carry these burdens" (1992:157). Williams (1992) describes Amerasians as having "prism lives," their experiences refracted through several cultural lenses. For some, that is a source of pride, but all experience frustrations, within their families, in the Vietnamese community, and in the larger white society.

All of the issues and historical experiences affecting Vietnamese refugees described here create personal stresses, some of which are debilitating. But the vocabulary, even the idea, of "mental health" is not in the inventory of most Vietnamese. Rutledge quotes a Vietnamese physician on the subject:

> *You cannot talk about mental health. I know what you mean, but you will offend people [Vietnamese] if you use those words. In Vietnam, you are crazy if you have mental health [problems]. You can be depressed, or lonely, or afraid. That is okay, but you cannot have a mental health problem. Depression and mental health are not the same to Vietnamese. (1992:103)*

Matsuoka believes Vietnamese refugees "experience a significant degree of fatalism and helplessness" (1991:127) and to cope with that they may need skill building, assertiveness training, opportunities to express feelings of survivor's guilt, and activities that promote self-esteem. Unfortunately, how these things are to be done in culturally meaningful ways has yet to be made explicit in the human services literature. A very small number of dedicated Vietnamese have gone into social services. But their knowledge of their own community, and their suggestions for culturally appropriate intervention, have yet to be systematically collected and made available to the larger professional community. Until that happens, social services for the Vietnamese will remain an area of uncertainty, guided more by good intentions than real ethnographic insight and understanding.

CONCLUSION

The diversity of countries and cultures subsumed under the label "Asian and Pacific Islanders" suggests both the unreality of that phrase and the future it portends. It is "unreal" in that it takes in too much; it identifies almost nothing except a huge geographical expanse. The clinician never confronts an Asian or a Pacific Islander. Clients are specific human beings, bearers of a localized and complex tradition in addition to their individual concerns. These clients, as Asians, are also on the leading edge of a century-long trend creating new interconnections among the countries of the Pacific Rim. That trend is more than commerce in cars, cameras, and foodstuffs. It is a new settlement in the United States, but with people from the East instead of the West. The demographics of their resettlement in America are already in place: in just a decade or two the baby boomers will be moving out of the job market and they have not produced enough children to replace themselves, their labor, or their skills. Asians will do that for them. People from Hong Kong, China, Korea, the Philippines, and India, blue collar workers and highly educated professionals, will occupy many of the economic niches the baby boomers leave behind. They will create the commercial and cultural ties that extend American interests across the Pacific, even to the Indian Ocean. And they *will* be American interests, because these Asian and Pacific Islanders will be the new Americans.

They will not, however, be like the old Americans. We delude ourselves if we believe that melting pots, acculturation, or the more recently celebrated pluralism will resolve fundamental differences in outlook, and that given time, "they" will become more like "us." Asian communities in America are not easily accessed by outsiders; they will not be accessed easily when their numbers are larger and their needs greater. Social and health service professionals must be ready to serve populations that will be more diverse in the future, not less so. That diversity, combined with intergenerational conflicts, elders at risk, children lacking nutrition and adequate schools, youth gangs, unemployment and underemployment, can lead to even more dangerous forms of ethnic and racial warfare than we have now. The productive society these future Americans might create will never be possible unless care providers of all kinds begin working now for the ethnic and cultural transformation that is only a few decades away. That work must include nothing less than the ability to help others live their lives according to their own best traditions.

FOLLOW-UP

1. Considering Cases

Somatization is well known as a feature of psychiatric disturbances in Asians. It is also routine to link Asian patients with clinicians of the same cultural background in the expectation that this will lead to quicker, more accurate diagnoses and better outcomes. As general rules of practice these concepts are useful, but they are no guarantee of better treatment or outcomes. A case reported by Russell F. Lim and Keh-Ming Lin (1996) makes this clear and demonstrates how complex the interaction of differing cultural traditions in mental health services can be.

In their case, "Mr. A," a 57-year-old Chinese American engineer, was born in China and at age 18 migrated with his family to Taiwan. Later, he completed his education with a Ph.D. from an American university and, while in this country, met his wife. He has a successful marriage of thirty years and two adult children and is functionally bicultural, speaking two dialects of Chinese as well as English. With no prior psychiatric history and in otherwise good health, he went to a physician complaining of auditory hallucinations, delusions, and acute backaches. With the onset of these symptoms, he was unable to continue working. He was diagnosed with kidney stones, for which the usual treatments did not work, and so he went to a practitioner of *Qi-gong*, a traditional folk medicine. But his delusional experiences intensified so his wife, a nurse, referred him to a Chinese American psychiatrist.

After extensive medical evaluation, he was diagnosed under the *DSM-IV* system with a schizophreniform disorder with good possibilities of recovery and given medications that reduced his hallucinations and made hospitalization unnecessary. Both he and his wife fully accepted the Western biomedical model but pursued a bicultural help-seeking path because the initial diagnosis failed to consider the backaches as potential signifiers of life stresses.

> *Many Chinese patients are reluctant to express distress in other than somatic terms since psychological difficulties may be experienced as potentially stigmatizing.... Somatization may in fact be facultative, allowing the patient access to the health care system, and seen only in the initial evaluation or in other selected settings, such as a physician's office. Provided the somatic nature of the ailment is accepted by the clinician, the person may feel free to explain his/her life difficulties without fear of being stigmatized as a mental patient.*

Just as the original physician failed to appreciate the somatizing import of the backaches, the Chinese American psychiatrist preferred the biomedical model and did not inquire systematically into the patient's experiences with *Qi-gong*. Had he done so, he would have known that Mr. A presented an idiom of distress commonly recognized in the Chinese community that it is indicative of a psychosis in the *Qi-gong* as well as Western systems, but that within the *Qi-gong* system Mr. A's experiences were not as bizarre as the psychiatrist seemed to think they were. In effect, Mr. A was perceived as "more sick" in the Western system than in the Chinese. In addition, the interaction between Mr. A and his psychiatrist was never comfortable nor did the doctor ever ask Mr. A how he integrated the two medical models to account for what was happening to him. While psychological tests could have been given, they too would have been misleading because they are based on Western models and administered in a Western language. Mr. A spoke fluent English but, in explaining his symptoms, sometimes used Chinese, in which he could state more accurately what he was experiencing.

- If Mr. A's first doctor, the Chinese American psychiatrist, came to you saying he wanted to know how he could have worked with Mr. A more effectively, what would you want to tell him? How would you advise him to proceed with future patients like Mr. A?
- If you were to go to the practitioner of *Qi-gong* seen by Mr. A, what would you want to know about that system of healing? List your global questions for interviewing the practitioner and explain why each one might be appropriate in cases like that of Mr. A.

Mr. A's case is more complex than I have described here. To get a full sense of it, and to appreciate better how patients can integrate quite different systems of explanation, you can consult the original article in *Culture, Medicine and Psychiatry* (20:369–378, 1996), where Lim and Lin present a detailed analysis.

2. Test Drive an Idea

One of the criticisms commonly made of the way cases are presented in the social service literature is that they are too brief, lack ethnographic detail, and only hint at the cultural variables implicit in symptoms and help seeking. Consequently, individual clients and patients are artificially presented in technical works as "examples" of selected clinical issues. In postmodernist terms, in their transcription to the academic page those who are in pain lose their voice and are subsumed by that of the author.

The help-seeking behavior model is one way of breaking through academic conventions that limit how we perceive the experiences of others. In fact, the more "other" someone is from us—whatever our beginning point might be—the more valuable the model becomes as a way of seeing how cultural traditions provide all kinds of resources and support for people in distress. Writing on help seeking among Asian and Pacific Americans in *Social Work* (1997), Yamashiro and Matsuoka describe an expanded version of the model, one that in its comprehensiveness could become the standard for future work on the topic. Areas they see as critical for good, ethnographic description of help seeking include the following:

- Human ecology, the major socioeconomic spheres in which everyday life is carried on
- Interpersonal ecology, the dynamics of family, friendships, and work life
- Worldview, relationships to others and to the natural world, and the language and symbols that signify what these relationships ought to be
- Sociohistory and cohort experiences, the events that influence people's lives and the beliefs and ideologies that come from them
- Acculturation, its relationship to service utilization, and the varieties of acculturation that can exist in a single, seemingly homogeneous community
- Social Learning, integration of what one has experienced over a life trajectory, and how that leads one to choices and actions when coping with illness and distress

Choose any article related to Asians from the social services literature, preferably one that includes at least one case, however briefly presented. (Some of those listed below would be useful.) Look at the article as a whole, and the writing up of the case in particular, and determine how much material for each of the six aspects of Yamashiro and Matsuoka's comprehensive help-seeking model is supplied. Where the case is weakly presented on any one of the six points named, list what additional information you would want to know if you could talk with the person in the case yourself. If this is done as a class project, list the areas of the model that seem to get the most attention in the cases examined, and those that are relatively ignored. Explain why you think this happens, and what in the ideology and practices of the service professions accounts for how the voices of others are reported.

In fairness, the authors of the cases you find in books and journals are not usually writing to meet your or my expectations about help-seeking issues. They have expectations of their own, as do their editors, and that is legitimate. What is at issue here is how the ethnographic context of pathology is usually slighted in social and health services accounts; how authors' theoretical agendas and styles of representation sometimes deform (if that is not too strong a word) the lived reality of those who are offered to us as "cases"; and how we might improve our investigations and reporting so that we become better advocates for them. With that in mind, you should consider how the case you are examining could be strengthened. Specifically, and using the six points of the model, how would you present the case to readers differently so that more of the client's voice is heard?

3. More on the Issues

- Counseling Chinese Clients

Guidelines to counseling Chinese clients and families are offered in Oye-Nam Christine Wong and Niva Piran, "Western Biases and Assumptions as Impediments in Counseling Traditional Chinese Clients," *Canadian Journal of Counselling* (29:107–119, 1995). A related article in the same issue, on depression, is that of Dan Zhang, "Depression and Culture—A Chinese Perspective" (29:227–233, 1995).

- Japanese American Family Roles

Clinical aspects of work with Japanese Americans are discussed in June W. J. Ching et al., "Perceptions of Family Values and Roles among Japanese Americans: Clinical Considerations," *American Journal of Orthopsychiatry* (65:216–224, 1995).

- Working with Filipino Families

Family practice guidelines for working with Filipino Americans are discussed in a well-documented article by Pauline Agbayani-Siewert, "Filipino American Culture and Family: Guidelines for Practitioners," *Families in Society* (75:429–438, 1994). The article includes an extensive bibliography, an especially useful addition since the literature on Filipino Americans is scattered and not as great as that of other Asians.

- Korean Immigrants

Koreans are receiving more attention in the recent social services literature. Practical aspects of resettlement are discussed by Kyung-Hee Nah, "Perceived Problems and Service Delivery for Korean Immigrants," *Social Work* (38:289–296, 1993). Contrasting immigrant experiences are described in Diane Drachman, Young Hee Kwon-Ahn, and Ana Paulino, "Migration and Resettlement Experiences of Dominican and Korean Families," *Families in Society* (77:626–638, 1996).

Koreans in the United States have high church attendance, participating in Korean branches of various Christian denominations, and their churches are often the focal institutions of their community. Consequently, Korean pastors are "gateway" individuals for their constituents. The implications of this for social services are considered in Mikyong Kim-Goh, "Conceptualization of Mental Illness among Korean-American Clergymen and Implications for Mental Health Service Delivery," *Community Mental Health Journal* (29:405–412, 1993).

- Immigrant Communities

A special issue of the *Journal of Multicultural Social Work* (2:1, 1992) is devoted to "Social Work with Immigrants and Refugees." The articles present cases and discuss practice applications. Southeast Asians are well represented as are topical issues including planning and service delivery. Also see Phyllis Hulewat, "Resettlement: A Cultural and Psychological Crisis," *Social Work* (41:129–137, 1996).

Many recent immigrants retain folk models of illness and healing, models unfamiliar to Western practitioners. For an example, with ways of working with such groups, see Barbara A. Frye and Carolyn D'Avanzo, "Themes in Managing Culturally Defined Illness in the Cambodian Refugee Family," *Journal of Community Health Nursing* (11:89–98, 1994).

- The Legacy of Elders

Documenting oral histories is one way of working with elders and, in immigrant populations, it can be a particularly effective one. The importance of the technique, and how it is used, is discussed in Noreen Mokuau and Collette Browne, "Life Themes of Native Hawaiian Female Elders: Resources for Cultural Preservation," *Social Work* (39:43–49, 1994).

- Asian Medicine in the West

When cultural traditions meet, they mix, and Asian medicine is a good example with growing numbers of non-Asians making use of it. At the local level, new explanatory models of health and self-care are appearing. See Martha L. Hare, "The Emergence of an Urban U.S. Chinese Medicine," *Medical Anthropology Quarterly* (7:30–49, 1993).

- Personal Points of View

Reading individual points of view, rather than academic articles, can give the kinds of issues discussed in books like this a more human dimension. Literature is always a valuable supplement (and sometimes a corrective) to social science writing. You might enjoy the essays compiled by Japanese American poet Garrett Hongo, *Under Western Eyes: Personal Essays from Asian America* (1995).

BIBLIOGRAPHY

Aberle, David F.
   1951   "The Psychological Analysis of a Hopi Life-History." *Comparative Psychology Monographs* 21:80–138.

Acosta-Belen, Edna, and Barbara R. Sjostrom, eds.
   1988   *The Hispanic Experience in the United States.* New York: Praeger.

Agbayani-Siewert, Pauline
   1994   "Filipino American Culture and Family: Guidelines for Practitioners." *Families in Society* 75:429–438.

Aitchison, Jean
   1987   *Words in the Mind.* Oxford: Basil Blackwell.

Akutsu, Phillip D., Lonnie R. Snowden, and Kurt C. Organista
   1996   "Referral Patterns in Ethnic-Specific and Mainstream Programs for Ethnic Minorities and Whites." *Journal of Counseling Psychology* 43:56–64.

Alasuutari, Pertti
   1992   *Desire and Craving: A Cultural Theory of Alcoholism.* Albany: State University of New York Press.

Alba, Richard D.
   1990   *Ethnic Identity: The Transformation of White America.* New Haven, CT: Yale University Press.

Alba, Richard D., and Mitchell B. Chamlin
   1983   "A Preliminary Examination of Ethnic Identification among Whites." *American Sociological Review* 48:240–247.

Albert, Steven M.
   1990   "Caregiving as a Cultural System." *American Anthropologist* 92:319–331.

Allison, Maria T., and Charles W. Geiger
    1993   "The Nature of Leisure Activities among the Chinese-American Elderly." *Leisure Sciences* 15:309–319.

Amaro, Hortensio, and Nancy Felipe Russo
    1987   "Hispanic Women and Mental Health, an Overview of Contemporary Issues in Research and Practice." *Psychology of Women Quarterly* 11:393–407.

Amaro, Hortensio, Nancy Felipe Russo, and Jose A. Pares-Avila
    1987   "Contemporary Research on Hispanic Women: A Selected Bibliography of the Social Science Literature." *Psychology of Women Quarterly* 11:523–532.

American Psychiatric Association
    1994   *Diagnostic and Statistical Manual of Mental Disorders, DSM-IV.* Washington, DC: American Psychiatric Association.

Amodeo, Maryann, and L. Kay Jones
    1997   "Viewing Alcohol and Other Drug Use Cross-Culturally: A Cultural Framework for Clinical Practice." *Families in Society* 78:241–254.

Applewhite, Steven Lozano
    1995   "Curanderismo: Demystifying the Health Beliefs and Practices of Elderly Mexican Americans." *Health and Social Work* 20:247–253.

Asamoah, Yvonne, Alejandro Garcia, Carmen Ortiz Hendricks, and Joe Walker
    1991   "What We Call Ourselves: Implications for Resources, Policy, and Practice." *Journal of Multicultural Social Work* 1:7–23.

Atkin, Karl, and Janet Rollings
    1992   "Informed Care in Asian and Afro/Caribbean Communities: A Literature Review." *British Journal of Social Work* 22:405–418.

Atkinson, Donald R.
    1983   "Ethnic Similarity in Counseling Psychology: A Review of the Research." *Counseling Psychologist* 11:79–92.

Attneave, Carolyn
    1982   American Indian and Alaska Native Families: Emigrants in Their Own Homeland. In Monica Mc Goldrick, John K. Pearce, and Joseph Giordano, eds. *Ethnicity and Family Therapy.* New York: The Guilford Press.

Aviera, Aaron
    1996   "'Dichos' Therapy Group: A Therapeutic Use of Spanish Language Proverbs with Hospitalized Spanish-Speaking Psychiatric Clients." *Cultural Diversity and Mental Health* 2:73–87.

Axinn, June, and Herman Levin
    1997   *Social Welfare, a History of the American Response to Need.* New York: Longman.

Baer, Hans A.
  1981   "Black Spiritual Churches: A Neglected Socio-Religious Institution." *Phylon* 42:207–223.

Baer, Hans A., and Merrill Singer
  1981   Toward a Typology of Black Sectarianism as a Response to Racial Stratification. *Anthropological Quarterly* 54:1–14.

Baer, Robert D., and Marta Bustillo
  1993   "*Susto* and *Mal de Ojo* among Florida Farmworkers: Emic and Etic Perspectives." *Medical Anthropology Quarterly* 7:90–100.

Banner-Haley, Charles T.
  1994   *The Fruits of Integration, Black Middle-Class Ideology and Culture, 1960–1990.* Jackson: University of Mississippi Press.

Barker, Philip
  1990   *Clinical Interviews With Children and Adolescents.* New York: W.W. Norton.

Barnow, Victor
  1963   *Culture and Personality.* Homewood, IL: Dorsey Press.

Bataille, Gretchen M., and Charles L. P. Silet
  1980   *The Pretend Indians: Images of Native Americans in the Movies.* Ames, IA: Iowa State University Press.

Bausch, Robert S., and Richard T. Serpe
  1997   "Negative Outcomes of Interethnic Adoption of Mexican American Children." *Social Work* 42:136–143.

Beauvais, Fred, and Steve LaBoueff
  1985   Drug and Alcohol Abuse Intervention in American Indian Communities. *International Journal of Addictions* 2:139–171.

Becker, Howard S., and James W. Carper
  1956   "The Development of Identification with an Occupation," *American Journal of Sociology* 61:289–298.

Bee-Gates, Donna, Beth Howard-Pitney, and Teresa LaFramboise
  1996   "Help-Seeking Behavior of Native American Indian Highschool Students." *Professional Psychology: Research and Practice* 27:495–499.

Bellah, Robert N., Richard Madsen, William M. Sullivan, Ann Swindler, and Steven M. Tipton
  1985   *Habits of the Heart.* Berkeley: University of California Press.

Benedek, Emily
  1993   *The Wind Won't Know Me: A History of the Navajo-Hopi Land Dispute.* New York: Vintage Books.

Benjamin, Alfred
1981   *The Helping Interview.* Boston: Houghton Mifflin.

Bennett, John W., ed.
1975   *The New Ethnicity: Perspectives from Ethnology.* St. Paul: West Publishing Co.

Billingsley, Andrew
1969   "Family Functioning in the Low Income Black Community." *Social Casework* 50:536–572.
1968   *Black Families in White America.* Englewood Cliffs, NJ: Prentice Hall.

Blanchard, Evelyn
1983   "The Growth and Development of American Indian and Alaska Native Children." In Gloria Johnson Powell, ed. *The Psychosocial Development of Minority Group Children.* New York: Brunner/Mazel.

Blanchard, Evelyn, and Steven Unger
1977   "Destruction of American Indian Families." *Social Casework* 58:312–314.

Bloch, Julia B.
1968   "The White Worker and the Negro Client in Psychotherapy." *Social Work* 13:36–42.

Blount, Mary
1996   "Social Work Practice with Native Americans." In Dianne Harrison, et al. *Cultural Diversity and Social Work Practice.* Springfield, IL: Charles C. Thomas.

Boekestijn, C.
1984   "Intercultural Migration and the Development of Personal Identity." Presented at the Seventh International Congress of Cross-Cultural Psychology, Acapulco, Mexico.

Bogdan, Robert
1972   *Participant Observation in Organizational Settings.* Syracuse, NY: Syracuse University Press.

Boyd-Franklin, Nancy, Tawn Smith Morris, and Brenna H. Bry
1997   "Parent and Family Support Groups with African American Families: The Process of Family and Community Empowerment." *Cultural Diversity and Mental Health* 3:83–92.

Brice, Janet
1982   "West Indian Families." In Monica McGoldrick, John K. Pearce, and Joseph Giordano, eds. *Ethnicity and Family Therapy.* New York: The Guilford Press.

Briggs, Jean
1986   "Kapluna Daughter." In Peggy Golde, ed. *Women in the Field: Anthropological Experiences.* Berkeley: University of California Press.

Brissett-Chapman, Sheryl
1997   "Child Protection Risk Assessment and African American Children: Cultural Ramifications for Families and Communities." *Child Welfare* 76:45–64.

Brookhiser, Richard
1991 *The Way of the Wasp.* New York: The Free Press.

Brown, Phil
1993 "Psychiatric Intake as a Mystery Story." *Culture, Medicine and Psychiatry* 17:255–280.

Buchwald, Dedra, Panagista V. Caralis, Francesca Gany, Eric J. Hardt, Marjorie A. Muecke, and Robert W. Putsch
1993 "The Medical Interview Across Cultures." *Patient Care* 27:141–144.

Bullis, Ronald K.
1996 *Spirituality in Social Work Practice.* Washington, DC: Taylor and Francis.

Bullock, Henry
1967 *A History of Negro Education in the South from 1619 to the Present.* Cambridge: Harvard University Press.

Bunkley, Crawford B.
1996 *The African American Network.* New York: Penguin Books.

Burciaga, José Antonio
1993 *Drink Cultura: Chicanismo.* Santa Barbara, CA: Capra Press.

Buriel, Raymond
1984 "Integration with Traditional Mexican-American Culture and Sociocultural Adjustment." In Joe L. Martinez, Jr., and Richard H. Mendoza, eds. *Chicano Psychology.* Orlando, FL: Academic Press.

Burnette, Denise
1997 "Grandmother Caregivers in Inner-City Latino Families: A Descriptive Profile and Informal Social Supports." *Journal of Multicultural Social Work* 5:121–138.

Candib, Lucy M.
1994 "Reconsidering Power in the Clinical Relationship." In Ellen Singer More and Maureen A. Milligan, eds. *The Empathic Practitioner, Empathy, Gender, and Medicine.* New Brunswick, NJ: Rutgers University Press.

Canino, Glorisa J., Maritza Rubio-Stipec, Patrick Shrout, Milagros Bravo, Robert Stolberg, and Hector R. Bird
1987 "Sex Differences and Depression in Puerto Rico." *Psychology of Women Quarterly* 11:443–459.

Caplan, Nathan, Marcella H. Choy, and John K. Whitmore
1992 "Indochinese Refugee Families and Academic Achievement." *Scientific American* February:36–42.

Carroll, John B., ed.
1956 *Language, Thought, and Reality: Selected Writings of Benjamin Lee Whorf.* Cambridge: MIT Press.

Cervantes, Richard C., and William Arroyo
1994   "*DSM-IV*: Implications for Hispanic Children and Adolescents." *Hispanic Journal of Behavioral Sciences* 16:8–27.

Chan, Sucheng
1991   *Asian Americans: An Interpretive History.* Boston: Twayne Publishers.

Chavez, John M., and Collette E. Roney
1990   "Psychocultural Factors Affecting the Mental Health Status of Mexican American Adolescents." In Arlene Rubin Stiffman, and Larry E. Davis, eds. *Ethnic Issues in Adolescent Mental Health.* Newbury Park, CA: Sage.

Cheung, Monit
1989   "Elderly Chinese Living in the United States: Assimilation or Adjustment?" *Social Work* 34:457–461.

Chin, Jean Lau
1983   "Diagnostic Considerations in Working With Asian-Americans." *American Journal of Orthopsychiatry* 53:100–109.

Ching, June W. J., John F. McDermott, Jr., Chantis Fukunaga, Evelyn Yanagida, Eberhard Mann, and Jean A. Waldron
1995   "Perceptions of Family Values and Roles among Japanese Americans: Clincial Considerations." *American Journal of Orthopsychiatry* 65:216–224.

Christian, Charles M., Mary Dufour, and Darryl Bertolucci
1989   "Differential Alcohol-Related Mortality Among American Indian Tribes in Oklahoma, 1968–1978." *Social Science and Medicine* 28:274–285.

Christodoulou, Costas
1991   "Racism—a Challenge to Social Work Education and Practice: The British Experience." *Journal of Multicultural Social Work* 1:99–107.

Chung, Douglas K.
1992   "Asian Cultural Commonalities: A Comparison with Mainstream American Culture." In Sharlene Maeda Furuto, Renoka Biswas, Douglas K. Chung, Kenji Murase, and Fariyal Ross-Sheriff, eds. *Social Work Practice with Asian Americans.* Newbury Park, CA: Sage.

Clark, Margaret
1959   *Health in the Mexican–American Culture: A Community Study.* Berkeley: University of California Press.

Clarke, Edith
1957   *My Mother Who Fathered Me.* London: George Allen and Unwin.

Cloward, Richard, and Frances Fox Piven
1975   "Notes Toward a Radical Social Work." In Roy Bailey, and Mike Brake, eds. *Radical Social Work.* New York: Random House.

Cochrane, Glynn
    1979   *The Cultural Appraisal of Development Projects.* New York: Praeger.

Cogan, Morris L.
    1953   "Toward a Definition of Profession." *Harvard Educational Review* 23: 33–50.

Comas-Diaz, Lillian
    1987   "Feminist Therapy with Mainland Puerto Rican Women." *Psychology of Women Quarterly* 11:461–474.

Comas-Diaz, Lillian, and Amado M. Padilla
    1992   "The English-Only Movement: Implications for Mental Health Services." *American Journal of Orthopsychiatry* 62:1–6.

Cordova, Fred
    1983   *Filipinos: Forgotten Asian Americans.* Dubuque: Kendall/Hunt.

Cornell, Stephen
    1984   "Crisis and Response in Indian-White Relations: 1960–1984." *Social Problems* 32:44–59.

Cowger, Charles D.
    1977   "Alternative Stances in the Relationship of Social Work to Society." *Journal of Education for Social Work* 13:25–29.

Crawford, James
    1992   *Language Loyalties: A Sourcebook on the Official English Controversy.* Chicago: University of Chicago Press.
    1989   *Bilingual Education: History, Political Theory, and Practice.* Trenton, NJ: Crane.

Csikszentmihalyi, Mihalyi
    1982   "Leisure and Socialization." *Social Forces* 60:332–340.
    1975   *Beyond Boredom and Anxiety.* San Francisco: Jossey-Bass.

Csikszentmihalyi, Mihalyi, and Selega Csikszentmihalyi
    1988   *Optimal Experience: Psychological Studies of Flow Consciousness.* Cambridge: Cambridge University Press.

Csordas, Thomas J., and Arthur Kleinman
    1990   "The Therapeutic Process." In Thomas M. Johnson and Carolyn F. Sargent, eds. *Medical Anthropology, Contemporary Theory and Method.* New York: Praeger.

Curry, Andrew E.
    1964   "The Negro Worker and the White Client: A Commentary on the Treatment Relationship." *Social Casework* 45:131–136.

Daly, Kerry
    1992   "The Fit Between Qualitative Research and Characteristics of Families." In Jane F. Gilgun, Kerry Daly, and Gerald Handel, eds. *Qualitative Methods in Family Research.* Newbury Park, CA: Sage.

Dana, Richard H.
  1993   *Multicultural Assessment for Professional Psychology.* Boston: Allyn and Bacon.

Dana, Richard H., ed.
  1981   *Human Services for Cultural Minorities.* Baltimore: University Park Press.

Daniel, G. Reginald
  1992   "Beyond Black and White: The New Multiracial Consciousness." In Maria P. P. Root, ed. *Racially Mixed People in America.* Newbury Park, CA: Sage.

Davidson, Ann Locke
  1994   "Student's Situated Selves: Ethnographic Interviewing as Cultural Therapy." In George Spindler, and Louise Spindler. *Pathways to Cultural Awareness: Cultural Awareness with Teachers and Students.* Thousand Oaks, CA: Corwin Press.

Davis, Cary, Carl Haub, and JoAnne L. Willette
  1988   "U.S. Hispanics: Changing the Face of America." In Edna Acosta-Belen, and Barbara R. Sjostrom, eds. *The Spanish Experience in the United States.* New York: Praeger.

Davis, Dona Lee, and Setha M. Low, eds.
  1989   *Gender, Health, and Illness: The Case of Nerves.* New York: Hemisphere Publications.

Davis, Larry E.
  1984a   "Essential Components of Group Work with Black Americans." *Social Work with Groups* 7:97–107.
  1984b   *Ethnicity in Social Work Practice.* New York: Haworth Press.

Davis, Ossie
  1969   "The Language of Racism: The English Language Is My Enemy." In Neil Postman, Charles Weingartner, and Terence P. Moran, eds. *Language in America.* New York: Pegasus.

Day, Mary W.
  1987   "Harlem Youth Opportunities Unlimited." In Gladys Walton Holly, Grace C. Clark, Michael A. Creedon, eds. *Advocacy in America: Case Studies in Social Change.* Lanham, MD: University Press of America.

Deal, Terrence E., and Allen A. Kennedy
  1982   *Corporate Cultures: The Rites and Rituals of Corporate Life.* Reading, MA: Addison-Wesley.

Dedmon, Rachel, and William Saur, eds.
  1983   *Rural Mental Health in North Carolina: Social Work Practice and Ethnocultural Issues.* Chapel Hill, NC: University of North Carolina, School of Social Work.

De La Cancela, Victor
  1986   "A Critical Analysis of Puerto Rican Machismo: Implications for Clinical Practice." *Psychotherapy* 23:291–296.

Delaney, Anita J.
   1979   *Black Task Force Report: Project on Ethnicity.* New York: Family Service Association of America.

Delgado-Gaitan, Concha
   1994   "Consejos: The Power of Cultural Narratives." *Anthropology and Education Quarterly* 25:298–316.

Deloria, Vine
   1973   *God is Red.* New York: Grosset and Dunlap.

Desjarlais, Robert
   1994   "Struggling Along: The Possibilities for Experience among the Homeless Mentally Ill." *American Anthropologist* 96:886–901.

DeVerthelyi, Renata Frank
   1996   "Intercountry Adoption of Latin American Children: The Importance of Early Bilingual/Bicultural Services." *Cultural Diversity and Mental Health* 2:53–63.

Devore, Wynetta
   1983   "Ethnic Reality: The Life Model and Work with Black Families." *Social Casework* 64:525–531.

Devore, Wynetta, and Elfriede G. Schlesinger
   1996   *Ethnic-Sensitive Social Work Practice.* Boston: Allyn and Bacon.

Dhooper, Surjit Singh
   1991   "Toward an Effective Response to the Needs of Asian-Americans." *Journal of Multicultural Social Work* 1:65–81.

Douglas, Mary
   1968   "Pollution." *Encyclopedia of the Social Sciences* 12:336–341.
   1966   *Purity and Danger.* London: Routledge and Kegan Paul.

Dow, James
   1986   "Universal Aspects of Symbolic Healing: A Theoretical Synthesis." *American Anthropologist* 88:56–69.

Drachman, Diane, Young Hee Kwon-Ahn, and Ana Paulino
   1996   "Migration and Resettlement Experiences of Dominican and Korean Families." *Families in Society* 77:626–638.

Dressler, William W.
   1985   "Extended Family Relationships, Social Support, and Mental Health in a Southern Black Community." *Journal of Health and Social Behavior* 26:39–48.

Dressler, William W., Susan Hoeppner, and Barbara Pitts.
   1985   "Household Structure in a Southern Black Community." *American Anthropologist* 87:853–862.

Driver, Harold E.
    1969   *Indians of North America.* Chicago: University of Chicago Press.

Dufort, Molly E.
    1992   "Disability Management in Cross-Cultural Contexts." *Practicing Anthropology* 14:14–16.

Dugan, Margaret A.
    1996   "Participation and Empowerment Evaluation." In David Fetterman et al., *Empowerment Evaluation.* Thousand Oaks, CA: Sage.

Dungee-Anderson, Dolores, and Joyce O. Beckett
    1995   "A Process Model for Multicultural Social Work Practice." *Families in Society* 78:459–468.

Eastman, Carol M.
    1984   "Language, Ethnic Identity and Change." In John Edwards, ed. *Linguistic Minorities, Policies and Pluralism.* London: Academic Press.

Eastmond, Marita
    1993   "Reconstructing Life: Chilean Refugee Women and the Dilemmas of Exile." In Gina Buijs, ed. *Migrant Women: Crossing Boundaries and Changing Identities.* Oxford: Berg.

Edwards, E. Daniel, and Margie Egbert-Edwards
    1990   "American Indian Adolescents: Combating Problems of Substance Use and Abuse Through a Community Model." In Arlene Rubin Stiffman and Larry E. Davis, eds. *Ethic Issues in Adolescent Mental Health.* Newbury Park, CA: Sage.
    1984   "Group Work Practice with American Indians." *Social Work with Groups* 7:7–22.

Edwards, John, ed.
    1988   *Linguistic Minorities, Policies and Pluralism.* London: Academic Press.
    1985   *Language, Society and Identity.* Oxford: Basil Blackwell.

Efired, Cathy M.
    1988   "Enhancing the Use of Mental Health Services." In Susan E. Keefe, ed. *Appalachian Mental Health.* Lexington: University Press of Kentucky.

Egan, Gerard
    1986   *The Skilled Helper: A Systematic Approach to Effective Helping.* Pacific Grove, CA: Brooks/Cole.

Eisner, Elliot W.
    1991   *The Enlightened Eye.* New York: Macmillan.

Epstein, Laura
    1985   *Talking and Listening: A Guide to the Helping Interview.* St. Louis: Times Mirror/Mosby.

Espin, Oliva M.
  1987   "Psychological Impact of Migration on Latinas." *Psychology of Women Quarterly* 11:489–503.

Espiritu, Yen Le
  1992   *Asian American Panethnicity: Bridging Institutions and Identities.* Philadelphia: Temple University Press.

Estroff, Sue E.
  1981   *Making It Crazy.* Berkeley: University of California Press.

Evans, A. Donald
  1991   "Maintaining Relationships in a School for the Deaf." In William B. Shaffir, and Robert A. Stebbins. *Experiencing Fieldwork.* Newbury Park, CA: Sage.
  1988   "Strange Bedfellows: Language, Deafness, and Knowledge." *Symbolic Interaction* 11:235–255.

Fabrega, Horacio, Jr.
  1990   "Hispanic Mental Health Research: A Case for Cultural Psychiatry." *Hispanic Journal of Behavioral Sciences* 12:339–365.

Ferguson, Frances N.
  1976   "Stake Theory as an Explanatory Device in Navajo Alcoholism Treatment Response." *Human Organization* 35:65–78.

Fernandez, Carlos A.
  1992   "La Raza and the Melting Pot: A Comparative Look at Multiethnicity." In Maria P. P. Root, ed. *Racially Mixed People in America.* Newbury Park, CA: Sage.

Fetterman, David M., Shakeh J. Kaftarian, and Abraham Wandersman, eds.
  1996   *Empowerment Evaluation.* Thousand Oaks, CA: Sage.

Fibush, Esther
  1965   "The White Worker and the Negro Client." *Social Casework* 46:271–277.

Fibush, Esther, and Bealva Turnquest
  1970   "A Black and White Approach to the Problem of Racism." *Social Casework* 51:459–466.

Fine, Mark, Andrew I. Schwebel, and Linda James-Myers
  1987   "Family Stability in Black Families: Values Underlying Three Perspectives." *Journal of Comparative Family Studies* 18:1–23.

Finkler, Kaja
  1985   *Spiritualist Healers in Mexico.* South Hadley, MA: Bergin and Garvey.

Fleming, Candace M.
  1996   "Case No. 01, An American Indian Woman Suffering from Depression, Alcoholism and Childhood Trauma." *Culture, Medicine and Psychiatry* 20:145–154.

Foner, Nancy
1994   *The Caregiving Dilemma, Work in an American Nursing Home.* Berkeley: University of California Press.

Foner, Philip S., and Daniel Rosenberg
1993   *Racism, Dissent and Asian Americans from 1850 to the Present.* Westport, CT: Greenwood Press.

Fong, Lillian G. W., and Jewelle Taylor Gibbs
1995   "Facilitative Services to Multicultural Communities in a Dominant Cultural Setting: An Organization Perspective." *Administration in Social Work* 19:1–24.

Fook, Jan, Martin Ryan, and Linette Hawkins
1997   "Towards a Theory of Social Work Expertise." *British Journal of Social Work* 27:399–417.

Foster, George M.
1965   "Peasant Society and the Image of Limited Good." *American Anthropologist* 67:293–315.

Foster, George M., and Barbara Gallatin Anderson
1978   *Medical Anthropology.* New York: John Wiley and Sons.

Foster, Madison, and Lorraine R. Perry
1982   "Self-Valuation among Blacks." *Social Work* 27:60–66.

Franklin, Cynthia, and Catheleen Jordan
1995   "Qualitative Assessment: A Methodological Overview." *Families in Society* 76: 281–295.

Franklin, Donna L.
1985   "Differential Clinical Assessments: The Influence of Class and Race." *Social Service Review* 59:44–61.

Fraser, Steven, ed.
1995   *The Bell Curve Wars: Race, Intelligence and the Future of America.* New York: Basic Books.

Frye, Barbara A., and Carolyn D'Avanzo
1994   "Themes in Managing Culturally Defined Illness in the Cambodian Refugee Family." *Journal of Community Health Nursing* 11:89–98.

Fugita, Stephen, Karen L. Ito, Jennifer Abe, and David T. Takeuchi
1991   "Japanese Americans." In Noreen Mokuau, ed. *Handbook of Social Services for Asian and Pacific Islanders.* New York: Greenwood Press.

Furnham, Adrian, and Stephen Bochner
1989   *Culture Shock: Psychological Reactions to Unfamiliar Environments.* London: Routledge.

Furuto, Sharlene Maeda
  1991   "Family Violence among Pacific Islanders." In Noreen Mokuau, ed. *Handbook of Social Services for Asian and Pacific Islanders.* New York: Greenwood Press.

Galanti, Geri-Ann
  1991   *Caring for Patients from Different Cultures: Case Studies from American Hospitals.* Philadelphia: University of Pennsylvania Press.

Gallegos, Joseph S.
  1984   "The Ethnic Competence Model for Social Work Education." In Barbara W. White, ed. *Color in a White Society.* Silver Spring, MD: National Association of Social Workers.

García-Castañon, Juan
  1994   "Training among Refugee Students: Chicano Anthropologist as Cultural Therapist." In George Spindler, and Louise Spindler. *Pathways to Cultural Awareness: Cultural Awareness with Teachers and Students.* Thousand Oaks, CA: Corwin Press.

Gates, Bee D., Howard B. Pitney, Teresa LaFromboise, and Wayne Rose
  1996   "Help-Seeking Behavior of Native American Indian High School Students." *Professional Psychology—Research and Practice* 27:495–499.

Geertz, Clifford
  1983   *Local Knowledge.* New York: Basic Books.
  1975   "On the Nature of Anthropological Understanding." *American Scientist* 63:47–53.

Ghali, Sonia Badillo
  1977   "Cultural Sensitivity and the Puerto Rican Client." *Social Casework* 58:459–468.

Gibbs, Jewelle Taylor
  1981   "The Interpersonal Orientation in Mental Health Consultation: Toward a Model of Ethnic Variations in Consultation." In Richard H. Dana, ed. *Human Services for Cultural Minorities.* Baltimore: University Park Press.
  1988   *Young, Black and Male in America: An Endangered Species.* Dover, MA: Auburn House.

Gibbs, Jewelle Taylor, and Larke Nahme Huang
  1989   *Children of Color: Psychological Interventions with Minority Youth.* San Francisco: Jossey-Bass.

Gibson, Cynthia M.
  1993   "Empowerment Theory and Practice with Adolescents of Color in the Child Welfare System." *Families in Society* 74: 387–396.

Gibson, Margaret, and Steven F. Arvizu
  1977   *Demystifying the Concept of Culture: Methodological Tools.* Sacramento: Sacramento State University.

Gilgun, Jane F.
  1994   "A Case for Case Studies in Social Work Research." *Social Work* 39:371–380.

Gilgun, Jane F., Kerry Daly, and Gerald Handel, eds.
    1992   *Qualitative Methods in Family Research*. Newbury Park, CA: Sage.

Gilligan, Carol
    1982   *In a Different Voice*. Cambridge: Harvard University Press.

Gilligan, Carol, and Mary F. Belenky
    1980   "A Naturalistic Study of Abortion Decisions." In Robert L. Selman, and Regina Yande, eds. *Clinical-Developmental Psychology*. San Francisco: Jossey-Bass.

Gilligan, Carol, and John Murphy
    1979   "Development from Adolescence to Adulthood: The Philosopher and the 'Dilemma of the Fact.'" In Deanna Kuhn, ed. *Intellectual Development beyond Childhood*. San Francisco: Jossey-Bass.

Giménez, Marta E., Fred A. López, and Carlos Muñoz, Jr.
    1992   "The Politics of Ethnic Construction: Hispanic, Chicano, Latino?" *Latin American Perspectives* 19:1–106.

Ginsburg, Faye D.
    1989   *Contested Lives, the Abortion Debate in an American Community*. Berkeley: University of California Press.

Glasser, Irene
    1994   *Homelessness in Global Perspective*. New York: Maxwell Macmillan.
    1988   *More Than Bread: An Ethnography of a Soup Kitchen*. Tuscaloosa: University of Alabama Press.
    1983   "Guidelines for Using an Interpreter in Social Work." *Child Welfare* 57:468–470.

Glazer, Nathan, and Daniel Patrick Moynihan
    1963   *Beyond the Melting Pot*. Cambridge: MIT Press.

Gleave, Danica, and Arturo S. Manes
    1990   "The Central Americans." In Nancy Waxler-Morrison, Joan Anderson, and Elizabeth Richardson, eds. *Cross-Cultural Caring: A Handbook*. Vancouver: University of British Columbia Press.

Goffman, Erving
    1961   *Asylums*. Garden City, NY: Doubleday.
    1959   *The Presentation of Self in Everyday Life*. New York: Doubleday.

Gómez, Manuel R.
    1990   "Biculturalism and Subjective Mental Health among Cuban Americans." *Social Service Review* 64:375–389.

Gonsalves, Carlos J.
    1990   "The Psychological Effects of Political Repression on Chilean Exiles in the U.S." *American Journal of Orthopsychiatry* 60:143–153.

Good, Mary-Jo DelVecchio, Paul E. Brodwin, Byron Good, and Arthur Kleinman, eds.
1992   *Pain as a Human Experience: An Anthropological Perspective.* Berkeley: University of California Press.

Good Tracks, Jimm G.
1973   "Native-American Non-Interference." *Social Work* 18:30–34.

Goode, William J.
1957   "Community Within a Community: The Professions." *American Sociological Review* 22:194–200.

Gopaul-McNicol, Sharon-Ann
1993   *Working with West Indian Families.* New York: Guilford Press..

Gopaul-McNicol, Sharon-Ann, Stephanie Clark-Castro, and Karen Black
1997   "Cognitive Testing and Culturally Diverse Children" (Special Section). *Cultural Diversity and Mental Health* 3:113–115.

Grafton, Jr., Hull H.
1982   "Child Welfare Services to Native Americans." *Social Casework* 63:340–347.

Graves, Theodore D.
1967   "Acculturation, Access and Alcohol in a Tri-Ethnic Community." *American Anthropologist* 69:306–321.

Green, James W.
1989   "Aging and Ethnicity: An Emergent Issue in Social Gerontology." *Journal of Cross-Cultural Gerontology* 4:377–383.
1973   "The British West Indian Alien Labor Problem in the Virgin Islands." *Caribbean Studies* 12:56–75.

Green, James W., and James Leigh
1989   "Teaching Ethnographic Methods to Social Service Workers." *Practicing Anthropology* 11:8–10.

Green, James W., and Linda Wilson
1983   "An Experiential Approach to Cultural Awareness Training." *Child Welfare* 63:303–311.

Green, Vera
1978   "The Black Extended Family in the United States: Some Research Suggestions." In Demitri B. Shimkin, Edith M. Shimkin, and Dennis A. Frate, eds. *The Extended Family in Black Societies.* The Hague: Mouton.
1970   "The Confrontation of Diversity in the Black Community." *Human Organization* 29:267–272.

Greenbaum, Susan
1991   "What's in a Label? Identity Problems of Southern Tribes." *Journal of Ethnic Studies* 19:107–126.

1985   "In Search of Lost Tribes: Anthropology and the Federal Acknowledgement Process." *Human Organization* 44:361–367.

Grossman, Daniel C., Carol Milligan, and Richard A. Deyo
1991   "Risk Factors for Suicide Attempts among Navaho Adolescents." *American Journal of Public Health* 81: 870–874.

Guarnaccia, Peter J.
1993   *"Ataques de Nervios* in Puerto Rico: Culture-Bound Syndrome or Popular Illness?" *Medical Anthropology* 15:157–170.

Guarnaccia, Peter J., Victor De La Cancela, and Emilio Carrillo
1989   "The Multiple Meanings of Ataques de Nervios in the Latino Community." *Medical Anthropology* 11:47–62.

Guarnaccia, Peter J., Melissa Rivera, Felipe Franco, and Charlie Neighbors
1996   "The Experience of *Ataques de Nervios:* Towards an Anthropology of Emotions in Puerto Rico." *Culture, Medicine and Psychiatry* 20:343–367.

Gubrium, Jaber F.
1991   "Recognizing and Analyzing Local Cultures." In William B. Shaffir, and Robert A. Stebbins. *Experiencing Fieldwork.* Newbury Park, CA: Sage.

Gumperz, John J., and Dell Hymes, eds.
1972   *Directions in Sociolinguistics.* New York: Holt, Rinehart and Winston.

Gunaratnam, Yasmin
1997   "Culture Is Not Enough: A Critique of Multiculturalism in Palliative Care." In David Field, Jenny Hockey, and Neil Small, eds. *Death, Gender and Ethnicity:* London: Routledge.

Gutierrez, Ann R. A., Howard Nemon, and Edith A. Lewis
1997   "Multicultural Community Organizing, A Strategy for Change." *Social Work* 41:501–508.

Gutiérrez, Lorraine M.
1990   "Working with Women of Color: An Empowerment Perspective." *Social Work* 35:149–153.

Gutman, Herbert G.
1984   "Afro-American Kinship Before and After Emancipation in North America." In Hans Medick and David Warren Sabeam, eds. *Interest and Emotion.* Cambridge: Cambridge University Press.
1976   *The Black Family in Slavery and Freedom.* New York: Random House.

Gwyn, Felisha S., and Allie C. Kilpatrick
1981   "Family Therapy with Low-Income Blacks: A Tool or Turn-Off?" *Social Casework* 62:259–266.

Haley, Alex
1976   *Roots.* Garden City, NY: Doubleday.

Hannerz, Ulf
   1986   "Theory in Anthropology: Small is Beautiful? The Problem of Complex Cultures." *Comparative Studies in Society and History* 28:362–367.

Hare, Martha L.
   1993   "The Emergence of a U.S. Chinese Medicine." *Medical Anthropology Quarterly* 7:30–49.

Hare-Mustin, Rachel
   1994   "Discourses in the Mirrored Room: A Postmodern Analysis of Therapy." *Family Process* 33:19–35.

Harris, Diane J., and Sue A. Kuba
   1997   "Ethnocultural Identity and Eating Disorders in Women of Color." *Professional Psychology: Research and Practice* 28:341–347.

Hartman, Ann
   1991   "Words Create Worlds." *Social Work* 36:275–276.
   1990   "Many Ways of Knowing." *Social Work* 35:3–4.

Harwood, Alan
   1987   *Rx: Spiritist as Needed, a Study of Puerto Rican Community Mental Health.* Ithaca, NY: Cornell University Press.

Hayes-Bautista, David E.
   1978   "Chicano Patients and Medical Practitioners: A Sociology of Knowledge Paradigm of Lay-Professional Interaction." *Social Science and Medicine* 12:83–90.

Hayes-Bautista, David E., and Jorge Chapa
   1987   "Latino Terminology: Conceptual Bases for Standardized Terminology." *American Journal of Public Health* 77:61–68.

Hayes-Bautista, David E., Werner O. Schink, and Jorge Chapa
   1988   *The Burden of Support: Young Latinos in an Aging Society.* Stanford: Stanford University Press.

Herrnstein, Richard J., and Charles Murray
   1994   *The Bell Curve: Intelligence and Class Structure in American Life.* New York: Free Press.

Hess, David J.
   1993   *Science in the New Age: The Paranormal, Its Defenders and Debunkers, and American Culture."* Madison: University of Wisconsin Press.

Hill, Robert B.
   1971   *The Strengths of Black Families.* New York: National Urban League.

Hilliard, Asa G.
   1996   "Either a Paradigm Shift or No Mental Measurement: The Nonscience and the Nonsense of *The Bell Curve*." *Cultural Diversity and Mental Health* 2:1–20.

Ho, Man Keung
    1992   *Minority Children and Adolescents in Therapy.* Newbury Park, CA: Sage.
    1991   "Use of Ethnic Sensitive Inventory (ESI) to Enhance Practitioner Skills with Minorities." *Journal of Multicultural Social Work* 1:57–67.
    1987   *Family Therapy with Ethnic Minorities.* Newbury Park, CA: Sage.

Hogan, Robert
    1969   "Development of an Empathy Scale." *Journal of Counseling and Clinical Psychology* 33:307–316.

Hongo, Garrett K., ed.
    1995   *Under Western Eyes: Personal Essays from Asian America.* New York: Anchor Books.

Hopps, June G.
    1982   "Oppression Based on Color." *Social Work* 27:3–6.

Horejsi, Charles, Bonnie H. Craig, and Joe Pablo
    1992   "Reactions by Native American Parents to Child Protection Agencies: Cultural and Community Factors." *Child Welfare* 71:329–342.

Huang, Karen
    1991   "Chinese Americans." In Noreen Mokuau, ed. *Handbook of Social Services for Asian and Pacific Islanders.* New York: Greenwood Press.

Huang, Lucy Jen
    1988   "The Chinese Family in America." In Charles H. Mindel, Robert W. Habenstein, and Roosevelt Wright, Jr. *Ethnic Families in America: Patterns and Variations.* New York: Elesevier.

Hulewat, Phyllis
    1996   "Resettlement: A Cultural and Psychological Crisis." *Social Work* 41:129–137.

Hunt, Portia
    1987   "Black Clients: Implications for Supervision of Trainees." *Psychotherapy* 24:114–119.

Hurtado, Aída, and Raul Rodriguez
    1989   "Language as a Social Problem: The Repression of Spanish in South Texas." *Journal of Multilingual and Multicultural Development* 10:401–419.

Husaini, Baqar A., Stephen T. Moore, and Van A. Cain
    1994   "Psychiatric Symptoms and Help-Seeking Behavior among the Elderly: An Analysis of Racial and Gender Differences." *Journal of Gerontological Social Work* 21:177–195.

Ivey, Allen E.
    1983   *Intentional Interviewing and Counseling.* Monterey, CA: Brooks/Cole.
    1971   *Microcounseling.* Springfield, IL: Charles C Thomas.

Jackson, Eileen M.
    1993   "Whiting Out Difference: Why U.S. Nursing Research Fails Black Families." *Medical Anthropology Quarterly* 7:363–385.

Jackson, Jacquelyne J.
 1982   "Death Rates of Aged Blacks and Whites, 1964–1978." *The Black Scholar* 13:36–48.
 1980   *Minorities and Aging.* Belmont, CA: Wadsworth.
 1977   "The Black Aging: A Demographic Overview." In Richard A. Kalish, ed. *The Later Years: Social Applications of Gerontology.* Monterey, CA: Brooks/Cole.

Jacobs, Carolyn, and Dorcas D. Bowles, eds.
 1988   *Ethnicity and Race: Critical Concepts in Social Work.* Silver Spring, MD: National Association of Social Workers.

Jacobs, Sue-Ellen
 1979   "Our Babies Shall Not Die: A Community's Response to Medical Neglect." *Human Organization* 38:120–133.
 1974a "Action and Advocacy Anthropology." *Human Organization* 33:209–214.
 1974b "Doing It Our Way and Mostly for Our Own." *Human Organization* 33:380–382.

Jacoby, Russell, and Naomi Glauberman, eds.
 1995   *The Bell Curve Debate: History, Documents, Opinions.* New York: Times Books.

Jemison, T. J.
 1982   "As Christians We Must Do More to Help Other People." *The Crisis* 89:9.

Joans, Barbara
 1992   "Problems in Pocatello: A Study in Linguistic Understanding." In Aaron Podolefsky, and Peter J. Brown, eds. *Applying Anthropology.* Mountain View, CA: Mayfield.

John, Robert
 1988   "The Native American Family." In Charles H. Mindel, Robert W. Habenstein, and Roosevelt Wright, Jr. *Ethnic Families in America: Patterns and Variations.* New York: Elsevier.
 1985   "Service Needs and Support Networks of Elderly Native Americans: Family, Friends, and Social Service Agencies." In Warren A. Peterson, and Jill Quadagno, eds. *Social Bonds in Later Life: Aging and Independence.* Beverly Hills, CA: Sage.

Johnson, Colleen L.
 1989   "In-law Relationships in the American Kinship System: The Impact of Divorce and Remarriage." *American Ethnologist* 16:87–99.

Jones, Alison, and Arthur A. Seagull
 1977   "Dimensions of the Relationship between the Black Client and the White Therapist: A Theoretical Overview." *American Psychologist* 32:850–855.

Jones, Dorothy M.
 1976   "The Mystique of Expertise in the Social Services." *Journal of Sociology and Social Welfare* 3:332–346.
 1974   *The Urban Native Encounters the Social Service System.* Fairbanks: University of Alaska.

Jones, Michael O., Michael D. Moore, and Richard C. Snyder
  1988 *Inside Organizations: Understanding the Human Dimension.* Newbury Park, CA: Sage.

Jones, Richard L.
  1983 "Increasing Staff Sensitivity to the Black Client." *Social Casework* 64:419–425.

Juarez, Reina
  1985 "Core Issues in Psychotherapy with Hispanic Children." *Psychotherapy* 22:441–448.

Kadushin, Alfred
  1990 *The Social Work Interview: A Guide for Human Service Professionals.* New York: Columbia University Press.
  1972 *The Social Work Interview.* New York: Columbia University Press.

Kahn, Marvin W., Cecil Williams, Eugene Galvez, Linda Lejero, Rex Conrad, and George Goldstein
  1981 "The Papago Psychology Service, a Community Mental Health Program on an American Indian Reservation." In Richard H. Dana, ed. *Human Services for Cultural Minorities.* Baltimore: University Park Press.

Kaneshige, Edward
  1973 "Cultural Factors in Group Counseling and Interaction." *Personnel and Guidance Journal* 51:407–412.

Keefe, Susan E., ed.
  1988 *Appalachian Mental Health.* Lexington: University Press of Kentucky.

Keefe, Susan E., and Amado M. Padilla
  1987 *Chicano Ethnicity.* Albuquerque: University of New Mexico Press.

Kelly, G. P.
  1977 *From Vietnam to America: A Chronicle of Vietnamese Immigration to the United States.* Boulder, CO: Westview Press.

Keyes, Charles F.
  1977 *The Golden Peninsula.* New York: Macmillan.

Kim-Goh, Mikyong
  1993 "Conceptualization of Mental Illness among Korean-American Clergymen and Implications for Mental Health Services Delivery." *Community Mental Health Journal* 29:405–412.

Kirmayer, Laurence J., Allan Young, and Barbara C. Hayton
  1995 "The Cultural Context of Anxiety Disorders." *The Psychiatric Clinics of North America* 18:503–521.

Kitano, Harry H. L.
  1988 "The Japanese American Family." In Charles H. Mindel, Robert W. Habenstein, and Roosevelt Wright, Jr. *Ethnic Families in America: Patterns and Variations.* New York: Elsevier.

Klein, Richard E.
  1989   *The Human Career.* Chicago: University of Chicago Press.

Kleinman, Arthur
  1992   "Pain as a Human Experience: An Introduction." In Mary-Jo DelVecchio, Paul E. Brodwin, Byron Good, and Arthur Kleinman, eds. *Pain as a Human Experience: An Anthropological Perspective.* Berkeley: University of California Press.
  1988a *The Illness Narratives: Suffering, Healing and the Human Condition.* New York: Basic Books.
  1988b *Rethinking Psychiatry: From Cultural Category to Personal Experience.* New York: The Free Press.
  1986   *Social Origins of Distress and Disease: Depression, Neurasthenia and Pain in Modern China.* New Haven, CT: Yale University Press.
  1982   "Neurasthenia and Depression: A Study of Socialization and Culture in China." *Culture, Medicine, and Psychiatry* 6:117–190.
  1980   *Patients and Healers in the Context of Culture.* Berkeley: University of California Press.
  1978a "Concepts and a Model for the Comparison of Medical Systems as Cultural Systems." *Social Science and Medicine* 12:85–93.
  1978b International Healthcare Planning from an Ethnomedical Perspective: Critique and Recommendations for Change."*Medical Anthropology* 2:71–94.
  1978c "Rethinking the Social and Cultural Context of Psychopathology and Psychiatric Care." In Theo C. Manschreck, and Arthur Kleinman, eds. *Renewal in Psychiatry.* New York: John Wiley and Sons.
  1977   "Lessons from a Clinical Approach to Medical Anthropology Research." *Medical Anthropology Newsletter* 8:11–16.

Kleinman, Arthur, and Byron Good, eds.
  1985   *Culture and Depression.* Berkeley: University of California Press.

Kleinman, Arthur, and Joan Kleinman
  1991   "Suffering and Its Professional Transformation: Toward an Ethnography of Interpersonal Experience." *Culture, Medicine, and Psychiatry* 15:275–301.

Kluckhohn, Florence R., and Fred L. Strodtbeck
  1961   *Variations in Value Orientations.* Evanston, IL: Row, Peterson.

Korbin, Jill
  1981   *Child Abuse and Neglect: Cross-Cultural Perspectives.* Berkeley: University of California Press.
  1976   "Anthropological Contributions to the Study of Child Abuse." Manuscript.

Koss-Chioino, Joan
  1992   *Women as Healers, Women as Patients: Mental Health Care and Traditional Healing in Puerto Rico.* Boulder, CO: Westview.

Koss-Chioino, Joan, and Jose M. Canive
  1993   "The Interaction of Popular and Clinical Diagnostic Labeling: The Case of Embrujado." *Medical Anthropology* 15:171–188.

Kozol, Jonathan
   1991   *Rachel and Her Children: Homeless Families in America.* New York: Crown.
   1988   *Savage Inequalities: Children in America's Schools.* New York: Crown.

Kracke, Waud H.
   1994   "Reflections on the Savage Self: Introspection, Empathy, and Anthropology." In Marcelo Suarez-Orozco, George Spindler, and Louise Spindler, eds. *The Making of Psychological Anthropology II.* Fort Worth: Harcourt Brace.

Kroeber, A. L., and C. Kluckhohn
   1952   *Culture: A Critical Review of Concepts and Definitions.* Cambridge, MA: Papers of the Peabody Museum, No. 47.

Kunitz, Stephen J., and Jerrold E. Levy
   1994   *Drinking Careers: A Twenty-Five-Year Study of Three Navajo Populations.* New Haven: Yale University Press.

Kupferer, Harriet J.
   1979   "A Case of Sanctioned Drinking: The Rupert's House Cree." *Anthropological Quarterly* 52:198–203.

Laird, Joan
   1995   "Family-Centered Practice in the Postmodern Era." *Families in Society* 76:150–162.

Lakoff, George
   1972   "Hedges: A Study of Meaning Criteria and the Logic of Fuzzy Concepts." *Papers of the Eighth Regional Meeting.* Chicago: Chicago Linguistics Society.

Lakoff, George, and Mark Johnson
   1980   *Metaphors We Live By.* Chicago: University of Chicago Press.

Landrine, Hope
   1992   "Clinical Implications of Cultural Differences: The Referential vs. Indexical Self." *Clinical Psychology Review* 12:401–415.

Landsman, Gail H.
   1987   "Indian Activism and the Press: Coverage of a Conflict at Ganienkeh." *Anthropological Quarterly* 60:101–113.
   1985   "Ganienkeh: Symbol and Politics in an Indian/White Conflict." *American Anthropologist* 87:826–839.

Lang, Gretchen C.
   1990   "Talking About a New Illness with the Dakota: Reflections on Diabetes, Food and Culture." In Robert H. Winthrop, ed. *Culture and the Anthropological Tradition.* Lanham, MD: University Press of America.

Lappin, Jay, and Sam Scott
   1982   "Intervention in a Vietnamese Refugee Family." In Monica McGoldrick, John K. Pearce, and Joseph Giordano, eds. *Ethnicity and Family Therapy.* New York: The Guilford Press.

Lave, Jean, and Etienne Wenger
  1991   *Situated Learning, Legitimate Peripheral Participation.* Cambridge: Cambridge University Press.

Leach, Edmund
  1968   *A Runaway World?* New York: Oxford University Press.

Le-Doux, Cora, and King S. Stephens
  1992   "Refugee and Immigrant Social Service Delivery: Critical Management Issues." *Journal of Multicultural Social Work* 2:31–45.

Lee, Jik-Joen, Michael R. Patchner, and Pallassana R. Balgopal
  1991   "Essential Dimensions for Developing and Delivering Service for the Asian American Elderly." *Journal of Multicultural Social Work* 1:3–11.

Lee, Joanne Faung Jean
  1991   *Asian American Experiences in the United States.* Jefferson, NC: McFarland.

Lee, Mo-Yee
  1996   "A Constructivist Approach to the Help-Seeking Process of Clients: A Response to Cultural Diversity." *Journal of Clinical Social Work* 24:187–202.

Lemert, E. M.
  1954   *Alcohol and the Northwest Coast Indians.* Berkeley: University of California Press.

Leonard, Karen Isaksen
  1992   *Making Ethnic Choices: California's Punjabi Mexican Americans.* Philadelphia: Temple University Press.

Leong, Frederick T. L.
  1986   "Counseling and Psychotherapy with Asian Americans: Review of the Literature." *Review of Counseling Psychology* 33:196–206.

Levin, Jeffrey, and H. Vanderpool
  1987   "Is Frequent Religious Attendance Really Conducive to Better Health? Toward an Epidemiology of Religion." *Social Science and Religion* 24:589–600.

Levy, Jerrold E., and Stephen J. Kunitz
  1987   "A Suicide Prevention Program for Hopi Youth." *Social Science and Medicine* 25:931–940.
  1974   *Indian Drinking: Navajo Practices and Anglo-American Theories.* New York: John Wiley and Sons.

Lewis-Fernandez, Roberto
  1996a "Cultural Formulation of Psychiatric Diagnoses." *Culture, Medicine and Psychiatry* 20:133–144.
  1996b "Case No. 02, Diagnosis and Treatment of *Nervios* and *Ataques* in a Female Puerto Rican Migrant." *Culture, Medicine and Psychiatry* 20:155–163.

Lide, Pauline D.
  1971   "Dialogue on Racism: A Prologue to Action?" *Social Casework* 52:432–437.

Lieberman, Alicia F.
  1990   "Culturally Sensitive Intervention with Children and Families." *Child and Adolescent Social Work* 7:101–120.

Lieberson, S.
  1985   "Stereotypes: Their Consequences for Race and Ethnic Interaction." In Cora Bagley Merrett, and Cheryl Leggon, eds. *Research in Race and Ethnic Relations.* Greenwich, CT: JAI Press.

Liebow, Elliot
  1967   *Tally's Corner.* Boston: Little, Brown.

Lim, Russell F., and Keh-Ming Lin
  1996   "Cultural Formulation of Psychiatric Diagnosis—Case No. 03, Psychosis Following Qi-Gong in a Chinese Immigrant." *Culture, Medicine, and Psychiatry* 28:369–378.

Lipson, Juliene, Suzanne L. Dibble, and Pamela A. Minarik, eds.
  1996   *Culture and Nursing Care: A Pocket Guide.* San Francisco: UCSF Nursing Press.

Lofland, John
  1971   *Analyzing Social Settings.* Belmont, CA: Wadsworth.

Logan, Sadye L., ed.
  1996   *The Black Family: Strengths, Self-Help, and Positive Change.* Boulder, CO: Westview.

Lomawaima, K. Tsianina
  1993   "Domesticity in the Federal Indian Schools: The Power of Authority over Mind and Body." *American Ethnologist* 20:227–240.

Long, Kathleen Ann
  1986   "Cultural Considerations in the Assessment and Treatment of Intrafamilial Abuse." *American Journal of Orthopsychiatry* 56:131–136.

Longres, John F.
  1991   "Toward a Status Model of Ethnic Sensitive Practice." *Journal of Multicultural Social Work* 1:41–57.

López, Steven, and Priscilla Hernandez
  1986   "How Culture Is Considered in Evaluations of Psychopathology." *Journal of Nervous and Mental Disease* 176:598–606.

Lukoff, David, Francis G. Lu, and Robert Turner
  1995   "Cultural Considerations in the Assessment and Treatment of Religious and Spiritual Problems." *The Psychiatric Clinics of North America* 18:467–485.

Lum, Doman
  1996   *Social Work Practice and People of Color: A Process-Stage Approach.* 3rd ed. Pacific Grove, CA: Brooks/Cole.
  1986   *Social Work Practice and People of Color: A Process-Stage Approach.* Monterey, CA: Brooks/Cole.

Lutz, Catherine A.
  1988   *Unnatural Emotions.* Chicago: University of Chicago Press.

MacAndrew, Craig, and Robert B. Edgerton
  1969   *Drunken Comportment.* Chicago: Aldine.

Madsen, William
  1964   *Mexican-Americans of South Texas.* New York: Holt, Rinehart and Winston.

Maduro, Renaldo
  1983   "Curanderismo and Latin Views on Disease and Curing." *Western Journal of Medicine* 139:64–70.

Mandelbaum, David G., ed.
  1949   *Language, Culture and Personality: Selected Writings of Edward Sapir.* Berkeley: University of California Press.

Mannes, Marc
  1993   "Seeking the Balance between Child Protection and Family Preservation in Indian Child Welfare." *Child Welfare* 72:141–152.

Manson, Spero M.
  1996   "The Wounded Spirit: A Cultural Formulation of Post-Traumatic Stress Disorder." *Culture, Medicine and Psychiatry* 20:489–498.
  1995   "Culture and Major Depression, Current Challenges in the Diagnosis of Mood Disorders." *The Psychiatric Clinics of North America* 18:487–501.
  1989   "Provider Assumptions about Long-Term Care in American Indian Communities." *The Gerontologist* 29:355–358.

Manson, Spero M., J. Beals, R. W. Dick, and C. Duclos
  1989a   "Risk Factors for Suicide Among Indian Adolescents at a Boarding School." *Public Health Report* 104:609–614.
  1989b   "Long-Term Care in American Indian Communities: Issues for Planning and Research." *The Gerontologist* 29:38–44.

Mariano, Anthony J., Dennis M. Donovan, Patricia Silk Walker, Mary Jean Mariano, and R. Dale Walker
  1989   "Drinking-Related Locus of Control and the Drinking Status of Urban Native Americans." *Journal of Studies of Alcohol* 50:331–338.

Marín, Gerardo
  1993   "Defining Culturally Appropriate Community Interventions: Hispanics as a Case Study." *Journal of Community Psychology* 21:149–161.

Marín, Gerardo, and Barbara VanOss Marín
    1991   *Research with Hispanic Populations.* Newbury Park, CA: Sage.

Marsella, Anthony J.
    1993   "Counseling and Psychotherapy with Japanese Americans: Cross-Cultural Considerations." *American Journal of Orthopsychiatry* 63:200–208.

Martin, Elmer P., and Joanne M. Martin
    1978   *The Black Extended Family.* Chicago: University of Chicago Press.

Martin, Joanne M., and Elmer P. Martin
    1985   *The Helping Tradition in the Black Family and Community.* Silver Spring, MD: National Association of Social Workers.

Martinez, Cervando, and Harry W. Martin
    1966   "Folk Diseases among Urban Mexican-Americans: Etiology, Symptoms and Treatment." *Journal of the American Medical Association* 196:147–150.

Maser, Jack D., and Norman Dinges
    1992   "Comorbidity: Meaning and Uses in Cross-Cultural Clinical Research." *Culture, Medicine, and Psychiatry* 16:409–425.

Mass, Amy Iwasaki
    1981   "Asians as Individuals—the Japanese Community." In Richard H. Dana, ed. *Human Services for Cultural Minorities.* Baltimore: University Park Press.
    1976   "Asians as Individuals: The Japanese Community." *Social Casework* 57:160–164.

Matheson, Lou
    1986   "If You Are Not An Indian, How Do You Treat An Indian?" In Harriet P. Lefley, and Paul P. Pedersen eds. *Cross-Cultural Training for Mental Health Professionals.* Springfield, IL: Charles C Thomas.

Matsuoka, Jon K.
    1993   "Demographic Characteristics as Determinants of Qualitative Differences in the Adjustment of Vietnamese Refugees." *Journal of Social Services Research* 17: 1–21.
    1991   "Vietnamese Americans." In Noreen Mokuau, ed. *Handbook of Social Services for Asian and Pacific Islanders.* New York: Greenwood Press.

Mayes, Nathaniel H.
    1978   "Teacher Training for Cultural Awareness. In David S. Hoopes, Paul B. Pedersen, and George Renwick, eds. *Overview of Intercultural Education, Training and Research.* Washington, DC: SIETAR

McAdoo, Harriette P.
    1988   *Black Families.* Beverly Hills, CA: Sage.
    1979   "Black Kinship." *Psychology Today* 12:64ff.
    1977   "Family Therapy in the Black Community." *American Journal of Orthopsychiatry* 47:75–79.

McAdoo, Harriette P., and John P. McAdoo
   1985   *Black Children.* Beverly Hills, CA: Sage.

McGoldrick, Monica
   1996   *Ethnicity and Family Therapy.* New York: Guilford Press.

McGoldrick, Monica, and Randy Gerson
   1985   *Genograms in Family Assessment.* New York: W. W. Norton.

McGoldrick, Monica, John K. Pearce, and Joseph Giordano, eds.
   1982   *Ethnicity and Family Therapy.* New York: The Guilford Press.

McLeod, Beverly
   1981   "The Mediating Person and Cultural Identity." In Stephen Bochner. *The Mediating Person.* Cambridge, MA: Schenkman.

McLeod, Donna L., and Henry J. Meyer
   1967   "A Study of the Values of Social Workers." In E. J. Thomas, ed. *Behavioral Science for Social Workers.* New York: Collier-Macmillan: 401–416.

McLeod, John
   1996   "Working with Narratives." In Rowan Bayne, Ian Horton, and Jenny Bimrose, eds. *New Directions in Counseling.* London: Routledge.

McMahon, Anthony, and Paula Allen-Meares
   1992   "Is Social Work Racist? A Content Analysis of Recent Literature." *Social Work* 37:533–539.

McMiller, William P., and John R. Weisz
   1996   "Help-Seeking Preceding Mental Health Clinic Intake among African-American, Latino, and Caucasian Youths." *Journal of the American Academy of Child and Adolescent Psychiatry* 35:1086–1094.

McPhatter, Anna R.
   1997   "Cultural Competence in Child Welfare: What is It? How Do We Achieve It? What Happens Without It?" *Child Welfare* 50:255–278.

McRoy, Ruth G., Zena Oglesby, and Helen Grape
   1997   "Achieving Same-Race Adoptive Placements for African American Children: Culturally Sensitive Practice Approaches." *Child Welfare* 76:85–106.

Mehrabian, Albert, and Norman Epstein
   1972   "A Measure of Emotional Empathy." *Journal of Personality* 40:525–543.

Meketon, Melvin Jerry
   1983   "Indian Mental Health: An Orientation." *American Journal of Orthopsychiatry* 53:110–115.

Menicucci, Linda C., and Laurie Wermuth
    1989   "Expanding the Family Systems Approach: Culture, Class, Developmental and Gender Influences in Drug Abuse." *American Journal of Family Therapy* 17:129–142.

Mezzich, Juan E.
    1995   "Cultural Formulation and Comprehensive Diagnosis, Clinical and Research Perspectives." *The Psychiatric Clinics of North America* 18:649–657.

Mezzich, Juan E., Arthur Kleinman, Horacio Fabrega, Jr.
    1994   *Cultural Issues and* DSM-IV: *Support Papers.* Washington, D.C.: NIMH.

Moffatt, Michael
    1989   *Coming of Age in New Jersey: College and American Culture.* New Brunswick, NJ: Rutgers University Press.
    1986   "The Discourse of the Dorm: Race, Friendship and 'Culture' among College Youth." In Herve Varenne. *Symbolizing America.* Lincoln: University of Nebraska Press.

Moffie, H. Steven, and J. David Kinzie
    1996   "The History and Future of Cross-Cultural Psychiatric Services." *Community Mental Health Journal* 32:581–592.

Mokuau, Noreen, ed.
    1991   *Handbook of Social Services for Asian and Pacific Islanders.* New York: Greenwood Press.

Mokuau, Noreen, and Collette Browne
    1994   "Life Themes of Native Hawaiian Female Elders: Resources for Cultural Preservation." *Social Work* 39:43–49.

Montero, Darrell
    1979   "Vietnamese Refugees in America: Toward a Theory of Spontaneous International Migration." *International Migration Review* 13:624–648.

Moore, Pat
    1989   "The Incredible Aging Woman." *The Guardian.* August 1, page 17.

Morinis, E. Alan
    1982   "'Getting Straight': Behavioral Patterns in a Skid Row Indian Community." *Urban Anthropology* 11:193–214.

Moynihan, Daniel P.
    1965   *The Negro Family: The Case for National Action.* Washington, DC.: Department of Labor.

Murase, Kenji
    1992   "Models of Service Delivery in Asian American Communities." In Sharlene Maeda Furuto, Renuka Biswas, Douglas K. Chung, Kenji Murase, Fariyal Ross-Sheriff, eds. *Social Work Practice with Asian Americans.* Newbury Park, CA: Sage.

Myerhoff, Barbara
  1982   "Rites of Passage: Process and Paradox." In Victor Turner. *Studies in Festivity and Ritual.* Washington, DC: Smithsonian Institution Press.
  1978   *Number Our Days.* New York: Simon and Schuster.

Myerhoff, Barbara, and Andrei Simic, eds.
  1978   *Life's Career.* Beverly Hills, CA: Sage.

Nah, Kyung-Hee
  1993   "Perceived Problems and Service Delivery for Korean Immigrants." *Social Work* 38:289–296.

Nakanishi, Manuel, and Barbara Rittner
  1992   "The Inclusionary Cultural Model." *Journal of Social Work Education* 28:27–35.

Nash, Manning
  1989   *The Cauldron of Ethnicity in the Modern World.* Chicago: University of Chicago Press.

National Center for American Indian and Alaska Native Mental Health Research
  1987   *American Indian and Alaska Native Mental Health Research.* Denver: University of Colorado Health Sciences Center.

Neighbors, Harold W., and Robert J. Taylor
  1985   "The Use of Social Service Agencies by Black Americans." *Social Service Review* 59:258–268.

Neumann, Alfred K., Velma Mason, Emmett Chase, and Bernard Albaugh
  1991   "Factors Associated with Success among Southern Cheyenne and Arapaho." *Journal of Commmunity Mental Health* 16:103–115.

Norton, Dolores G., et al.
  1978   *The Dual Perspective.* New York: Council on Social Work Education.

Olson, James S., and Raymond Wilson
  1984   *Native Americans in the Twentieth Century.* Urbana: University of Illinois Press.

Omni, Michael, and Howard Winant
  1986   *Racial Formation in the United States from the 1960s to the 1980s.* New York: Routledge and Kegan Paul.

O'Nell, Carl W.
  1976   "An Investigation of Reported 'Fright' as a Factor in the Etiology of Susto, 'Magical Fright'." *Ethos* 3:41–63.

O'Nell, Theresa D.
  1992   "'Feeling Worthless': An Ethnographic Investigation of Depression and Problem Drinking at the Flathead Reservation." *Culture, Medicine and Psychiatry* 16:447–469.

Oquendo, Maria
    1994   "Differential Diagnosis of Ataques des Nervios." *American Journal of Orthopsychiatry* 65:60–65.

Ordaz, Maricela, and Diane DeAnda
    1996   "Cultural Legacies: Operationalizing Chicano Cultural Values." *Journal of Multicultural Social Work* 4:57–68.

Ortiz, Karol R.
    1985   "Mental Health Consequences of the Life History Method." *Ethos* 9:99–120.

Pachter, Lee M., Bruce Bernstein, and Adalberto Osorio
    1992   "Clinical Implications of a Folk Illness: *Empacho* in Mainland Puerto Ricans." *Medical Anthropology* 13:285–299.

Padilla, Amado M.
    1995   *Hispanic Psychology, Critical Issues in Theory and Research.* Thousand Oaks, CA: Sage.

Padilla, Amado M., Kathryn Lindholm, and Andrew Chen
    1991   "The English-Only Movement: Myths, Reality, and Implications for Psychology." *American Psychologist* 46:120–130.

Padilla, Felix M.
    1985   "On the Nature of Latino Ethnicity." In Rodolpho O. De La Garza, et al., eds. *The Mexican American Experience: An Interdisciplinary Anthology.* Austin: University of Texas Press.

Padilla, Yolanda C.
    1996   "Incorporating Social Science Concepts in the Analysis of Ethnic Issues in Social Work: The Case of Latinos." *Journal of Multicultural Social Work* 4:1–12.

Page, J. Bryan, Dale D. Chitwood, Prince C. Smith, Narmie Kane, and Duane C. McBride
    1990   "Intravenous Drug Use and HIV Infection in Miami." *Medical Anthropology Quarterly* 4:56–71.

Palacios, Maria, and Juan N. Franco
    1986   "Counseling Mexican-American Women." *Journal of Multicultural Counseling and Development* 14:124–131.

Pardeck, John T., John W. Murphy, and Jung Min Choi
    1994   "Some Implications of Postmodernism for Social Work Practice." *Social Work* 39:343–346.

Payne, Monica A.
    1989   "Use and Abuse of Corporal Punishment: A Caribbean View." *Child Abuse and Neglect* 13:389–401.

Pearlmutter, Lynn
    1996   "Using Culture and the Intersubjective Perspective as a Resource: A Case Study of an African American Couple." *Clinical Social Work Journal* 24:389–401.

Pedersen, Paul B.
  1997   *Culture-Centered Counseling Interventions.* Thousand Oaks, CA: Sage.
  1989   *Counseling Across Cultures.* Honolulu: University of Hawaii Press.

Pedersen, Paul, ed.
  1985   *Handbook of Cross-Cultural Counseling and Therapy.* Westport, CT: Greenwood Press.
  1976   "The Field of Intercultural Counseling." In Paul Pedersen, Walter J. Lonner, and Juris G. Draguns, eds. *Counseling across Cultures.* Honolulu: University of Hawaii Press: 17–41.

Pedersen, Paul B., and Daniel Hernandez
  1996   *Decisional Interviewing in a Cultural Context.* Thousand Oaks, CA: Sage.

Pérez-Stable, E. J.
  1987   "Issues in Latino Health Care." *Western Journal of Medicine* 146:213–218.

Phelan, Michael, and Sue Parkman
  1995   "Work with an Interpreter." *British Medical Journal* 311:555–557.

Philips, Susan V.
  1974   "Warm Springs 'Indian Time.'" In Richard Bauman, and Joel Sherzer, eds. *Explorations in the Ethnography of Speaking.* New York: Cambridge University Press.

Pinderhughes, Elaine
  1995   "Empowering Diverse Populations: Family Practice in the 21st Century." *Families in Society* 76:131–140.
  1982a   "Family Functioning of Afro-America." *Social Work* 27:91–96.
  1982b   "Afro-American Families and the Victim System." In Monica McGoldrick, John K. Pearce, and Joseph Giordano, eds. *Ethnicity and Family Therapy.* New York: The Guilford Press.
  1979   "Afro-America and Economic Dependency." *Urban and Social Change Review* 12:24–27.

Ponterotto, Joseph G., and J. Manuel Casas, eds.
  1991   *Handbook of Racial/Ethnic Minority Counseling Research.* Springfield, IL: Charles C Thomas.

Ponterotto, Joseph G., and Haresh B. Sabnani
  1989   "'Classics' in Multicultural Counseling: A Systematic Five-Year Content Analysis." *Journal of Multicultural Counseling and Development* 17:23–37.

Portes, Alejandro, and Cynthia Truelove
  1987   "Making Sense of Diversity: Recent Research on Hispanic Minorities in the United States." *Annual Review of Sociology* 13:359–385.

Pozatek, Ellie
  1994   "The Problem of Certainty: Clinical Social Work in the Postmodern Era." *Social Work* 39:396–403.

Price, John A.
    1975   "An Applied Analysis of North American Indian Drinking Patterns." *Human Organization* 34:17–26.

Price, Laurie
    1987   "Ecuadoran Illness Stories: Cultural Knowledge in Natural Discourse." In Dorothy Holland, and Naomi Quinn, eds. *Cultural Models in Language and Thought.* Cambridge: Cambridge University Press.

Putsch, Robert W. III
    1985   "Cross-Cultural Communication: The Special Case of Interpreters in Health Care." *Journal of the American Medical Association* 254:3344–3348.

Rahe, R. H., et al.
    1976   "Psychiatric Consultation in a Vietnamese Refugee Camp." *American Journal of Psychiatry* 135:185–190.

Rainwater, Lee
    1970   *Behind Ghetto Walls.* Chicago: Aldine.

Rainwater, Lee, and William Yancey, eds.
    1967   *The Moynihan Report and the Politics of Controversy.* Cambridge: MIT Press.

Ratliff, Nancy
    1988   "Stress and Burnout in the Helping Professions." *Social Casework* 69:147–154.

Red Horse, John G., Ronald Lewis, Marvin Feit, and James Decker
    1981   "Family Behavior of Urban American Indians." In Richard H. Dana, ed. *Human Services for Cultural Minorities.* Baltimore: University Park Press.

Rhodes, Lorna
    1991   *Emptying Beds: The Work of an Emergency Psychiatric Unit.* Berkeley: University of California Press.

Robbins, Susan P.
    1984   "Anglo Concepts and Indian Reality: A Study of Juvenile Delinquency." *Social Casework* 65:235–241.

Robinson, Lena
    1995   *Psychology for Social Workers: Black Perspectives.* London: Routledge.

Rodriguez, Orlando
    1987   *Hispanics and Human Services: Help-Seeking in the Inner City."* Bronx, NY: Fordham University Hispanic Research Center.

Rodriguez, Orlando, and Luis H. Zayas
    1990   "Hispanic Adolescents and Antisocial Behavior: Sociocultural Factors and Treatment Implications." In Arlene Rubin Stiffman, and Larry E. Davis, eds. *Ethnic Issues in Adolescent Mental Health.* Newbury Park, CA: Sage.

Rodwell, Mary K.
    1995   "Constructivist Research: A Qualitative Approach." In Peter J. Pecora, Mark W. Fraser, Kristine F. Nelson, Jacquelyn McCroskey, and William Meezan, eds. *Evaluating Family-Based Services*. New York: Aldine de Gruyter.

Rodwell, Mary K., and Adell Blankebaker
    1992   "Strategies for Developing Cross-Cultural Sensitivity: Wounding as a Metaphor." *Journal of Social Work Education* 28:153–165.

Rogler, Lloyd H.
    1996   "Framing Research on Culture in Psychiatric Diagnosis: The Case of *DSM-IV*." *Psychiatry* 59:145–155.

Rogler, Lloyd H., and August B. Hollingshead
    1985   *Trapped: Puerto Rican Families and Schizophrenia*. Maplewood, NJ: Waterfront Press.

Rogler, Lloyd, Robert G. Malgady, Giuseppe Costantino, and Rena Blumenthal
    1987   "What Do Culturally Sensitive Mental Health Services Mean? The Case of Hispanics." *American Psychologist* 42:565–570.

Rogler, Lloyd H., and Rosemary Santana-Cooney
    1984   *Puerto Rican Families in New York City: Intergenerational Processes*. Maplewood, NJ: Waterfront Press.
    1983   *A Conceptual Framework for Mental Health Research on Hispanic Populations*. New York: Fordham University.

Root, Maria P. P., ed.
    1996   *The Multiracial Experience, Racial Borders as the New Frontier*. Thousand Oaks, CA: Sage.
    1992   *Racially Mixed People in America*. Newbury Park, CA: Sage.

Rose, Stephen M., and Bruce L. Black
    1985   *Advocacy and Empowerment: Mental Health Care in the Community*. Boston: Routledge and Kegan Paul.

Rosenberg, M. L., J. C. Smith, L. E. Davidson, and J. M. Conn
    1987   "The Emergence of Youth Suicide: An Epidemiologic Analysis and Public Health Perspective." *American Review of Public Health* 8:417–440.

Ross, Thomas E., and Tyrel G. Moore
    1987   *A Cultural Geography of North American Indians*. Boulder, CO: Westview Press.

Rounds, Kathleen A., Maria Weil, Kathleen Kirk Bishop
    1994   "Practice with Culturally Diverse Families of Young Children with Disabilities." *Families in Society* 75:3–15.

Rubel, Arthur J.
    1984   *Susto, a Folk Illness*. Berkeley: University of California Press.

1966   *Across the Tracks: Mexican-Americans in a Texas City.* Austin: University of Texas Press.

1964   "The Epidemiology of a Folk Illness: Susto in Hispanic America." *Ethnology* 3:268–283.

1960   "Concepts of Disease in Mexican-American Culture." *American Anthropologist* 62:795–814.

Rubin, Herbert J., and Irene S. Rubin
1995   *Qualitative Interviewing.* Thousand Oaks, CA: Sage.

Rumelhart, Marilyn Austin
1984   "When Understanding the Situation is the Real Problem." *Social Casework* 65:27–33.

Rutledge, Paul James
1992   *The Vietnamese Experience.* Bloomington: Indiana University Press.

Ryan, William
1969   *Blaming the Victim.* New York: Pantheon Press.

Saenz, Rogelio, and Benigno E. Aguirre
1991   "The Dynamics of Mexican Ethnic Identity." *Ethnic Groups* 9:17–32.

Sandoval, Mercedes C., and Maria C. De La Roza
1986   "A Cultural Perspective for Serving the Hispanic Client." In Harriet P. Lefley, and Paul B. Pedersen, eds. *Cross-Cultural Training for Mental Health Professionals.* Springfield, IL: Charles C Thomas.

Sands, Robert G.
1988   "Sociolinguistic Analysis of a Mental Health Interview." *Social Work* 33:149–154.

Saunders, Lyle
1954   *Cultural Differences and Medical Care: The Case of Spanish Speaking People of the Southwest.* New York: Russell Sage Foundation.

Schiele, Jerome H.
1997   "The Contour and Meaning of Afrocentric Social Work." *Journal of Black Studies* 27:800–819.

1996   "Afrocentricity: An Emerging Paradigm in Social Work Practice." *Social Work* 41:284–295.

Schlesinger, Elfriede G., and Wynetta Devore
1995   "Ethnic Sensitive Social Work Practice: The State of the Art." *Journal of Sociology and Social Welfare* 22:29–58.

Schubert, Margaret
1982   *Interviewing in Social Work Practice: An Introduction.* New York: Council on Social Work Education.

Schusky, Ernest L.
1970   "Cultural Change and Continuity in the Lower Brule Community." In Ethel C. Nurge. *The Modern Sioux: Social Systems and Reservation Culture.* Lincoln: University of Nebraska Press.

Schwarz, Maureen
    1997a "Unraveling the Anchoring Cord, Navajo Relocation, 1974 to 1996." *American Anthropologist* 99:43–55.
    1997b *Molded in the Image of Changing Woman.* Tucson: University of Arizona Press.

Sciarra, Daniel T., and Joseph G. Ponterotto
    1991 "Counseling the Hispanic Bilingual Family: Challenge to the Therapeutic Process." *Psychotherapy* 28:473–479.

Sewell-Coker, Beverly, Joyce Hamilton-Collins, and Edith Fein
    1985 "Social Work Practice with West Indian Immigrants." *Social Casework* 66:563–568.

Shomaker, Dianna J.
    1990 "Health Care, Cultural Expectations and Frail Elderly Navajo Grandmothers." *Journal of Cross-Cultural Gerontology* 5:21–34.
    1989 "Transfer of Children and the Importance of Grandmothers among Navaho Indians." *Journal of Cross-Cultural Gerontology* 4:1–18.

Shon, Steven P., and Davis Y. Ja
    1982 "Asian Families." In Monica McGoldrick, John K. Pearce, and Joseph Giordano, eds. *Ethnicity and Family Therapy.* New York: The Guilford Press.

Shore, James H., and Spero Manson
    1983 "American Indian Psychiatric and Social Problems." *Transcultural Psychiatric Research Review* 20:159–179.

Shweder, Richard A.
    1991 *Thinking Through Cultures: Expeditions in Cultural Psychology."* Cambridge: Harvard University Press.
    1985 "Menstrual Pollution, Soul Loss, and the Comparative Study of Emotions." In Arthur Kleinman, and Byron Good, eds. *Culture and Depression.* Berkeley: University of California Press.

Simmons, Leonard C.
    1963 "'Jim Crow': Implications for Social Work." *Social Work* 8:24–30.

Singer, Merrill, Freddie Valentin, Hans Baer, and Zhongke Jia
    1992 "Why Does Juan Garcia Have a Drinking Problem? The Perspective of Critical Medical Anthropology." *Medical Anthropology* 14:77–108.

Smith, Maria A., and Marco A. Mason
    1995 "Developmental Disability Services and Caribbean Americans in New York City." *Journal of Community Practice* 21:87–106.

Smith, Raymond T.
    1988 *Kinship and Class in the West Indies.* Cambridge: Cambridge University Press.

Snow, Loudell F.
    1993 *Walkin' over Medicine.* Boulder, CO: Westview Press.

1978   "Sorcerers, Saints, and Charlatans: Black Folk Healers in Urban America." *Culture, Medicine and Psychiatry* 2:69–106.

1977   "Popular Medicine in a Black Neighborhood." In Edward H. Spicer, ed. *Ethnic Medicine in the Southwest.* Tucson: University of Arizona Press.

1974   "Folk Medical Beliefs and Their Implications for Care of Patients." *Annals of Internal Medicine* 81:82–96.

1973   "'I was Born Just Exactly with the Gift.' An Interview with a Voodoo Practitioner." *Journal of American Folklore* 86:272–281.

Social Casework
1964   "Editorial Notes: Race Relations in Social Work." *Social Casework* 45:155.

Sokolovsky, Jay
1990a   "Bringing Culture Back Home: Aging, Ethnicity, and Family Support." In Jay Sokolovsky. *The Cultural Context of Aging.* New York: Bergin and Garvey.
1990b   *The Cultural Context of Aging.* New York: Bergin and Garvey.

Solomon, Barbara B.
1985   "The Inner-City Church: A Non-traditional Setting for Mental Health Services." In Aminifur R. Harvey, ed. *The Black Family: An Afro-Centric Perspective.* New York: United Church of Christ.
1982   "The Delivery of Mental Health Services to Afro-American Individuals and Families: Translating Theory into Practice." In Barbara Ann Bass, Gail Elizabeth Wyatt, and Gloria Johnson Powell, eds. *The Afro-American Family: Assessment, Treatment, and Research Issues.* New York: Grune and Stratton.
1976   *Black Empowerment: Social Work in Oppressed Communities.* New York: Columbia University Press.

Song-Kim, Young I.
1992   "Battered Korean Women in [the] Urban United States." In Sharlene Maeda Furuto, Renoka Biswas, Douglas K. Chung, Kenji Murase, and Fariyal Ross-Sheriff, eds. *Social Work Practice with Asian Americans.* Newbury Park, CA: Sage.

Sormanti, Mary, and Judith August
1997   Parental Bereavement: Spiritual Connections with Deceased Children." *American Journal of Orthopsychiatry* 67:460–469.

Sowers-Hoag, Karen M., and Patricia Sandau-Beckler
1996   "Educating for Cultural Competence in the Generalist Curriculum." *Journal of Multicultural Social Work* 4:37–56.

Spindler, George
1987   *Interpretive Ethnography of Education at Home and Abroad.* Hillsdale, NJ: Erlbaum.
1982   *Doing the Ethnography of Schooling: Educational Anthropology in Action.* New York: Holt, Rinehart and Winston.

Spindler, George, and Louise Spindler
1994   *Pathways to Cultural Awareness: Cultural Awareness with Teachers and Students.* Thousand Oaks, CA: Corwin Press.

Spradley, James P.
   1980   *Participant Observation.* New York: Holt, Rinehart and Winston.
   1979   *The Ethnographic Interview.* New York: Holt, Rinehart and Winston.
   1972   *Culture and Cognition.* San Francisco: Chandler Publishing Co.
   1970   *You Owe Yourself a Drunk: An Ethnography of Urban Nomads.* Boston: Little, Brown.

Spradley, James P., and David W. McCurdy
   1975   *Anthropology: The Cultural Perspective.* New York: John Wiley and Sons.
   1972   *The Cultural Experience.* Chicago: Science Research Associates.

Squier, Roger W.
   1990   "A Model of Empathic Understanding and Adherence to Treatment Regimes in Practitioner-Patient Relationships. *Social Science and Medicine* 30:325–339.

Stack, Carol B.
   1975   *All Our Kin: Strategies for Survival in the Black Community.* New York: Harper and Row.
   1970   "The Kindred of Viola Jackson: Residence and Family Organization of an Urban Black Family." In Norman E. Whitten, and John F. Szwed, eds. *Afro-American Anthropology: Contemporary Perspectives.* New York: Free Press.

Stanford, E. Percil
   1990   "Diverse Black Aged." In Zev Harel, Edward A. McKinney, and Michael Williams, eds. *Black Aged: Understanding Diversity and Service Needs.* Newbury Park, CA: Sage.

Statham, Daphne
   1978   *Radicals in Social Work.* London: Routledge and Kegan Paul.

Steele, Shelby
   1989   "Being Black and Feeling Blue." *The American Scholar* 3:497–513.
   1988   "I'm Black, You're White, Who's Innocent?" *Harpers*, June.

Stewart, E. C., J. Danielian, and R. J. Festes
   1969   *Simulating Intercultural Communication through Role Playing.* Alexandria, VA: Human Resources Research Organization.

Strickland, Lee
   1994   "Autobiographical Interviewing and Narrative Analysis: An Approach to Psychosocial Assessment." *Clinical Social Work Journal* 22:27–41.

Sue, Derald Wing, and David Sue
   1990   *Counseling the Culturally Different.* New York: John Wiley and Sons.

Sue, Stanley
   1988   "Psychotherapeutic Services to Ethnic Minorities: Two Decades of Research Findings." *American Psychologist* 43:301–308.

Sue, Stanley, and Herman McKinney
    1975   "Asian Americans in the Community Mental Health Care System." *American Journal of Orthopsychiatry* 45:111–118.

Sue, Stanley, and Nolan Zane
    1987   "The Role of Culture and Cultural Techniques in Psychotherapy." *American Psychologist* 42:37–45.

Sykes, Donald K., Jr.
    1987   "An Approach to Working with Black Youth in Cross Cultural Therapy." *Clinical Social Work Journal* 15:260–271.

Taft, Ronald
    1981   "The Role and Personality of the Mediator." In Stephen Bochner. *The Mediating Person.* Cambridge, MA: Schenkman.
    1977   "Coping with Unfamiliar Cultures." In Neil Warren, ed. *Studies in Cross-Cultural Psychology.* New York: Academic Press.

Tamura, Takeshi, and Annie Lau
    1992   "Connectedness versus Separateness: Applicability of Family Therapy to Japanese Families." *Family Process* 31:319–340.

Taylor, Eleanor D.
    1987   *From Issue to Action: An Advocacy Program Model.* Lancaster, CA: Family and Children's Services.

Thorne, Barrie, Cheris Kramarae, and Nancy Henly, eds.
    1983   *Language, Gender and Society.* Rowley, MA: Newbury House.

Thrasher, Shirley, and Gary Anderson
    1988   "The West Indian Family: Treatment Challenges." *Social Casework* 69:171–176.

Thyer, Bruce A.
    1997   *Controversial Issues in Social Work Practice.* Boston: Allyn and Bacon.

Tran, Thanh Van
    1988   "The Vietnamese American Family." In Charles H. Mindel, Robert W. Habenstien, and Roosevelt Wright, Jr. *Ethnic Families in America: Patterns and Variations.* New York: Elsevier.

Trimble, Joseph E.
    1981   "Value Differences among American Indians: Concerns for the Concerned Counselor." In Paul Pedersen, Juris G. Draguns, Walter J. Lonner, and Joseph E. Trimble, eds. *Counseling across Cultures.* Honolulu: University of Hawaii Press.

Trimble, Joseph E., Teresa D. LaFromboise, Duane H. Mackey, and Gary A. France
    1983   "American Indians, Psychology and Curriculum Development: A Proposed Reform with Reservations." In Jay C. Chunn III, Patricia J. Dunston, and Fariyal Ross-Sheriff, eds. *Mental Health and People of Color.* Washington, DC: Howard University Press.

Tsui, Philip, and Gail L. Schultz
    1988   "Ethnic Factors in Group Process: Cultural Dynamics in Multi-Ethnic Therapy Groups." *American Journal of Psychotherapy* 58:136–142.
    1985   "Failure of Rapport: Why Psychotherapeutic Engagement Fails in the Treatment of Asian Clients." *American Journal of Psychotherapy* 55:561–569.

Tung, May
    1991   "Life Values, Psychotherapy, and East-West Integration." *Psychiatry* 47:285–292.
    1984   "Insight-Oriented Psychotherapy and the Chinese Patient." *American Journal of Orthopsychiatry* 61:186–194.

Tyler, Forrest B., Deborah Ridley Sussewell, and Janice Williams-McCoy
    1985   "Ethnic Validity in Psychotherapy." *Psychotherapy* 22:311–320.

Uba, Laura, and Stanley Sue
    1991   "Nature and Scope of Services for Asian and Pacific Islander Americans." In Noreen Mokuau, ed. *Handbook of Social Services for Asian and Pacific Islanders.* New York: Greenwood Press.

Ucko, Lenora Greenbaum
    1983   "The Use of Folktales in Social Work Practice." *Social Casework* 64:414–418.

U.S. Department of Commerce
    1993a   *We the American...Blacks.* Washington, DC: U.S. Government Printing Office.
    1993b   *We the American...Hispanics.* Washinton, DC: U.S. Government Printing Office.

U.S. Department of Health and Human Services
    1985   *Health Status of Minorities and Low Income Groups.* Washington, DC: Government Printing Office.
    1984   *Fifth Special Report to the U.S. Congress on Alcohol and Health.* Washington, DC: U.S. Government Printing Office.

Valverde, Kieu-Linh Caroline
    1992   "From Dust to Gold: The Vietnamese Amerasian Experience." In Maria P. P. Root, ed. *Racially Mixed People in America.* Newbury Park, CA: Sage.

Varenne, Herve
    1986   *Symbolizing America.* Lincoln: University of Nebraska Press.
    1977   *Americans Together.* New York: Teachers College Press.

Vasquez, Melba J. T.
    1984   "Power and Status of the Chicana: A Social-Psychological Perspective." In Joe L. Martinez, Jr., and Richard H. Mendoza, eds. *Chicano Psychology.* Orlando, FL: Academic Press.

Vega, William A., Bohdan Kolody, Ramon Valle, and Judy Weir
    1991   "Social Networks, Social Support, and Their Relation to Depression among Immigrant Mexican Women." *Human Organization* 50:154–162.

Vigil, James Diego

    1988a *Barrio Gangs: Street Life and Identity in Southern California.* Austin: University of Texas Press.

    1988b "Group Processes and Street Identity: Adolescent Chicano Gang Members." *Ethos* 16:421–445.

    1983 "Chicano Gangs: One Response to Mexican Urban Adaptation in the Los Angeles Area." *Urban Anthropology* 12:45–75.

Waldram, James B.

    1994 "Aboriginal Spirituality in Corrections: A Canadian Case Study in Religion and Therapy." *American Indians Quarterly* 18:197–214.

Walker, R. Dale, M. Dow Lambert, Patricia Silk Walker, Daniel R. Kivlahan, Dennis M. Donovan, and Matthew O. Howard

    1996 "Alcohol Abuse in Urban Indian Adolescents and Woman: A Longitudinal Study for Assessment and Risk Evaluation." *American Indian and Alaska Native Mental Health Research* 7:1–47.

Wallace, Anthony F. C.

    1970 *Culture and Personality.* New York: Random House.

    1956 "Mazeway Resynthesis: A Bio-Cultural Theory of Religious Inspiration." *Transactions of the New York Academy of Science* 18:626–638.

Wallman, Sandra

    1979 *Ethnicity at Work.* London: Macmillan.

Watts-Jones, Darielle

    1992 "Cultural and Integrative Therapy Issues in the Treatment of a Jamaican Woman with Panic Disorder." *Family Process* 31:105–113.

Wax, Rosalie, and Robert K. Thomas

    1961 "American Indians and White People." *Phylon* 22:305–317.

Waxler-Morrison, Nancy, Joan Anderson, and Elizabeth Richardson, eds.

    1990 *Cross-Cultural Caring: A Handbook for Health Professionals in Western Canada.* Vancouver: University of British Columbia Press.

Weaver, Hilary N.

    1996 "Social Work with American Indian Youth Using the Orthogonal Model of Cultural Identification." *Journal of Contemporary Human Services* 77:98–107.

Weaver, Jerry L.

    1977 *National Health Policy and the Underserved.* St. Louis: C.V. Mosby.

Weibel-Orlando, Joan

    1990 "Grandparenting Style: Native American Perspectives." In Jay Sokolovsky. *The Cultural Context of Aging.* New York: Bergin and Garvey.

    1989 "Hooked on Healing: Anthropologists, Alcohol and Intervention." *Human Organization* 48:148–155.

Weick, Karl E.
1984   "Small Wins: Redefining the Scale of Social Problems." *American Psychologist* 39:40–49.

Weisner, Thomas S., Joan Crofut Weibel-Orlando, and John Long
1984   " 'Serious Drinking,' 'White Man's Drinking' and 'Teetotling': Drinking Levels and Styles in an Urban American Indian Population." *Journal of Studies on Alcohol* 45:237–250.

Weiss, Mitchell G.
1995   "Eating Disorders and Disordered Eating in Different Cultures." *The Psychiatric Clinics of North America* 18:537–553.

Wellman, David T.
1993   *Portraits of White Racism.* London: Cambridge University Press.

Wharton, Carol S.
1989   "Splintered Visions: Staff/Client Disjunctions and Their Consequences for Human Service Organizations." *Journal of Contemporary Ethnography* 18:50–71.

White, Barbara W., ed.
1984   *Color in a White Society.* Silver Spring, MD: National Association of Social Workers.

Whitten, Norman E.
1962   "Contemporary Patterns of Malign Occultism among Negroes in North Carolina." *Journal of American Folklore* 75:311–325.

Whitten, Norman E., and John F. Szwed, eds.
1970   *Afro-American Anthropology: Contemporary Perspectives.* New York: Free Press.

Wiener, Carolyn L., and Jeanie Kayser-Jones
1989   "Defensive Work in Nursing Homes: Accountability Gone Amok." *Social Science and Medicine* 28:37–44.

Williams, Brackette F.
1989   "A Class Act: Anthropology and the Race to Nation across Ethnic Terrain." In Bernard J. Siegel, Alan R. Beals, and Stephen A. Tyler, eds. *Annual Review of Anthropology, 18.* Palo Alto, CA: Annual Reviews, Inc.

Williams, Melvin D.
1992   *The Human Dilemma: A Decade Later in Belmar.* Forth Worth, TX: Harcourt Brace Jovanovich.
1981   *On the Street Where I Lived.* New York: Holt, Rinehart and Winston.

Williams, Teresa Kay
1992   "Prism Lives: Identity of Binational Amerasians." In Maria P. P. Root, ed. *Racially Mixed People in America.* Newbury Park, CA: Sage.

Wilson, Terry P.
1992   "Blood Quantum: Native American Mixed Bloods." In Maria P. P. Root, ed. *Racially Mixed People in America.* Newbury Park, CA: Sage.

Wilson, William Julius
  1996   *When Work Disappears: The World of the New Urban Poor.* New York: Knopf.
  1987   *The Truly Disadvantaged: The Inner City, the Underclass, and Public Policy.* Chicago:
         University of Chicago Press.
  1980   *The Declining Significance of Race: Blacks and Changing American Institutions.* Chi-
         cago: University of Chicago Press.

Wintrob, R. M.
  1973   "The Influence of Others: Witchcraft and Rootwork as Explanations of Behavior
         Disturbances." *Journal of Nervous and Mental Disorders* 156:318–326.

Wise, Fred, and Nancy B. Miller
  1983   "The Mental Health of American Indian Children." In Gloria Johnson Powell, ed.
         The Psychosocial Development of Minority Group Children. New York: Brunner/
         Mazel.

Wong, Morrison G.
  1988   "The Chinese American Family." In Charles H. Mindel, Robert W. Habenstein,
         and Roosevelt Wright, Jr. *Ethnic Families in America: Patterns and Variations.* New
         York: Elsevier.

Wong, Morrison G., and Charles Hirschman
  1983   "The New Asian Immigrants." In William McCready, ed. *Culture, Ethnicity, and
         Identity.* New York: Academic Press.

Wong, Oye-Nam Christine, and Niva Piran
  1995   "Western Biases and Assumptions as Impediments in Counseling Traditional
         Chinese Clients." *Canadian Journal of Counselling* 17:107–119.

Woolfson, Peter, Virginia Hood, Roger Secker-Walker, and Ann C. Macaulay
  1995   "Mohawk English in the Medical Interview." *Medical Anthropology Quarterly*
         9:503–509.

Yamashiro, Greg, and Jon K. Matsuoka
  1997   "Help-Seeking among Asian and Pacific Americans: A Multiperspective Analy-
         sis." *Social Work* 42:176–186.

Yanagisako, Sylvia Junko
  1985   *Transforming the Past: Tradition and Kinship among Japanese Americans.* Stanford:
         Stanford University Press.
  1975   "Two Processes of Change in Japanese-American Kinship." *Journal of Anthropo-
         logical Research* 31:196–224.

Ying, Yu-wen
  1990   "Explanatory Models of Major Depression and Implications for Help Seeking
         among Immigrant Chinese American Women." *Culture, Medicine and Psychiatry*
         14:393–408.

Youngman, Geraldine, and Margaret Sadongei
   1974   "Counseling the American Indian Child." *Elementary School Guidance and Counseling* 8:272–277.

Zambrana, Ruth E., ed.
   1995   *Understanding Latino Families.* Thousand Oaks, CA: Sage.

Zayas, Louis, and Nancy A. Busch-Rossnagel
   1992   "Pregnant Hispanic Women: A Mental Health Study." *Families in Society* 73:515–521.

Zhang, Dan
   1995   "Depression and Culture—A Chinese Perspective." *Canadian Journal of Counselling* 29:227–233.

Zintz, M. V.
   1963   *Education across Cultures.* Dubuque, IA: William Brown.

Zola, I. K.
   1972   "The Concept of Trouble and Sources of Medical Assistance." *Social Science and Medicine* 6:673–680.

Zollar, Ann Creighton
   1985   *A Member of the Family: Strategies for Black Family Continuity.* Chicago: Nelson-Hall.

Zuniga, Maria E.
   1992   "Using Metaphors in Therapy: Dichos and Latino Clients." *Social Work* 37:55–60.
   1991   "'Dichos' as Metaphorical Tools for Resistant Latino Clients." *Psychotherapy* 28:480–483.

INDEX

Note: Page numbers in *italics* indicate illustrations; those followed by t indicate tables.